T0220817

Communications
in Computer and Information Science **1599**

Editorial Board Members

Joaquim Filipe ⓘ
Polytechnic Institute of Setúbal, Setúbal, Portugal

Ashish Ghosh
Indian Statistical Institute, Kolkata, India

Raquel Oliveira Prates ⓘ
Federal University of Minas Gerais (UFMG), Belo Horizonte, Brazil

Lizhu Zhou
Tsinghua University, Beijing, China

More information about this series at https://link.springer.com/bookseries/7899

Sandeep Joshi · Amit Kumar Bairwa ·
Amita Nandal · Milena Radenkovic ·
Cem Avsar (Eds.)

Cyber Warfare, Security and Space Research

First International Conference, SpacSec 2021
Jaipur, India, December 9–10, 2021
Revised Selected Papers

 Springer

Editors
Sandeep Joshi (iD)
Manipal University Jaipur
Jaipur, India

Amit Kumar Bairwa (iD)
Manipal University Jaipur
Jaipur, India

Amita Nandal (iD)
Manipal University Jaipur
Jaipur, India

Milena Radenkovic (iD)
University of Nottingham
Nottingham, UK

Cem Avsar
beSpace GmbH
Berlin, Germany

ISSN 1865-0929   ISSN 1865-0937 (electronic)
Communications in Computer and Information Science
ISBN 978-3-031-15783-7   ISBN 978-3-031-15784-4 (eBook)
https://doi.org/10.1007/978-3-031-15784-4

© The Editor(s) (if applicable) and The Author(s), under exclusive license
to Springer Nature Switzerland AG 2022
This work is subject to copyright. All rights are reserved by the Publisher, whether the whole or part of the material is concerned, specifically the rights of translation, reprinting, reuse of illustrations, recitation, broadcasting, reproduction on microfilms or in any other physical way, and transmission or information storage and retrieval, electronic adaptation, computer software, or by similar or dissimilar methodology now known or hereafter developed.
The use of general descriptive names, registered names, trademarks, service marks, etc. in this publication does not imply, even in the absence of a specific statement, that such names are exempt from the relevant protective laws and regulations and therefore free for general use.
The publisher, the authors, and the editors are safe to assume that the advice and information in this book are believed to be true and accurate at the date of publication. Neither the publisher nor the authors or the editors give a warranty, expressed or implied, with respect to the material contained herein or for any errors or omissions that may have been made. The publisher remains neutral with regard to jurisdictional claims in published maps and institutional affiliations.

This Springer imprint is published by the registered company Springer Nature Switzerland AG
The registered company address is: Gewerbestrasse 11, 6330 Cham, Switzerland

Preface

This volume contains the papers from the 1st International Conference on Cyber Warfare, Security & Space Research (SpacSec 2021). The event was organized at Manipal University Jaipur (MUJ), India, during December 9–10, 2021, under a conference grant received by the All India Council for Technical Education (AICTE) New Delhi. MUJ is a private research-oriented higher education institution participating in a wide variety of nationally and internationally funded research projects. The sponsoring partners involved in this conference were AICTE and DRDO. SpacSec 2021 provided an opportunity for researchers, educators, professionals, practitioners, scientists, satellite and space researchers, space agency executives, geophysicists, spacecraft ground control operators, agencies, earth science researchers, geologists, spacecraft and satellite engineers, satellite launch vehicle manufacturers/operators, marshals and admirals in the army, artists, and students around the world who are involved in the study, management, development, and implementation of systems and concepts to combat information warfare and all aspects of space technology and research to come together and exchange ideas. There are several strong strands of research developing in the cyber warfare, cyber security, and space research area, including the understanding of threats and risks to systems, the development of a strong innovative culture, and incident detection and post-incident investigation.

New threats brought about by social networking and cloud computing are gaining interest from the research community, and the conference aimed to tackle these issues. It provided an excellent opportunity for students and researchers worldwide to interact and share ideas face to face. This knowledge sharing may inspire and thrill many young minds and help us bring about collaborations and global partnerships to work together. This will enable us to solve challenging problems in our society to contribute to our world. The whole idea of the forum is to exchange thoughts and ideas and transform these in real-time to solve the problems. Another aim of the conference was to create awareness in students about the importance of scientific research in related fields and synchronizing with the product market. The highly diversified audience allowed us to achieve a good understanding of the mutual needs, requirements, and technical means available in this field of research. The topics included in the first edition of this event focused on the areas of cyber warfare and cyber security, and space research. All accepted papers were peer-reviewed by three qualified reviewers chosen from our Technical Committee based on their qualifications and experience. The proceedings editors wish to thank the dedicated Technical Committee members and other reviewers for their contributions. We also thank Springer for their trust and for publishing the proceedings of SpacSec 2021.

May 2022

Sandeep Joshi
Amita Nandal
Amit Kumar Bairwa

Organization

Organizing Committee

Patrons

K. Ramnarayan	Manipal University Jaipur, India
Gopalkrishna K. Prabhu	Manipal University Jaipur, India
Niti Nipun Sharma	Manipal University Jaipur, India
Nitu Bhatnagar	Manipal University Jaipur, India

Honorary Chair

Rajveer Singh Shekhawat	Manipal University Jaipur, India

General Chair

Sandeep Joshi	Manipal University Jaipur, India

Program Chairs

Amita Nandal	Manipal University Jaipur, India
Amit Kumar Bairwa	Manipal University Jaipur, India

Publication Chairs

Milena Radenkovic	University of Nottingham, UK
Cem Avsar	beSpace GmbH, Germany

Promotion Chairs

Arjun Singh	Manipal University Jaipur, India
Arvind Kumar Dhaka	Manipal University Jaipur, India
Anubha Parashar	Manipal University Jaipur, India
Bali Devi	Manipal University Jaipur, India

Space Research Chairs

Manish Tiwari	Manipal University Jaipur, India
Prathistha Mathur	Manipal University Jaipur, India

Cyber Warfare and Security Chairs

| Dinesh Kumar Saini | Manipal University Jaipur, India |
| Vijandra Singh | Manipal University Jaipur, India |

Local Organization Team

Sandeep Chaurasia	Manipal University Jaipur, India
Anita Shrotriya	Manipal University Jaipur, India
Vineeta Soni	Manipal University Jaipur, India
Smaranika Mohapatra	Manipal University Jaipur, India
Prakash Ramani	Manipal University Jaipur, India
Kusum Lata	Manipal University Jaipur, India
Satyabrata Roy	Manipal University Jaipur, India
Jaya Krishna	Manipal University Jaipur, India
Santosh Kumar	Manipal University Jaipur, India
Neha V. Sharma	Manipal University Jaipur, India
Ankit Srivastava	Manipal University Jaipur, India
Saket Acharya	Manipal University Jaipur, India
Nitesh Pradhan	Manipal University Jaipur, India
Mahesh Jangid	Manipal University Jaipur, India
Vidyadhar Aski	Manipal University Jaipur, India
Satpal Singh Kushwaha	Manipal University Jaipur, India
Vaishali Yadav	Manipal University Jaipur, India
Anjana Syamla	Manipal University Jaipur, India
Prashant Hemrajani	Manipal University Jaipur, India
Linesh Raja	Manipal University Jaipur, India
Aditya Sinha	Manipal University Jaipur, India
Harish Sharma	Manipal University Jaipur, India
Neha Chaudhary	Manipal University Jaipur, India
Sunita Singhal	Manipal University Jaipur, India

Technical Committee Members

Adel Al-Jumaily	University of Technology Sydney, Australia
Vidhyacharan Bhaskar	San Francisco State University, USA
Amit Mahesh Joshi	MNIT Jaipur, India
Avatar Singh	National Institute of Technology, Jalandhar, India
Eduard Babulak	Fort Hays State University, USA
Basant Agarwal	Indian Institute of Information Technology, Kota, India
Bharanidharan Shanmugam	Charles Darwin University, Australia
Chhagan Charan	National Institute of Technology, Kurukshetra, India

Chithral Ambawatte	University of Ruhuna, Sri Lanka
Dimitrios A. Karras	University of Athens, Greece
Mohamed Firdhous	University of Moratuwa, Sri Lanka
Kambiz Ghazinour	State University of New York at Canton, USA
G. S. Mahapatra	National Institute of Technology, Puducherry, India
Thusitha Gunawardana	University of Sri Jayewardenepura, Sri Lanka
Brij B. Gupta	National Institute of Technology, Kurukshetra, India
Jafar A. Alzubi	Wake Forest University, USA
Anshuman Kalla	University of Oulu, Finland
Kalpana Dhaka	Indian Institute of Information Technology, Guwahati, India
Krishna Kumar Sharma	University of Kota, India
Kuldeep Singh	MNIT Jaipur, India
Maninder Singh Nehra	Government Engineering College Bikaner, India
M. A. R. M. Fernando	University of Peradeniya, Sri Lanka
Mohiuddin Ahmed	University of New South Wales, Australia
Mohamed Ismail Roushdy	Future University, Egypt
Muzathik Abdul Majeed	Southeastern University of Sri Lanka
A. Nagaraju	Central University of Rajasthan, India
Narpat Singh Shekhawat	Government Engineering College Bikaner, India
Nilesh Bhaskarrao Bahadure	BIT Raipur, India
Nishtha Kesswani	Central University of Rajasthan, Rajasthan
Nitin Gupta	National Institute of Technology, Hamirpur, India
Parag Narkhede	SIT Pune, India
Pardeep Singh	National Institute of Technology, Hamirpur, India
Prakash Choudhary	National Institute of Technology, Hamirpur, India
Prashant Kumar	National Institute of Technology, Jalandhar, India
P. Sakthivel	Anna University, India
Rajeev Kumar	National Institute of Technology, Hamirpur, India
Ravi Saharan	Central University of Rajasthan, India
Sotiris Moschoyiannis	University of Surrey, UK
Samantha Thelijjagoda	Sri Lanka Institute of Information Technology, Sri Lanka
Guathilaka Samantha	University of Ruhuna, Sri Lanka
Saurabh Kumar Pandey	Indian Institute of Technology, Patna, India
Saurabh Kumar	National Institute of Technology, Hamirpur, India
Shashank Gupta	BITS Pilani, India
Satyasai Jagannath Nanda	MNIT Jaipur, India
Sujala Deepak Shetty	BITS Pilani, Dubai, UAE
V. G. Tharinda N. Vidanagama	Wayamba University of Sri Lanka, Sri Lanka

Silva A. T. P.	University in Moratuwa, Sri Lanka
Urvashi Bansal	National Institute of Technology, Jalandhar, India
Vigneswaran T.	VIT, India
Aynur Unal	DigitalMonozukuri, USA
Deepika Koundal	UPES Dehrdun, India
Rahul Dixit	IIIT Pune, India
Somya Ranjan Sahoo	VIT, Andhra Pradesh, India
Subhash Panwar	Government Engineering College, Bikaner, India
Wilfred Lin	PuraPharm, Hong Kong
Xianglin Wei	Nanjing Telecommunication Technology Research Institute, China
Ekaterina Pakulova	Southern Federal University, Russia
Cesar Collazos	Universidad del Cauca, Colombia
Reza Malekin	Malmö University, Sweden
Johnny Öberg	KTH Royal Institute of Technology, Sweden
Natasa Sladoje	Uppsala University, Sweden
Aleksander Karadimche	UIST, North Macedonia
Carlos E. Galvan-Tejada	UAZ, Mexico
Oliver Jokisch	HSF Meißen, Germany
Jorge I. Galvan-Tejada	UAZ, Mexico
Max Henrique Machado Costa	University of Campinas, Brazil
Eva Volna	University of Ostrava, Czech Republic
Dijana C. Bogatinoska	UIST, North Macedonia
Tomas Sochor	University of Ostrava, Czech Republic
Ninoslav Marina	UIST, North Macedonia
Huizilopoztli Luna-Garcia	UAZ, Mexico
Arturo Moreno-Baez	UAZ, Mexico
Eustrat Zupa	Rochester Institute of Technology, USA
Monika Polak	Rochester Institute of Technology, USA
Jaime Portugheis	University of Campinas, Brazil
Zizung Yoon	TU Berlin, Germany
Cihangir Tezcan	Middle East Technical University, Turkey
Ekaterina Maro	Southern Federal University, Russia
Sedat Akleylek	Ondokuz Mayis University, Turkey
Selwyn Piramuthu	University of Florida, USA
Rajeev Tiwari	UPES Dehradun, India
Dmitry Namiot	Lomonosov Moscow State University, Russia
Jibitesh Mishra	College of Engineering and Technology, Bhubaneswar, India
Victor Govindaswamy	Concordia University Chicago, USA
Thangadurai N.	Jain University, India

Muthukumar S.	National Institute of Technology, Puducherry, India
Nisheeth Joshi	Banasthali University, India
Rasib Khan	Northern Kentucky University, USA
Shivnath Ghosh	Maharana Pratap College of Technology, India
Saurabh Mukherjee	Banasthali Vidyapeeth, India
Anil Kumar Gupta	CDAC, India
Muhammad Mostafa	King Abdulaziz University, Saudi Arabia
Sanjay Bansal	Acropolis Institute of Technology and Research, India
Jagannathan Sarangapani	Missouri University of Science and Technology, USA
Nurilla Avazov	Inha University, South Korea
Abhineet Anand	Galgotias University, India
M. Shanmugasundaram	R.M.K. College of Engineering and Technology, India
Elena Basan	Southern Federal University, Russia
Maxim Anikeev	Southern Federal University, Russia
Pushpendra Singh	JIIT, India
Snehanshu Shekhar	BIT Mesra, India
Mohiuddin Ahmed	University of New South Wales, Australia
Syed Hassan Ahmed	Kyungpook National University, South Korea
Bhupendra Singh	DRDO, India
Satyendra Singh	BSDU Jaipur, India
Sonu Lamba	Thapar Institute of Engineering and Technology, India
Parvinder Singh	Central University of Punjab, India
Sumitra Singar	BSDU Jaipur, India

Technical Advisory Members

Jalel Ben Othman	Université Sorbonne Paris Nord, France
Adel Al-Jumaily	University of Technology, Sydney, Australia
Krithi Ramamritham	IIT Bombay, India
Lei Zhang	East China Normal University, China
Edmond C. Prakash	University of Westminster, UK
D. M. Akbar Hussain	Aalborg University, Denmark
Prabhaker Mateti	Ohio University, USA
Vijay Laxmi	Malaviya National Institute of Technology, Jaipur, India
Olariu Stephan	Old Dominion University, USA
Atilla Elci Aksaray	Aksaray University, Turkey
Mouhamed Abdulla	Chalmers University of Technology, Sweden

Gowrish B.   Indian Space Research Organization, India
Alok Kumar   DRDO, India
M. Subramanyam   National Institute of Technology, Puducherry,
                                        India
Syed Nisar Bukhari   NIELIT Srinagar, India
Bert-Jan van Beijnum   University of Twente, The Netherlands

Keynote Speakers

Gaurav Gupta   Ministry of Electronics and Information
                                        Technology, India
Somitra Kumar Sanadhya   Indian Institute of Technology, Jodhpur, India
Milena Radenkovic   University of Nottingham, UK
Hari Hablani   Indian Institute of Technology, Indore, India
Surendra Sunda   Airports Authority of India, India
Geeta Sikka   National Institute of Technology, Jalandhar, India
Pushpendu Kar   University of Nottingham, UK
Cem Avsar   beSpace GmbH, Germany

Contents

Creation of Novel Database for Knowledge Repository on Cyber Security 1
Kunal Sinha and Kishore Kumar Senapati

Brain Tumor Classification via UNET Architecture of CNN Technique 18
Arpit Kumar Sharma, Amita Nandal, Arvind Dhaka,
and Dijana Capeska Bogatinoska

Analysis of Various Supervised Machine Learning Algorithms
for Intrusion Detection 34
Kabir Nagpal, Niyati Jain, Ayush Patra, Arnav Gupta, Anjana Syamala,
and Sunita Singhal

Enhanced Security Mechanism for Cryptographic File Systems Using
Trusted Computing 51
Umashankar Rawat, Satyabrata Roy, Saket Acharya, Ravinder Kumar,
and Krishna Kumar

Critical Analysis of IoT Ecosystem to Understand Security Threats
and Challenges 64
N. Renya Nath and Hiran V. Nath

Hyper-parameters Study for Breast Cancer Datasets: Enhancing Image
Security and Accuracy for Prediction Class 75
Neha Panwar and D. P. Sharma

An Efficient Image Encryption Technique Using Logistic Map
and 2D-TCLM 87
Krishna Kumar, Satyabrata Roy, Umashankar Rawat, and Ishan Mishra

Learning Co-occurrence Embeddings for Sentence Classification 97
Triveni Lal Pal and Kamlesh Dutta

Preventing Fault Attacks on S-Boxes of AES-Like Block Ciphers 105
Swapan Maiti, Deval Mehta, and Dipanwita Roy Chowdhury

Privacy Preserving of Two Local Data Sites Using Global Random Forest
Classification 117
Latha Gadepaka and Bapi Raju Surampudi

Privacy Preserving and Secured Clustering of Distributed Data Using Self
Organizing Map 130
  Latha Gadepaka and Bapi Raju Surampudi

Implementation of Intrusion Detection Systems in Distributed Architecture 144
  *Dhrumil Malani, Jimit Modi, Siddharth Lilani, Yukta Desai,
  and Ritesh Dhanare*

Practical Phase Shift Model for RIS-Assisted D2D Communication
Systems 156
  Samuel Jia Sheng Lee and Choo W. R. Chiong

Recent Trend of Transform Domain Image Steganography Technique
for Secret Sharing 171
  *Jyoti Khandelwal, Vijay Kumar Sharma, Jaya Krishna Raguru,
  and Hemlata Goyal*

Design of a High Efficiency Access Control and Authentication Analysis
Model for Cloud Deployments Using Pattern Analysis 186
  Anagha Raich and Vijay Gadicha

A Study on Cyber Security in Various Critical IT Infrastructure
Organizational Sectors: Challenges and Solutions 201
  Sachin Kumar Sharma, Arjun Singh, and Manoj Kumar Bohra

Short-Delay Multipath Errors in NavIC Signals for Stationary Receivers 213
  Kartik Tiwari, A. Althaf, and Hari Hablani

Point Clouds Object Classification Using Part-Based Capsule Network 239
  Jonathan Then Sien Phang and King Hann Lim

Study of Various Attacks Over Images Transferred Optically Through
Communication Channel 248
  Anshika Malsaria and Pankaj Vyas

Satellite Image Classification Using ANN 263
  Pratistha Mathur and Kavita

Power Quality Disturbance Classification Using Transformer Network 272
  Dar Hung Chiam and King Hann Lim

On-Orbit, Non-destructive Surface Surveillance and Inspection
with Convolution Neural Network 283
  *Sanjay Lakshminarayana, Shubham Bhaskar Thakare,
  and Krishna Vamshi Duddukuru*

Ramadan Group Transform Fundamental Properties and Some its Dualities 294
  A. A. Soliman, K. R. Raslan, and A. M. Abdallah

Enhancing Security Mechanism in Smart Phones Using Crowdsourcing 303
  Shivani Gupta, Srinivas Ravipati, Ranjeet Kumar, and V. Vani

INTELLIBOT - Intelligent Voice Assisted Chatbot with Sentiment
Analysis, COVID Dashboard and Offensive Text Detection 311
  Gadiparthy Harika Sai, Meghna Manoj Nair, V. Vani, and Shivani

Author Index 325

Creation of Novel Database for Knowledge Repository on Cyber Security

Kunal Sinha[1](✉) [iD] and Kishore Kumar Senapati[2](✉) [iD]

[1] Birla Institute of Technology and Science, Pilani 333031, India
Kunals.iitd@gmail.com
[2] Birla Institute of Technology Mesra, Ranchi 835215, India
kksenapati@bitmesra.ac.in

Abstract. The use of cyberspace, internet and server governed services has grown exponentially in the past decade and is expected to rise higher in coming future. Numerous transactions of different forms and properties are executed continuously. As a law of nature, this innovation, development and use of technology has counteracted digital crimes which hinders the different processing's using the cyberspace for an illegal benefit. Data and information security are an important concern in this technology leaded digital era of the world today and it becomes important for end-users to accomplish, understand and analyze the occurrence of digital crimes to safeguards themselves. The implementation of this security logic for an awareness of cyber security, an analysis of different occurred cyber-crime is covered followed by the characterization of cyber-crime actors. In this work we propose a method for creating a Cyber Security database with semantics search functions. The characterization of actors thus helps in identification of entities, attributes and their relations. An Entity Relationship Diagram is sketched based upon the results which opens a path to design and develop a data model for cyber security. The data model allows to create schema followed by database preparation for cyber security. The databases can become an effective tool and proven technology to let the world recognize the patterns of cyber-crime and patterns by virtue of its property to warehouse and mine a collection of related information called data. The database is validated through a training set of data.

Keywords: Cyber-attack · Cyber-crime · Cyber-threat · Prevention · Attack patterns · Threat resource · Database · schemas

1 Introduction

Cyber-attacks are a continuous problem in Computer and IT industry. Survey shows approximately 66% of industry had faced these attacks. Repelling these attacks are not easy and a tedious task. This increase in cyber-attacks had brought analysts to not only analyse cyber accidents but also to study hacker's intention and purpose of incidents from a long-term perspective.

In the process of prevention of cyber-crime and handling the cyber threats, databases can become one of an important application in the field of the computer science that can

© The Author(s), under exclusive license to Springer Nature Switzerland AG 2022
S. Joshi et al. (Eds.): SpacSec 2021, CCIS 1599, pp. 1–17, 2022.
https://doi.org/10.1007/978-3-031-15784-4_1

help in focusing research on cyber-crime and hacker's interpretation. Databases can help in understanding the patterns of cyber-crime. It helps in providing adequate knowledge in understanding the future cyber-attacks through its logical and physical models and query processing techniques.

A database management system provides a method that makes process of explaining, building, operating and distributing database among its users and applications [14, 16]. Databases can be proved as an excellent tool for analysis and prevention of cyber-crime.

Major concept in database knowledge repository for cyber security is providing information to its intended users about different types of cyber-crime activities that took place in the near future and help in interpretation to predict upcoming near future threats and retrieve various information related to cyber-crimes.

It helps in cyber decision making and response by developing proofs of concepts that will be transformed in form a data model and will fed into a database giving it a defence capability that supports the existing algorithms of cyber security [4] and also serves as informative repository in the field of cyber threat.

2   Related Work

The main investigating question is - How to represent a cyber-attack? The target is to design a representation that clearly shows what it means by cyber-attacks and its allied concepts. Also, the designed cyber-attack representation must be capable to characterize cyber-attacks using open information's via any media.

The representation shall be capable of:-

1. Eradicating the ambiguities and inconsistencies in various concepts of the cyber-attack uses.
2. Developing a multidisciplinary theory of cyber-attacks that may be applied for understanding and predicting future attacks.
3. Developing cyber-attack databases that holds theory development.

To follow it, samples of previously occurred cyber-attacks were collected and studied to understand the different types of cyber-crimes and how an attacker targets a victim. Literatures, research papers and technical journals were collected and referred. The study resulted in gaining a knowledge on how these attacks are performed. How does a victim of these attacks face loss? An attempt is made to corelate the available data with the desired planned outcomes of the repository.

In order to understand cyber threat, we need to understand the difference between data, information and intelligence [5].

1. Data - is an individual item that has atomicity.
2. Information - is a processed data.
3. Intelligence - is the information about how to detect and defend cyber incidents and threats.

In purview of cyber threat, the above definition can be explained in such a way as [5]:-

1. Data - is IP, domain, URL and email etc. that can be collected from the web or network.
2. Information - as URL exploited for Phishing, domain that spread malicious code and IP that establishes connection.
3. Intelligence - is the comprehensive analysis result, which reports a cyber incident or crime.

Thus, an interpretation of these data and its allied information along with its intelligence provides a path in creation of a new information security area that explains how and why a cyber-attack becomes threat.

2.1 Data Collection

A brief background of cyber incidents, cyber-crimes, cyber threat and cyber intelligence is searched, collected and studied. An intensive literature review is conducted. The objective is to understand different types of cyber threats, incidents, occurring patterns. On the basis of studies conducted, an intensive analysis on the collected data is performed to identify the basics of cyber threat.

The recorded basics thus help in identification of cyber-crime and threat, it's entities and its allied attributes [2, 3, 8].

2.2 Material and Methods

There exists no single approach that may addresses all the requirements to construct a database repository on cyber-crimes. Based on existing survey a cyber threat characterization framework is outlined and used in preparation of the repository [4, 8, 11].

2.3 Mapping of Threats with Data Objects

Summary of data objects with its threat characterization categories (Table 1).

Table 1. Mapping of threats with data objects

Data objects	Threat characterization categories
Actor	Adversary/Type
	Adversary/Commitment
	Adversary/Resources
Adversary	Adversary/Motivation (non-hostile)
	Attack/Delivery mechanisms
	Attack/Tools
	Attack/Automation
Significant incident	Attack/Actions
Intent	Adversary/Motivation (hostile)
	Effect/Cyber effects
Impact	Effect
Resource	Asset/Container
	Asset/Vulnerability
Target	Asset/Profile
Victim	Suffer/Loss

2.4   Characterization Framework Categories

The above shown characterization of the cyber threat are broken down into four major categories, these are Adversary, Attack, Asset, Effect [4, 8, 11]:-

2.4.1   Adversary

Adversaries can be categorized into various types viz - Script Kiddies, newbies, novices, Hackers, Cyber Punks, crashers, thugs, Insiders, user malcontent, Insiders/outside collusion, Coders, writers, Black hat hackers, Professionals, elite, Cyber Terrorists.

2.4.2   Attack

Attacks can be categorized into four different types like Delivery Mechanism, Tools, Automation and Actions. These further categorized as follows:-

Delivery Mechanism - Local Access, Remote Delivery, Distributed Delivery and Social Engineering
Tools - Physical attack, Information exchange, User command, Script or program, Autonomous agent and Distributed tool
Automation – Automatic, Semi-automatic ad Manual
Actions – Spoof, Read, Copy, Steal, Modify and Delete

2.4.3 Asset

Assets can be categorized into various types like Profile, Features, Quality, Characteristics and Value. Out of these values can further be defined in two different categories, these are Hardware – Workstations, Servers, Network devices, Storage devices and Mobile devices. And Software –Applications, Operating systems and Virtual images.

2.4.4 Effect

Effects can be categorized into various types viz - Cyber effects, Interruption, Modification, Degradation, Fabrication and Interception.

3 Data Model

It is a technical idea used to describe structure and design of a database. It speaks about the data types, relationships and constraints that are applied to a data in a database. It gives us necessary methods to achieve abstraction. Data models are of various types and almost most of them contains a basic set of operations to specify retrievals and updates on a database. These are [6, 16]:-

1. High Level or Conceptual Data Model – Describes the concepts on how users recognise a data.
2. Low Level or Physical Data Model – Describes the concepts on how data is stored in a system.
3. Entity Relationship Model – A high level conceptual data model that describe relations between an entity, its attributes and its relationship.
4. Relational Data Model – This represents databases in form of collections of relations. The relations are tables with values and each row of a table represents a collection of related values.
5. Hierarchal Model – The model where the data is represented in a tree structure.
6. Record Based Data Model – Contains the representation of data by using record structures.
7. Object Data Model – These are model based upon object-oriented programming. It extends program space into object management and shareability.
8. Self-Describing Data Models – It is a data model that constitutes a combination of data description with data values themselves.

4 Mathematical Modelling

Mathematical modelling studies are increasingly recognized as an important tool for evidence synthesis and to inform cyber and security, particularly when data from systematic reviews of primary studies do not adequately answer any question. However, systematic reviewers and guideline developers may struggle with using the results of modelling studies, because, at least in part, of the lack of a common understanding of concepts and terminology between evidence synthesis experts and mathematical modelers. The use of a common terminology for modelling studies across different cyber research fields that spans over several cybercrimes. The characterization, comparison, and use of mathematical modelling studies will help the researchers and other computer domain experts to used terms in mathematical modelling studies that are particularly salient to evidence synthesis and knowledge translation in Cyber domain. A mathematical model is a "mathematical framework representing variables and their interrelationships to describe observed phenomena or predict future events". We define a mathematical modelling study as a study that uses mathematical modelling to address specific cybercrime questions. For the modelling studies that are most relevant to evidence synthesis and cybercrime decision-making, the framework of the mathematical model represents interrelationships among Adversaries, Cyberspace, Victim, Crime, Info or Software, Action, Physical System and Extrinsic (all of these are variables) where their interrelationships are typically described by the parameters of Motivation, Objective, Firewall, Service Provider, Infrastructure, Browser, Technology, Name, Age, Gender, Location, Origin, Date and Time, Type, Degree, Software Name, License Type, App, Type, Objective, Duration, Type, Network Hardware, Organization and Cost. Mathematical modelers can use different methods to specify these parameters; they can use theoretical values, values reported in the scientific literature, or estimate the parameters from data using methods from statistical modelling. There are various models available such as Agent based model, compartmental model, Computational model, Continuous time model (Dynamic model), Discrete time model (Static model), Decision Analytic model, Parsimony model, Stochastic model, Markov model [17].

This paper will adopt any of these model strategies only when it will fully develop all schemas, entities (variables) methods and procedures. Then the rule of evidence combination will correspond to the several operators of the relational database theory. The interpretation of the variables and relation between the variables will fit to any of the model after the model fully evolved. Utilizing the model, the databases will be optimized and ready to refer by the research communities. The different tables will also connect with different functionalities.

5   Instances and Schemas

The collection of information's that are stored in a database at a particular moment of time is called an instance of a database. And the overall design of a database is called a schema. Instances and schemas depend upon the programming language on which a program is written. Schemas are related to variable declaration in a program. Each variable has a specific value at a given instant. The values of the variables in a program at a point corelates to an instance of database schema.

There are several types of schemas in a database system. These are physical schemas that describes designs at physical levels. Logical schemas that describe designs at logical levels. Databases has several other schemas at view levels known as sub schemas, it describes the different views of a database [1, 16].

6 Data Model Preparing Techniques

To advance the theory of design and develop the cyber-attack data model an analysis based upon cyber-attack observations is carried out to understand different classes of cyber-attacks. An important step in the study is recognition of concepts in cyber-attacks. To represent these concept of cyber-crime entities is identified and ER Diagrams is prepared and used to study cyber-attacks concepts. The identification of entities and knowledge of cyber-crime is done through the collected literature and information gathered from the internet [5].

This work is a study which is an exploratory research and contributes towards the presentation and resolution of ways and concepts of cyber-attacks are performed. The study tries to organize available data on cyber-attacks which are available on internet as entities, its attributes and the relationship between them.

In this study an Adversary identified as an attacker. Attack identified as delivery mechanism of the attacker. Assets identified as hardware, network system, software, information and the physical asset that is controlled. Victim identified as the individual or an organization that is affected by an attack.

An adversary to attack may utilize cyberspace that may be affected by the factors both intrinsic or extrinsic to their organizations. The assets that are affected by the attacks towards the victim may be intrinsic or extrinsic to an organization or an individual [7, 12].

7 Entity Relationship Introduction

Entity Relationship Diagram or ERDs is a data modelling technique that helps in preparation of database design which further allows to sketch schemas which are the representation of overall database structure of a chosen subject or topic [9]. The better is the entity relationship diagram the better is the database structure. There are three main components of ER Diagrams, these are Entity, Attribute and Relationship.

Entity - An entity is something that exist in real world and data are required to be stored about it. Entities can be anything like peoples, places, an action or objects that are correlated in a system. There can be five types of entities, these are:-

1. Role
2. Event
3. Location
4. Anything Tangible

Attributes - An attribute are components of an entity or an attribute too. Attribute may be a component of particular entity or may be common to multiple entities.

Relationship - A relationship defines how the entities connects with each other and also exhibit relations that are in between the entities.

7.1   ER Diagram Research

The research on entity relationship modeling of cyber-crimes or attacks uses an elementary reasoning, approach and information's on cyber-attacks and crimes from reliable sources and internet. A principal theoretical possibility on cyber-crimes may not exist. Therefore, this is an exploratory research [9].

7.1.1   Research Methodology

Summary of description of steps taken in work (Table 2).

Table 2. Research methodology

SL No	Steps	Description of steps
1	Identification of entities	Identify subject's role, event, location and concepts
2	Identification of attributes	Identify entity details
3	Finding relationships	Identify correlations between entities
4	Sketching an ERD	Drawing the ER Diagram as per defined rules
5	Preparing schema based upon ERD	Preparation of schema with keys identification

7.1.2   Knowledge Repository Preparation Techniques

Summary of description of steps taken in repository preparation (Table 3).

Table 3. Preparation technique

SL No	Steps	Description of steps
1	Identification of entities	Identify subject's role, event, location and concepts
2	Identification of attributes	Identify entity details
3	Finding relationships	Identify correlations between entities
4	Sketching an ERD	Drawing the ER diagram as per defined rules
5	Preparing schema based upon ERD	Preparation of schema with keys identification

7.1.3   Identification of ERD Components

Summary of ER Diagram Component (Table 4).

Table 4. ERD components

SL No	Cyber-attack definition	Entities	Attributes	Relationships
1	Actions to damage the functionality of a computer system	• Action • Adversary • Net or System	• Type • Objective Durations	Adversary executes Actions damages Net or Systems
2	Use of actions to disrupt or destroy a computer system	• Action • Adversary • Victim • Net or System • Info and Software	• Software Name • License Type • Apps • Type Network Hardware	Adversary executes Actions damages Net or Systems Action damages Software Net or System run transit Info and Software
3	Operations performed to disrupt or destroy a computer system and an independent or organizational network	• Action • Adversary • Victim • Extrinsic • Physical • Net or System • Info and SW	• Software Name • License Type • Apps • Costs	Adversary executes Action damages Net or Systems Action damages Info and Software Action damages Physical System Action Damages Extrinsic
4	Illegal use of cyberspace for unauthorized access	• Cyberspace • Net or Systems • Info and Software	• Firewall • Service Provider • Infrastructure • Technology • Browser	Adversary uses Cyberspace damages Net or System Action damages Info and Software
5	Aggressive use of technology to interfere and destroy a cyber system, its assets and functions	• Action • Adversary • Victim • Cyberspace	• Origin • Type • Date and Time • Type Degree	Adversary executes Action Adversary uses Cyberspace Action damages Net or Systems Action damages Info and Software
6	Efforts destroy a cyber system, its assets and functions	• Action • Net or System • Info and Software	• Software Name • License Type • Apps • Type • Network Hardware Costs	Adversary execute Action Action damages Net or System

8   Result and Discussion

Based upon the ER-Diagram research below is an ER-Diagram designed for the data repository and further the related Schema [9, 10, 13].

8.1   ER Diagram

This designed ER diagram of the data the said data repository illustrates the basic ER model concepts and their use in schema design. The current data requirements for the database are studied and collected. Based upon the current literature studies and data collection the following entities with their attributes are designed which will be evolved gradually with the progress on the topic of research.

1. Adversary – It is the cyber criminals who are intended towards the cyber-crime activities. Motivation and objective of these are the primary concerns.
2. Cyberspace – This defines the basic infrastructure that a cyber-criminal uses to operate its intentions. These are the firewall, internet service providers, browsers used, technology and other infrastructure as and when required.

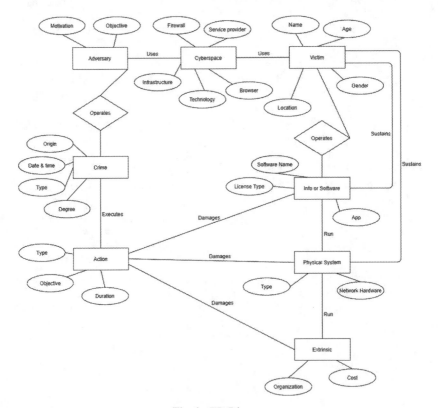

Fig. 1. ER-Diagram

3. Victims – It is the persons or peoples who suffer the loss done to them due to a cyber-attack on their e-data's.
4. Info or Software – This defines which applications or software's were targeted by the cyber-criminals to fulfil their illegal intentions.
5. Physical System – It defines the hardware that is destroyed due to an attack.
6. Extrinsic – It defines external entities that faced the loss like organizations etc.
7. Action – It defines the entity for which a crime was planned, its objective and the duration of the attacks and losses.
8. Crime – It defines the type of crime committed for a cyber-attack (Fig. 1).

8.2 Schema

The ER diagram design provides the path for the schema preparation [15]. The current designed schema constitutes the tables with attributes of the database per table extracted from the ER diagram. The current schema is duly normalized to obtain the results of question of its users through the data query processing languages (Fig. 2).

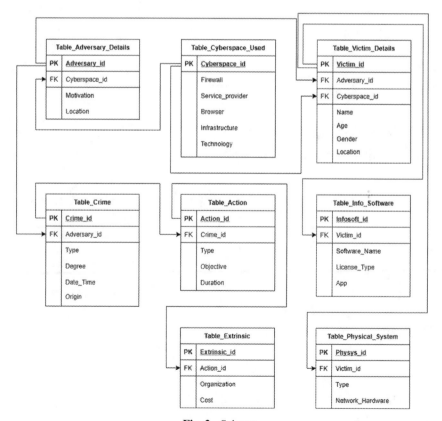

Fig. 2. Schema

8.3   Design of Database Model Tables

Schema preparation prepares the database structure and makes it ready for use. To test the authenticity of the designed database a list of training data is being used to populate data into respective tables used for the data model. Query processing language had been used to populate these training data and the same has been shown below in a sample of five tuples for the demonstration of data model results.

8.3.1   Table Adversary Details

Training data of adversary (Table 5).

Table 5. Adversary table

Motivation	Location
Richness	USA
Rivalry	India
Crime	Pakistan
National security	China
Data breach	Canada

8.3.2   Table Cyberspace Used

Training data of used cyberspace (Table 6)

Table 6. Cyberspace used table

Firewall	Service_provider	Browser	Infrastructure	Technology
ZoneAlarm	Airtel	Opera	Cloud	VB 6
Tinywall	Bsnl	Chrome	Internet	Java
Comdo	Reliance	Chrome	Internet	DotNet
PeerBlock	Tata	Chrome	Server	Python
Cyberraom	Lic	Chrome	Server	Azure

8.3.3   Table Victim Details

Training data of victims (Table 7).

Table 7. Victim table

Name	Age	Gender	Location
Jhon	27	Male	USA
Ravi	32	Male	India
Sarfraj	45	Male	Pakistan
Ju Chin Van	23	Female	China
Mocanaro	54	Male	Canada

8.3.4   Table Physical System

Training data of utilized system (Table 8).

Table 8. Physical system table

Type	Network hardware
Laptop	Switch
Desktop	Hub
Laptop	Routers
Server	Bridge
Desktop	Switch

8.3.5   Table Info Software

Training data of used info software (Table 9).

Table 9. Info software table

Software name	License type	App
Software A	Personal	A
Software B	Corporate	B
Software A	Free	A
Software B	Corporate	B
Software A	Personal	A

8.3.6   Table Extrinsic

Training data of Extrinsic (Table 10).

Table 10. Extrinsic table

Organization	Cost
Public sector	1 Crore
Public sector	5 Crore
Private sector	4 Crore
Defence	5 Crore
Private sector	3 Crore

8.3.7 Table Crime

Training data of crime (Table 11).

Table 11. Crime table

Type	Degree	Date time	Origin
Ransomware	First degree	20/11/1987	USA
Botnet	Second degree	12/12/1998	India
DoS attack	First degree	14/02/1978	Pakistan
Phishing	Second degree	15/03/1972	Canada
Cyberstalking	First degree	02/02/1965	China

8.3.8 Table Action

Training data of actions (Table 12).

Table 12. Action table

Type	Objective	Duration
Black hat	Money	2 Weeks
Grey hat	State rivalry	1 Year
White hat	Illegal desires	2 Years
Black hat	Money	3 Months
White hat	Money	4 Years

8.4 Query Processings

Query processing also helps the users of the data model to fetch desired outcomes based upon the schema of the designed database.

The A sample set of five questions are taken to understand the exploratory uses of the designed data model, these are:-

1. What was the location from where the crime was done?

Solution Query: -

SELECT Adversary_Details.Location, Victim_Details.Name
FROM Adversary_Details INNER JOIN
Victim_Details ON Adversary_Details.Adversary_ID = Victim_Details.Adversary_ID
WHERE Victim_Details.Name = 'Ravi'

Query Result: -

Location: India
Name: Ravi

2. Who was the service provider for the crime?

Solution Query: -

SELECT Cyberspace.Service_Provider, Action_ID
FROM Cyberspace INNER JOIN
Crime ON Cyberspace.Cyberspace_ID = Crime.Cyberspace_ID INNER JOIN
Action ON Crime.Crime_ID = Action.Crime_ID
WHERE Crime.Crime_ID = '2'

Query Result: -

Service Provider: Bsnl

3. What type of crime it was?

Solution Query: -

SELECT Crime.Type, Action.Crime_ID
FROM Action INNER JOIN
Crime ON Action.Crime_ID = Crime.Crime_ID
Where Crime.Crime_ID = '3'

Query Result: -

Type: DoS Attack

4. What was the loss victim suffered?

Solution Query: -

SELECT Physical_System.Network_Hardware, Physical_System.Victim_ID
FROM Physical_System INNER JOIN
Vicitim_Details ON Physical_System.Victim_ID = Victim_Details.Victim_ID
Where Victim_Details.Victim_ID = '2'

Query Result: -

Network Hardware: Hub

5. What type of extrinsic losses occurred?

Solution Query: -

SELECT   Extrinsic.Organization,   Extrinsic.Cost,   Extrinsic.Action_ID,
Action.Objective, Action.Duration
FROM Extrinsic INNER JOIN
Action ON Extrinsic.Action_ID = Action.Action_ID
Where Action.Action_ID = '3'

Query Result: -

Organization: Private Sector
Cost: 4 Crore
Objective: Illegal Desires
Duration: 2 Years

A numerous number of questions can be framed and its query can be written to get desired results.

9 Conclusion

The work analyses the cybercrime and cyber-criminal available data. It focuses on design techniques, understand cyber-crimes and how these crimes affect digital era to eradicate the professional work culture of organizations, data breach individual personal details and sometimes even endangers national security by embedding crime ideologies in states e-infrastructure.

The ideology of designing and developing data model for cyber threat initiates a way to gain knowledge of these cyber-crime through a data repository serving the questionnaire of its users to know details of cyber-crime, its occurrences, how it was implemented and by providing a knowledge on how to safeguard from these in futures.

The data model preparation was followed through a study of database system, modelling techniques, preparation of tables and query processing that results the answer to the title. The research also provides an introductory path for future enhancements and deep research on the topic for design and development of a robust model.

References

1. Bao, K.-M., Cheng, G.-G.: Design the database of laboratory management system. In: IEEE First International Conference on Information Science and Engineering, pp. 26–28, December 2009
2. Jing, S., Liu, X., Cheng, C., Shang, X., Xiong, G.: Study on a process safety management system design of a chemical accident database. In: IEEE International Conference on Service Operations and Logistics, and Informatics (2014)
3. Cho, H., Lee, S., Kim, B., Lee, T.: The data indexing for cyber threat resources. In: IEEE, Eighth International Conference on Ubiquitous and Future Networks (ICUFN) (2016)
4. Kellette, M., Bernier, M.: Cyber Threat Data Modeling high level model and use cases, Defence Research and Development Canada, Reference Document, DRDC-RDDC-2016-D080, December 2016
5. Kim, N., Kim, B., Lee, S., Cho, H., Park, J.-H.: Design of a cyber threat intelligence framework. Int. J. Innov. Res. Technol. Sci. (IJIRTS) 5(6) (2017)
6. Komarkova, J., Lastovicka, M., Husak, M., Tovarnak, D.: CRUSOE: data model for cyber situational awareness. In: International Conference on Availability, Reliability, and Security, 27–30 August 2018, Hamburg, Germany, p. 10. ACM, New York (2018)
7. Ch, R., Gadekallu, T.R., Abidi, M.H., Al-Ahmari, A.: Computational System to classify cyber crime offences using machine learning, MPDI, 16 May 2020
8. Agana, M.A., Inyiama, H.C.: Cyber crime detection and control using the cyber user identification model. IRACST – Int. J. Comput. Sci. Inf. Technol. Secur. (IJCSITS) 5(5), October 2015. ISSN: 2249-9555
9. Kadivar, M.: Entity relationship diagram approach to defining cyber attacks, a thesis Carleton University (2015)
10. Griffin, M.P., Mitchell, R.J.: Regenerating database techniques for real-time creation and maintenance of very large scale databases. In: IEE Colloquium on Using Virtual Worlds, 15 April 1992
11. Telnarova, Z.: Relational database as a source of ontology creation. In: Proceedings of the International Multiconference on Computer Science and Information Technology, pp. 18–20, October 2010
12. Choi, D.-L., Kim, B.-W., Lee, Y.-J., Um, Y., Chung, M.: Design and creation of dysarthric speech database for development of QoLT software technology. In: 2011 International Conference on Speech Database and Assessments (Oriental COCOSDA), pp. 26–28, October 2011
13. Boulahia-Cuppens, N., Cuppens, F., Gabillon, A., Yazdanian, K.: Multiview model for object-oriented database. In: Proceedings of 9th Annual Computer Security Applications Conference, 06–10 December 1992
14. Elmasri, R., Navathe, S.B.: Fundamentals of Database Systems, 7th edn. Pearson, London (2019)
15. Ponniah, P.: Data Warehousing Fundamentals for IT Professionals, Student Wiley, Hoboken (2019)
16. Silberschatz, A., Forth, H.F., Sudarshan, S.: Database System, 4th edn. McGraw Hill, New YOrk (2006)
17. Porgo, T.V., et al.: The use of mathematical modeling studies for evidence synthesis and guideline development: a glossary. Res. Synth. Methods 10, 125–133 (2018)

Brain Tumor Classification via UNET Architecture of CNN Technique

Arpit Kumar Sharma[1], Amita Nandal[1(✉)], Arvind Dhaka[1], and Dijana Capeska Bogatinoska[2]

[1] Department of Computer and Communication Engineering, Manipal University Jaipur, Jaipur, India
amita.nandal@jaipur.manipal.edu
[2] UIST Ohrid, Ohrid, Republic of North Macedonia
dijana.c.bogatinoska@uist.edu.mk

Abstract. The key step of early diagnosis in the brain tumor classification highly depends on the accurate estimation through the CT images or the other datasets. The precise results can effectively enhance the survival rate of patients. However, it becomes a difficult task to achieve a robust classification model with the help of traditional deep learning approaches due to differences in texture, shape and size of tumor masses with visual similarities. Therefore, this paper proposed a new algorithm of UNET that address such an important issue with the three core ideas as: 1) the construction of U-shaped classification framework for brain tumor recognition, 2) integration of adaptive histogram equalization approach with the suggested truncated normalization method for the enhancement of image contrast and 3) transfer learning approach to sort out the issue of insufficient training data. The proposed scheme shows superior performance by evaluating the public datasets of brain tumor. UNET architecture becomes a trending topic among the researchers and broadly utilized as a tool for medical image segmentation. Although, the conventional level set approaches still remained an issue as experts fail to completely understand the tumor regions due to their low-level features with complex characteristics. Thus, it is important to consider the contextual features that can deliver the complementary discriminative data to low-level characteristics for brain tumor segmentation. It starts with the designing of an UNET algorithm for encoder-decoder framework that acquire the knowledge of semantic information as high-level contextual features. Afterwards, the outcomes depicts the novel contextual energy terms with the potential to integrate the high-level contextual information in the level set framework. Such semantic information with learned contextual features can deliver the accurate distinctive information that can directly connect the category labels rather with original intensity. Thus, it can enhance the segmentation performance as it becomes robust to serious intensity inhomogeneity.

Keywords: Brain tumor · Machine learning · FCN Brain tumor segmentation · MRI · UNET · CNN · ROI

1 Introduction

Several computer-aid medical image assessment approaches require the segmentation of brain with region-of-interest (ROI) [1–3]. For example, the diagnosis of brain disease

© The Author(s), under exclusive license to Springer Nature Switzerland AG 2022
S. Joshi et al. (Eds.): SpacSec 2021, CCIS 1599, pp. 18–33, 2022.
https://doi.org/10.1007/978-3-031-15784-4_2

needs the thorough assessment of the brain network pipeline. Usually, the MR images of brain have the segmentation of multiple ROIs in order to build the brain networks. Afterwards, the subsequent assessment and diagnosis require the utilization of constructed brain networks. Although, the task becomes time consuming as the manual labeling ROIs of brain MR images is a tedious process. It also has the chances of error-prone even for experts. Therefore, researchers have developed several efficient techniques that automatically provide the ROIs of brain MRIs by using segmentation. Initial diagnosis is critical for several diseases resulting as human vision deterioration (e.g. diabetic retinopathy, hypertension and glaucoma) [1, 2]. Retinal blood vessels can be clinically examined as well as assessed with "Ophthalmologists" by taking the retinal fundus images. Such process is a significant indicator for several ophthalmic diseases diagnosis. Although, such images need high clinical experience for accurate diagnosis. Furthermore, the efficient process requires manual labeling of retinal vessels that is a tedious and time-consuming task. Therefore, experts need the real-time automatic segmentation process for the assessment of retinal blood vessels [3, 4]. Prevailing segmentation techniques to analyze retinal vessels are categorized as supervised and unsupervised systems [5]. In case of unsupervised approach, the unlabeled data samples are showing the features by distinguishing between background tissues with blood vessels, clustering and extracting the images.

In recent time, computer-aided brain disease diagnosis and medical image segmentation have shown the excellent results with the help of great success in deep learning approaches [6–12]. Experts developed numerous end-to-end networks to extract the image via automated segmentation involving the two sections as encoding and decoding of the data. Such data needs the high-level extraction of contextual feature maps with the employment of encoding path from the input image. Whereas, such high level feature maps require the decoding of up sample to estimate the to-be segmented image by using dense label map. As the brain of human features the complex anatomical structure. The usual images of brain via MR images consist the low intensity contrast nearby the ROIs boundary as well as great variance among different subjects. Although, current approaches in deep learning are generally excluding the data related with anatomical structure of brain. Therefore, susceptible to deliver the performance of sub-optimal segmentation of brain ROI.

Last decade witnessed the superior performance of ROI segmentation by using the techniques of multi-atlas system employed in ROI segmentation [13–16] with respect to the traditional single-atlas based approaches of brain MR images. The labeled set of atlases are primarily registered onto the common space of to-be-segmented image in case of multi-atlas based segmentation framework. Further, the multiple atlas labels lead to estimate the final label map of the segmented image. Multi-atlas based segmentation framework has the major advantage of having the abundant of anatomical data about human brain delivered by several registered atlases (apart from single atlas). Although, such techniques generally carry the MR images of brain represented by handcrafted features such as image intensity. Also, such handcrafted characteristics depicts the lacking of coordination with consequent label propagation algorithms resulting as the degradation in segmentation performance. The accurate ROI segmentation requires the task-oriented feature extraction approaches for brain MR images. However, the segmentation approaches consisting the multi-atlas mapping are usually a tedious and time-consuming task as it consists an enormous volume of atlas images [17]. It is important to note that the clinical applications always consider the computation time as most significant factor.

2 UNET Architecture and Training

Olaf et al. introduced and developed the *UNET* approach for the segmentation of bio images. The architecture of UNET has two paths including the contraction path or en coder and symmetric expanding path or decoder. Encoder can capture the context in image. Contraction path just depicts the conventional stack of max pooling and con volution layers. Whereas, decoder enables the accurate localization by utilizing the transposed convolutions. Therefore, the UNET framework becomes an end-to-end fully convolutional network (FCN) [18–20]. It only includes the Convolutional layers without any dense layer due to which it can work with data of any size.

The core architecture of UNET is as follows:

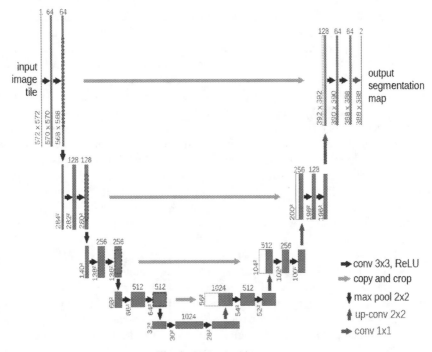

Fig. 1. UNet Architecture

Figure 1 depicts the original architecture of UNET having the input image as 572 × 572 × 3 in size. Although, several researchers also use the image size of 128 × 128 × 3. Therefore, experts need to carefully analyze the several locations of images in order to achieve the optimized results.

Deep learning techniques widely use CNN architecture with UNET approach. It is the post-processing method used in the reconstruction of sparse tomographic image

[21–23]. UNET features several characteristics appropriated for the removal of artifact used in multichannel filtering and multilevel decomposition [24]. Furthermore, UNET architecture depicts the high compatibility with the iterative approaches for sparse photoacoustic tomography (PAT). It can efficiently remove the image artifact from the experimental/synthetic data [21, 22]. Researchers can consider the prior work on CNN with advanced post-processing techniques such as dense connectivity to attain the superior performance with better results. The training process can be accelerated with the use of batch normalization method with respect to conventional UNET implementations [25, 26].

"DD-Net" is another advanced version of UNet that represents the dense connectivity. It is applicable for the reconstruction of sparse-view CT images with the outperforming of iterative approaches [27]. However, the FD-UNet also involves dense connectivity but with numerous differences in execution such as;

1) DD-Net consists only dense connectivity in contracting path/encoding of UNet architecture. While, FD-UNet involves the dense connectivity in both contracting/encoding as well as the expanding/decoding paths. Such approach initiates the advantages of dense connectivity in the entire network.
2) DD-Net has the constant "growth rate" of dense block (as a hyper-parameter) throughout the network. While, FD-UNET requires the constant upgradation of such hyper-parameter to the entire CNN for the advancement of computational effectiveness.

3 Related Work

Feng et al. [28] assessed the 3D directional scores collected from retinal images that is further enhanced the blood vessels via multi-scale derivatives. Roy Chowdhury et al. [29] utilized the segmentation approaches as adaptive thresholding as well as fundus vascular morphology techniques. Jiang et al. worked on the vessel segmentation by introducing a centerline detection methodology [30]. CNN architecture with unsupervised strategies have the merits of low data acquisition cost and the requirement of low sample data. However, the small dataset features are generally carrying the individual traits without reflecting the complications of vessel boundaries.In case of CNN with supervised approaches, a classification issue arises in form of retinal vessel segmentation. Such an issue consider the blood vessels and other tissues as in two groups based on pixel-by-pixel classification. For instance, Strisciuglio et al. [31] suggested COSFIRE filter sets in order to estimate the most discriminative filter subset with the training of a support vector machine (SVM) classfier for vessel delineation. Furthermore, Orlando et al. [32] suggested the structured-output of SVM learning technique as fully-connected conditional-random-field vessel segmentation system. In recent times, Zhang et al. [33] integrated the wavelet and vascular characteristics by utilizing the random forest classifier with the processing of twenty-nine feature sets for vessel segmentation. Supervised approaches have often the strong influence of the engineered features and expert labeling with high computational cost with respect to unsupervised methods. Several computer vision operations have the deep learning model that can achieve state-of-the-art performance e.g. developing image subtitles, motion tracking, target recognition, image segmentation and image classification [33]. Specifically, the assessment of medical image has the deep CNN performance that is nearly equivalent to several semantic operations for the radiologists. U-Net [34] is most broadly featured the deep learning framework for the assessment of medical image, majorly due to the presence of codec architecture with jump joints that permits the effective data flow as well as superior performance under the condition of insufficiently large files of dataset. Therefore, researchers proposed several UNET attributes. Alom et al. [35] provided a novel architecture of UNET segmentation with recurrent convolutional neural network (RCNN) (also known as RU-NET).

Oktay et al. [36] offered a technique by integrating the UNET with an attention module for the segmentation of pancreas. Jégou et al. [37] suggested another UNET architecture named as Tiramisu that include the dense blocks in place of cascaded convolutional layers. Here, feed-forward sequence makes the direct connection between every convolutional layer with other layers. Although, such process shows extremely unbalanced nature to extract the fundus image data including just twenty cases of the training dataset. Such framework only has 10-20% of positive cases [38]. Thus, it becomes risky to apply the classic U-Net architecture in such cases. Image patches extraction can solve the issue of data imbalance including the random selection of data from 3,000 to 10,000 training samples [27, 39–42]. Although, such patch-based methods has several limitations such as failure to achieve real-time outcomes, long testing times and slow convergence rates, due to which it becomes less selective for clinical applications. However, the results of BTS-DSN approach are inferior to patch-based approach as it fails to discriminate the fundus images into patches. Prior approaches implemented diverse forms of data augmentation processes for small datasets extraction. For example, Bandara and Giragama [43] proposed a technique by using the concept of spatially adaptive contrast enhancement for vessel segmentation to extract the retinal fundus images. Furthermore, Oliveira et al. [39] preprocessed the retinal fundus images 3by utilizing the stationary wavelet transform (SWT) technique. Although the preprocessing via SWT is a slow and complicated approach.

4   Dataset Description Data Acquisition

4.1   Data Acquisition

The brain tumor classification involves the images with the gray value ranges from 0-65535 of the original brain CT or MRI images. Usually, such images consists numerous worthless zero-value sections. The data acquisition requires an accurate CNN-based approach that initiates the simple normalization operations by pre-processing the input information [25–27]. Although, the main concentration of the tumor masses (represented by gray distribution) reflecting the sections that have the gray level of higher than 10,000. Such distribution shows no alterations if the linear normalization operation directly conducted on the CT/MRI images. The brain tumor region can be highlighted by arranging the gray level pixels in ascending order (starts with '0'). Normally, such pixels are normalized to attain the efficient truncated normalization as it is placed from the initial 1% to the final 5%. Figure 1 depicts the original images of the human brain with gray representation by using truncated normalization approach. It illustrates the image contrast among several tissues of brain region.

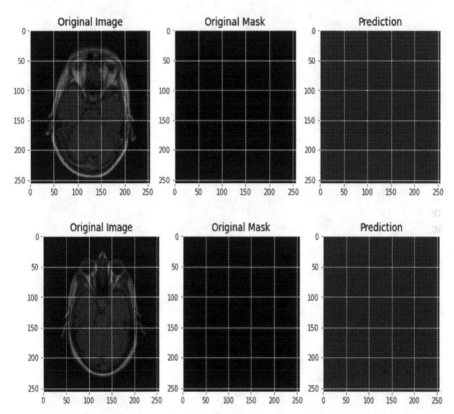

Fig. 2. Original image and the masking effect due to preprocessing

4.2   Pre-processing

Figure 2 shows the original image and the masking effect due to preprocessing the data with their prediction. The original CT/MRI image has the single-channel as shown in Fig. 1. While, the pre-processed data has the three-channel image as the original image, original mask and prediction. The first channel always goes for the truncation normalization process. On the other hand, the contrast limited adaptive histogram equalization can enhance the image by processing the remaining two channels. Figure 2 depicts the more visible boundaries of several sections as compared to the Fig. 1.

The primary step in medical image assessment is the pre-processing of data that can enhance the diagnostic effectiveness by developing the images as more intuitive. Medical image analysis has the segmentation approach as the most crucial step. The pathology research and clinical diagnosis needs a reliable procedure in order to assist the doctor for achieving precise diagnosis. It provides the relevant feature extraction by

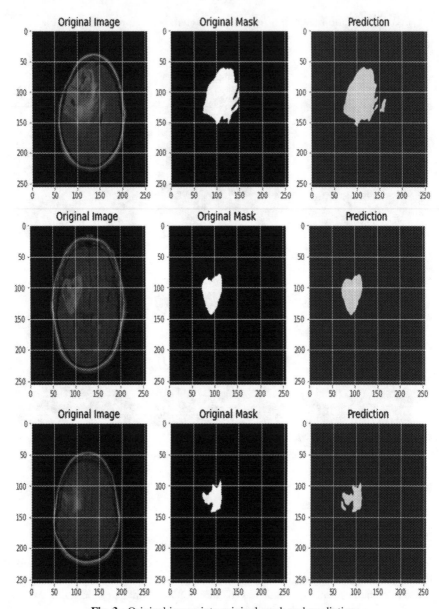

Fig. 3. Original image into original mask and prediction

segmenting the required sections of medical images. Primarily, low-level pixel process-ing with sequential application can assess the medical images such as threshold based or region based approaches. Afterwards, the construction of compound rule based sys-tems through mathematical modeling can sort out the specific tasks [3]. The data has the absence of semantic label based segmentation outcomes. However, image segmentation often refers the semantic segmentation in the domain of deep learning. It represents the image recognition at pixel level (image has the object category with the marking of each pixel) [4, 5]. Currently, image analysis has CNN as the most successful type of deep learning approach.

Conventional CNNs usually work with fully connected layer to achieve the fixed-length feature vectors by putting them into a classifier such as softmax layer. On the contrary, the fully convolutional layers (FCNs) can receive the input image of any size as the up-sampling layer. Such process happens after restoring the input dimensions by last convolutional layer to be equivalent as the input image. Afterwards, the system generates the prediction for every pixel, simultaneously conserving the spatial information in the original input image. In last, up-sampling feature maps can deliver the pixel-by-pixel classification into the expected image segmentation. UNET [8] includes the convolutional layers, up as well as down-sampling layers as similar to the FCNs. However, UNET approach has the equivalent numbers of up-sampling layers, down-sampling layers and convolution layers as differ from FCNs process. Furthermore, U-net provides the more accurate segmentation outcomes by directly applying the spatial information to the much deeper layers as it utilizes the skip connection process to make connection between every pair of up/down-sampling layer.

4.3 Transfer Learning

Transfer learning technique can solve the issue of insufficient labeled data by classifying the brain tumor in regions. The testing as well as training data carry the similar and independent prior assumptions at the time of training method while using the CNN models. Therefore, deep learning approaches have the most serious issue as data dependency. Several operations need the different data types. Such information have almost linear correlation between the scale of required training data and CNN model size. It means that the lacking of information in deep CNN models training leads to the prone to overfitting. Transfer learning phenomenon can easily remove such issue by assuming that no difference in the highlighting characteristics learned by CNN model. At the time of training, the model can be trained by information having the uneven distribution from testing dataset. Therefore, the model carries the training data with superior initialization variants along with similar distribution resulting as the fine-tuning of testing dataset. Figure 3 illustrates the images with large dataset training with high labeling quality. Afterwards, some pre-trained variants can initialize such new model (usually the feature extraction section), and in last performed the fine-tuning of novel model with target dataset (Fig. 4).

Transfer learning can eliminate the requirement of similar and independent distribution of testing and training the information. The datasets of medical images also includes the record privacy of the patient that becomes a tough task to collect. Also, the data annotation always requires the consultation from professional doctors. As such kind of datasets have not much data annotation. Thus, transfer-learning approaches play significant role in medical field due to their broad applications with superior results [36–38]. In addition, few research works have depicted the high efficiency of transfer learning algorithms applicable for brain tumor classification [39]. Particularly, UNET architecture of CNN model can train the datasets from ImageNet in order to initialize the encoding part.

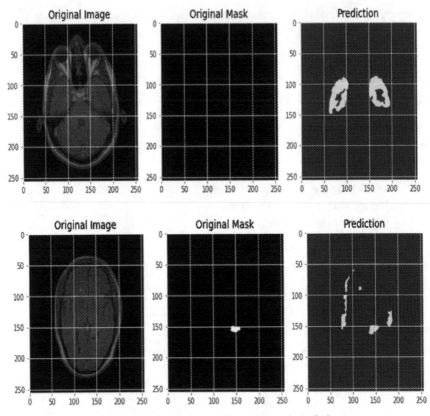

Fig. 4. Original image, original mask and prediction

5   System Model

Research works have illustrated the significance of computer-aid diagnostic models that can deliver the reproducible as well as speedy assessment results. In addition, such procedures highly enhancing the diagnostic accuracy of the brain tumor by lessening the work pressure of radiologists [10, 11]. Nevertheless, it becomes difficult to achieve a robust classification framework for brain tumor due to the presence of heterogeneity in tumor sections from CT/MRI images. Figure 1 and 2 depicts several discriminations in tumor sections as differ in texture, shape and size. Apart from great resemblance among the malignant and benign regions, there is the need to create a robust classification model. For example, Fig. 3 shows the high resemblance between the datasets, but all are belong to different classes. Such issue can be easily addressed with the help of UNET architecture involving the two key modules as classification module (or an encoder depending on the residual block and segmentation module (or a decoder depending on the convolution block). This research has the technical contributions as:

1. Integration of conventional classification architecture with a decoder in order to achieve the classification module by performing the feature extraction. Such procedure can extract the truly efficient features by indirectly assisting the classification module.
2. This research has the extension of core UNET architecture by involving the adaptive histogram equalization process and truncated normalization approach for image contrast. It can extract the features of brain tumor (along with the surrounding tissues) consisting the low contrast with better results.
3. Such work involves the transfer learning based approach on datasets to sort out the issue of difficult convergence developed by lacking of training data that can be further enhance the generalization capability of the model.

UNet Model as Security: As per security in UNet model, majorly two reason behind that:

- Converting a picture into a vector, currently scholarly the element planning of the picture so why not utilize a similar planning to change over it again to picture.
- The reason it can confine and recognize borders is by doing order on each pixel, so the information and yield share a similar size.

This is the strategy behind the UNet model engineering or all in all, this is the security system of UNet. Utilize similar component maps that are utilized for withdrawal to extend a vector to a fragmented picture. This would protect the primary uprightness of the picture which would lessen contortion hugely according to security purposes.

6   Proposed Methodology

This section provides the design detailing of the UNET architecture that uses the bridge format of the framework. Research work involves the cascading architecture with the applications of foreground characteristics to the earlier network block. Such significant information of the next network block can boost the quality of input images along with inherit the learning experience of the prior network blocks. The methodology involves the usage of full images with vertical as well as horizontal performance of data augmentation. The summarization of proposed framework is presented in this section. UNET architecture with its attributes consist the encoder-decoder framework in order to attain the outstanding outcomes with fundus vascular segmentation. Although, such segmentation issue leads to the excessive down sampling with the loss of vascular information. Also, the presence of several attributes can develop the problem of overfitting. Thus, this research presents the simplified version of UNET architecture with classical framework that uses the core building block of the segmentation system.

Proposed Methodology:

1. Step 01: OpenCV function read the image and visualise the plot.

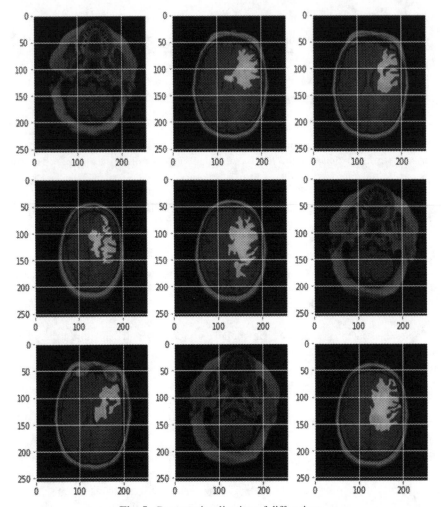

Fig. 5. Dataset visualization of diff patients

As shown in Fig. 5, the datasets of three patients depicts the tumour growth in the brain. First step involves the tumour detection with high visualization. The datasets shows the growth in the tumour with constant rate. It has also the image reconstruction quality that removes many artifacts and provides the clear picture.

Step 02: using few function in this step (dice_coef, dice_coef_loss, iou, jac_distance).

dice_coef (F1 Score) = Dice Coefficient is 2 * the Area of Overlap divided by the total number of pixels in both images.

iou = IoU is the area of overlap between the predicted segmentation and the ground truth divided by the area of union between the predicted segmentation and the ground truth.

$$IoU = \text{Area of overlap/Area of Union}$$

jac_distance = This loss is useful when you have unbalanced classes within a sample such as segmenting each pixel of an image.

This step performs the quantification of image reconstruction by utilizing the structural similarity index (SSIM) as well as peak signal-to-noise ratio (PSNR) [43]. SSIM computes the similarities in the pixel intensities as local patterns, while PSNR delivers the global measurement of image quality. CNN technique provides both testing as well as training datasets in this initial experiment by utilizing the sequential dataset. CNN has the opportunity to learn all the features as such experiment consists the ideal data scenario where the testing and training data are compatible [44]. It means the testing data to perform well on training data. Such condition delivers the initial point for the performance assessment of CNNs excluding the data-related issues [45].

Step 03: UNet Architecture (Conv 01 to 05, up 06 to 09) (Image 01: UNet architecture diagram)

The initial process of this step starts with the training of neural networks depending on the encoder-decoder model. UNet architecture generates the contextual feature map by providing the building block that acquire knowledge about the intrinsic characteristics of brain tumor. Such model shows high accuracy and better performance with respect to the other techniques that can restore the contextual feature map. Tumors detection requires the pixel tracking ultimately resulting as in the improvement of segmentation process.

Step 04: Train Generator (Adjust as standard image data size, epochs 50, 100 iteration in each epoch)

The process initiates with the convolution of the encoder. Each convolutional layer consists the 3 × 3 kernel and applies the convolution operation in order to generate the feature maps. Afterwards, max-pooling layer retains the robust rotation information and lessens the size of feature map. The max pool operation uses five layers consisting the window size of 2 × 2 with a stride-size of 2. Encoder as the local details of the convolutional layers extract. On the other hand, max pooling layers works on the extraction of global features. Input image has the spatial resolution that become 32 times shorten after feature extraction.

Decoder forms with the help of skip-layers, deconvolution operation and un-pooling that can attain the equivalent resolution level from input image. Feature maps has a broader view of resolution due to the un-pooling mechanism. Encoder as well as deconvolution layers have the relatable operations. Skip layers forwards the feature maps of every pooling layer at the encoder. It can simultaneously link the layers with the relative feature maps at decoder. Such process can restore the spatial information that is missing from max pooling. In last, a convolution layer with 1 × 1 dimensions produces the contextual feature map following Google Inception and U-Net. Decoder provides the final outcome with respect to the conventional fully connected layer. Convolution layer involves the single channel that carries the channels of features or input image. Convolution layer usage can lessen the estimation time during testing. Furthermore, it has the potential to deplete in dimensions, high-performance computational operations and effective feature pooling characteristics.

Step 05: Load the Model

Loading the images after achieving the results from UNet architecture (encoder-decoder).

Step 06: Predict the Result

7   Result and Discussion

UNet architecture for brain tumor classification process totally depends on the highly encoding, decoding on the datasets with transfer learning techniques in order to overcome with the designed algorithm shows the accuracy of 99% that is the superior outcome in its range. The suggested algorithm involves the pre-trained datasets with the training of separate approach as well as an off-the-shelf feature extractor (without training). It also presents the transferability of learning from natural images to medical brain MR images. According to the structure of UNet model is shown in Fig. 1 clearly all the layers of model and its working way and process to solve the challenges to classified. In that Model loss, Binary Accuracy, IoU and model dice coefficient as shown in table (Table 1).

Table 1. Resultant parameter of work

Resultant parameter	Final result
Loss	0.12243861705064774
binary_accuracy	0.9975486397743225
Iou	0.7829025387763977
dice_coef	0.8771856427192688

8   Conclusion

In this research work, we developed a novel UNET architecture for brain tumor classification with accurate performance. The process highly depends on the encoding, decoding of the datasets with transfer learning technique in order to overcome the issue of insufficient datasets. The clinical diagnosis becomes simpler as it segments the data sets with accurate illustration of brain tumor regions. The designed algorithm shows the accuracy of 99% that is the superior outcome in its range. The suggested algorithm involves the pre-trained datasets with the training of separate approach as well as an off-the-shelf feature extractor (without training). It also presents the transferability of learning from natural images to medical brain MR images. This approach may be used to develop CBIR for other body organ MRI images and other medical imaging domains, such as X-rays, PET, and CT. Our CBIR is more generic because it requires only MR images as a query to retrieve the relevant tumor images from the database. The experimental results revealed that the proposed CBIR outperformed state-of-the-art methods on CE-MRI dataset.

References

1. Karpecki, P., Bowling, B.: Kanski's clinical ophthalmology: a systematic approach. In: Optometry and Vision Science, 8th edn., vol. 92, no. 10, Art. no. e386. LWW, Philadelphia, October 2015
2. Furtado, P., Travassos, C., Monteiro, R., Oliveira, S., Baptista, C., Carrilho, F.: Segmentation of eye fundus images by density clustering in diabetic retinopathy. In: Proceedings of IEEE EMBS International Conference on Biomedical and Health Informatics (BHI), Orlando, FL, USA, pp. 25–28, February 2017
3. Kirbas, C., Quek, F.: A review of vessel extraction techniques and algorithms. ACM Comput. Surv. **36**(2), 81–121 (2014)
4. Fraz, M.M., et al.: Blood vessel segmentation methodologies in retinal images-a survey. Comput. Methods Progr. Biomed. **108**(1), 407–433 (2012)
5. Mo, J., Zhang, L.: Multi-level deep supervised networks for retinal vessel segmentation. Int. J. Comput. Assist. Radiol. Surg. **12**(12), 2181–2193 (2017). https://doi.org/10.1007/s11548-017-1619-0
6. Liu, M., Zhang, J., Adeli, E., Shen, D.: Landmark-based deep multiinstance learning for brain disease diagnosis. Med. Image Anal. **43**, 157–168 (2018)
7. Chen, Y., Gao, H., Cai, L., Shi, M., Shen, D., Ji, S.: Voxel deconvolutional networks for 3D brain image labeling. In: Proceedings of the 24th ACM SIGKDD International Conference on Knowledge Discovery and Data Mining, pp. 1226–1234. ACM (2018)
8. Lian, C., et al.: Multi-channel multi-scale fully convolutional network for 3D perivascular spaces segmentation in 7T MR images. Med. Image Anal. **46**, 106–117 (2018)
9. Iakovidis, D.K., Georgakopoulos, S.V., Vasilakakis, M., Koulaouzidis, A., Plagianakos, V.P.: Detecting and locating gastrointestinal anomalies using deep learning and iterative cluster unification. IEEE Trans. Med. Imaging **PP**(99), 2196–2210 (2018)
10. Lin, H., Chen, H., Graham, S., Dou, Q., Rajpoot, N., Heng, P.-A.: Fast ScanNet: fast and dense analysis of multi-gigapixel whole-slide images for cancer metastasis detection. IEEE Trans. Med. Imaging **38**(8), 1948–1958 (2019)
11. Lian, C., Liu, M., Zhang, J., Shen, D.: Hierarchical fully convolutional network for joint atrophy localization and Alzheimer's disease diagnosis using structural MRI. IEEE Trans. Pattern Anal. Mach. Intell. **42**, 880–893 (2018)
12. Islam, J., Zhang, Y.: Brain MRI analysis for Alzheimer's disease diagnosis using an ensemble system of deep convolutional neural networks. Brain Inform. **5**(2), 1–14 (2018). https://doi.org/10.1186/s40708-018-0080-3
13. Artaechevarria, X., Munozbarrutia, A., Ortizdesolorzano, C.: Combination strategies in multi-atlas image segmentation: application to brain MR data. IEEE Trans. Med. Imaging **28**(8), 1266–1277 (2009)
14. Coupe, P., Manjon, J.V., Fonov, V., Pruessner, J.C., Robles, M., Collins, D.L.: Patch-based segmentation using expert priors: application to hippocampus and ventricle segmentation. Neuroimage **54**(2), 940–954 (2011)
15. Tong, T., Wolz, R., Coupe, P., Hajnal, J.V., Rueckert, D.: Segmentation of MR images via discriminative dictionary learning and sparse coding: application to hippocampus labeling. Neuroimage **76**, 11–23 (2013)
16. Wang, H., Suh, J.W., Das, S.R., Pluta, J., Craige, C., Yushkevich, P.A.: Multi-atlas segmentation with joint label fusion. IEEE Trans. Pattern Anal. Mach. Intell. **35**(3), 611–623 (2013)
17. Kirisli, H.A., et al.: Fully automatic cardiac segmentation from 3D CTA data: a multi-atlas based approach. In: Medical Imaging 2010: Image Processing, vol. 7623, p. 762305 (2010)

18. Ronneberger, O., Fischer, P., Brox, T.: U-Net: convolutional networks for biomedical image segmentation. In: Proceedings of International Conference on Medical Image Computing and Computer-Assisted Intervention, Münich, Germany, pp. 234–241, November 2015

19. Alom, M.Z., Hasan, M., Yakopcic, C., Taha, M.T., Asari, V.K.: Recurrent residual convolutional neural network based on U-Net (R2U-Net) for medical image segmentation, February 2018

20. Oktay, O., et al.: Attention U-Net: learning where to look for the pancreas, April 2018

21. Antholzer, S., Haltmeier, M., Schwab, J.: Deep learning for photoacoustic tomography from sparse data, ArXiv170404587 Cs, April 2017

22. Schwab, J., Antholzer, S., Nuster, R., Haltmeier, M.: DALnet: high-resolution photoacoustic projection imaging using deep learning, ArXiv180106693 Phys, January 2018

23. Han, Y.S., Yoo, J., Ye, J.C.: Deep residual learning for compressed sensing CT reconstruction via persistent homology analysis, ArXiv161106391 Cs, November 2016

24. Jin, K.H., McCann, M.T., Froustey, E., Unser, M.: Deep convolutional neural network for inverse problems in imaging. IEEE Trans. Image Process. **26**(9), 4509–4522 (2017)

25. Ioffe, S., Szegedy, C.: Batch normalization: accelerating deep network training by reducing internal covariate shift, ArXiv150203167 Cs, February 2015

26. Santurkar, S., Tsipras, D., Ilyas, A., Madry, A.: How does batch normalization help optimization? (No, it is not about internal covariate shift), ArXiv180511604 Cs Stat, May 2018

27. Zhang, Z., Liang, X., Dong, X., Xie, Y., Cao, G.: A sparse-view CT reconstruction method based on combination of DenseNet and deconvolution. IEEE Trans. Med. Imaging **37**, 1 (2018)

28. Feng, Z., Yang, J., Yao, L.: Patch-based fully convolutional neural network with skip connections for retinal blood vessel segmentation. In: Proceedings of IEEE International Conference on Image Processing (ICIP), Beijing, China, pp. 1742–1746, September 2017

29. Roychowdhury, S., Koozekanani, D.D., Parhi, K.K.: Iterative vessel segmentation of fundus images. IEEE Trans. Biomed. Eng. **62**(7), 1738–1749 (2015)

30. Jiang, Z., Yepez, J., An, S., Ko, S.: Fast, accurate and robust retinal vessel segmentation system. Biocybern. Biomed. Eng. **37**(3), 412–421 (2017)

31. Strisciuglio, N., Azzopardi, G., Vento, M.: Supervised vessel delineation in retinal fundus images with the automatic selection of B-COSFIRE filters. Mach. Vis. Appl. **27**(8), 1137–1149 (2016). https://doi.org/10.1007/s00138-016-0781-7

32. Orlando, J.I., Prokofyeva, E., Blaschko, M.B.: A discriminatively trained fully connected conditional random field model for blood vessel segmentation in fundus images. IEEE Trans. Biomed. Eng. **64**(1), 16–27 (2017)

33. Zhang, J., Chen, Y., Bekkers, E., Wang, M., Dashtbozorg, B., ter Haar Romeny, B.M.: Retinal vessel delineation using a brain-inspired wavelet transform and random forest. Pattern Recognit. **69**, 107–123 (2017)

34. LeCun, Y., Bengio, Y., Hinton, G.: Deep learning. Nature **521**, 436–444 (2015)

35. Alom, M.Z., Hasan, M., Yakopcic, C., Taha, M.T., Asari, V.K.: Recurrent residual convolutional neural network based on U-Net (R2U-Net) for medical image segmentation, February 2018. arXiv:1802.06955 https://arxiv.org/abs/1802.06955

36. Oktay, O., et al.: Attention U-Net: learning where to look for the pancreas, April 2018 arXiv: 1804.03999 https://arxiv.org/abs/1804.03999

37. Jegou, S., Drozdzal, M., Vazquez, D., Romero, A., Bengio, Y.: The one hundred layers tiramisu: fully convolutional densenets for semantic segmentation. In: Proceedings of IEEE Conference on Computer Vision and Pattern Recognition Workshops, pp. 11–19, July 2017

38. Staal, J., Abramoff, M.D., Niemeijer, M., Viergever, M.A., van Ginneken, B.: Ridge-based vessel segmentation in color images of the retina. IEEE Trans. Med. Imag. **23**(4), 501–509 (2004)
39. Pereira, O.S., Silva, C.A.: Retinal vessel segmentation based on fully convolutional neural networks. Expert Syst. Appl. **112**, 229–242 (2018)
40. Yan, Z., Yang, X., Cheng, K.-T.: A three-stage deep learning model for accurate retinal vessel segmentation. IEEE J. Biomed. Health Inform. **23**(4), 1427–1436 (2019)
41. Zhang, Y., Chung, A.C.S.: Deep supervision with additional labels for retinal vessel segmentation task. In: Proceedings of International Conference on Medical Image Computing and Computer-Assisted Intervention, Granada, Spain, pp. 83–91, September 2018
42. Guo, S., Wang, K., Kang, H., Zhang, Y., Gao, Y., Li, T.: BTS-DSN: deeply supervised neural network with short connections for retinal vessel segmentation. Int. J. Med. Inform. **126**, 105–113 (2019)
43. Bandara, M.R.R., Giragama, P.W.: A retinal image enhancement technique for blood vessel segmentation algorithm. In: Proceedings of IEEE International Conference on Industrial and Information Systems (ICIIS, Peradeniya, Sri Lanka, pp. 1–5, December 2017
44. Wang, Z., Bovik, A.C., Sheikh, H.R., Simoncelli, E.P.: Image quality assessment: from error visibility to structural similarity. IEEE Trans. Image Process. **13**(4), 600–612 (2004)
45. Sharma, A.K., Nandal, A., Dhaka, A., Dixit, R.: A survey on machine learning based brain retrieval algorithms in medical image analysis. Health Technol. **10**(6), 1359–1373 (2020). https://doi.org/10.1007/s12553-020-00471-0
46. Sharma, A.K., Nandal, A., Dhaka, A., et al.: Medical image classification techniques and analysis using deep learning networks: a review. In: Patgiri, R., Biswas, A., Roy, P. (eds.) Health Informatics: A Computational Perspective in Healthcare, vol. 932, pp. 233–258. Springer, Cham (2021). https://doi.org/10.1007/978-981-15-9735-0_13

Analysis of Various Supervised Machine Learning Algorithms for Intrusion Detection

Kabir Nagpal, Niyati Jain, Ayush Patra, Arnav Gupta, Anjana Syamala,
and Sunita Singhal$^{(\boxtimes)}$

Department of Computer Science and Information Technology, Manipal University Jaipur,
Jaipur, Ajmer Expressway, Jaipur, Jaipur, Rajasthan, India
```
{kabir.189301041,niyati.189301051,ayush.189301006,
arnav.189303180}@muj.manipal.edu, {anjana.syamala,
sunita.singhal}@jaipur.manipal.edu
```

Abstract. Computer network intrusion detection systems help recognize unauthorized access and abnormal attacks over secured networks. It is an important research domain with the advent of internet technologies and cybersecurity. Several past research includes decision-based methods to detect intrusion. However, with advancing technologies, intrusions are becoming more sophisticated. Machine learning algorithms are the panacea to improve detection accuracy and reduce false alarm rate. An Anomaly-based intrusion detection system is one type that uses supervised machine learning techniques to train the system to detect and classify an attack. The paper includes feature extraction and selection methods that considerably reduce time in detecting an anomaly without compromising the accuracy. The UNSW-NB15 dataset, which represents communications in a network, is used for the research. Performance of several known algorithms is compared along with feature engineering, aiding us to achieve an unparalleled accuracy of 88.7%, F-score of 88.3%, and false alarm rate of 0.014.

Keywords: Intrusion detection · UNSW-NB15 dataset · Machine learning · Feature selection

1 Introduction

The exponential growth of technologies like the Cloud, Internet-of-Things, Big Data, and Cryptography has attracted hackers and encouraged them to create new forms of crime orders. Due to critical information, secrets and user privacy, organizations must prevent their systems from being hacked. Hence, Intrusion Detection Systems (IDS) unquestionably proves a key invention to overcome security management concerns [1].

As described by Panda et al. [2] an IDS is a system to monitor the activities occurring in a computer system or network and analyses them for possible intrusions. An IDS is capable of managing audit data, rectifying system configurations and maintaining information about intruders. Intruders are categorized as external and internal. An external intruder is an unauthorized user of the machine they attack, whereas internal intruders

© The Author(s), under exclusive license to Springer Nature Switzerland AG 2022
S. Joshi et al. (Eds.): SpacSec 2021, CCIS 1599, pp. 34–50, 2022.
https://doi.org/10.1007/978-3-031-15784-4_3

have the rights to access the system with slight restrictions [3]. Such attacks need to be recognized by an IDS for effective prevention and control.

IDS can be, broadly classified into two types under detection methods i.e. Anomaly-based detection [4] and Misuse detection [5]. Misuse detection, also called Signature-based detection detect intrusion by constructing anomaly behavior character libraries and mapping network data. They cannot identify new attacks in the network even after having a high detection rate. On the other hand, an Anomaly-based System establishes models as per normal network behavior and performs operations based on whether the behaviors match the normal behavior. These type of system have unparalleled accuracy for unknown anomalies, but their overall detection rate is low with a high False Alarm Rate (FAR) [6] Detection of intrusion is a classification task, which categories the behavior of the network traffic into normal and anomalous. If anomalous, it predicts the type of intrusion. The main challenges of IDS philosophically are to reduce false positives alarm and to increase detection accuracy.

Over the last few years, Machine Learning-based IDS (ML) have proved to be a primary area of research. ML gives the system the ability to learn and improve using predefined data. These systems do not rely much on domain knowledge; hence, they are simple to plan and build. These are largely deployed as depicted in Fig. 1. The incoming network traffic is filtered within the IDS system and forwarded based on IP address. Detected packages are dropped and hence prevent any network intrusions in time. Machine Learning algorithms can be Supervised, Unsupervised or Semi-Supervised. These categories are due to data which can be labelled, unlabeled or partially labelled. Furthermore, this paper puts forward various Feature Engineering strategies intending to create optimal features that improve the system's efficiency helping in nearly real-time detection.

Supervised ML methodologies as given in the Fig. 1. Our work is leveraged the power of XGBoost [7] and Light Gradient Boosting Machine [8] over the UNSW-NB15 dataset [9]. To evaluate the importance of features, the other supervised models to engender a reduced and a capitalized feature vector. All the processing is done in the Python [10] programming language using packages Scikit-Learn [11] and Pandas [12].

The encapsulation of the entire text is as follows: Firstly, the report of related work is introduced in Sect. 2. That is followed by methodology the research work where Feature engineering and Machine learning models are precisely described in Sect. 3. Section 3

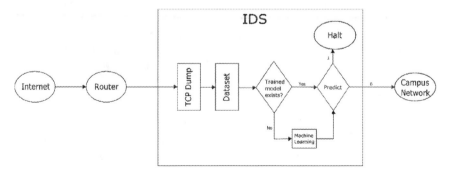

Fig. 1. A pictorial representation of internet setup with IDS

highlights the UNSW-NB15 dataset with an emphasis on its data objects, features, and advantages over other datasets. Section 4 shows results of different methodology. Finally Sect. 5, the last segment concludes the paper while paving the way for future experiments in this domain.

2 Related Work

An integrated rule-based methodology was used by V. Kumar et al. [13], on the UNSW-NB15 dataset. The method is faster to implement and achieves the FAR of 2.01%. RTNITP18, a new dataset, was also introduced by the researchers to test the rules. However, the system is unable to detect any zero-day attacks which are blatantly unknown. Therefore, there is no sign found for those attacks. Hence there is no signature found for those attacks.

Feature selection methods are imperative in improving the performance of a classification problem. Better results can be achieved from classification by choosing a reduced feature subset from the main set. This reduced feature subset is usually free of multi collinearity and consists of the most optimal variables, thus producing a better depiction of patterns belonging to different classes.

Authors of [14], a GA-LR wrapper strategy is used for feature selection, to choose a set that expands the precision of classification. The paper tested the approach on KDD99 and UNSW-NB15 datasets. Their methodology permitted them to accomplish the False Alarm Rate of 6.39%, with the subset having 20 features.

Ambusaidi et al. introduced [15] Flexible Mutual Information Feature Selection (FMIFS), a supervised filter-based feature selection algorithm, was introduced. The selected features trained with Least Squares Support Vector Machine [16] showed an improvement easily surpassing other algorithms present then, in terms of FAR and efficiency in training. However, there is a scope of improvement by reducing unbalance in the dataset and improving feature search.

Hadeel et al. [17] proposes the use of Pigeon inspired Optimizer. The datasets used to test the method were KDDCUPP99, NSL-KDD and UNSW-NB15. This technique reduced the feature count in the UNSW-NB15 dataset from 49 to 5 and achieved an accuracy of 91.3%.

Omar Almomani et al. purposes [18], uses several feature selection methods such as Genetic algorithms and optimization techniques such as PSO, GWO and FFA. The methodology produces 13 sets of rules for choosing features from the UNSW-NB15 dataset. The subset thus obtained is trained on Support Vector Machine (SVM) [16]. Each of the 13 rules contained a different subset of features and achieved varying accuracy and F-scores.

3 Methodology

A schematic approach of solving supervised Machine learning problems is followed. First the UNSW-NB15 dataset and then went on to perform feature engineering. This is followed by feature extraction and feature selection to eliminate unnecessary columns and elevate the efficiency and speed of our model. Thereafter multiple machine learning algorithms were tested and evaluation metrics, Accuracy, F score and FAR score were calculated.

3.1 The UNSW-NB15 Dataset

The UNSW-NB 15 dataset created in the Cyber Range Lab of the Australian Centre for Cyber Security (ACCS) to generate a hybrid of the realistic modern normal activities and the synthetic contemporary attack behaviors from network traffic [19]. The dataset is collected from the IDS systems as in Fig. 1 and deployed at the same location.

The UNSW-NB15 comprises 42 features out of which 3 instances that are categorical features and 39 are numeric which are described explicitly. The dataset incorporates a greater number of sorts of attacks than does the KDD99 dataset [20], and its highlights are more abundant. The features include flow features, basic features, content features, time features, additional features, and labelled features [21].

The data categories include normal data and nine types of attacks. The UNSW-NB15 includes the following types of network attacks: Backdoor, Shellcode, Reconnaissance, Worms, Fuzzers, DoS, Generic, Analysis, Shellcode and Exploits. It represents the latest IDS and is hence preferred in recent studies. Though its effectiveness is limited, it is essential to come up with new datasets for working on the new IDS using machine learning.

3.2 Feature Engineering

The performance of any machine learning model is highly dependent on the quality of the dataset. As discussed earlier, dataset KDD99 was not an appropriate dataset to represent the current day network intrusion, and hence UNSW-NB15 dataset is used.

Feature Engineering not only improves the accuracy of an algorithm but also increases the efficiency of the model. However, the dataset itself contains several issues that need to be addressed first before applying the algorithms.

Issues with the Dataset

1. Unbalanced: The dataset consists of 56,000 samples of label 0 (no attack) and 119,341 of label 1. Its effect is noticeable in the hypothesis of the baseline accuracy of the algorithm. However, this influence remains undocumented by researchers. To represent the score, F-score and FAR are used.

   a. F-score is the balanced mean of recall and precision. [22]. It is computed as Eq. 1

$$F - Measure = \frac{2 * Precision * Recall}{Precision + Recall} \qquad (1)$$

The score is in the range of 0–1 and defines the actual performance of the algorithm.

b. FAR is the probability of falsely rejecting the null hypothesis for a particular test [23]. This work considers FAR as the ratio of the number of samples wrongly predicted attack to the total number of samples with the label attack. A smaller FAR value represents our greater chances of perfectly classifying an attack.

2. Column ID is a unique identifier for all the samples and hence is independent of the dependent variable. The correlation of the ID showed no significance with the label and therefore dropped from the dataset.
3. Feature "is_ftp_login" which must be a boolean containing values greater than 1. These values are rounded to 1.

3.3 Preprocessing

1. Column proto, service and state are categorical variables with different proportions of categories. Column proto consists of more than 190 categories, most of which only contribute to less than 1% of the dataset. Only the following categories are kept in the dataset for each column while others are renamed to "Others" and then one hot encoded as displayed in Fig. 2.a, Fig. 2.b and Fig. 2.c.

   a. Service: 'dns', 'http', 'smtp', 'ftp-data', 'ftp'
   b. Proto: 'tcp', 'udp', 'unas'
   c. State: 'FIN', 'INT', 'CON'

2. Most   columns in the dataset are right-skewed. 'trans_depth' and 'response_body_len' have the highest skewness of 176.3 and 76.3, respectively. 30 more columns have a right skewness of greater than 1. The right skewness is corrected using log transformation while left is corrected using cubic function.
3. New columns are created using the following transformation between sender and destination features. These are explained in Table 1.
4. Quantile Transformation: The quantile transformation [11] arranges or smooths out the connection among perceptions and can be planned onto different distributions, such as the uniform or normal distribution. This helps spread out the most frequent values and remove outliers. A cumulative density function of a feature is used to project the original values. Features values of new/concealed data act as an input to the machine learning model where those that fall below or above the identified range will be then plotted to the bounds of the output distribution.
5. Standard Scaling: All the columns were standardized, using the Z-score as shown in Eq. 2.

$$\frac{x - \underline{x}}{\sigma} \tag{2}$$

Here X denotes value, $\underline{x}$ denotes feature wise mean and σ denotes feature wise standard deviation. Standardization is the necessary equipment for many algorithms like support vectors, as they assume the dataset is centered, on 0 with a unit standard deviation. Columns with a higher standard deviation have a higher effect in influencing the target variable.

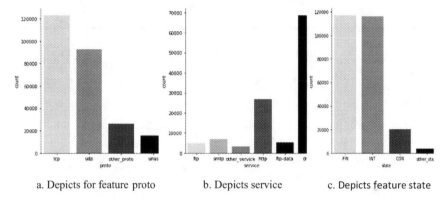

a. Depicts for feature proto   b. Depicts service   c. Depicts feature state

Fig. 2. Represents distribution of categories in columns

Table 1. Feature engineering of certain features to create new features

New feature	Formula	Description
Mean	Smean - dmean	Difference of average transmitted packet size
Pkts	Spkts - Dpkts	Difference in number of packers sent
Bytes	Sbytes - Dbytes	Difference in number of bytes sent
Loss	Sloss + Dloss	Total Packets retransmitted or dropped
Inkpt	Sinkpt - Dinkpt	Different in inter packet arrival time
Load	Sload- Dload	difference in bits transmitted per second
Jit	Sjit + djit	Total jitter
Tcpb	Stcpb - Dtcpb	Difference in TCP window advertisement
Ttl	Sttl + Dttl	Total time to live

3.4   Feature Selection

Random Forest [31] classification is used for feature selection which is a sub category of embedded methods. Embedded methods are like filter and wrapper methods wherein every algorithm has their own built-in feature selection method. Random forests includes numerous random decision trees, each of them built over random observations from the dataset. Each tree is actually a sequence of yes-no questions based on a single or combination of features. The features that are chosen at the highest point of the trees are overall more significant than highlights that are chosen toward the end nodes of the trees, as by and lead to greater data gains [24].

The list of twenty one selected features selected after applying Random forest feature selection is shown in Table 2.

Table 2. Selected features

1. Sbytes	2. Dbytes	3. Rate	4. Sttl
5. Dttl	6. Sload	7. Dload	8. Dinpkt
9. Tcprtt	10. Synack	11. Ackdat	12. Dmean
13. Ct_sry_src	14. Ct__state_ttl	15.Ct_dst_src_ltm	16. Ct_sry_dst
17. Bytes	18. Ttl	19. Load	20. Mean
21. State_INT			

3.5 Machine Learning Algorithms

Several Machine learning algorithms were tested on tenfold stratified sampling to determine train accuracy, FAR and F-score. The experiment was first conducted on raw data with minimum processing addressing the issues of the dataset. This is followed by feature engineered data and repeated after feature selection.

The first algorithm chosen for the experiment was Logistic Regression [25]. Logistic regression is an OLS based algorithm where the regression linear equation formed as in the equation is passed through a sigmoid activation as in Eqs. 3 and 4.

$$y = \beta_0 + \beta_1 X \tag{3}$$

$$\underline{y} = \frac{1}{1 + e^{-y}} \tag{4}$$

Here, in Eq. 3, β_1 denotes slope, β_0 denotes intercept, y denotes regression result and in Eq. 4, y denotes probabilistic output. The obtained value is in the range of 0 and 1 and a threshold of 0.5 was chosen to classify an anomaly.

Another algorithm used is SVM. SVM is a widely preferred classification model which separates data points by customizing suitable hyper planes in an N-dimensional space. It does this while maintaining the maximum distance between different sets of classification in order to allow more room for future data points. If the predicted and actual value are of the same sign, the cost obtained will be 0. If that isn't the case, we will calculate the loss value using the hinge loss.

Next, we tried the Naive Bayes [26] algorithm, a probabilistic classifier that classifies by calculating the conditional probability for each class. It takes in the conjecture that the features are not related to each other and have an equal impact on the outcome. Its computation is shown in Eqs. 5 and 6.

$$P(c|x) = \frac{P(x|c) \times P(c)}{P(x)} \tag{5}$$

$$P(c|x) = P(x_1|c) \times P(x_2|c) \times P(x_3|c) \times \ldots \times P(x_n|c) \times P(c) \qquad (6)$$

Here Eq. 6 x represents feature and c represents class. Equation 5 is a classical Bayes theorem which is multiplied for all the features in Eq. 6 to generate final output.

K-Nearest Neighbor (KNN) [27] on the other hand, works on the assumption that similar things exist in close proximity. KNN captures k number of samples in training data which are closest to the test sample and allocates the most frequent class label for the considered train to test samples. The distance is based on Standard Euclidean Metric (EM).

Passive Aggressive [28] works on the concept of incremental learning, i.e. the input data is updated step-by-step in sequential order unlike batch learning where the entire train set is uploaded all at once. It is hence an effective tool for real time data as the dataset then becomes very large. It makes use of a regularization parameter to correct the model if it makes an incorrect prediction.

Another incremental learning algorithm, the Stochastic Gradient Descent classifier [29] is an optimization technique which trains logistic regression and linear SVM. It creates a learning mechanism by working with different loss functions and penalties for classification. The gradient loss function is calculated for every sample at a time (learning rate) and penalties are estimated via a regularization parameter.

A Multilayer Perceptron [35] is a class of feed forward artificial neural networks. They are the classical type of neural networks composed of one or more layers of neurons. The input layer is responsible for the data that is fed. There may be one or more layers providing levels of abstraction and results are predicted on the output layer. Each neuron performs a similar task as logistic regression with different activation.

A Decision Tree [30] is a map of all the various possible outcomes of a series of related choices. A decision tree typically begins with a single node, which limbs itself into various possible outcomes. The algorithm chooses a feature and makes a split. It then looks at the subsets and measures their Gini Impurity I_G given in the Eq. 7.

$$I_G = 1 - \sum_{i=1}^{n} (p_i^2) \qquad (7)$$

p_i is the proposition of samples that belongs to class c for a particular node. It does this for multiple thresholds and determines the best split. The process is repeated for the next node. This supervised algorithm achieved an accuracy of

Random Forest algorithm is an algorithm that randomly generates decision trees and then averages the result. However, manufacturing the forest is not the same as forming the decision with the information gain or gain index approach. Taking an average case instead of a greedy approach, random forest is able to make better decisions than the decision tree itself.

Extra Trees Classifier [36] is a decision tree based ensemble learning method. Bootstrap is used to build multiple trees, which is false by default indirectly meaning that it samples without replacement. Like Random forest, split depending on random subset features is applied; however, Extra-Tree method comes up with piecewise multi linear approximations, rather than the piecewise constant ones of random forests.

Bootstrap Aggregating, known as Bagging Classifier [37], is again an ensemble ML technique that fits standard classifiers on arbitrary subsets from the original dataset and then combines the respective predictions to give a final prediction. This eliminates the challenge of over fitting by using averaging or voting. Unlike Extra tree, sampling is done with replacement and the decision tree is used by default as learner.

Gradient Boosting [32] is a machine learning technique for regression and classification problems, which created a prediction model in the form of an entity of weak prediction models, typically decision trees. This likewise implies that they are difficult to classify increasing larger load until the algorithm identifies a model that correctly classifies these samples.

Adaptive Boosting [38] technique is used to boost the performance of weak learners. Most widely used learner is the decision tree. After training on learners, the misclassification rate is calculated using weighted sums. This provides weighting of wrong predictions which are retrained hence boosting the accuracy of the learner.

Ridge regression [33] is a powerful technique that is generally used for creating models in presence of an enormous number of features. Ridge regression is valuable in solving problems where you have less than one hundred thousand samples or when you have more restrictions than samples. It performs L2 regularization, i.e. adding sanction that is equivalent to square of the magnitude of coefficients to prevent over fitting.

XGBoost [7] has been one of the most popular algorithms with state of the art performance in most real world applications. This is due the large parallel capability and an efficient implementation of Gradient Boosted tree and several regularizations. The objective function which includes regularization combines the convex loss function and cannot be minimized using classical methods such as Euclidean distance. The training is done by adding a new learner which calculates the loss from the previous tree. As the learner with maximum reduction in loss is computationally and time expensive, a greedy method is chosen to select and proceed to the next tree.

Light Gradient Boosting Machine (LGBM) [34] developed by Microsoft is another decision tree based Approach which iterates over multiple trees each trying to minimize error of previous. In each tree gradients of features are calculated. Small gradient means the features are well trained while clothes are currently being trained. This leads to down sampling of data which results in reducing complexity. It achieves down sampling by combining features. The model achieved similar accuracy in both feature selection and raw data as discussed in later papers.

Learning rate of LGBM and XGBoost was set to be 0.1 with maximum depth of tree as 7. All other classifiers were set to default arguments as in Scikit-Learn. Logistic Regression and Ridge Classifier are automatically fine-tuned using cross validation scores.

4   Results

As briefed earlier the analysis is performed thrice. First the machine models are applied on raw data after performing basic preprocessing and removing categorical data. As noted from Table 3, bagging classifier had the best F-score of 87% with an FAR of 0.03. While the best FAR was the Ridge Classifier, XGB and Light gradient boosting machines performed great with a balance between F-score and FAR is seen in Fig. 3.

Table 3. Results of ML models on raw data

Model	F-score	FAR	Accuracy
Bagging classifier	**0.87079**	0.0308	**0.87554**
XGB classifier	0.86745	0.01436	0.8734
LGBM classifier	0.86721	0.01379	0.87322
Random forest classifier	0.86513	0.01511	0.87127
Extra trees classifier	0.85933	0.0165	0.86596
Decision tree classifier	0.85776	0.04454	0.86286
Extra trees classifier	0.85933	0.0165	0.86596
Decision tree classifier	0.85776	0.04454	0.86286
Gradient boosting classifier	0.84713	0.01361	0.85528
Ada boost classifier	0.84216	0.03609	0.84927
MLP classifier	0.82786	0.04535	0.83585
KNN classifier	0.81665	0.06066	0.82471
Ridge classifier CV	0.76847	**0.00609**	0.78995
Passive aggressive classifier	0.76688	0.11219	0.77633
Linear SVC	0.7644	0.02142	0.78463
SGD classifier	0.76325	0.00818	0.78551
Logistic regression CV	0.75732	0.06168	0.77367
Bernoulli NB	0.71544	0.2245	0.72051

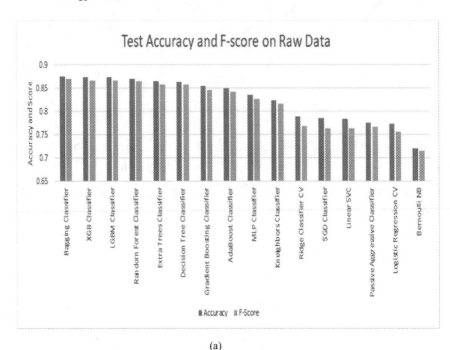

(a)

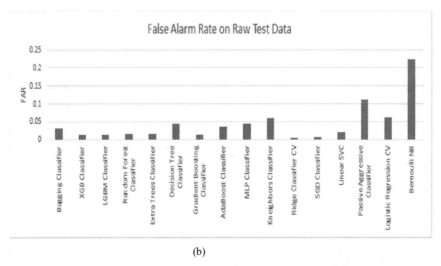

(b)

Fig. 3. a. Graphical representation of accuracy and f-score results obtained on raw data. b. Graphical representation of FAR results obtained on raw data.

Second, classifiers are applied on processed data. Results are shown in Table 4. XGB Classifier topped the F-score and accuracy with 88.35% and 88.78% respectively. This is closely followed by the Bagging Classifier with 87.37%. The best tradeoff between F-score and FAR is observed for LGBM classifiers is shown in Fig. 3 (Fig. 4).

Table 4. Results of ML models on processed data

Model	F-score	FAR	Accuracy
XGB classifier	**0.8835**	0.0178	**0.88787**
Bagging classifier	0.87375	0.02841	0.87838
SGD classifier	0.87147	0.05052	0.8752
LGBM classifier	0.87091	0.01445	0.87654
Random forest classifier	0.86874	0.01637	0.87446
Extra trees classifier	0.8682	0.01672	0.87395
Decision tree classifier	0.86207	0.04185	0.86695
KNN classifier	0.86108	0.02722	0.86688
MLP classifier	0.85316	0.02371	0.85996
Gradient boosting classifier	0.84692	0.01204	0.85521
Logistic regression CV	0.84659	0.01507	0.8547
Ada boost classifier	0.84012	0.03124	0.84779
Linear SVC	0.8324	0.01114	0.84258
Passive aggressive classifier	0.80171	0.05943	0.81166
Ridge classifier CV	0.79595	**0.00185**	0.8127
Bernoulli NB	0.69769	0.33912	0.69795

Third, different classifiers are employed on the reduced data is shown in Table 5. That includes 21 columns. The XGB classifier again outperformed in terms of Accuracy and F-score with F-score of 87.74% and accuracy of 88.2% described in Fig. 5.

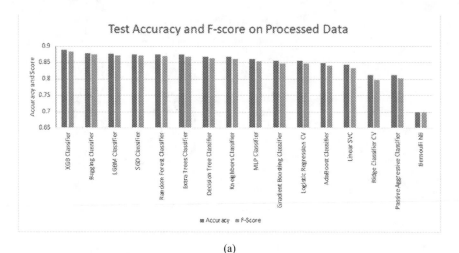

(a)

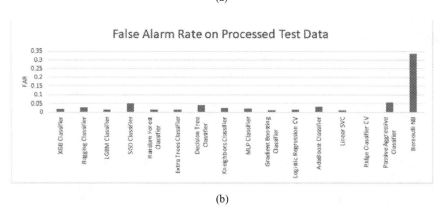

(b)

Fig. 4. a. Graphical representation of accuracy and f-score results obtained on processed data. b. Graphical representation of FAR results obtained on processed data.

Table 5. Results of ML classifier models on reduced data

Model	F-score	FAR	Accuracy
XGB classifier	**0.8774**	0.01729	**0.88229**
Extra trees classifier	0.86771	0.02038	0.87329
Bagging classifier	0.86748	0.04262	0.87188
Random forest classifier	0.86684	0.01853	0.87261
LGBM classifier	0.86646	0.01454	0.8725

(*continued*)

Table 5. (*continued*)

Model	F-score	FAR	Accuracy
KNN classifier	0.85821	0.03373	0.86389
MLP classifier	0.84501	0.03309	0.85203
Ada boost classifier	0.83021	0.03002	0.83911
Decision tree classifier	0.82919	0.10472	0.83318
Gradient boosting classifier	0.82619	0.01271	0.83706
Logistic regression CV	0.78962	0.02402	0.80494
Linear SVC	0.7742	0.01211	0.79374
Passive aggressive classifier	0.76962	0.03545	0.78706
SGD classifier	0.7641	**0.00243**	0.787
Ridge classifier CV	0.7634	0.00377	0.78626
Bernoulli NB	0.7362	0.34234	0.73624

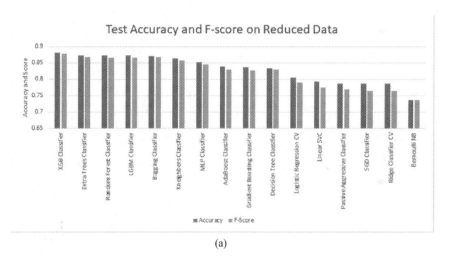

(a)

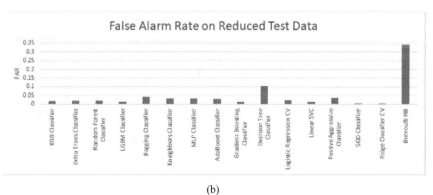

(b)

Fig. 5. a. Graphical representation of accuracy and f-score results obtained on reduced data. b. Graphical representation of FAR results obtained on reduced data.

5 Conclusion

This paper presented analysis of the UNSW-NB15 dataset with several ML models. Critical analysis and preprocessing of data along with State of the art Machine learning algorithms of XGBoost and LGBM outperformed traditional methods and scores till date. While XGBoost possessed better accuracy and F-score, LGBM may be preferred because of lower FAR. Additionally analysis of Feature selection using Random Forest, substantially decreased the size of the dataset. This however did not affect the scores and accuracy achieved.

While other works have focused more on feature election methods, this paper has focused on critical preprocessing. This helps increase the correlation between features and target. Previous research using complex feature selection methods, may be recon ducted with mentioned preprocessing techniques to increase accuracy of detection. More decision tree based approaches may be invented to reduce time complexity and increase efficiency of the model to perform in real time. Decision trees are able to effectively depict the reason of decision taken and hence can be used to trace back intrusions. Although this research includes UNSW NB-15 dataset, which is a great depiction of real time intrusion and network activities, with upcoming new generation of Intrusions and Network devices, require updated datasets to perform analysis.

References

1. Kasongo, S.M., Sun, Y.: Performance analysis of intrusion detection systems using a feature selection method on the UNSW-NB15 dataset. J. Big Data **7**(1), 1–20 (2020). https://doi.org/10.1186/s40537-020-00379-6
2. Mrutyunjaya, P., Abraham, A., Das, S., Patra, M.R.: Network intrusion detection system: a machine learning approach. Intell. Decis. Technol. **5**(4), 347–356 (2011)
3. Kumar, S.: Survey of current network intrusion detection techniques, pp. 1–18. Washington University, St. Louis (2007)
4. Aljawarneh, S., Monther, A., Yassein, M.B.: Anomaly-based intrusion detection system through feature selection analysis and building hybrid efficient models. J. Comput. Sci. **25**, 152–160 (2018)
5. Wikipedia contributors: misuse detection. Wikipedia, the Free Encyclopedia,7 January 2020. Accessed 16 Apr 2021
6. Maji, S.: Building an intrusion detection system on UNSW-NB15 dataset based on machine learning algorithm. https://medium.com/@subrata.maji16/building-an-intrusion-detection-system-on-unsw-nb15-dataset-based-on-machine-learning-algorithm-16b1600996f5. Accessed 19 Sept 2020
7. Tianqi, C., Guestrin, C.: XGBoost: a scalable tree boosting system. In: Proceedings of the 22nd ACM SIGKDD International Conference on Knowledge Discovery and Data Mining (2016)
8. Guolin, K., et al.: LightGBM: a highly efficient gradient boosting decision tree. Adv. Neural Inf. Process. Syst. **30**, 3146–3154 (2017)
9. Nour, M., Slay, J.: UNSW-NB15: a comprehensive data set for network intrusion detection systems (UNSW-NB15 network data set). In: IEEE Conference Proceedings on Military Communications and Information Systems (MilCIS) (2015)
10. Guido, V.R., Drake Jr, F.L.: Python reference manual. Centrum voor Wiskunde en Informatica, Amsterdam (1995)

11. Pedregosa, F., et al.: Scikit-learn: machine learning in Python. J. Mach. Learn. Res. **12**, 2825–2830 (2011)
12. Wes, M.: Data structures for statistical computing in python. In: Proceedings of the 9th Python in Science Conference, p. 445 (2010)
13. Kumar, V., Sinha, D., Das, A.K., Pandey, S.C., Goswami, R.T.: An integrated rule based intrusion detection system: analysis on UNSW-NB15 data set and the real time online dataset. Cluster Comput. **23**(2), 1397–1418 (2019). https://doi.org/10.1007/s10586-019-03008-x
14. Chaouki, K., Krichen, S.: A GA-LR wrapper approach for feature selection in network intrusion detection. Comput. Secur. **70**, 255–277 (2017)
15. Ambusaidi, M.A., He, X., Nanda, P., Tan, Z.: Building an intrusion detection system using a filter-based feature selection algorithm. IEEE Trans. Comput. **65**(10), 2986–2998 (2016)
16. Noble, W.S.: What is a support vector machine? Nat. Biotechnol. **24**(12), 1565–1567 (2006)
17. Hadeel, A., Ahmad Sharieh, A., Sabri, K.E.: A feature selection algorithm for intrusion detection system based on pigeon inspired optimizer. Expert Syst. Appl. **148**, 113–249 (2020)
18. Almomani, O.: A feature selection model for network intrusion detection systems based on PSO, GWO, FFA and GA algorithms. Symmetry **12**(6), 1046 (2020)
19. Moustafa, N., Slay, J.: The evaluation of network anomaly detection systems: statistical analysis of the UNSW-NB15 data set and the comparison with the KDD99 data set. Inf. Secur. J.: Glob. Perspect. **25**(1–3), 18–31 (2016)
20. Tavallaee, M., Bagheri, E., Lu, W., Ghorbani, A.A.: A detailed analysis of the KDD CUP 99 data set. In: 2009 IEEE Symposium on Computational Intelligence for Security and Defense Applications (2009)
21. Liu, H., Lang, B.: Machine learning and deep learning methods for intrusion detection systems: a survey. Appl. Sci. **9**(20), 4396 (2019)
22. Wikipedia contributors. F-score. Wikipedia, the free encyclopedia. Wikipedia, the Free Encyclopedia, 24 March 2021. Accessed 16 Apr 2021
23. Wikipedia contributors. False positive rate. Wikipedia, the free encyclopedia, 21 March 2021. Accessed 16 Apr 2021
24. Dubey, A.: Feature selection using random forest. https://towardsdatascience.com/feature-selection-using-random-forest-26d7b747597f. Accessed 15 Dec 2018
25. Hosmer Jr, D.W., Lemeshow, S., Sturdivant, R.X.: Applied Logistic Regression, vol. 398. Wiley, Hoboken (2013)
26. Irina, R.: An empirical study of the naive Bayes classifier. In: IJCAI 2001 Workshop on Empirical Methods in Artificial Intelligence, vol. 3, no. 22 (2001)
27. Peterson, L.E.: K-nearest neighbor. Scholarpedia **4**(2), 1883 (2009)
28. Crammer, K., Dekel, O., Keshet, J., Shalev-Shwartz, S., Singer, Y.: Online passive aggressive algorithms (2006)
29. Gardiner, C.W.: Handbook of Stochastic Methods, vol. 3. Springer, Berlin (1985)
30. Rasoul, S.S., Landgrebe, D.: A survey of decision tree classifier methodology. IEEE Trans. Syst. Man Cybern. **21**(3), 660–674 (1991)
31. Nabila, F., Jabbar, M.A.: Random forest modeling for network intrusion detection system. Procedia Comput. Sci. **89**, 213–217 (2016)
32. Natekin, A.N., Knoll, A.: Gradient boosting machines, a tutorial. Front. Neurorobot. **7**, 21 (2013)
33. McDonald, G.C.: Ridge regression. Wiley Interdiscip. Rev.: Comput. Stat. **1**(1), 93–100 (2009)
34. Ke, G., et al.: LightGBM: a highly efficient gradient boosting decision tree. Adv. Neural Inf. Process. Syst. **30**, 3146–3154 (2017)
35. Tang, J., Deng, C., Huang, G.: Extreme learning machine for multilayer perceptron. IEEE Trans. Neural Netw. Learn. Syst. **27**(4), 809–821 (2015)

36. Bhati, B.S., Rai, C.S.: Ensemble based approach for intrusion detection using extra tree classifier. In: Solanki, V.K., Hoang, M.K., Lu, Z., Pattnaik, P.K. (eds.) Intelligent Computing in Engineering. AISC, vol. 1125, pp. 213–220. Springer, Singapore (2020). https://doi.org/10.1007/978-981-15-2780-7_25
37. Gaikwad, D.P., Thool, R.C.: Intrusion detection system using bagging ensemble method of machine learning. In: 2015 International Conference on Computing Communication Control and Automation. IEEE (2015)
38. Alexander, V., Vezhnevets, V.: Modest AdaBoost-teaching AdaBoost to generalize better. In: Graphicon, vol. 12, no. 5 (2005)

Enhanced Security Mechanism for Cryptographic File Systems Using Trusted Computing

Umashankar Rawat[1], Satyabrata Roy[1(✉)], Saket Acharya[1], Ravinder Kumar[2], and Krishna Kumar[2]

[1] Department of Computer Science and Engineering, Manipal University Jaipur, Rajasthan, India
`satyabrata.roy@jaipur.manipal.edu`
[2] Department of Information Technology, Manipal University Jaipur, Rajasthan, India

Abstract. Trusted Computing Platform (TCP) using Trusted Platform Module (TPM) cryptographic microcontroller system was introduced by the Trusted Computing Group (TCG). It can produce, store and manage the keys used for cryptographic purpose on the hardware itself. A number of companies, including HP, IBM, Apple, Dell, etc. now release their systems with an inbuilt TPM component. This paper elucidates the method of using TPM chip for efficient management of cryptographic keys in Enterprise-class Cryptographic File System (ECFS) through Linux operating systems. It provides an extra layer of superior quality security when it comes to security based on hardware devices. The proposed security architecture is deployed using TPM tools version 1.3.8 packages and TrouSerS, a Public Key Infrastructure (PKI) API with version number 0.3.9. A comparison analysis in terms of performance using TPM based ECFS with the state-of-art ECFS is presented in this paper. The results of the proposed scheme outperforms the existing systems.

Keywords: Machine learning · Cryptographic file system · Trusted platform module · Trusted computing group · Public key infrastructure · Pluggable authentication module · Trusted computing platform · Data mining

1 Introduction

Cryptographic File Systems (CFS's) are the most popular and secure file systems [8]. CFS provides data encryption before passing the data to untrusted components, and decrypts the data when it is about to enter the trusted components. The users make directories and add keys to the directories to achieve security. Each and every file created in these directories is automatically encrypted. The major challenge with the existing CFS's is efficient and secure key management. Most of the CFS's implement basic password protection methods, disregarding

© The Author(s), under exclusive license to Springer Nature Switzerland AG 2022
S. Joshi et al. (Eds.): SpacSec 2021, CCIS 1599, pp. 51–63, 2022.
https://doi.org/10.1007/978-3-031-15784-4_4

multi-factor authentication method. Majority of the passwords can be successfully obtained by the attackers with the help of brute force and dictionary attack methods [1]. Smart card chips are used for the purpose of storing secret keys in CFS, such as eCryptfs [3]. Smart chips are more secure over rudimentary password preservation techniques, as these block access with the combination of passphrase and hardware. Furthermore, the implementation cost of deploying smart card chips is very high and the computational complexity is also high [6].

Multi-factor authentication in CFS can be achieved by using a secure technology like trusted computing without including additional cost. TCG has developed a TCP based on TPM. The TCG is a charitable organization which was established to create, define and extend open standards for security technologies that were hardware-based. The TCP has both software and hardware modules. The methods rendered by hardware modules are known as TPM functions and those offered by software modules are termed as Trusted Software Stack (TSS)[1] methodologies. TPM is a small hardware chip installed in the computers to attain greater security mechanisms. It was not possible before with so called basic security methodologies. Most of the computer manufacturers embed such TPM chips in the product's hardware to efficiently perform access-control to the keys. The TPM gives a foundation of trust based on hardware and has many cryptographic utilities to create, reserve and administer secret keys within hardware. It offers validated booting technique by estimating the boot-loader and other crucial segments of the machine, limiting keys to a carefully characterized framework and release them only when the system boots in its trusted state. This methodology also prevents assaults that include boot-loader hacking. In this way, TPM can be used for safety applications like memory protection and remote validation [14]. TSS is an application needed to deal with TPM chips. TrouSerS[2] and Trusted Computing for the Java Platform[3] are among the most prevalent available publicly available TSS bundles. dmCrypt [2] and latest versions of eCryptfs [4] provide TPM support for key administration.

This paper explicates the application of trusted computing in managing keys in the ECFS file systems [9], which profit by a more significant layer of security by utilizing trust based on hardware. In such situation, a TPM chip is designed to produce a key pair having public key and private key, where it is not possible to obtain the secret private key from the TPM chip. The public key which is used to encrypt ECFS file should be provided to the TPM chip for ensuring accurate decoding by the secured private key. Such hardware level encryption adds more strength to security for key management than any software based security deployment. Publicly available TrouSerS PKI API version 0.3.13 and the TPM tools version 2.0 [10] bundle have been used for implementing the proposed methodology.

Remaining segments of the paper is written in this fashion. Section 2 presents a survey on two principle parts of TCP/TPM and TSS. Section 3 portrays the

---

[1] https://trustedcomputinggroup.org/resource/tcg-software-stack-tss-specification.

[2] http://sourceforge.net/projects/trousers/files/trousers.

[3] http://trustedjava.sourceforge.net.

TPM key progression with the Root of Trust for Storage (RTS) and important instructions for storage of keys in a secure way. Section 4 clarifies how TPM evaluates the machine state with the RoT for Measurement (RTM) and manages access to different keys depending on machine state. Section 5 specifies some trusted computing application in key administration in case of ECFS. Section 6 explains the deployment part. Results obtained during implementation are shown in Sect. 7 and finally, Sect. 8 provides conclusion and some future research directions.

2 Modules of Trusted Computing

This segment presents a survey about TCP hardware and software modules, more specifically known as the TSS and TPM. Section 2.1 first explains the TPM chip as well as related functionalities, and Sect. 2.2 describes the software module, TSS in brief.

2.1 Hardware Module – TPM Chip

The TPM offers each machine a protected domain having the capabilities of saving confidential data, producing secret keys and executing cryptographic operations, for example, digital signatures and encryption. Linux Journal distributed a prologue to the chip [7], which empowers Linux users to emulate and create applications. From a developer's point of view, a TPM chip resembles as displayed in Fig. 1. It contains five cryptographic modules which are very useful. It consists of a Random Number Generator (RNG) module that generates random numbers for generating on-device chip keys. It consists of a SHA-1 hashing module and a related HMAC module for producing Message Authentication Code (MAC) on the basis of SHA-1 hash code. It additionally consists a RSA key producing component which can produce keys of size 256 bytes, based on the output provided by the RNG module. At last, RSA engine is there to perform encryption, decryption and providing digital signatures.

The TPM saves three significant keys in permanent memory (non-volatile). The 2048-bit endorsement or backup key is a private-public key pair RSA, generated in a random fashion on the chip at the manufacturing time and cannot be altered. The private key always remains on chip, but the publicly available key is used for verification and encipherment of critical information forwarded to the chip, as happens while using *"TPM_ TakeOwnership"*.

The Storage Root Key (SRK) is a 256 Byte key pair. Initially it remains blank and is made as a component of the command *"TPM_ TakeOwnership"*. This key remains on chip and is used to encode private keys for external TPM storage as well as to decode when they are stacked over the TPM. The framework owner has the privilege to refresh the SRK. The owner authorization private key is a 160-bit key shared mutually with the owner who loads this key on the chip as a module of the command *"TPM_ TakeOwnership"*. This confidential key authorizes the requests of critical owner commands.

The temporary memory (volatile) area contains ten slots as illustrated in Fig. 1. But, it may vary among different chip manufacturers. The wrapped keys are kept remotely and restored into these slots as and when required for usage. The keys which are stored in such slots are temporary and are not ascertained to persist even after power loss. This also varies among various chip makers.

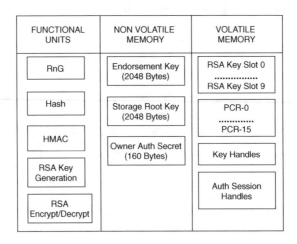

Fig. 1. View of the TPM chip

The volatile segment consist of several Platform Configuration Registers (PCRs) of size 160-bits and these are used to save hash values of the software boot modules such as MBR, BIOS, bootstrap loader, kernel portion, initial disk image and so forth. At this point the enciphering and deciphering keys can be attached to precise PCRs to detect and block then and there any alteration of software. In TPM phrasing, encryption of a particular PCR value is known as "sealing", and the corresponding decoding is termed as "unsealing". PCRs are composed of a procedure called "extending" which is further clarified in Sect. 4.

Temporary memory also stores both types of handles. The loaded keys are given interim names using Key handles so that next sequence of commands can use a specific key at time of loading multiple keys. Key handle is deleted as soon as the corresponding key gets removed. "Authorization session handles" recognize the confidential information among several commands.

2.2   Software Module – TSS

It takes care of the hardware module, TPM chip. It transforms TPM function request to a input stream identified by TPM. TrouSerS and Trusted Computing for the Java Platform[4] provide free TPM and TSS tools. The important modules associated are depicted in Fig. 2 and are explained below:

---

[4] http://trustedjava.sourceforge.net.

- "TCG Service Provider Interface (TSPI)": It is used to permanently store the keys, managing authentication requests, managing authorization sessions, encrypting and hashing.
- "TCG Core Service (TCS)": It provides synchronization of several access requests to the hardware module, gives key and caching facility for authorization along with services for transitions of TPM in power mode.
- "TPM Device Driver Library (TDDL)": It provides user interface. It should be ensured that all commands sent to this module must be sent in a sequential.
- "TPM Device Driver (TDD)": It is a component of kernel mode accepting input byte stream from the TDDL and forwards it to the chip. The chip sends the response back to the TDDL via this module. It also handles device power state variations ($S_0 - S_5$).

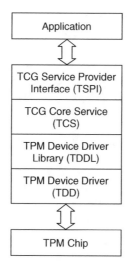

Fig. 2. Trusted Software Stack (TSS) modules

3   Safe Storage with TPM

This segment illustrates safe data storage using on chip cryptographic keys using different commands exclusively used for TPM. Section 3.1 describes the hierarchical structure of TPM key having Storage Root Key as the RoT for Storage (RTS). Section 3.2 demonstrates different commands to produce, install, save and for maintenance of on chip keys for encrypting and decrypting the user information.

3.1   RoT for Storage

TPM-produced keys are used to encipher user related data as described in Sect. 2. Apart from the mentioned keys, several other keys might be there that could be saved in small TPM chip. In this situation, keys are placed in external part on a disk after encrypting them by the keys already stored in the TPM. The Storage Root Key (SRK) is the RTS which secures every key externally stored in the disk. The SRK stays in the permanent memory of the TPM. Figure 3 exhibits the TPM Key hierarchy that regulates the encryption using external key. Storage Root Key is the root of the hierarchy. When the "TPM_TakeOwnership" command is initiated by the owner, external key is also generated. Decryption is performed only within the TPM chip. However, authorization must be granted when generating and using a key. Two types of keys are there and they are:

– **Storage key:** It is the key based on RSA and it encrypts other RSA keys.
– **Binding key:** This key is also based on RSA and it encrypts other symmetric keys. However, this key is not used to encipher further RSA keys.

There are two ways to protect the data from masquerading attack:

1. **Data binding:** A permanent key is created and used to provide encryption.
2. **Data sealing:** Encrypted data is bound to a particular TPM with a specific configuration.

The input to "sealing" is binding key and PCR value and the output is sealed data bundle. To decrypt the bundle, same key and same PCR must be provided. For instance, let a user signs an Adobe PDF document by using a "binding" key, with PCR values indicating Adobe Reader and McAfee antivirus software are installed. In order to read the PDF, other users must have key access and they must use the very TPM with Adobe Reader and McAfee installed; or else, the PDF remains sealed.

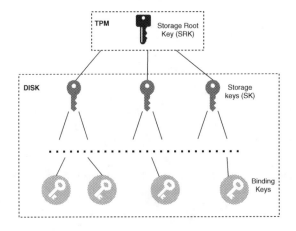

Fig. 3. The TPM key hierarchy

3.2   Secure Storage TPM Commands

This section explains various TPM commands that are used for achieving secure data storage [14]. These commands generate TPM keys which are used to perform data encryption. The TPM keys are maintained in a hierarchical manner as described before. After TPM starts, a process initiates the *"TPM_ TakeOwnership"* command to generate the cache key. After this, *"TPM_ CreateWrapKey"* command is called to generate a slave key from the existing key. Once the key is generated, it is installed using the *"TPM_ LoadKey"* command.

The *"TPM_ CreateWrapKey"* command generates a new key Wk(Pk, *"auth_ data"*, *"key_ type"*), where Pk is the parent key and *"key_ type"* contains information like sealing, binding, HMAC(based on *"auth_ data"*) and digital signature. The command returns a blob containing portion of new public key and an encoded bundle. The bundle, which is scrambled with the generator key, contains private portion and *"auth_ data"* of the new key. To utilize the above generated TPM key, it needs to be installed using the *"TPM_ LoadKey"* command, which accepts key blob as the parameter and provides a pointer to the key saved in memory of the TPM. The SRK is for all time stored in the permanent memory and it has its own handle.

When a key is loaded, *"TPM_ Seal"* command is used for encryption process. It calls the handle of the scrambling key, the information to be encrypted, seal bounded PCR's data, and encrypted *"auth_ data"* as parameters. Obviously, it additionally requires an approval HMAC dependent on the *"auth_ data"* of the scrambling key. *TPM_ Unseal* works in opposite way i.e. it receives the handle of the scrambling key and the fixed blob, and it restores the original information. This command needs two approved HMACs – 1) dependent on the scrambling key *"auth_ data"* and 2) dependent on the sealed blob. At last, the *TPM_ UnBind* decodes the information that is encoded with the public key; the associated private key is saved in the memory of the TPM.

4   Measurements of Platform

The TPM consists several 160-bit registers known as PCRs, that give data regarding the state of platform that cannot be exploited. A module can "measure" another module (calculate its hash) and save that estimation in a PCR. This saving cannot be reversed and it is known as "extending" the PCR [14]. A PCR 'Pr' is extended with the estimation 'E' as:

$$Pr = SHA - 1(Pr \parallel E)$$

A PCR can be increased with any number of estimations. The last estimation of the PCR gives the summation of all measurements. A safe chain of trust can be set up by expanding a PCR with an estimation of the principal code fragment implemented on power-up. In the event that each module A that heaps another module B guarantees that an estimation of B is extended into a PCR before granting control, at that point the PCRs record the historical backdrop of executed code.

Figure 4 demonstrates the verified booting with boot square code of BIOS taken as the "Core Root of Trust for Measurement (CRTM)". It is an expansion of the ordinary BIOS executed first to gauge different BIOS block parts ahead of transferring control. Boot code is dependable as it dependably verifies the trustworthiness of different modules and is unaltered during the span of the machine platform. When the measurement is finished, the control is passed to the boot-loader. The boot-loader assesses kernel and afterward it transfers control to the system.

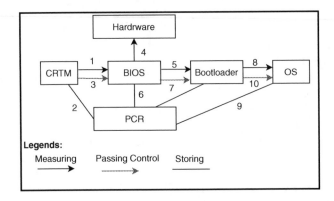

Fig. 4. The estimation process, starting with CRTM

After the booting process, values in the PCR are examined to guarantee that the machine is functioning in a desired specification. *TPM_ SignKey* (made by *"TPM_ CreateWrapKey"*) are used to sign the PCR values with the help of *TPM_ Quote* command. Thus, application programming can guarantee an outsider about the platform state. Also, PCR values guarantee that specific information are applicable only to the approved applications. For this situation, the *"TPM_ Seal"* command seals the information by taking (PCR, value) as arguments, and after that, the *TPM_ Unseal* command unlocks the information for approved applications.

5   TPM in CFS's

Modified ECFS for efficient key management using TPM is shown in Fig. 5. The TrouSerS PKI module are utilized as trusted software stack for interacting with the TPM. The TrouSerS programming suite gives a freely available TCG Software Stack. It is authorized under the "Common Public License" (CPL). Following are the services provided by TrouSerS [5]:

- Generation of RSA key pair.
- RSA encoding and decoding using PKCS v2.40 and OAEP padding
- RSA signature/verification
- Logging of events
- Data sealing to arbitrary PCRs.
- Generating Random Numbers using RNG Module.
- Secure key storage

The altered ECFS produces a key pair for every framework user with the help of TPM, where the private key is ensured securely by SRK (i.e., the SRK encoded private key). The private SRK key is stored in the TPM chip as discussed in the previous sections. At the point when the client needs to get to the file, the FEK is unscrambled with the client's private key, stacked in the TPM. The user also locks his private key by sealing it to a set of PCR values. The hash values of the boot chain are stored in the 160-bit PCRs. Malicious modifications to the MBR, boot-loader, kernel, or initrd are always detected by the PCR values, because the metric assessments are performed always on the subsequent boot process, before transferring the control, as discussed before.

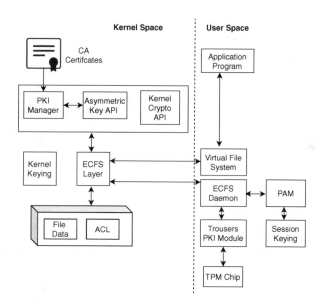

Fig. 5. TPM utilization for managing key in ECFS architecture

Trusted GRUB estimates random files in the duration of the booting and expands the PCR. Trusted GRUB is an expansion of the basic GRUB boot-loader that has been altered to identify and include the TPM specifications. PCR registers stored inside TPM cache are refreshed at every boot. The PCRs usage is given in Table 1.

Table 1. PCRs usage

PCRs	Usage
PCR 0 to PCR 3	Used for the BIOS, GRUB, ROMS, CRTM, etc.
PCR 4 arguments (CLA'S)	Used to carry MBR data and stage 1
PCR 8, PCR 9	Used to carry boot-loader data
PCR 12	It consist of all Menu.Lst's command line arguments
PCR 13	It consists of all the files verified through the checkfile-method
PCR 14	It contains all actually loaded files (e.g. modules, kernels, etc.)
PCRs 15–23	They are generally not used

6   Implementation of Proposed Method

ECFS using TPM has been executed on Red Hat Enterprise Linux (RHEL) 7.6.
TrouSerS PKI API rendition 0.3.13 and the TPM freely available tools 2.0 were
utilized, and a test framework was installed on an Intel Core i9 7900x machine
(M arrangement, machine type 5474) with STMicroelectronics TPM 2.0 (TPM
module with I2C interface). The STM TPM 2.0 complies with the TCG 2.0
specifications. It has a total of 10 key slots and has following cryptographic
algorithms: RSA key generation algorithm, RSA encryption algorithm, HMAC
and SHA-256 for hashing, AES algorithm having keys of 128-192-256 bits and
ECC algorithm.

To store and encrypt the data, the TPM keys have to be created first. TPM
key hierarchy is discussed in Sect. 3.1. When TPM is booted, a process calls the
"TPM_TakeOwnership" command and the SRK is generated. The step by step
flowchart of TPM initialization process is demonstrated in Fig. 6:

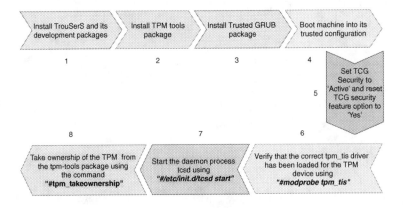

Fig. 6. TPM initialization process

7   Evaluation of Performance

In this segment, assessment of ECFS performance and proposed ECFS implementation using TPM support (ECFS_TPM) is described. The test cases have
been executed on a 2.5 GHz Intel Core i-9 7900x machine with STMicroelectronics TPM 2.0 (TPM module with I2C interface) with 24 GB RAM that runs
Red Hat Enterprise Linux 7. When a user mounts the ECFS_TPM, it takes
less than a second to initiate the *"TPM_LoadKey"* command to load the private
key of the user inside the TPM wrapped by Storage Root Key. Further, when a
user executes a write operation, FEK gets encrypted with the public key of the
user outside the TPM. Hence, there will be no write operation overhead. While
performing the read operation, it takes few milliseconds to decode FEK using
the private key of the user inside the TPM. Hence, some amount of overhead
will be there in the read throughput in the proposed implementation i.e. ECFS
using TPM. Read throughput measured by executing IOZone[5], on ECFS, Ext4
and ECFS using TPM (ECFS_TPM) file storage points is shown in Fig. 7 for
variable file sizes. In Fig. 7, ECFS_TPM is denoted by ECFS_T.

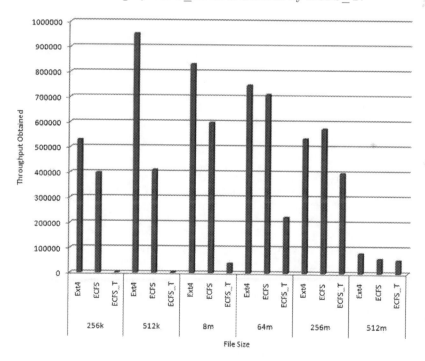

Fig. 7. Read throughput obtained (in KBPS) on Ext4, ECFS and ECFS_T file systems
with different file sizes

Throughput values for small sized files are very small in ECFS_TPM as every
read operation requires the FEK to be decoded inside the TPM. Larger files

---
[5] www.iozone.org.

require lesser TPM operations. The read throughput overhead in ECFS_TPM in comparison with ECFS for variable file sizes is demonstrated in Fig. 7. It can be analyzed from the diagram that overhead almost reaches to 100% in case of ECFS_TPM for small sized files (less than 2 MB), whereas for large sized files(greater than 512 MB), the overhead has been decreased and it is almost negligible.

8   Conclusions and Future Work

The architecture of ECFS has been extended to support TPM for achieving multifactor authentication and efficient key management. This enables ECFS to achieve a higher level of security as the TPM provides hardware-based RoT. The proposed ECFS scheme (ECFS_TPM) has been executed on a 2.5 GHz Intel Core i-9 7900x machine with STMicroelectronics TPM 2.0 (TPM module with I2C interface) and 24 GB RAM executing Red Hat Enterprise Linux 7. This has been concluded that by using ECFS_TPM, each read operation takes few milliseconds as compared to the file systems without TPM. Write operations, however, are not affected. Security is very high as the TPM provides hardware level security. The performance overhead in ECFS_TPM is more for small file sizes (less than 2 MB) but for large file sizes, the overhead is almost negligible. In future, the efficiency can be increased further by using advanced versions of kernel with TPM Module. The TPM can be used to provide security for IoT devices [11–13,15] in real time environments.

References

1. Ball, M.V., Guyot, C., Hughes, J.P., Martin, L., Noll, L.C.: The XTS-AES disk encryption algorithm and the security of ciphertext stealing. Cryptologia **36**(1), 70–79 (2012)
2. Fruhwirth, C.: LUKS on-disk format specification version 1.1. Changes 1, 22-01 (2005)
3. Halcrow, M.A.: eCryptfs: an enterprise-class encrypted filesystem for Linux. In: Proceedings of the 2005 Linux Symposium, vol. 1, pp. 201–218 (2005)
4. Jeong, W.S., Jeong, J., Jeong, I.R.: The vulnerability improvement research using pseudo-random number generator scheme in EncFS. J. Korea Inst. Inf. Secur. Cryptol. **26**(6), 1539–1550 (2016)
5. Miller, K.: The Cartographer Tries to Map a Way to Zion. Carcanet, Manchester (2014)
6. Nepal, S., Zic, J., Hwang, H., Moreland, D.: Trust extension device: providing mobility and portability of trust in cooperative information systems. In: Meersman, R., Tari, Z. (eds.) OTM 2007. LNCS, vol. 4803, pp. 253–271. Springer, Heidelberg (2007). https://doi.org/10.1007/978-3-540-76848-7_17
7. Pirker, M., Toegl, R., Gissing, M.: Dynamic enforcement of platform integrity. In: Acquisti, A., Smith, S.W., Sadeghi, A.-R. (eds.) Trust 2010. LNCS, vol. 6101, pp. 265–272. Springer, Heidelberg (2010). https://doi.org/10.1007/978-3-642-13869-0_18

8. Rawat, U., Roy, S., Acharya, S., Kumar, K.: An efficient technique to access cryptographic file system over network file system. In: Sharma, M.K., Dhaka, V.S., Perumal, T., Dey, N., Tavares, J.M.R.S. (eds.) Innovations in Computational Intelligence and Computer Vision. AISC, vol. 1189, pp. 463–471. Springer, Singapore (2021). https://doi.org/10.1007/978-981-15-6067-5_52

9. Rawat, U., Kumar, S.: ECFS: an enterprise-class cryptographic file system for Linux. Int. J. Inf. Secur. Privacy (IJISP) 6(2), 53–63 (2012)

10. Roghanian, P., Rasli, A., Kazemi, M., Gheysari, H.: Productivity tools: TPM and TQM. Int. J. Fundam. Psychol. Soc. Sci. 2(4), 65–69 (2012)

11. Roy, S., Rawat, U., Sareen, H.A., Nayak, S.K.: IECA: an efficient IoT friendly image encryption technique using programmable cellular automata. J. Ambient Intell. Humaniz. Comput. 11(11), 5083–5102 (2020)

12. Roy, S., Shrivastava, M., Pandey, C.V., Nayak, S.K., Rawat, U.: IEVCA: an efficient image encryption technique for IoT applications using 2-D Von-Neumann cellular automata. Multimedia Tools Appl. 80(21), 31529–31567 (2021)

13. Roy, S., Shrivastava, M., Rawat, U., Pandey, C.V., Nayak, S.K.: IESCA: an efficient image encryption scheme using 2-D cellular automata. J. Inf. Secur. Appl. 61, 102919 (2021)

14. Ryan, M.: Introduction to the TPM 1.2. Draft of March 24 (2009)

15. Shrivastava, M., Roy, S., Kumar, K., Pandey, C.V., Grover, J.: LICCA: a lightweight image cipher using 3-d cellular automata. Nonlinear Dyn. 106(3), 2679–2702 (2021)

Critical Analysis of IoT Ecosystem to Understand Security Threats and Challenges

N. Renya Nath$^{(\boxtimes)}$ and Hiran V. Nath

Department of Computer Science and Engineering,
National Institute of Technology Calicut, Kozhikode 673601, Kerala, India
{renya_p190141cs,hiranvnath}@nitc.ac.in

Abstract. The rapid growth of IoT devices in recent years have given more pervasiveness to IoT services. But the inherent resource constraints and lack of proper security designs make them an easy target to attackers. As a result, the number of threats and attacks on IoT devices and services are increasing nowadays. As the IoT ecosystem is not just a homogeneous network of devices and related services, the isolated layers of an IoT architecture will be insufficient to investigate IoT security. Hence we present a holistic view of the IoT ecosystem by considering it as a collaboration of the object ecosystem and service ecosystem. We then analyse the security threats and challenges of each ecosystem thoroughly. The critical analysis reveals that significant attacks on the object and service ecosystems often occur because of the vulnerability in authentication and access control models. Besides, IoT-specific lightweight security solutions and innovative defensive mechanisms are required to secure IoT devices and services effectively.

Keywords: IoT security · Threats · Challenges

1 Introduction

Internet of Things (IoT) is an emerging communication paradigm that envisions the connectivity of the physical world to the digital world and thus gives ubiquitous access to information. The decrease in the IoT component cost, improved wireless services and speed, battery life, and improved business models have made IoT vision a reality. As a result, recent years have seen an explosion in the number and variety of IoT applications such as smart city, Smart grid, Smart home, Smart health care, etc. Moreover, predictions show that this count will rise more in the coming years. For example, according to Cisco, the number of Internet-connected devices will exceed 30 billion by 2023.

IoT has the potential to create a vast database of knowledge and shared user experiences. However, the same technology can be act as a weapon in the hands of an adversary if not correctly designed. Hence, for broader acceptance,

© The Author(s), under exclusive license to Springer Nature Switzerland AG 2022
S. Joshi et al. (Eds.): SpacSec 2021, CCIS 1599, pp. 64–74, 2022.
https://doi.org/10.1007/978-3-031-15784-4_5

IoT enabling technologies must ensure security, privacy, reliability and quality of service.

Although the security requirements vary with different IoT applications, the core concepts remain the same while considering IoT as an ecosystem. Therefore a deeper understanding of the IoT ecosystem will give more flexibility in the innovative development of security solutions. Researches biased to either layered IoT architecture or systematic approaches are insufficient to address the security issues holistically. Hence in this survey, we try to understand major IoT security threats and challenges based on the most affected elements in the IoT ecosystem.

The contribution of this paper can be summarized as follows: Firstly, an analysis of the IoT ecosystem by dividing it into object ecosystem and service ecosystem. Secondly, security analysis of both object and service ecosystems covers respective threats and challenges. Finally, we conclude our paper with some existing research gaps and future directions in this field.

The rest of the paper is structured as follows: Sect. 2 reviews the existing surveys on IoT security. Section 3 introduces the IoT architecture. Section 4 and 5 analyze security threats and challenges of both object and service ecosystems. With discussions and findings in Sect. 6, Sect. 7 concludes the paper.

2 Related Works

Many survey papers have been published in the area of IoT security until now. Most of the survey papers [13,14,18,23,24] on IoT security have analysed isolated layers of IoT architecture. However, the non-uniformity in the presentation of IoT architecture often creates confusion in understanding the IoT ecosystem.

Very few papers have adopted systematic approaches to analyse IoT security. In [25] authors cover the security issues from the perspective of users, devices, mobility, communication and integration of resources. Whereas the paper [16] covers the security issues based on three levels: object, network and communication and application. However, the paper focuses on very few threats, namely side-channel attacks and firmware update attacks. Meanwhile, authors in [1] provide a comprehensive survey that covers attacks and challenges of core technologies of IoT such as ZigBee, NFC, BLE and WiFi. However, the paper does not include any details on service level security issues.

We concentrate on the object and service ecosystem of IoT architecture to analyse concerning security threats and challenges. In this way, our paper will give more flexibility in framing effective security policies than the layered approach and other systematic approaches mentioned above.

3 Architecture

The IoT architecture embraces the way how different components of the IoT ecosystem communicate with each other. However, the non-uniformity in the presentation of IoT architecture throughout the literature [13,14,18,23,24] poses a significant challenge in understanding the security issues. A holistic approach can give more insight into this realm. Hence, we present a systematic app-roach for analysing IoT architecture, which contains two ecosystems closely connected through communication networks, namely *IoT object ecosystem* and *service ecosystem* as shown in Fig. 1. Every IoT product comprises both these ecosystems irrespective of its complexity.

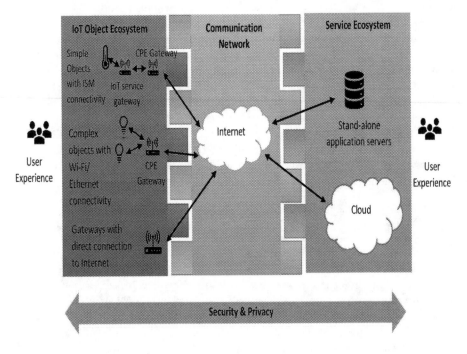

Fig. 1. IoT architecture

The *IoT object-ecosystem* encompasses *simple to complex devices* and *gate-ways* which connects the physical world to the digital world. For example, smart lighting systems, smart door locking systems, industrial control systems, etc. The objects sense and collect data from the surrounding environments and transmit them to the service ecosystem in different data formats via communication net-works. The service ecosystem, in turn, acts as the platform for providing the desired services to the IoT object ecosystem. In other words, the service ecosys-tem gathers data from objects and store them in respective servers for fur-ther processing to render desired end-user experience. The subsequent section explains each ecosystem and associated security threats and challenges in detail.

3.1   IoT Object Ecosystem

The *simple objects* in the IoT object ecosystem use short-range protocols such as IEEE 802.15.4, ZigBee, Z-Wave, NFC, Radio Frequency Identification (RFID),

Bluetooth Low Energy (BLE) or Thread for connectivity and use very cheap processing units such as eight-bit micro-controllers with low power batteries. Smart-watches, thermostats, motion sensors and more are examples of simple devices. These devices are connected to the service ecosystem via IoT service gateways or hub and Customer Premises Equipment (CPE) gateways. Due to severe resource and power constraints, simple devices can not accommodate complex security solutions. However, lightweight security solutions can provide trust and robustness to these devices.

The *complex objects* have continuous connectivity to the service ecosystem using Wi-Fi or Ethernet via CPE gateways. In addition, these devices can run more robust processing units as they are connected to a direct power supply-for example, Wi-Fi-enabled bulbs, refrigerators, and washing machines. As a result, these devices can include more security solutions such as lightweight trust computing entities and Public Key Infrastructure (PKI).

Gateways are complex devices with a dedicated power supply, intricate chip design, and direct communication links such as satellite, optical fibre cable (OFC), or Ethernet. Furthermore, the gateways act as an aggregation point between the object ecosystem and the service ecosystem. The primary functions of gateways include protocol translation, device discovery, authentication and security, run time monitoring and management [12]. Unlike simple and complex objects, IoT service providers manage IoT service gateway, and network provider controls the CPE gateway. Complex gateways thus have more scope to include more lightweight security solutions than complex objects.

3.2 Service Ecosystem

The *service ecosystem* provides value to the data received from the object ecosystem. Database clusters, Application servers and proxy servers and other enabling infrastructures are the sub-components of the service ecosystem [11]. The object ecosystem depends on the service ecosystem for authentication, service availability and user management. Furthermore, the composition of different services and service access points makes the service ecosystem more complex or straightforward IoT applications. Cloud infrastructure-based solutions, Container-based applications, web application service clusters and more are examples of service ecosystem.

Sub-components of the service ecosystem, such as application servers, generally provide service access points as a point of entry into their system. For example, a simple IoT application such as an intelligent lighting system needs to get service from web servers, specific application servers, and authentication servers for its functioning. Therefore secure and reliable environments for their functioning and interactions can only ensure the success of the IoT application. The main challenges of the service ecosystem include proper service segmentation and isolation, solid authentication, and authorisation.

4   Object-Ecosystem Security

The inherent characteristics of IoT devices often create unique security threats
and challenges. Table 1 shows the significant constraints and challenges that are
unique to any IoT object. However, the security threats that profoundly affect
the IoT object ecosystem can be categorised into four:

1. Hardware attacks.
2. Attacks from console access points
3. Internal network service attacks
4. External network and communication infrastructure attacks

Table 1. IoT object constraints and challenges

Constraints	Challenges
Power constraints	Efficient lightweight cryptography algorithms
Cost constraints	Better low processing and memory capability Operating Systems
Durability constraints	Management of system vulnerability and robustness of security choices
Accessibility constraints	Protection of network components and interfaces from attacks

Hardware Attacks. In Hardware attacks [17] adversary will have direct access
to the chip-set or circuit board for manipulation; hence such attacks have the
potential to compromise the confidentiality and integrity of IoT devices. The
main goal of this type of attack includes gathering security information such
as encryption keys, firmware features and messages from internal memory to
identify device vulnerability and manipulate accordingly. A one-time hardware
attack can disrupt the entire product line if the objects are not provisioned
with unique secret keys. In other words, hardware attacks raise confidentiality
threats to deployed technology on the device. Physical tampering [2], Reverse
engineering attacks [10], node cloning, relay attacks [25] side-channel attacks
[33], local bus communication attacks [12], firmware update attacks [21] and
malicious data injection attacks [23] are the significant hardware attacks.

Identifying all open interfaces and protecting them with strong authentication credentials is necessary as a primary step toward securing these devices.
Probing on busses and signals can be thwarted by obfuscating the data that
is transmitted over them [17]. In addition, encryption of device memory and
sensitive data can protect devices from reverse engineering attacks [29].

Furthermore, as a security measure against SCAs, some researchers put forward the use of Physical Unclonable Functions (PUF) to generate keys for identification instead of storing them in memory [16]. Moreover, secure firmware
updates will protect these devices from known vulnerabilities.

Attacks from Console Access Points. All endpoint devices will generally have console access points to diagnose anomalies in hardware or software by their developers and the Quality Assurance team. However, console points can give valuable information to an adversary. An adversary can access console points locally via analysing port pins. For example, a five-pin header on the circuit board indicates a TTL serial port [12]. Console ports often provide direct access to the device. In addition, a thorough analysis of network protocols and console access protocols such as SSH and Telnet can provide remote console access to an adversary. However, lack of proper authentication mechanisms often creates an easy entry for an adversary into the system-for example, default login credentials, easily guessable login credentials etc.

Once the adversary gains access to the device, they can perform data theft, reprogram attack, node capture attack [14], malicious code injection attack and more. For example, in 2016, the most disruptive distributed denial of service attack constructed by Mirai malware remotely gained access to telnet ports of home routers and digital video recorders through the Dictionary attack [7].

Internal Threats that Exploit Network Services. Internal threats are perpetrated by authorised/non-authorised persons having access within the security perimeter of an IoT application network [34]. The adversary evaluates accessible network services for extracting valuable information such as login credentials. For example, eavesdropping [3] of wireless/wired channels that lacks sound encryption mechanisms can provide helpful information to the adversary. Once the adversary gets into the system, they can manipulate the local operating system and potentially abuse vulnerabilities to escalate privileges.

Wireless sensor network as a constituent of the IoT object system, attacks that disrupt trust of WSN also affects IoT object system. Black-hole attack [27], grey-hole attack [27], worm-hole attack [9], sink-hole attack [22] and Sybil attack [27] are the prominent WSN inherited insider threats. All these attacks aim to exploit vulnerabilities of the multi-hop protocols used in the object ecosystem. In addition, vulnerabilities of IoT specific routing protocols such as Routing Protocol for Low-Power and Lossy Networks (RPL) also occur in this respect.

Moreover, an adversary can make jamming attacks [28] by disrupting radio signals to launch a denial of service to or from the device. Another type of attack found inside the network is battery drainage attack and sleep deprivation attack [20] which aims to disrupt the energy harvesting mechanism of a device.

Trust management systems help to ensure the authenticity of objects that take part in communication. The design principle of trust management systems works on either policy-based or reputation based [26]. In which recent researches explain the applicability of blockchain technology for policy-based trust management systems [32]. Meanwhile, many papers employ trust scores to detect insider attacks in IoT systems [4,19]. Furthermore, a trust anchor associated with individual device hardware will improve the trust management system associated with a network.

External Network and Communication Infrastructure Attacks. Network and communication infrastructure plays a crucial role in IoT security as it is a channel that connects the IoT object ecosystem to the service ecosystem. All the threats that exploit the Internet framework hence affect IoT as well. For example, an SQL injection attack [5] takes place by injecting commands over gateway interfaces, resulting in code execution on their local operating system. [35]. Another example is a phishing attack [24] where an adversary gains login credentials by directing the users to perpetrated web interfaces pretending as legitimate sites. Table 2 summarises the attacks in object ecosystem.

Table 2. Object ecosystem: attack overview

Category	Attack vector	Attacks
Object ecosystem	Hardware attacks	Physical tampering, reverse engineering attacks, node cloning, relay attack, side channel attack, local bus communication attack, firmware update attack, malicious code injection attack
	Attacks from console access points	Data theft, reprogram attack, node capture, malicious code injection, access control attacks
	Internal network service attacks	Black hole attack, worm hole attack, sink hole attack, grey hole attack, Sybil attack, jamming attack, battery drainage attack
	External network and communication infrastructure attacks	SQL injection, Phishing, malware

Meanwhile, the availability of IoT devices on a large scale and their poor security designs have made these devices an attractive platform for launching massive DDoS attacks [30]. IoT malware is another major threat to the IoT ecosystem. Recent years have seen an exponential increase in IoT malware with increased variety and complexity- for example, Mirai [8], VPNFilter [36], Hajime [15], etc.

Secure communication models incorporating additional security protocols such as IPSec and DTLS can protect IoT object ecosystems from external attacks. However, the resource constraints of devices often pose a challenge in this realm. Moreover, security mechanisms specific to IoT architecture needs to get more attention from the research world.

5 Service-Ecosystem Security

The security of the service ecosystem strongly depends on the policies enforced on each service component and their interaction. Like IT systems, most IoT products also use cloud platforms for data processing and storage. However, unlike IT systems, IoT requires to meet specific requirements such as hetero-geneity, scalability and mobility. Table 3 summarises the attacks on the service ecosystem.

The virtualised provision of computing resources using cloud technology facil-itates distributed processing of massively generated data. However, data security, exploitation of the virtual environment and authorisation techniques are major security problems to the service ecosystem. Major data security issues are (i) data breach [3] where the adversary succeeds to disclose users' confidential data, and (ii) data lock-in problem [6], which hinders data portability between cloud service providers.

Table 3. Service ecosystem attacks overview

Category	Attacks
Service ecosystem	Data breach, data lock-in problem, VM poaching, VM sprawl, malicious code injection, side channel attack, DDoS attack

Secondly, exploitation of the virtual machines (VM) includes [3,31]: (i) VM poaching occurs when malicious VM uses more resources than allocated, causing availability issues to other VMs, (ii) VM sprawl takes place when unused VMs consume resources (iii) malicious code injection to gain control over hypervisor (iv) Side-channel attack on cloud servers (v) DDoS attacks on servers and more.

Finally, authorisation and access control models have to be advanced to cover the IoT requirement, such as group accessibility of services, multi-service acces-sibility, etc.

6   Discussion

This section discusses the findings and learnings from our analysis. While analysing the literature, we found that most IoT threats occur by exploiting existing authentication and authorisation models on both the object and ser-vice ecosystem. More focus has to be given to improve such models to meet IoT specific requirements.

Each interface acts as an entry to an adversary as objects interact with users, peers, and services. Moreover, the inherent nature of IoT demands a multi-user and multi-controller models object ownership over a single user and single device model. As a result, assurance of the identity of an object can only bring trust in the heterogeneous IoT object ecosystem.

Rather than using hard-coded or default credentials, adopting a crypto-graphically proven authentication mechanism at the object level can improve confidence in the identity of objects. Incorporating a unique trust computing module at the circuit level will help to meet this requirement. Such a mechanism will also help to protect the object ecosystem from internal threats. However, lightweight cryptographic algorithms suitable to IoT specific requirements need to be improved to preserve data confidentiality. Furthermore, an innovative peripheral defence mechanism can also help to protect the object ecosystem from external threats.

Like the object ecosystem, all the interfaces at the service ecosystem have to be protected with proper authentication and authorisation mechanisms. Preserving user privacy is an essential concern in the service ecosystem. However, enforcement of adequate policies to ensure user privacy is still a challenging issue.

7   Conclusion

The advancement in IoT technology has brought down the gap between the physical world and the digital world. As a result, digital security directly affects the physical world than ever before. This paper analyses the IoT ecosystem more deeply by dividing it into object and service ecosystem. The individual analysis of each ecosystem will help to understand their respective security issues in depth. Furthermore, the research shows the pressing need for IoT specific authentication and authorisation models. We believe our study will give more flexibility in designing security solutions for IoT systems in future.

References

1. Abdul-Ghani, H.A., Konstantas, D., Mahyoub, M.: A comprehensive IoT attacks survey based on a building-blocked reference model. Int. J. Adv. Comput. Sci. Appl. **9**(3), 355–373 (2018)
2. Alladi, T., Chamola, V., Sikdar, B., Choo, K.K.R.: Consumer IoT: security vulnerability case studies and solutions. IEEE Consum. Electron. Mag. **9**(2), 17–25 (2020)
3. Aly, M., Khomh, F., Haoues, M., Quintero, A., Yacout, S.: Enforcing security in internet of things frameworks: a systematic literature review. Internet of Things **6**, 100050 (2019)
4. Ambili, K., Jose, J.: Trust based intrusion detection system to detect insider attacks in IoT systems. In: Kim, K., Kim, H.Y. (eds.) Information Science and Applications, pp. 631–638. Springer, Cham (2020). https://doi.org/10.1007/978-981-15-1465-4_62
5. Barcena, M.B., Wueest, C.: Insecurity in the internet of things. Security Response, Symantec (2015)
6. Chen, Y., et al.: Time-reversal wireless paradigm for green internet of things: an overview. IEEE Internet Things J. **1**(1), 81–98 (2014)
7. Costin, A., Zaddach, J.: IoT malware: comprehensive survey, analysis framework and case studies. BlackHat USA (2018)
8. De Donno, M., Dragoni, N., Giaretta, A., Spognardi, A.: DDoS-capable IoT malwares: comparative analysis and Mirai investigation. Security Commun. Netw. **2018** (2018)

9. Deshmukh-Bhosale, S., Sonavane, S.S.: A real-time intrusion detection system for wormhole attack in the RPL based internet of things. Procedia Manuf. **32**, 840–847 (2019)
10. Fernández-Caramés, T.M., Fraga-Lamas, P., Suárez-Albela, M., Castedo, L.: Reverse engineering and security evaluation of commercial tags for RFID-based IoT applications. Sensors **17**(1), 28 (2017)
11. GSMA: IoT Security Guidelines for IoT Service Ecosystem, pp. 1–61 (2016). https://www.gsma.com/iot/wp-content/uploads/2016/02/CLP.12-v1.0.pdf
12. GSMA Association: IoT Security Guidelines for Endpoint Ecosystem, p. 82 (2016). https://www.gsma.com/iot/wp-content/uploads/2016/02/CLP.13-v1.0.pdf
13. Hassan, W.H., et al.: Current research on internet of things (IoT) security: a survey. Comput. Netw. **148**, 283–294 (2019)
14. Hassija, V., Chamola, V., Saxena, V., Jain, D., Goyal, P., Sikdar, B.: A survey on IoT security: application areas, security threats, and solution architectures. IEEE Access **7**, 82721–82743 (2019)
15. Herwig, S., Harvey, K., Hughey, G., Roberts, R., Levin, D.: Measurement and analysis of Hajime, a peer-to-peer IoT botnet. In: Network and Distributed Systems Security (NDSS) Symposium (2019)
16. Hou, J., Qu, L., Shi, W.: A survey on internet of things security from data perspectives. Comput. Netw. **148**, 295–306 (2019)
17. Hutle, M., Kammerstetter, M.: Resilience against physical attacks. In: Smart Grid Security, pp. 79–112. Elsevier (2015)
18. Iqbal, W., Abbas, H., Daneshmand, M., Rauf, B., Bangash, Y.A.: An in-depth analysis of IoT security requirements, challenges, and their countermeasures via software-defined security. IEEE Internet Things J. **7**(10), 10250–10276 (2020)
19. Khan, Z.A., Herrmann, P.: A trust based distributed intrusion detection mechanism for internet of things. In: 2017 IEEE 31st International Conference on Advanced Information Networking and Applications (AINA), pp. 1169–1176. IEEE (2017)
20. Kumar, V., Jha, R.K., Jain, S.: NB-IoT security: a survey. Wirel. Pers. Commun. **113**(4), 2661–2708 (2020)
21. Kvarda, L., Hnyk, P., Vojtěch, L., Neruda, M.: Software implementation of secure firmware update in IoT concept (2017)
22. Liu, Y., Ma, M., Liu, X., Xiong, N.N., Liu, A., Zhu, Y.: Design and analysis of probing route to defense sink-hole attacks for internet of things security. IEEE Trans. Netw. Sci. Eng. **7**(1), 356–372 (2018)
23. Mrabet, H., Belguith, S., Alhomoud, A., Jemai, A.: A survey of IoT security based on a layered architecture of sensing and data analysis. Sensors **20**(13), 3625 (2020)
24. Ogonji, M.M., Okeyo, G., Wafula, J.M.: A survey on privacy and security of internet of things. Comput. Sci. Rev. **38**, 100312 (2020)
25. Pal, S., Hitchens, M., Rabehaja, T., Mukhopadhyay, S.: Security requirements for the internet of things: a systematic approach. Sensors **20**(20), 5897 (2020)
26. Pourghebleh, B., Wakil, K., Navimipour, N.J.: A comprehensive study on the trust management techniques in the internet of things. IEEE Internet Things J. **6**(6), 9326–9337 (2019)
27. Raoof, A., Matrawy, A., Lung, C.H.: Routing attacks and mitigation methods for RPL-based internet of things. IEEE Commun. Surv. Tutor. **21**(2), 1582–1606 (2018)

28. Sharma, M., Tandon, A., Narayan, S., Bhushan, B.: Classification and analysis of security attacks in WSNs and IEEE 802.15. 4 standards: a survey. In: 2017 3rd International Conference on Advances in Computing, Communication & Automation (ICACCA) (Fall), pp. 1–5. IEEE (2017)

29. Shwartz, O., Mathov, Y., Bohadana, M., Elovici, Y., Oren, Y.: Reverse engineering IoT devices: effective techniques and methods. IEEE Internet Things J. 5(6), 4965–4976 (2018)

30. Sonar, K., Upadhyay, H.: A survey: DDoS attack on internet of things. Int. J. Eng. Res. Dev. 10(11), 58–63 (2014)

31. Subramanian, N., Jeyaraj, A.: Recent security challenges in cloud computing. Comput. Electr. Eng. 71, 28–42 (2018)

32. Tang, B., Kang, H., Fan, J., Li, Q., Sandhu, R.: IoT passport: a blockchain-based trust framework for collaborative internet-of-things. In: Proceedings of the 24th ACM Symposium on Access Control Models and Technologies, pp. 83–92 (2019)

33. Tsague, H.D., Twala, B.: Practical techniques for securing the internet of things (IoT) against side channel attacks. In: Dey, N., Hassanien, A.E., Bhatt, C., Ashour, A.S., Satapathy, S.C. (eds.) Internet of Things and Big Data Analytics Toward Next-Generation Intelligence. SBD, vol. 30, pp. 439–481. Springer, Cham (2018). https://doi.org/10.1007/978-3-319-60435-0_18

34. Tukur, Y.M., Ali, Y.S.: Demonstrating the effect of insider attacks on perception layer of internet of things (IoT) systems. In: 2019 15th International Conference on Electronics, Computer and Computation (ICECCO), pp. 1–6. IEEE (2019)

35. Tweneboah-Koduah, S., Skouby, K.E., Tadayoni, R.: Cyber security threats to IoT applications and service domains. Wirel. Pers. Commun. 95(1), 169–185 (2017)

36. Vignau, B., Khoury, R., Hallé, S.: 10 years of IoT malware: a feature-based taxonomy. In: 2019 IEEE 19th International Conference on Software Quality, Reliability and Security Companion (QRS-C), pp. 458–465. IEEE (2019)

Hyper-parameters Study for Breast Cancer Datasets: Enhancing Image Security and Accuracy for Prediction Class

Neha Panwar$^{(\boxtimes)}$ ⓘ and D. P. Sharma

School of Computing and IT, Manipal University Jaipur, Jaipur, Rajasthan 303007, India
nehapanwar1994@gmail.com

Abstract. This study is all about to propose a method for prediction of Breast Cancer (BC) classification which is a very important field for diagnosis of cancer diseases in medical field. All the research studies that have done earlier are centered to get better accuracy in prediction level of BC using different Machine Learning (ML) algorithms. The earlier paper of the same study proposed comparative study chart of different supervised machine learning algorithm in which SVM found to be good for classification. Now this study proposed a comparative study of selection of different kernel categories and Grid Search (GS) implementation for optimal selection for hyper-parameters which is very important to get better results for prediction in classification process. The choices of hyper-parameters affect the rate of accuracy of algorithm. This study used three datasets WBC (Wisconsin Breast Cancer), WDBC (Wisconsin Breast Cancer for Diagnosis) and WPBC (Wisconsin Breast Cancer for Prognosis) in which a for loop structure and GS is used to get best hyper-parameter choices for model training for better accuracy prediction in classification problem of breast cancer. For the diagnosis of breast cancer the most important part is medical image data and its privacy, security is also very important. Due to the use of cloud computing approaches health care sector is also going to store data to the third party server.

Keywords: Support vector machine · Grid search · WBC · WDBC · WPBC · Breast cancer · Image data security

1 Introduction

Now day's cancer is very pandemic and considerable diagnosis field which is spreading all over the world due to so many reasons of using tobacco, infection, obesity and many more. There are so many categories of cancer found in which Breast Cancer is mostly found in women which is reducing the health criteria of happy living and increasing the rate of death of women every year. So this is very important field for research in medical that leads to reduction in death due to this hazardous disease.

Support Vector Machine (SVM), k-Nearest Neighbors (k-NN), Naïve Bayes (NB), Decision-Tree (DT) and Logistic Regression (LR) are implemented for the Wisconsin Diagnostic Breast Cancer (WDBC) dataset which is the measurements taken by the Fine

© The Author(s), under exclusive license to Springer Nature Switzerland AG 2022
S. Joshi et al. (Eds.): SpacSec 2021, CCIS 1599, pp. 75–86, 2022.
https://doi.org/10.1007/978-3-031-15784-4_6

Needle Aspirate (FNA) Test. In which SVM is measured to have highest accuracy in all to 99.12% [1]. Now this study leads to find how hyper-parameter choices affect SVM accuracies ratio.

SVM is very good algorithm when dealing with high dimensional data and proven to be good with all its default values however accuracies can be measure and study by using parameter optimization. Learning process is very critical and variant situation for estimation of correct output for the model where value of node weights typically known responsible parameters that derived through learning process plays important role. The control of learning process is manage by value of hyper-parameters that effect the speed and quality of learning process that result for the better prediction time and correctness of outcome study. These hyper-parameters help to find best estimated model parameter by tuning for a predictive modeling problem. Hyper-parameter includes learning rate, C, sigma, gamma or k value. The controlling properties of hyper-parameter impact so much on behavior and performance significance of model is going to trained. If the values of hyper-parameter are good it will possible to find efficient search space and experimental large set is managed accordingly for hyper-parameter best tuning. This method is referred hyper-parameter optimization.

1.1 Related Work

All Although SVM work well with default values but resultant accuracies and speed can be increased by the use of parameter optimization. There is no exact range of parameter like penalty parameter C, degree or gamma so if there is wide range of parameter than also have more possibilities for Grid Search to get perfect combination of parameters. Support vector machine based on recursive feature elimination and parameter optimization (SVM-RFE-PO). The grid search (GS) algorithm, the particle swarm optimization (PSO) algorithm, and the genetic algorithm (GA) are applied to search the optimal parameters in the feature selection process [2]. SVM Classifier and SVM ensembles classifier used for with different kernel functions and different combinational methods for prediction in classification. In this study Arcane and Micro-Mass dataset used on which RBF kernel SVM classifier is worst measured and Linear kernel SVM classifier is measured good baseline classifier. SVM Classifier and SVM ensembles classifier used for with different kernel functions and different combinational methods. RBF kernel SVM classifier is worst measured and linear kernel SVM classifier is measured good baseline classifier [3].

SVM is considered good classifier method and embedded with feature selection procedure in higher dimensional space with right kernel function that lead to reasonable feature selection of model parameters i.e. width of SVM kernel and penalty parameter, in which Gaussian kernel used with SVM [4]. WBC with, Heterogeneous ensembles machine learning algorithms were used to classify the given data set 10-fold cross-validation, SVM, KNN, gradient boosting classifier, RF, LR, AdaBoost classifier, Gaussian Naive Bayes, and linear discriminant analysis [11]. A broad survey of the different types of machine learning methods being used for cancer prediction and prognosis including a growing dependence on protein biomarkers and microarray data. Decision Tree, Naïve Bayes, k-Nearest Neighbour, Neural Network, Support Vector and Genetic algorithm [19].

Table 1. Comparative research study

Author	Title	Method	Accuracy
Neha Panwar, Naina Narang, D.P.Sharma,2020	"Breast Cancer Classification with Machine Learning Classifier Techniques"	5-fold cross validation classification using SVM, k-NN, DT, NB, LR	99.12%
Shutao Li, Xixian et al. 2008	"Selection using Genetic Algorithm and Support Vector Machines"	Classification performance of optimal feature subset using SVM different parameters using any type of kernel (Rbf, Polynomial and Linear)	Colon Rbf and Polynomial (93.6%) performs better than Linear classifier (87.1%)
Shokoufeh Aalaei et al. 2016	"Feature selection using genetic algorithm for breast cancer diagnosis: experiment on three different datasets"	SVM, ANN	SVM implemented on WBC dataset and yield 96.5% accuracy, where for WDBC and WPBC, ANN yield highest accuracies (97.3% and 79.2%)
Ch. Shravya et al. 2019	"Prediction of Breast Cancer Using Supervised Machine Learning Techniques"	SVM, ANN, LR	SVM in among SVM, ANN and Logistic Regression to 92.7%
Akshya Yadav et al. 2019	"Comparative Study of Machine Learning Algorithms for Breast Cancer Prediction - A Review"	ANN, DT, Random Forest (RF), Naïve Bayes Classifier (NBC), SVM and KNN	Highest accuracy with SVM 97.2%
Bichen Zheng et al. 2014	"Breast Cancer Diagnosis Based on Feature Extraction using Hybrid of k-means and Support Vector Machine Learning Algorithm"	k-means, SVM,10-fold cross validation applied	Accuracy with SVM is 97.38% [9]
Zafiropoulos, Elias et al. 2006	"A Support Vector Machine Approach to Breast Cancer Diagnosis and Prognosis"	SVM	WPBC (96.91%) and for WDBC (90%)

(*continued*)

Table 1. (*continued*)

Author	Title	Method	Accuracy
Y. Qiu, G. Zhou1 et al. 2018	"Comparative Study on the Classification Methods for Breast Cancer Diagnosis"	ML method	93.0% and 62.5%
HibaAsri et al. 2016	"Using Machine Learning Algorithms for Breast Cancer Risk Prediction and Diagnosis"	SVM, C4.5, NB, K-NN, 10-fold cross-validation	SVM (97.13%)
MadhuKumari, VijendraSingh, 2018	"Breast Cancer Prediction system"	K-NN, LR, SVM	K-NN (99.28%)
Abien Fred M. Agarap et al. 2018	"On Breast Cancer Detection:An Application of Machine Learning Algorithms on the Wisconsin Diagnostic Dataset"	SVM + RBF	99.04%
Mogana Darshini Ganggayah et al. 2019	"Predicting factors for survival of breast cancer patients using machine learning techniques"	DT, Random Forest	DT (accuracy = 79.8%) and RF (accuracy = 82.7%)
Carlo Boeri et al. 2020	"Machine learning techniques in breast cancer prognosis prediction: A primary evaluation"	ANN, SVM	(=95.29%–96.86%), sensitivity (=0.35–0.64), specificity (=0.97–0.99), and AUC (=0.804–0.916)

2   Proposed Work

In this study Jupyter notebook with python language is used to implement machine learning algorithm SVM on three different breast cancer datasets. To implement support vector classifier SVC model imported with scikit libraries. There are also inbuilt libraries for implementing Grid Search algorithm for parameter optimization. We import all the scikit libraries necessary for implementing methods and models along with there we applied a nested for loop structure for parameter optimization for Kernels, C, degree, Gamma, coefficient and best score for each kernel by using SVC model [20].

Grid Search and loop structure compared for the values of hyper-parameters. There is also very important thing is to decide type of kernel function for model tuning, for that this study here a function is written in which initially for all kernels classifier accuracies can also measured. In this study all two methods compared for kernel suitability and best hyper-parameter study to find out better prediction accuracy for support vector classifier [21].

2.1 Dataset

In this study three dataset were used taken from UCI repository of Breast Cancer named WBC (Wisconsin Breast Cancer), WDBC (Wisconsin Breast Cancer for Diagnosis) and WPBC (Wisconsin Breast Cancer for Prediction) dataset. The original WBC dataset has 9 attributes and 2 attribute name id and class each having range value of 1–10 with total instances 699 which are divided into two classes malignant (M-> identified as cancer tumor cell) and benign (B-> identified as normal cell) with ratio of 24(M) and 458(B).

The next WDBC dataset having 10 real valued attribute described in Table 1 and for each attribute mean, standard error and worst (mean of three largest value) is computed that result in 30 attributes and along with that 2 attribute name id and diagnosis class for benign and malignant cell. The primary attribute are the result of fine needle aspirate of breast mass formed a digitized image form which attributes extracted. This dataset have 569 instances in which 212 are malignant and 357 benign.

The third one WPBC is having same attribute as WDBC accepts 2 more attribute named as tumor size and lymph node status where tumor size is diameter and lymph node is status of having positive nodes found during surgery time of patient (Table 2 and Table 3).

Table 2. Feature description for cell nuclei

WDBC dataset

Feature no	Features	Description
1	Radius	Mean of distance from centre to point on the perimeter
2	Texture	Standard deviation of grey-scale values
3	Perimeter	Mean size of core tumor
4	Area	The size of cell area
5	Smoothness	Mean of local variation in radius lengths
6	Compactness	Mean of $perimeter^2$/area-1.0
7	Concavity	Mean of severity of concave portions of the contour
8	Concave points	Number of concave portions of the contour
9	Symmetry	Symmetricity

(continued)

Table 2. (*continued*)

WDBC dataset

Feature no	Features	Description
10	Fractal dimension	"Coastline approximation"-1

WPBC dataset

Feature no	Features	Range
1	Sample code number	Id
2	Clump thickness	1–10
3	Uniformity of cell size	1–10
4	Uniformity of cell shape	1–10
5	Marginal adhesion	1–10
6	Single epithelial cell size	1–10
7	Bare nuclei	1–10
8	Bland chromatin	1–10
9	Normal nucleoli	1–10
10	Mitoses	1–10
11	Class	2 (Benign) and 4 (Malignant)

Table 3. Breast cancer datasets

Dataset	No. of attributes	No. of instances	No. of class
WBC	11	699	2
WDBC	32	569	2
WPBC	34	198	2

3   Method and Modeling

3.1 Support Vector Machine

Breast Cancer Classification is supervised problem in which an algorithm is modeled to learn from its training dataset and tested for labeled outcome of any input vector. This model has an activation function that classifies input data points based on its learning accuracies to get better predicted accuracies. Classification problem is determined as parameter optimization problem that helps to model the algorithm in best way to represent predictive relationship among all data points.

SVM is very important technique for classification which uses hypothesis space of linear function to map low dimensional data into high dimensional feature space and deal with vector representation of input variable they solved the problem for classification by using hyper plan which are more than 2 dimensional to n-dimensional and hence avoid over fit to data for maximizing predictive accuracy.

Parameter Optimization

Parameter Tuning plays a very important role for having an optimal solution for most of machine learning algorithms. There is need to have a powerful model as well as proper adjustment of parameters for better classification accuracies of prediction. Parameter optimization is a process that is time consuming if is applied manually in a case of high parameter range [2]. Here SVM classifier is implemented and there is problem of selection of good kernel function and other parameter to avoid bad classification results.

So here in this study two study compared to each other in which for each kernel function, very well known Linear, Polynomial, Rbf and Sigmoid setting up parameter value range externally and performing for each kernel with the help of for loop structure for each instance in training and testing to get better parameter optimization that lead to best accuracy measures and second one is to use Grid Search parameter optimization with the scikit learn inbuilt libraries implementation. All the methods are performed using 5-fold cross validation method [22].

Parameter Optimization with Grid Search

There is hyper-parameter space that has subset searched exhaustively. The hyper-parameter is defined with lower bound, upper bound and number of steps [2]. SVM hyper-parameter has C, Gamma, Degree, and Coefficient that are optimized with grid search by using cross-validation (CV) that can prevent over fitting problem. Different combination of parameters is used for calculating CV error in SVM classifier and for lower value of CV error, hyper-parameter selected for training model (Fig. 1).

3.2 Proposed Model

Here we have four kernels and the entire kernels have different parameter settings. Linear Kernel use only one parameter which C the penalty where Rbf and Sigmoid has two parameters C and Gamma settings, and the last Polynomial has three parameter setting for C, Gamma and degree. In SVM classifier there is no fixed range of using parameter so wider range of parameter gives a better possibility to have a best combination of selected parameters [23].

Feature Scaling

Data pre-processing is very important part of data cleaning and understanding of how the values are going to impact our prediction level accuracies and how values are correlated to each other and creating relationship among all. In data pre-processing and cleaning we have applied to remove all null values from all three data sets and conversion of data type i.e. object to numeric [24].

With all this a another important thing is to check that whether all the values are lying in same range, because there can be situation in which some values lies out range in

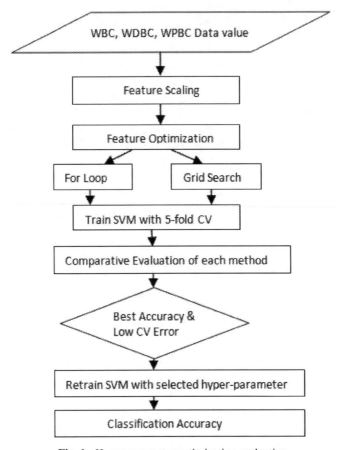

Fig. 1. Hyper-parameter optimization evaluation

comparison of others that lead to outlier condition that result in bad result for accuracies for solving this there is need to apply feature scaling that keep all the values in same range 0–1. In this study WBC dataset studied and found to a same domain range of 1–10 so there is no need to apply feature scaling whether in WDBC and WPBC there is need to apply Feature scaling to keep a domain range 0–1. Feature scaling can be done with Eqs. (1) and (2) for x_{train} and x_{test} from [1].

$$XTrainScaled = \frac{XTrain - XTrainMin}{XTrainMax - XTrainMin} \qquad (1)$$

$$XTestScaled = \frac{XTest - XTestMin}{XTestMax - XTestMin} \qquad (2)$$

4   Result Analysis

In this section we are discussing about experimental results and accuracies outcome for three different methods with a comparative study.

Table 4. Hyper-parameter for comparative study for optimization

Parameter	Kernel	Lower bound	Upper bound	Data type	Step
C	Linear		50.0	Real	1
Degree	Polynomial	3	8	Integer	1
Gamma	RBF, Sigmoid, Polynomial	Auto, scale			
Coefficient	RBF, Sigmoid, Polynomial	.001	10	Real	0.5

In this study two methods applied to study the impact of model hyper-parameter for the effectiveness measurement of the prediction in accuracy for all three Wisconsin dataset WBC, WPBC and WDBC. Here hyper-parameter optimization technique is applied which is grid search.

Feature scaling is also important technique to go through better accuracy result. In the first one method a loop structure is build to work for all kernels (Rbf, Polynomial, Sigmoid, and Linear) applied for all three datasets in two cases feature scaling and without feature scaling with all externally defined values for hyper-parameter in a domain range. In second case grid search is implemented with same values as well as defined in loop structure. This parameter setting is shown in Table 4 (Table 7).

4.1   Measure of Performance Evaluation

Table 5. Accuracy measures based on loop structure and grid search method from domain range

Dataset		WBC				
Parameter		C	Degree	Gamma	Coefficient	Accuracy
For loop	Polynomial	1.0	3	Scale	8.501	95.60%
	RBF	16.0	3	Scale	0.001	94.63%
	Sigmoid					
	Linear		93.65%			
Grid search	RBF	1.0	3	Scale	0.001	93.65%

Table 6. Accuracy measures based on loop structure and grid search method from domain range

Dataset		WDBC				
Parameters		C	Degree	Gamma	Coefficient	Accuracy
For loop	Polynomial	1.0	6	Auto	0.501	95.61%
	RBF	4.0	3	Auto	0.001	95.61%
	Sigmoid	1.0	3,6	Auto	1.001	95.61%
	Linear	1.0	95.61%			
Grid search	RBF	1.0	3	Scale	0.001	92.98%

Table 7. Accuracy measures based on loop structure and grid search method from domain range

Dataset		WPBC				
Parameter		C	Degree	Gamma	Coefficient	Accuracy
For loop	Polynomial	1.0	6	Auto	2.001	82.05%
	RBF	11.0	3	Scale	0.001	82.05%
	Sigmoid	18.0	3	Auto	0.001	79.48%
	Linear	1.0	74.35%			
Grid search	Polynomial	1.0	3	Auto	10	74.35%

Performance of all the kernels with different parameter settings in both two methods is measured and evaluated by classification report, Accuracy score and confusion metrics which are obtained and compared for selection of best combination of hyper-parameter.

5   Conclusion

Here in this research study Three Datasets (WBC, WDBC and WPBC) used for performance evaluation of classifier SVM for prediction accuracies with the different combination of Hyper-Parameters. In place of using default parameters externally domain range is provided for C, Degree, Gamma and Coefficient for four different kernels functions Linear, Sigmoid, Polynomial and Rbf. For different combination of hyper-parameters different accuracies measured that can be seen in Tables 4, 5 and 6.

This study shows that Grid search always try to find optimal parameter choice for classifier modeling but this is very time consuming too if combination of parameter is large set even if dimension of dataset is also high. Although this is good for small dimensional dataset because we want to optimize n parameter and there x steps are needed then xn combination will be calculated and it will take so much time to execute. At the same time we found somehow for loop giving higher accuracy at different value of parameter C, degree and coefficient which is also greater than Grid search.

Here Accuracies can be measured for all three datasets where in WBC loop exit to have greater accuracy for polynomial with 95.60% grid search select Rbf with only

93.65%, in WDBC dataset loop exit with 95.61% for all kernels but grid search select RBF with 92.98%. In third case where in WPBC, loop exit with highest accuracy for polynomial and Rbf with 82.05% grid search select Polynomial with only 74.35%. So this difference is need to conclude ahead with some more method that can overcome the problem related to grid search with higher dimensionality of data, these method can be Genetic Algorithm or PSO for feature selection with effectiveness in calculation of accuracies in prediction and reduce the dimensionality. After that comparison can be taken ahead to have a similarity result for accuracy or nearby.

References

1. Panwar, N., Narang, N., Sharma, D.P.: Breast cancer classification with machine learning classifier techniques. In: International Conference on Innovative Advancement in Engineering and Technology (IAET-2020). Jaipur National University, February 2020
2. Zhang, Y., Deng, Q., Liang, W., Zou, X.: An efficient feature selection strategy based on multiple support vector machines technology with gene expression data. Hindawi BioMed Res. Int. **2018** (2018)
3. Huang, M.W., Chen, C.W., Lin, W.C., Ke, S.W., Tsai, C.F.: SVM and SVM ensembles in breast cancer prediction. PLoS ONE (2017). https://doi.org/10.1371/journal.pone.0161501
4. Mao, Y., Zhou, X.-B., Pi, D.-Y., Sun, Y.-X., Wong, S.T.C.: Parameters selection in gene selection using Gaussian kernel support vector machines by genetic algorithm*. J. Zhejiang Univ. Sci. **6B**(10), 961–973 (2005). ISSN 1009-3095
5. Li, S., Wu, X., Hu, X.: Gene selection using genetic algorithm and support vector machines. Soft Comput. **12**, 693–698 (2008)
6. Aalaei, S., Shahraki, H., Rowhanimanesh, A., Eslami, S.: Feature selection using genetic algorithm for breast cancer diagnosis: experiment on three different datasets. Iran. J. Basic Med. Sci. **19**(5), 476 (2016)
7. Ch. Shravya, K. Pravalika, Shaik Subhani," Prediction of Breast Cancer Using Supervised Machine Learning Techniques",International Journal of Innovative Technology and Exploring Engineering (IJITEE), ISSN: 2278–3075, Volume-8 Issue-6, April 2019
8. Yadav, A., Jamir, I., Jain, R.R., Sohani, M.: Comparative study of machine learning algorithms for breast cancer prediction - a review. Int. J. Sci. Res. Comput. Sci. Eng. Inf. Technol. (IJSRCSEIT) **5**(2), 979–985 (2019)
9. Zheng, B., Yoon, S.W., Lam, S.S.: Breast cancer diagnosis based on feature extraction using hybrid of k-means and support vector machine learning algorithm. Expert Syst. Appl. **41**, 1476–1482 (2014)
10. Zafiropoulos, E., Maglogiannis, I., Anagnostopoulos, I.: A support vector machine approach to breast cancer diagnosis and prognosis. In: Maglogiannis, I., Karpouzis, K., Bramer, M. (eds.) AIAI 2006. IIFIP, vol. 204, pp. 500–507. Springer, Boston (2006). https://doi.org/10.1007/0-387-34224-9_58
11. Alfonso, G.: Cancer detection using support vector machines trained with linear kernels. Int. J. Sci. Res. (IJSR) 2319–7064 (2018)
12. Qiu, Y., Zhou1, G., Zhao, Q., Cichocki, A.: comparative study on the classification methods for breast cancer diagnosis. Bull. Pol. Acad. Sci. Tech. Sci. **66**(6) (2018)
13. Asri, H., Mousannif, H., Al Moatassime, H., Noel, T.: Using machine learning algorithms for breast cancer risk prediction and diagnosis. Procedia Comput. Sci. **83**, 1064–1069 (2016). The 6th International Symposium on Frontiers in Ambient and Mobile Systems (FAMS 2016)

14. Kumari, M., Singh, V.: Breast cancer prediction system. Procedia Comput. Sci. **132**, 371–376 (2018). International Conference on Computational Intelligence and Data Science (ICCIDS 2018)
15. Agarap, A.F.M., et al.: On breast cancer detection: an application of machine learning algorithms on the wisconsin diagnostic dataset. In: ICMLSC 2018, 2–4 February 2018
16. Ganggayah, M.D., et al.: Predicting factors for survival of breast cancer patients using machine learning techniques. BMC Med. Inform. Decis. Making **19**, 48 (2019)
17. Boeri, C., et al.: Machine learning techniques in breast cancer prognosis prediction: a primary evaluation. Cancer Med. **9**, 1–10 (2020)
18. Dhahri, H., et al.: Automated breast cancer diagnosis based on machine learning algorithms. Hindawi J. Healthc. Eng. **2019** (2019)
19. Omondiagbe, D.A., et al.: machine learning classification techniques for breast cancer diagnosis. IOP Conf. Ser.: Mater. Sci. Eng. **495**, 012033 (2019)
20. Sharma, A.K., Nandal, A., Dhaka, A., Dixit, R.: Medical image classification technique-sand analysis using deep learning networks: a review. In: Patgiri, R., Biswas, A., Roy, P. (eds.) Health Informatics: A Computational Perspective in Healthcare, vol. 932, pp. 233–258. Springer, Singapore (2021). https://doi.org/10.1007/978-981-15-9735-0_13
21. Wild, C.P., Weiderpass, E., Stewart, B.W.: World cancer report: cancer research for cancer prevention, world cancer reports (2020). ISBN: 978-92-832-0447-3
22. Sharma, A.K., Nandal, A., Dhaka, A., Dixit, R.: A survey on machine learning based brain retrieval algorithms in medical image analysis. Health Technol. **10**, 1359–1373 (2020)
23. Bishop, C.: Pattern Recognition and Machine Learning. Springer, Berlin (2006)
24. Deng, L., Yu, D.: Deep learning: methods and applications. Found. Trends Sign. Process. **7**(34), 197–387 (2014)

An Efficient Image Encryption Technique Using Logistic Map and 2D-TCLM

Krishna Kumar[1], Satyabrata Roy[1(✉)], Umashankar Rawat[1(✉)], and Ishan Mishra[2]

[1] Department of Computer Science and Engineering, Manipal University Jaipur, Jaipur, Rajasthan, India
{satyabrata.roy,umashankar.rawat}@jaipur.manipal.edu
[2] Department of Information Technology, Manipal University Jaipur, Jaipur, Rajasthan, India

Abstract. Nowadays, multimedia data transfer through internet has rapidly increased. This has drawn the interest of the miscreants towards theft and misuse of images for certain malign purpose. Image encryption can provide confidentiality to these images by restricting the miscreants from performing various security attacks. In this paper an image encryption technique using hybrid chaotic maps - Logistic Map and 2D - Tent Cascade Logistic Map (2D-TCLM) has been proposed. The result of the encryption is promising. Various performance analyses have confirmed the security features of the proposed technique. It has been also shown that the proposed image encryption technique is better than the existing techniques with respect to majority of the key parameters, making it suitable for implementation in real-time image communication over insecure public channel.

Keywords: Image encryption · Chaotic map · Ciphertext · Logistic map · 2D - TCLM

1 Introduction

Encryption is a method used to protect images from possible attacks when transmitted through insecure public channels. In the digital world, image encryption plays a massive role due to the number of images being sent at any moment. Encryption plays a vital role to ensure confidentiality of the sensitive images sent over the internet. There exist many image encryption algorithms that are mainly based on chaotic logistic maps, but these are often used in combination of other resource consumptive techniques such as deep neural networks [5,14]. In this paper we have proposed a method that uses chaotic logistic map and a 2D Tent-cascade-Logistic map (2D-TCLM) to encrypt a set of images. The proposed scheme is a symmetric key encryption technique. Hence, the same secret key has been used to encrypt and decrypt the images. The experimental results clearly demonstrate that encryption algorithm based on hybrid chaotic maps generate better results than the existing techniques.

© The Author(s), under exclusive license to Springer Nature Switzerland AG 2022
S. Joshi et al. (Eds.): SpacSec 2021, CCIS 1599, pp. 87–96, 2022.
https://doi.org/10.1007/978-3-031-15784-4_7

The proposed scheme has gone through various standard analyses such as histogram analysis, image quality analysis using Mean Square Error (MSE) and Peak Signal to Noise Ratio (PSNR), differential analysis using Number of Pixel Change Rate (NPCR) and Unified Average Changing Intensity (UACI). The scheme has been compared with existing techniques. The result of comparison confirmed the efficiency of the proposed technique.

2   Related Works

Over the years it have been studied that the traditional ciphers are not very much useful for the encryption of digital images. This is because of the large data volume of the digital images, high correlation between adjacent pixels and redundancy of the data. Chaotic map based image encryption techniques are pretty useful for encryption of the digital images because they provide a balanced combination of good speed, computational overhead, energy consumption, high level of security in terms of various standard parameters and large key space [10].

Anwar *et al.* [1] presented a pixel based image encryption scheme using chaotic maps that produced high correlation coefficient values, good structural similarity index (SSIM). Pak *et al.* [9] proposed an image encryption technique using 1-D chaotic maps. Their encryption system consisted linear-nonlinear-linear structure based on total shuffling and it achieved excellent performance in noise attacks.

Lu *et al.* [6] presented an image encryption scheme that used LSS chaotic map and single S-box. Their scheme achieved good resistance against chosen plaintext attacks. Sneha *et al.* [15] proposed an efficient algorithm for image encryption using the mixture of Walsh-Hadamard transform and Arnold-Tent maps. Their technique achieved large key space and good security features. Apart from the chaotic maps based image encryption, there are several other techniques such as cellular automata based encryption [11–13], DNA based image encryption [2,8], in the recent years. Majority of the works are based on chaotic maps because of the suitability of the encryption scheme in practical real-time uses.

Man *et al.* [7] presented a double image encryption technique where key generation was performed using a chaotic map, then convolution neural network based dual image encryption was performed. This achieved high resistivity against security attacks. In [16], dynamic row scrambling and zigzag transformation were used to generate encrypted image. It achieved excellent security features for image cipher. Wang *et al.* [17] proposed an encryption technique with scrambling based on 1D logistic chaotic map. Their scheme achieved bit level confusion property using random blocks.

3   Mathematical Preliminaries

This section provides some basic concepts required for understanding the proposed methodology. This section explains logistic map first. Subsequently, the required details of 2D-TCLM has been presented.

3.1   Logistic Map

Logistic map is a function given by Eq. (1) used to generate the first series. It is One Dimensional and is chaotic in nature. It is shown in Fig. 1. It is used in Eq. (1).

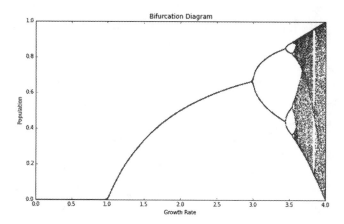

Fig. 1. Logistic map [3]

$$X_{n+1} = r \times X_n(1 - X_n) \tag{1}$$

'r' is the Bifurcation parameter and ranges between (0 to 4) and 'X0' is the initial value and ranges between (0 to 1) and elements $X_1, X_2, X_3 \ldots, X_n$ are generated using this Equation. It is known that when 'r' is 3.9999, a highly random sequence is formed. Using 3.99, a chaotic sequence X_i is generated with X_0 being a random number. Each element in this sequence is between 0 and 1, this is now converted to integer by multiplying the number by 255 and then rounded off. This sequence is now called K_1.

3.2   2D-TCLM

This section introduces the 2D Tent-cascade-Logistic map (2D-TCLM). Mathematically, it is represented as:

$$
\begin{cases}
x_{n+1} = \begin{cases} (3 + y_n) \times 2\mu x_n(1 - 2\mu x_n) & \text{if } x < 0.5 \\ (3 + y_n) \times 2\mu(1 - x_n)(1 - 2\mu(1 - x_n)) & \text{if } x > 0.5 \end{cases} \\[4ex]
y_{n+1} = \begin{cases} (3 + x_{n+1}) \times 2\mu y_n(1 - 2\mu y_n) & \text{if } y_n < 0.5 \\ (3 + x_{n+1}) \times 2\mu(1 - y_n)(1 - 2\mu(1 - y_n)) & \text{if } y_n > 0.5 \end{cases}
\end{cases}
\tag{2}
$$

x_n and y_n are iterative values, μ is the control parameter and exists between $[0, 1]$. We iteratively generate an array of the same dimensions as the image with the values $|x_n - y_n|$. Each element in the sequence is between 0 and 1, This is now converted to integer by multiplying by 255 and then rounded off. This forms the sequence, K_2.

4   Proposed Image Encryption and Decryption

In this section we describe at the techniques used for image encryption and decryption of a color image.

The proposed encryption model used in this paper is a combination of a chaos logistic map and the 2D-TCLM. Both have been chosen due to their chaotic nature. For the sake of the explanation, we will use one channel of the image, but the model can be used for RGB images by running it against the 3 channels, which we have done in the testing phase.

Encryption Process. We first import an image and convert it into a 2D sequence called "IMGSEQ". This is followed by generating a sequence using logistic maps of the same dimensions as IMGSEQ, 3.99 is used as the value of μ and generate a random first number, a list of numbers ranging between 0 and 1 are now formed, this is then multiplied by 255 and then convert it into 8bit binary. This is saved as "K_1". The encryption process has been written in Algorithm 1 (Fig. 2).

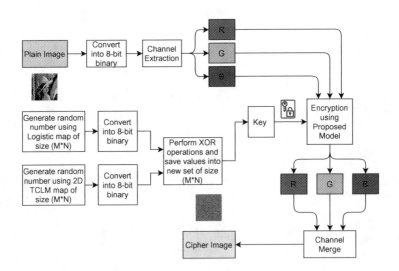

Fig. 2. Proposed encryption model

Algorithm 1. Proposed Encryption Algorithm

1: *Begin*
2: *The image (m × n) is imported and converted into a sequence of n, m sized elements, (2D array) called **IMGSEQ***
3: *A sequence K1 is generated using the Logistic Map function.*
4: *A sequence K2 is generated using the 2D-TCLM function.*
5: *XOR function is applied to all elements in **K1** and **K2**, This sequence is used as the **KEY**.*
6: *The XOR function is applied to all elements of **KEY** and **IMGSEQ** and the formed sequence is called **IMG**.*
7: ***IMG** is converted into an encrypted image.*
8: *End*

Another sequence is generated using 2D-TCLM of the same dimensions as IMGSEQ, The model consists of generating all 3 random values (x, y, u) and form a sequence consisting of values between 1 and 0, this is then multiplied by 255 and then convert it into 8bit binary. This is saved as "K_2".

The XOR function is applied between all elements of K1 and their corresponding values in K_2, This is saved as the final **"KEY"**. The XOR function is applied between all elements of the KEY and their corresponding values in IMGSEQ, this then saved as the final encrypted image or cipher image.

Decryption Process. The encrypted image is imported and converted into a 2D sequence called **"IMGSEQ"**. The XOR function is applied between all elements of IMGSEQ and their corresponding values in the KEY, This is saved as the the final decrypted image. the overall decryption process has been written in Algorithm 2.

Algorithm 2. Proposed Decryption Algorithm

1: *Begin*
2: *The encrypted image (m × n) is imported and converted into a sequence of n,m sized elements, (2D array) called **IMGSEQ**.*
3: *The KEY is imported.*
4: *The XOR function is applied to all elements of KEY and **IMGSEQ** and the formed sequence is called **IMG**.*
5: ***IMG** is converted into the decrypted image.*
6: *End*

The proposed encryption and decryption schemes are repeated three times for each channel (RGB) during the testing (Fig. 3).

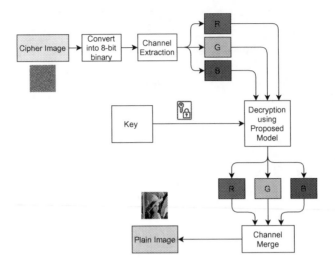

Fig. 3. Proposed decryption model

5   Experimental Results and Performance Analysis

Simulation of the proposed image encryption and decryption scheme is conducted in a computer having 4 GB RAM, Intel core i3 processor using python language. The proposed scheme was tested on Lena, Baboon and Pepper images. The original, encrypted and decrypted test images are shown in Fig. 4. All the test images were of 512×512 size.

5.1   Performance Analysis

In this section, the proposed scheme is presented with the following performance analyses – i) Histogram analysis ii) Mean Square Error (MSE) iii) Peak Signal-to-Noise Ratio (PSNR) iv) Mean Absolute Error (MAE), v) Structural Similarity Index (SSIM), vi) Root Mean Square Error (RMSE), vii) Number of Pixel Change Rate (NPCR) and Unified Average Changing Intensity (UACI) of plain, encrypted and decrypted images.

Results of other analyses are presented in Table 1. Additionally, the results of MSE and PSNR were compared with some of the existing techniques and the result is presented in Table 2.

Furthermore, the comparison results with respect to NPCR and UACI values are shown in Table 3. In the proposed method, key sequence $\{K_i\}$ is generated from the sequence of logistic map $\{K_1\}$ and sequence generated by 2D-TCLM $\{K_2\}$. The test results confirms the efficiency of the proposed technique.

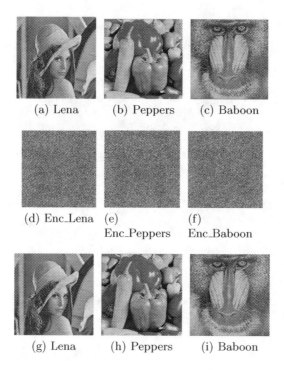

(a) Lena   (b) Peppers   (c) Baboon

(d) Enc_Lena   (e) Enc_Peppers   (f) Enc_Baboon

(g) Lena   (h) Peppers   (i) Baboon

Fig. 4. Decrypted images

Table 1. Result of various performance analysis of the proposed technique

Metrics/Images	Baboon	Lena	Pepper
MSE	8.593×10^3	9.203×10^3	10.337×10^3
PSNR	8.7888	8.4915	7.9868
MAE	0.0035	0.0036	0.0038
SSIM	0.0081	0.0048	0.0044
RMSE	0.3635	0.3762	0.3987
NPCR	99.6189	99.6158	99.6011
UACI	33.4711	33.4763	33.4699

Table 2. Comparison of MSE and PSNR with existing techniques for Lena image

Technique	MSE	PSNR
Proposed technique	9.203×10^3	8.4915
IESCA [13]	7.179×10^3	9.57
Zhu et al. [18]	7.817×10^3	9.23

Table 3. Comparison of NPCR and UACI values for Lena image

Technique	NPCR	UACI
Proposed technique	99.6158	33.4763
IESCA [13]	99.6347	33.4653
Dong et al. [4]	99.6159	33.4763

The result of histogram analysis for the plain and encrypted Lena, Peppers and Baboon images are shown in Fig. 5.

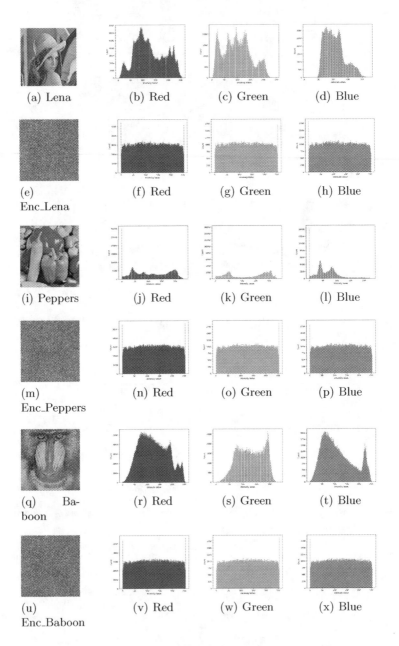

(a) Lena   (b) Red   (c) Green   (d) Blue

(e) Enc_Lena   (f) Red   (g) Green   (h) Blue

(i) Peppers   (j) Red   (k) Green   (l) Blue

(m) Enc_Peppers   (n) Red   (o) Green   (p) Blue

(q) Baboon   (r) Red   (s) Green   (t) Blue

(u) Enc_Baboon   (v) Red   (w) Green   (x) Blue

Fig. 5. Histograms of Red, Green and Blue channels of plain and cipher images of Lena, Peppers and Baboon using the proposed technique (Color figure online)

It can be noticed from the result of histogram analysis that the histograms of encrypted images contained uniform distribution of the pixel values as is desirable from a good quality encryption algorithm.

6 Conclusion and Future Works

The image encryption proposed in this paper used two chaotic maps – logistic map and 2D - Tent Cascade Logistic Map (2D-TCLM). The chaotic maps were used to generate the symmetric secret key used for both encryption and decryption. The key was applied to red, green and blue channels separately and then the channels were merged to obtain the cipher image. This method is a pixel-wise encryption method that has achieved good values of the standard parameters used in majority of the analyses.

In future, the technique can be enhanced to achieve more randomness, noise resistant and lightweight characteristics to be applied for IoT applications. The technique can be made public key based encryption technique. Furthermore, it can be combined with DNA sequences to infuse higher degree of randomness. Moreover, by using certain shuffling techniques in combination with cellular automata, the proposed method can achieve more confusion and diffusion properties.

References

1. Anwar, S., Meghana, S.: A pixel permutation based image encryption technique using chaotic map. Multimed. Tools Appl. **78**(19), 27569–27590 (2019). https://doi.org/10.1007/s11042-019-07852-2
2. Babaei, M.: A novel text and image encryption method based on chaos theory and DNA computing. Nat. Comput. **12**(1), 101–107 (2013)
3. Boeing, G.: Visual analysis of nonlinear dynamical systems: chaos, fractals, self-similarity and the limits of prediction. Systems **4**(4), 37 (2016)
4. Dong, C.: Color image encryption using one-time keys and coupled chaotic systems. Signal Process. Image Commun. **29**(5), 628–640 (2014)
5. He, Y., Li, W.: Image-based encrypted traffic classification with convolution neural networks. In: 2020 IEEE Fifth International Conference on Data Science in Cyberspace (DSC), pp. 271–278. IEEE (2020)
6. Lu, Q., Zhu, C., Deng, X.: An efficient image encryption scheme based on the LSS chaotic map and single s-box. IEEE Access **8**, 25664–25678 (2020)
7. Man, Z., Li, J., Di, X., Sheng, Y., Liu, Z.: Double image encryption algorithm based on neural network and chaos. Chaos Solit. Fractals **152**, 111318 (2021)
8. Mondal, B., Mandal, T.: A light weight secure image encryption scheme based on chaos & DNA computing. J. King Saud Univ.-Comput. Inf. Sci. **29**(4), 499–504 (2017)
9. Pak, C., Huang, L.: A new color image encryption using combination of the 1D chaotic map. Signal Process. **138**, 129–137 (2017)
10. Pareek, N.K., Patidar, V., Sud, K.K.: Image encryption using chaotic logistic map. Image Vis. Comput. **24**(9), 926–934 (2006)

11. Roy, S., Rawat, U., Sareen, H.A., Nayak, S.K.: IECA: an efficient IoT friendly image encryption technique using programmable cellular automata. J. Ambient. Intell. Humaniz. Comput. **11**(11), 5083–5102 (2020)

12. Roy, S., Shrivastava, M., Pandey, C.V., Nayak, S.K., Rawat, U.: IEVCA: an efficient image encryption technique for IoT applications using 2-D von-Neumann cellular automata. Multimed. Tools Appl. **80**, 1–39 (2020)

13. Roy, S., Shrivastava, M., Rawat, U., Pandey, C.V., Nayak, S.K.: IESCA: an efficient image encryption scheme using 2-D cellular automata. J. Inf. Secur. Appl. **61**, 102919 (2021)

14. Sirichotedumrong, W., Maekawa, T., Kinoshita, Y., Kiya, H.: Privacy-preserving deep neural networks with pixel-based image encryption considering data augmentation in the encrypted domain. In: 2019 IEEE International Conference on Image Processing (ICIP), pp. 674–678. IEEE (2019)

15. Sneha, P., Sankar, S., Kumar, A.S.: A chaotic colour image encryption scheme combining Walsh-Hadamard transform and Arnold-Tent maps. J. Ambient. Intell. Humaniz. Comput. **11**(3), 1289–1308 (2020)

16. Wang, X., Chen, X.: An image encryption algorithm based on dynamic row scrambling and zigzag transformation. Chaos Solit. Fractals **147**, 110962 (2021)

17. Wang, X., Guan, N., Yang, J.: Image encryption algorithm with random scrambling based on one-dimensional logistic self-embedding chaotic map. Chaos Solit. Fractals **150**, 111117 (2021)

18. Zhu, C.: A novel image encryption scheme based on improved hyperchaotic sequences. Opt. Commun. **285**(1), 29–37 (2012)

Learning Co-occurrence Embeddings for Sentence Classification

Triveni Lal Pal[✉] and Kamlesh Dutta

Department of Computer Science and Engineering, National Institute of Technology Hamirpur, Hamirpur, HP, India
trivenipal@gmail.com, kd@nith.ac.in

Abstract. The sequence and co-occurrence information of the words constituting the sentence is crucial for the sentence classification task. Distributed representations like word embeddings successfully learned for classification tasks. Learning longer word sequences like sentence embeddings for text classification incorporating word sequences and co-occurrence information remains a challenging task. This research article, proposed a CNN-based embedding learning for sentence classification that incorporates sequence as well as co-occurrence information of the words. The empirical result shows that the proposed approach performance better over other baseline models.

Keywords: Vector space model · RNN · LSTM · CNN · Embeddings · Naïve Bayes classifier · Support vector machine

1 Introduction

Text data is most common forms of representation for communication/storage. A terabytes of text data is generated daily but unfortunately it is unstructured in nature. This means managing text require special representation techniques which can incorporate meaning (semantics) of text. The conventional approach for text representation is vector space model (VSM) which considers numerical feature vectors in a Euclidean space. Numerical values of VSM are incapable of representing the complex relations between the words as it treats word in isolation. Another most recent representation technique which is gaining popularity is embeddings learning. Embeddings are also popularized due to their capability to learn complex relations between different units of text and availability of software packages which are open source like word2vec, GloVe and Deeplearning4j [1]. Usefulness of word embeddings is due to their capability of incorporating both syntactic and semantic information of words in learning high-quality continuous vectors such that semantically similar words are represented by vectors close to one another, in semantic space. The recent popularity of the embeddings is due to the fact that "they are able to capture surprisingly nuanced semantics even in the absence of sentence structure" [2].

Word embeddings find its applications in language models [3, 4], extractive summarization [5], machine translation [6, 7], named entity recognition [8], disambiguation [9],

© The Author(s), under exclusive license to Springer Nature Switzerland AG 2022
S. Joshi et al. (Eds.): SpacSec 2021, CCIS 1599, pp. 97–104, 2022.
https://doi.org/10.1007/978-3-031-15784-4_8

parsing [10], sentiment analysis [11], sentence classification [12] and lexical information retrieval [13].

Embeddings are task and domain specific and are able to capture the sequence information [14, 15], but learning embeddings for longer word sequences like phrases and sentences, is still a challenging task. Learning sentence embeddings require word sequence information as well as sentence structure (syntactic information). Embeddings thus learned are useful in text classification task.

In this paper, we proposed a CNN based model for sentence classification, capable of learning sequence information and co-occurrence information thereby learning sentence structure, classifies the sentence to appropriate class. The article in its next section (Sect. 2) presents related work followed by Sect. 3 in which we presented the proposed model. Section 4 contains experimental results and discussion. Conclusion and future scope is presented in last section (Sect. 5) of the paper.

2   Related Works

Word embeddings gain its popularization by word2vec, a family of energy-based modes [16–18]. RNN based embeddings are helpful in making a prediction within local context windows (shallow window-based method). However, the RNN embeddings are task and domain specific. Convolution neural networks have long history of being used in image processing applications. In text mining, researchers exercises on CNNs with window of varying sizes. [19] proposed hybrid text classification approach and claimed to solve sparse high dimensionality problem of matrix. The researchers employed deep belief network with softmax regression for feature extraction and training. Generalizable Sentence Classification [12] has been proposed using Cost-Sensitive BERT for automatic identification of propaganda. The window-based intra-weighing approach proposed in [20] is different from tradition CNN/RNN based models which works on primary assumption that key-words are more import than other words in deciding the class. Author extracted key-words to put some extra weight on key-words while embedding learning. [21] proposed a classification approach for sentiment classification using CNN and word2vec. However this model is trained to classify the short sentence only.

3   Proposed Model

This section contains architecture description of the proposed system staring with description and overview of the system.

3.1   Overview of the Proposed CNN Model

The model uses pre-trained Glove word vectors with 200 dimensions. The group of these word vectors represents a sentence and is passed to the input layer. The model basically has input layer, convolution layer, max-pooling layer, concatenation layer and finally classification layer (classifier). The system made to learn from training set and tested on testing set. Figure 1 illustrates the different layers in the proposed system.

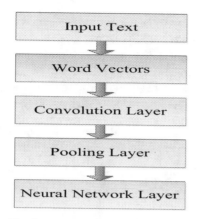

Fig. 1. Layers in the proposed system.

Algorithm 1: Sentence Embedding Learning
Input: Text collection (D) $\{w_1, w_2, \ldots\}$

Output: fixed size sentence vectors

Steps:

1. for each sentence $s_i \in D$,

    i.extract vectors get n×d matrix

    ii.do basic preprocessing to get reduced matrix

2.
    2×50,3×50,4×50) and ReLu as function, of varying sizes
3. perform convolution on matrix with stride=1 to get feature maps
4. perform pooling (max) to get max value out of feature maps corresponding to each region
5. concatenate pooled values to get fixed size feature vectors

3.2 CNN Architecture

The proposed CNN model consist of 1-input layer, one embedding layer, 9-convolutional layers (3 each with dimensions 2 × 50, 3 × 50, 4 × 50), 9-max-pooling layers corresponding to 9-convolutional layers, 3-averaging layers, 1-concatenation layer, 2-dense layers and 1-dropout layer. As maximum length of a sentence in the dataset is 200, so the dimension of input sentence is taken as 200. For the sentences short in length (<200), the remaining indexes are padded with zeros. At embedding layer group of pre-trained Glove word embeddings taken corresponding to each sentence. To capture fine details stride size is kept at 1 and 9 different filters at convolution layer provide extra to incorporate co-occurrence relation between the words. This is the uniqueness of this model which enable the model to learn co-occurrence embeddings. Output of the max-pooling layer is maximum value out of convolution vectors at each convolution layers. The averaging layer is used to get the average value out of 3-max-pooled value corresponding to each average convolution vector. Concatenation layer takes the input from previous layer and returns concatenated vector of 300 dimension. Two dense layers are fully connected layers. The first dense layer has 300 neurons with ReLu activation function whereas second in implemented having 5 neurons with softmax activation function. The second dense layer is also works as classifier, which classifies the output into 5 different classes.

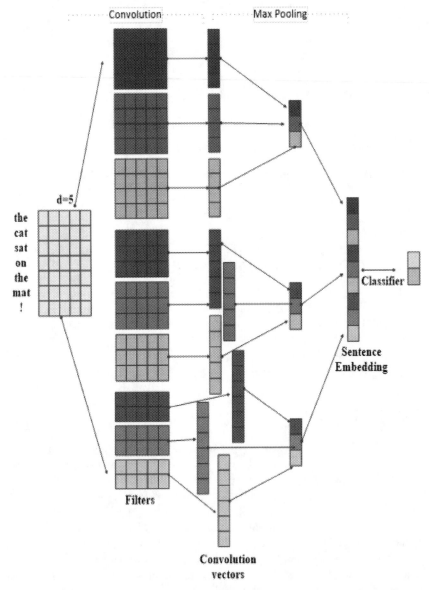

Fig. 2. Illustration of the model on example sentence "the cat sat on the mat!".

Dropout layer with dropout rate 0.2 is used to selectively dropping some values to avoid network overfitting. The model uses the categorical_crossentropy as our loss function and adam as the optimization function.

Figure 2 is simple illustration of the proposed model. Word embeddings corresponding to each word in the input sentence "the cat sat on the mat" is taken. At convolution layer 9 filters are taken. 9 convolution vectors corresponding to 9 convolution filters are obtained. At max-pooling layer these vectors are max-pooled to get 3 vectors that further concatenated to get sentence embeddings. Thus for each sentence we get one sentence embedding.

4   Experimental Results

This section presents about the datasets we used and the experimental result of our proposed CNN model.

4.1   Datasets

We used BBC full text document consisting of 2225 documents in five categories labelled as business, entertainment, politics, sport and tech. We used single label dataset due to research constraints. We train our model on 23735 labelled sentences and tested on 4117 new sentences. The training is performed for 10 epochs. Table 1 shows the percentage share of documents with different class labels towards training and test sets.

Table 1. Data partition.

Classes	Number of documents		Portion in the dataset
	Training	Testing	
Business	408	102	22.92%
Entertainment	309	77	17.35%
Politics	334	83	18.74%
Sports	409	102	22.97%
Tech	321	80	18.02%

4.2   Results and Discussion

We implement the baseline Naïve Bayes and Support Vector Machine for same dataset and found our model perform better than existing models on the evaluation metrics as precision, recall, f-measure and accuracy (Table 2 shows the same) (Fig. 3).

Table 2. Comparison between NB, SVM and proposed model.

Models	Classes	Precision	Recall	F-measure	Accuracy
NB	Business	74.51%	74.51%	74.51%	77.70%
	Entertainment	73.17%	77.92%	75.47%	
	Politics	77.27%	81.93%	79.53%	
	Sports	80.85%	74.51%	77.55%	
	Tech	74.71%	81.25%	77.84%	
SVM	Business	87.63%	83.33%	85.43%	82.88%
	Entertainment	81.25%	84.42%	82.80%	
	Politics	77.92%	72.29%	74.99%	
	Sports	88.00%	86.27%	87.13%	
	Tech	77.78%	87.50%	82.35%	
Proposed model	Business	87.50%	82.35%	84.85%	86.07%
	Entertainment	82.93%	88.31%	85.54%	
	Politics	79.78%	85.54%	82.56%	
	Sports	90.82%	87.25%	89.99%	
	Tech	88.61%	87.50%	88.05%	

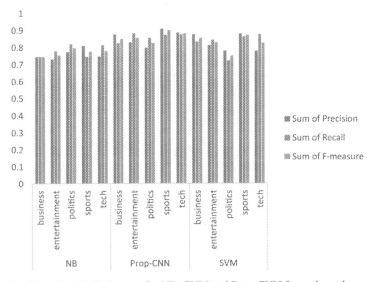

Fig. 3. Precision, Recall, F-Measure for NB, SVM and Prop-CNN for various classes of text.

Figure 4 is the comparison between NB, SVM and our model (Hy-CNN) showing the Precision, Recall, F-Measure and Accuracy values for different systems trained and evaluated on same dataset. The experimental results shows that our model converge at fine tuning stage and outperform Naïve Bayes and Support Vector Machine.

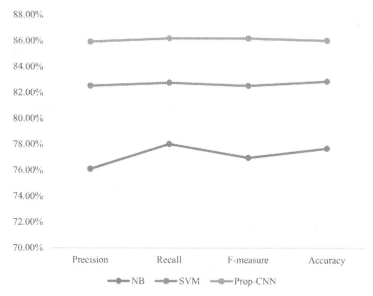

Fig. 4. Precision, Recall, F-Measure and Accuracy of various models.

5   Conclusion and Future Scope

The proposed CNN module able to learn sentence embeddings that further used to predict the class label of unknown document. The system trained on 23735 labelled sentences and tested on 4117 new sentences. The model shows considerable improvement on precision, recall and F-values over baseline (NB and SVM) models. The overall accuracy of the system when trained for 1000 epochs is 86.04% which is considerably good when compared with NB and SVM which is 77.70% and 82.88% respectively on same dataset. The result shows that the model is capable of incorporating word co-occurrence information in its representation useful for sentence classification. As a future scope, the model can be extended to learn document embeddings for document retrieval applications.

References

1. Singh, T., Kumari, M., Pal, T.L., Chauhan, A.: Current trends in text mining for social media. Int. J. Grid Distrib. Comput. **10**(6), 11–28 (2017)
2. Chen, Y., Perozzi, B., Al-Rfou, R., Skiena, S.: The expressive power of word embeddings. arXiv Prepr. arXiv1301.3226, vol. 28, pp. 2–9 (2013)
3. Collobert, R., Weston, J.: A unified architecture for natural language processing. In: Proceedings of the 25th International Conference Machine Learning - ICML 2008, vol. 20, no. 1, pp. 160–167 (2008)

4. Bengio, Y., Schwenk, H., Senécal, J.-S., Morin, F.: Neural probabilistic language models. In: Innovations in Machine Learning, pp. 137–186 (2006)
5. Kageback, M., Mogren, O., Tahmasebi, N., Dubhashi, D.: Extractive summarization using continuous vector space models. In: Proceedings of the 2nd Workshop on Continuous Vector Space Models and their Compositionality, pp. 31–39 (2014)
6. Zou, W.Y., Socher, R., Cer, D., Manning, C.D.: Bilingual word embeddings for phrase-based machine translation. In: Proceedings of the 2013 Conference on Empirical Methods in Natural Language Processing (EMNLP 2013), no. October, pp. 1393–1398 (2013)
7. Pal, T.L.: Anaphora resolution in Hindi: issues and challenges. Int. J. Comput. Appl. **42**(18), 7–13 (2012)
8. Ratinov, L., Turian, J.: Word representations : a simple and general method for semi-supervised learning. In: Acl, no. July, pp. 384–394 (2010)
9. Collobert, R., Weston, J., Bottou, L., Karlen, M., Kavukcuoglu, K., Kuksa, P.: Natural language processing (almost) from scratch (2011)
10. Socher, R., Lin, C.: Parsing natural scenes and natural language with recursive neural networks. In: Proceedings of the 28th International Conference on Machine Learning, pp. 129–136 (2011)
11. Ahsan, M., Kumari, M., Singh, T., Pal, T.L.: Sentiment based information diffusion in online social networks. In. J. Knowl. Discov. Bioinf. **8**(1), 60–74 (2018)
12. Generalisable, C.B.: Cost-sensitive BERT for generalisable sentence classification with imbalanced data (2014)
13. Gao, L., Dai, Z., Chen, T., Fan, Z., Van Durme, B., Callan, J.: Complement lexical retrieval model with semantic residual embeddings. In: Hiemstra, D., Moens, M.-F., Mothe, J., Perego, R., Potthast, M., Sebastiani, F. (eds.) ECIR 2021. LNCS, vol. 12656, pp. 146–160. Springer, Cham (2021). https://doi.org/10.1007/978-3-030-72113-8_10
14. Pal, T.L., Kumari, M., Singh, T., Ahsan, M.: Semantic representations in text data. Int. J. Grid Distrib. Comput. **11**(9), 65–80 (2018)
15. Pal, T.L., Kumari, M.: Semantic similarity metrics for analysing semantic representations: In Proceedings of International Conference on Emerging Trends in Engineering Innovations and Technology Management, ISBN- 978–93–86724–30–4, pp. 30–35 (2017)
16. Mikolov, T., Corrado, G., Chen ,K., Dean, J.: Efficient estimation of word representations in vector space. In: Proceedings of the International Conference Learning Representation (ICLR 2013), pp. 1–12 (2013)
17. Mikolov, T., Chen, K., Corrado, G., Dean, J.: Distributed Representations of Words and Phrases and their Compositionality. Adv. Neural Inf. Process. Syst. Nips **26**, 3111–3119 (2013)
18. Mikolov, T., Yih, W., Zweig, G.: Linguistic regularities in continuous space word representations. In: Proceedings of the NAACL-HLT, no. June, pp. 746–751 (2013)
19. Socher, R., Huang, E., Pennington, J.: Dynamic pooling and unfolding recursive autoencoders for paraphrase detection. Adv. Neural Inf. Process. Syst. **24**, 801–809 (2011)
20. Jiang, R., et al.: Text classification based on deep belief Network and softmax regression. Neural Comput. Appl. **29**, 61–70 (2018)
21. Huang, T., Deng, Z., Shen, G., Chen, X.: A window-based self-attention approach for sentence encoding neurocomputing a window-based self-attention approach for sentence encoding. Neurocomputing **375**, 25–31 (2019)
22. Sharma, A.K., Chaurasia, S., Srivastava, D.K.: ScienceDirect sentimental short sentences classification by using CNN deep learning model with fine tuned Word2Vec. Procedia Comput. Sci. **167**(2019), 1139–1147 (2020)

Preventing Fault Attacks on S-Boxes of AES-Like Block Ciphers

Swapan Maiti[1]([✉]), Deval Mehta[2], and Dipanwita Roy Chowdhury[1]

[1] Indian Institute of Technology Kharagpur, Kharagpur, India
swapankumar_maiti@yahoo.co.in, drc@cse.iitkgp.ac.in
[2] Space Applications Centre (SAC), ISRO, Ahmedabad, India
m_deval@sac.isro.gov.in

Abstract. Substitution functions (S-boxes) are essential for the design of AES-like cryptosystems as they play an important role in the security of the cryptosystems. Most of the cryptosystems are highly vulnerable against fault-attacks. So, countermeasures against fault-attacks are necessary to make the cryptographic devices secure. This paper presents a fault resilient design of S-boxes for AES-like block ciphers. It is done by fault detection and correction. The S-boxes are designed based on the synthesized nonlinear cellular automata. The proposed design guarantees 100% coverage of double-byte fault detection and single-byte fault correction.

Keywords: S-box · Nonlinear functions · Nonlinear cellular automata · Fault attack countermeasures

1 Introduction

In todays era of communication, secure transmission of information is utmost important. Fault is a problem that results in a complete failure in secure data transmission. The most common type of faults in hardware implementation, particular in FPGAs primarily affect digital circuits in aviation, space applications, and nuclear research where devices are subjected to higher levels of radiation.

Many cryptographic systems use block ciphers which are conventionally considered as the most important symmetric ciphers. The "Advanced Encryption Standard (AES)" [7] is a "NIST" standardized "symmetric cipher" that provides 128-bit security. Unfortunately, it is vulnerable to side-channel attacks. Fault attacks are implementation attacks where faults are injected deliberately into the cryptographic devices and faulty ciphertexts are exploited to break the security. Fault attacks have currently become the most effective, and successfully employed to break the ciphers. In 1997, Boneh et al. [1] introduced faults to find secret key of RSA. In [12,14,16] the authors proposed that a one-byte

This work is supported by Space Applications Centre (SAC), Ahmedabad, Indian Space Research Organization (ISRO) through an R&D project.

© The Author(s), under exclusive license to Springer Nature Switzerland AG 2022
S. Joshi et al. (Eds.): SpacSec 2021, CCIS 1599, pp. 105–116, 2022.
https://doi.org/10.1007/978-3-031-15784-4_9

fault injection on AES can derive a secret key. Unfortunately, all the standards of symmetric ciphers become vulnerable against a fault- attack. So, countermeasures against fault-attacks are necessary to make the cryptographic devices secure.

In literature [2,15,17], fault correction was not considered. This work detect as well as correct the faults using Cellular Automata (CA). CA has been widely preferred by many researchers for their low implementation cost. Furthermore, CA exhibit good "cryptographic properties" [5]. Moreover, CA can be suitable for good pseudorandom number generation [19]. There exist some CA-based S-boxes in literature [8,11,13].

This paper presents a novel design of 8×8 S-boxes based on CA capable of exhibiting good "cryptographic properties". The design is particularly developed to construct fault-resilient S-boxes. Below is a list of key contributions of this paper:

- Design and exploring of 8×8 S-boxes based on synthetic "Nonlinear Cellular Automata (NLCA)".
- A novel technique is proposed for preventing fault attacks on the S-boxes at substitution phase of AES-like block ciphers.

The organization of rest of the paper is as follows. Section 2 describes some related works. Section 3 presents the design of S-boxes, and also explores the rule vectors of NLCA for designing S-boxes, and shows their "cryptographic properties". The design strategy to prevent fault injection attacks on the S-boxes is presented in Sect. 4. Section 5 discusses the results. Finally, the paper is concluded in Sect. 6.

2   Related Work

In [10], NLCA based S-boxes are introduced, where the underlying NLCA are synthesized with Rules 90, 150, 30 followed by nonlinearity injection into some cells. For a n-cell, 3-neighborhood CA represented by $\langle q_0, q_1, \ldots, q_{n-1} \rangle$ where state of $i - th$ cell is represented by q_i. Rules 90, 150, and 30 are defined respectively as follows:

$$\text{For Rule 90,} \quad \varphi_i = q_{i-1} \oplus q_{i+1}$$
$$\text{For Rule 150,} \quad \varphi_i = q_{i-1} \oplus q_i \oplus q_{i+1}$$
$$\text{For Rule 30,} \quad \varphi_i = q_{i-1} \oplus (q_i \ OR \ q_{i+1}) = q_{i-1} \oplus q_i \oplus q_{i+1} \oplus (q_i \cdot q_{i+1})$$

where φ_i represents a combinational logic for the i-th cell, "$\oplus$" denotes Boolean XOR operation, and "OR" denotes Boolean OR operation. In the work, authors explore 17 S-boxes and compute their "cryptographic properties".

In the proposed work, we explore synthetic NLCA based 8×8 S-boxes on another variant of rule combinations (i.e., Rules 90, 150, 86) with nonlinearity injection, and present a design strategy for preventing fault injection attacks on the S-boxes of AES-like block ciphers.

3   Designing Synthesized S-Boxes Using CA

This work presents the design overview of 8×8 S-boxes based on synthetic non-linear cellular automata (NLCA), and that of the corresponding inverse S-boxes. Then we explore the S-boxes and their "cryptographic properties". For designing the S-boxes, a preliminary knowledge of CA is essential. Now we discuss few fundamental notions of CA before presenting our proposed works.

3.1   Basics of the Design Primitive: Cellular Automata

Cellular Automata (CA) are studied for pseudorandom sequence generation, and applications in cryptography by Wolfram [18,19]. Some basic terminologies and their respective definitions such as linear CA, nonlinear CA, maximum length CA, uniform and non-uniform CA, boundary conventions etc. can be found in [4,5,10].

Here, the S-boxes have been constructed using null-boundary CA with combinations of Rule 90, Rule 150 and Rule 86. Subsequently, nonlinear functions are used to inject nonlinearity. The state transition function of Rule 86 can be written as follows:

$$\varphi_i = (q_{i-1} \ OR \ q_i) \oplus q_{i+1} = q_{i-1} \oplus q_i \oplus q_{i+1} \oplus (q_{i-1} \cdot q_i)$$

where "OR", "$\oplus$" and "$\cdot$" denotes Boolean OR, XOR, and AND operations, respectively. Figure 1 shows a "null-boundary" nonlinear CA with rule vector [90, 86, 90, 150].

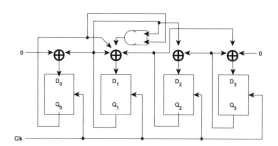

Fig. 1. A hybrid null-boundary non-linear CA

3.2   S-Box Design

Figure 2 shows an overview of the design of an 8×8 S-box using an 8-bit synthesized NLCA. We initially consider the NLCA of the rule vectors having three 3-neighborhood rules 90, 150 and 86. By the synthesis algorithm (ref. Algorithm 1), the state transition functions of the CA cells are updated as per the rules 90, 150, 86. Then, using some other nonlinear functions, state updating

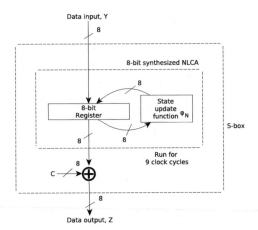

Fig. 2. Generalized view of the proposed S-box design

Algorithm 1. NLCA Synthesize Algorithm

Input: An NLCA of its present state denoted by $Q = \langle q_0, q_1, \ldots, q_7 \rangle$ with a state update function $\varphi = \langle \varphi_0, \varphi_1, \ldots, \varphi_7 \rangle$ of rules 90, 150, 86, and the set of positions $\{2, 3, 4, 5\}$ of the cells of the NLCA for nonlinearity injections
Output: A synthesized NLCA with a state update function φ_N

 1. **For** each $i \in \{0, 1, \ldots, 7\}$ **do**   ▷ Update the state updating function of i-th cell
 2.   **If** the i-th cell runs Rule 90
 3. $\varphi_i \leftarrow q_{i-1} \oplus q_{i+1}$
 4.   **If** the i-th cell runs Rule 150
 5. $\varphi_i \leftarrow q_{i-1} \oplus q_i \oplus q_{i+1}$
 6.   **If** the i-th cell runs Rule 86
 7. $\varphi_i \leftarrow q_{i-1} \oplus q_i \oplus q_{i+1} \oplus (q_{i-1}.q_i)$
 8. **end For**
 9. $\varphi_N \leftarrow \varphi$
10. Let $\mathcal{X} \subseteq \{2, 3, 4, 5\}$ ▷ $\mathcal{X}$ be the set of cell positions where nonlinearity injections are made using a nonlinear function $(q_{i-2}.q_{i+2})$ or $(\varphi_{i-2}.\varphi_{i+2})$
11. **For** each $i \in \mathcal{X}$ **do**   ▷ Update the state updating function of the i-th cell
12.   **If** the i-th cell initially runs Rule 90
13. $\varphi_i \leftarrow \varphi_i \oplus (\varphi_{i-2}.\varphi_{i+2})$
14.   **If** the i-th cell initially runs Rule 150
15. $\varphi_i \leftarrow \varphi_i \oplus (q_{i-2}.q_{i+2}) \oplus (\varphi_{i-2}.\varphi_{i+2})$
16.   **If** the i-th cell initially runs Rule 86
17. $\varphi_i \leftarrow \varphi_i \oplus (\varphi_{i-2}.\varphi_{i+2})$
18. **end For**
19. **Return** φ_N

---

functions are further updated by nonlinearity injection [6] either into single or multiple cell-location(s) of the NLCA. Eventually, the state updating function becomes $\varphi_N = \langle \varphi_0, \varphi_1, \ldots, \varphi_7 \rangle$ for a single clock cycle.

Algorithm 2 presents construction of the S-box based on the synthesized NLCA. The underlying NLCA of its present state Q is loaded with an 8-bit input Y, and then CA is executed for a total of nine clock cycles (ref. Fig. 2), and finally produce an 8-bit value denoted by $\varphi_N^9(Q)$. Since, $(0, 0, \ldots, 0)$ is generated

---

Algorithm 2. Designing the NLCA based S-box: **S-box(Y)**

Input: A synthesized NLCA denoted by $Q = \langle q_0, q_1, \ldots, q_7 \rangle$ with a state update function $\varphi_N = \langle \varphi_0, \varphi_1, \ldots, \varphi_7 \rangle$ and Y, an eight-bit input
Output: Z, an eight-bit output.

1. $Q \leftarrow Y$ ▷ Load the NLCA with the input Y
2. **For** j = 1 **to** 9 **do**   ▷ Run the NLCA for 9 clock cycles
3. $Q \leftarrow \varphi_N(Q)$
4. **end For**
5. $Z \leftarrow \varphi_N^9(Q) \oplus C$ ▷ Add an 8-bit nonzero constant C
6. **Return** Z

---

from $(0, 0, \ldots, 0)$ by the NLCA, an appropriate 8-bit non-zero constant $C = (c_0, c_1, \ldots, c_7)$ is XORed with $\varphi_N^9(Q)$ to generate S-box output Z. Thus, the output function of S-box can be written as $F = (f_0, f_1, \ldots, f_7)$, where $f_i \; \forall i \in \{0, 1, 2, \ldots, 7\}$ being "coordinate functions", and can be represented as $f_i = \varphi_i^9(Q) \oplus c_i$.

3.3   Inverse S-Box

Figure 3 shows the corresponding inverse S-box of the proposed design to generate an 8-bit output, Y from an 8-bit input Z. The output Y of inverse S-box after running the underlying CA for nine clock cycles is as follows:

$$(\varphi_N^I)^9(Z \oplus C) = (\varphi_N^I)^9(\varphi_N^9(Q) \oplus C \oplus C) = (\varphi_n^I)^9(\varphi_N^9(Q)) = Q, \quad Y \leftarrow Q$$

3.4   The Synthetic NLCA Based S-Boxes

The important "cryptographic properties" of an S-box can be found in [3,8]. In this work, the total $3^8 = 6561$ number of rule vectors have been studied. The rule vectors are formed with Rules 90, 150 and 86 along with nonlinearity injections at locations $\langle 2, 3, 4, 5 \rangle$ of the underlying 8-bit NLCA. After "Linear Cryptanalysis (LC)" and "Differential Cryptanalysis (DC)" [9], 79 S-boxes are found. Among these, 17 S-boxes are found where the associated linear CA (LCA) are group CA (Table 1). There exist NLCA based S-boxes on another variant of rule combinations (i.e., rules 30, 90, 150) in literature [10]. Among these, four S-boxes with rules 90, 150 are also found in this work.

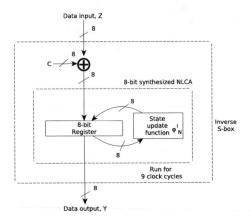

Fig. 3. The inverse S-box

3.5 Cryptographic Properties of the S-Boxes

Table 2 shows the "cryptographic properties" of the 17 S-boxes. The "cryptographic properties" of AES S-box is shown in Table 3.

Table 1. S-boxes with underlying NLCA

S-boxes	Rule vectors	Nonlinearity injection position(s)	L_{mn}	L_{mx}	D_{max}	LCA cycles (Associated to NLCA)
1	[150 90 90 150 150 86 150 150]	2	−36	36	10	(1 51 51 51 51 51)
2	[150 86 90 86 150 150 90 90]	2, 3	−38	34	10	(1 85 85 85)
3	[150 90 86 90 90 90 86 90]	2, 5	−32	36	10	(1 255)
4	[150 150 90 150 86 90 86 90]	2, 5	−34	36	10	(1 255)
5	[90 150 90 150 90 150 90 90]	3, 4	−32	36	10	(1 255)
6	[90 90 150 90 150 90 86 90]	3, 4	−32	34	10	(1 255)
7	[150 86 90 150 90 90 150 150]	3, 4	−34	34	10	(1 255)
8	[150 150 90 86 90 90 150 150]	3, 4	−34	32	10	(1 255)
9	[150 150 90 150 90 90 150 150]	3, 5	−34	36	10	(1 255)
10	[90 90 150 150 90 90 150 150]	3, 5	−36	36	10	(1 85 85 85)
11	[90 90 86 90 86 90 150 90]	2, 3, 4	−36	32	10	(1 255)
12	[90 90 86 150 90 150 86 90]	2, 3, 4	−36	32	10	(1 255)
13	[90 150 90 150 86 150 90 150]	2, 3, 4	−36	32	10	(1 255)
14	[150 150 90 90 150 90 90 150]	2, 3, 5	−32	34	10	(1 255)
15	[150 90 86 90 90 90 150 90]	2, 4, 5	−32	34	10	(1 255)
16	[150 90 86 90 90 90 86 90]	2, 4, 5	−36	32	10	(1 255)
17	[90 150 90 150 86 150 90 150]	2, 4, 5	−34	32	10	(1 255)

L_{mn}: Minimum value in the linear approximation table
L_{mx}: Max. value in the linear approximation table
D_{max}(Differential uniformity): Max. value in the Difference Distribution Table (DDT)

Table 2. Computing the "cryptographic properties" of 17 S-boxes

S-boxes	$|L_{mn}| + |L_{mx}|$	D_{max}	Nonlinearity	Balancedness	Alg. Deg.	BN_F
1	72	10	96	✓	7	2
2	72	10	100	✓	7	2
3	68	10	98	✓	7	2
4	70	10	98	✓	7	2
5	68	10	102	✓	7	2
6	66	10	100	✓	7	2
7	68	10	98	✓	7	2
8	66	10	100	✓	7	2
9	70	10	100	✓	7	2
10	72	10	102	✓	7	2
11	68	10	100	✓	7	2
12	68	10	100	✓	7	2
13	68	10	100	✓	7	2
14	66	10	98	✓	7	2
15	66	10	102	✓	7	2
16	68	10	100	✓	7	2
17	66	10	102	✓	7	2

✓: True BN_F : Differential branch number

Table 3. Computing the "cryptographic properties" of AES S-box

S-box	$|L_{mn}| + |L_{mx}|$	D_{max}	Nonlinearity	Balancedness	Alg. Deg.	BN_F
"AES S-box"	32	4	112	✓	7	2

✓: True

4   Designing Fault Resilient S-Boxes for AES-Like Block Ciphers

This section presents a development strategy to prevent fault-attacks on S-boxes in the substitution phase designed with S-boxes using synthetic NLCA.

4.1   Fault Model

In the fault model, we presume that the fault occurs (naturally or maliciously) in the S-boxes where we correct a one-byte fault, and detect a two-byte fault.

4.2   Design Approach

The design for preventing faults that occur in the 16-byte substitution phase using some check-bytes is shown in Fig. 4. The layer uses 16 instances of an S-box out of 17 S-boxes (ref. Table 1). The substitution is done after executing the

16 base NLCA for a total of 9 clock-cycles. In each clock cycle, few check-bytes are generated (ref. Algorithm 3) to detect the occurrences of faults (if any) in registers of NLCA. The check-bytes are then computed again (ref. Algorithm 4) depending on all the NLCA next states. The newly generated check-bytes are compared with the previously generated check-bytes. The faulty byte(s) can be identified by this comparison in case the fault arises in the NLCA as shown in Fig. 4. After fault detection in every clock cycle, the faulty byte is corrected by Fault Correction Circuit (FCT). The state updating function of CA uses the corrected byte to set up the next state for next clock cycle. The corrected byte is also used to configure the check-bytes of the subsequent state of the CA. After executing all NLCA for nine clock cycles, the substitution layer generates 16 correct bytes as output.

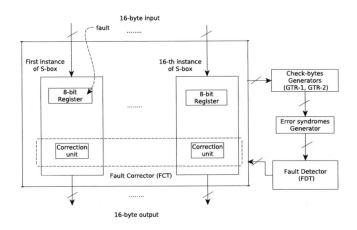

Fig. 4. The fault resilient design of the sub-layer

Let the 16-byte (i.e., 128-bit) message be defined as $\langle A_0, A_1, A_2, \ldots, A_{15} \rangle$ which are given as input to 16 8-bit NLCA. The check-bytes Generator, GTR-1 determines (ref. Algorithm 3) three check-bytes C_0, C_1 and C_2 based on $\langle A_0, A_1, A_2, \ldots, A_{15} \rangle$. The other check-bytes Generator, GTR-2 then computes (ref. Algorithm 4) the three check bytes C_0', C_1' and C_2' based on the computed values $D_i = (B_i' \oplus F_{NL}(A_i))$, $0 \le i \le 15$. Then the error syndromes S_0, S_1 and S_2 are computed (ref. Algorithm 5) by XORing the newly generated check bytes C_0', C_1', C_2' with C_0, C_1 and C_2.

Algorithm 3. Generating check-bytes by GTR-1

Input: A 16-byte message be defined as $\langle A_0, A_1, A_2, \ldots, A_{15} \rangle$ which is fed to the 16-byte substitution layer of the cipher
Output: Three check-bytes C_0, C_1 and C_2

1. Let an 8-bit S-box be used in 16 instances in the substitution layer, and the state transition function be φ_N, where $\varphi_N(A_i) = \varphi_L(A_i) \oplus \varphi_{NL}(A_i)$, and φ_L be the vectorial linear function of the associated linear CA and φ_{NL} be the vectorial nonlinear function operated on A_i

2. **Initialize** $C_0 \leftarrow 0, C_1 \leftarrow 0, C_2 \leftarrow 0$
3. **For** i = 0 **to** 15
4. $\quad C_0 \leftarrow C_0 \oplus \varphi_L(A_i)$
5. **end For**
6. **For** i = 15 **down to** 0
7. $\quad C_1 \leftarrow \varphi_L(C_1 \oplus A_i)$
8. **end For**
9. **For** i = 15 **down to** 1
10. $\quad C_2 \leftarrow \varphi_L^2(C_2 \oplus A_i)$ $\quad \triangleright \varphi_L^2$ represents the function composition φ_L with itself
11. **end For**
12. $C_2 \leftarrow \varphi_L(C_2 \oplus A_0)$
13. **Return** C_0, C_1, C_2

The fault in j-th NLCA register is detected (ref. Algorithm 6) by the fault detection circuit FDT based on the values of the generated error syndromes S_0, S_1 and S_2. After fault detection in the j-th NLCA register, FCT generates the correct outputs $\langle B_0, B_1, \ldots, B_{15} \rangle$ by

$$B_j = B_j' \oplus E_j$$
$$B_i = B_i' \text{ for all } i \in \{0, 1, 2, \ldots, 15\} \text{ and } i \neq j.$$

Here, $\langle B_0, B_1, \ldots, B_{15} \rangle$ is the correct 16-byte output for one clock cycle.

For the next run, the 16-byte output $\langle B_0, B_1, \ldots, B_{15} \rangle$ is used by the state updating functions of all the NLCA, and accordingly the check-bytes C_0, C_1, C_2 are generated based on the correct 16-byte output. The process is executed for 9 clock cycles to generate $\langle \varphi_N^9(B_0), \varphi_N^9(B_1), \ldots, \varphi_N^9(B_{15}) \rangle$. Consequently in the end, the "substitution-layer" generates 16 correct bytes $\langle (\varphi_N^9(B_0) \oplus C), (\varphi_N^9(B_1) \oplus C), \ldots, (\varphi_N^9(B_{15}) \oplus C) \rangle$, where C is an 8-bit non-zero constant as discussed in Sect. 3.2.

Algorithm 4. Generating check-bytes by GTR-2

Input: The 16-byte message be defined as $\langle A_0, A_1, A_2, \ldots, A_{15} \rangle$ and the output bytes for the 16 NLCA be $B' = \langle B'_0, B'_1, \ldots, B'_{15} \rangle$

Output: Three check-bytes C'_0, C'_1 and C'_2

1. Here, $B'_i = \varphi_N(A_i) = \varphi_L(A_i) \oplus \varphi_{NL}(A_i)$, $i \in \{0, 1, 2, \ldots, 15\}$ denotes correct output byte, and $B'_i = \varphi_N(A_i) \oplus E_i = \varphi_L(A_i) \oplus \varphi_{NL}(A_i) \oplus E_i$ denotes incorrect output byte, where E_i denotes the byte-error in the i-th byte.

2. Compute $(B'_i \oplus \varphi_{NL}(A_i))$ for all $i \in \{0, 1, \ldots, 15\}$, and store into D_i
3. **Initialize** $C'_0 \leftarrow 0, C'_1 \leftarrow 0, C'_2 \leftarrow 0$
4. **For** i = 0 **to** 15
5. $\quad C'_0 \leftarrow C'_0 \oplus D_i$
6. **end For**
7. **For** i = 15 **down to** 1
8. $\quad C'_1 \leftarrow \varphi_L(C'_1 \oplus D_i)$
9. **end For**
10. $C'_1 \leftarrow C'_1 \oplus D_0$
11. **For** i = 15 **down to** 1
12. $\quad C'_2 \leftarrow \varphi_L^2(C'_2 \oplus D_i)$ ▷ φ_L^2 represents the function composition φ_L with itself
13. **end For**
14. $C'_2 \leftarrow C'_2 \oplus D_0$
15. **Return** C'_0, C'_1, C'_2

Algorithm 5. Generating error syndromes

Input: Two sets of check-bytes $\langle C_0, C_1, C_2 \rangle$ and $\langle C'_0, C'_1, C'_2 \rangle$

Output: Three error syndrome bytes S_0, S_1 and S_2

1. $S_0 \leftarrow C_0 \oplus C'_0$
2. $S_1 \leftarrow C_1 \oplus C'_1$
3. $S_2 \leftarrow C_2 \oplus C'_2$
4. **Return** S_0, S_1, S_2

---

5   Result and Discussion

The design guarantees 100% coverage of double-byte fault detection and single-byte fault correction in the S-boxes with redundant hardware and memory. This paper also explores 17 S-boxes based on synthetic nonlinear CA. The underlying NLCA are synthesized with Rules 90, 150, 86 followed by nonlinearity injection. Among the 17 S-boxes, Sbox-15 and Sbox-17 (ref. Table 2) have the best non-linearity. The proposed fault resilience can be accomplished at the cost of extra memory and hardware redundancy. The results furnished in Table 2 and Table 3 reveals that the "cryptographic properties" of AES S-box are superior than that of the proposed S-boxes. Further, the proposed design is lightweight too.

Algorithm 6. Detecting fault

Input: The error syndrome bytes S_0, S_1 and S_2
Output: Fault location j if fault occurs in j-th NLCA register

1. Let fault occurs in j-th NLCA register, therefore
   $S_0 = E_j$
   $S_1 = \varphi_L^j(E_j)$
   $S_2 = \varphi_L^{2j}(E_j)$
2. **If** $(S_0 = S_1 = S_2 = 0)$ ▷ No fault in the NLCA registers
3.   there is no fault in the NLCA registers
4. **If**$((S_0 \neq 0)\&\&(S_1 = S_2 = 0))$ ▷ Fault in check-bytes
5.   then check-byte C_0 is faulty
6. **If**$((S_1 \neq 0)\&\&(S_0 = S_2 = 0))$ ▷ Fault in check-bytes
7.   then check-byte C_1 is faulty
8. **If**$((S_2 \neq 0)\&\&(S_0 = S_1 = 0))$ ▷ Fault in check-bytes
9.   then check-byte C_2 is faulty
10. **If** (two or more syndrome bytes are nonzero)
11.   **For** $i = 0$ to 15 **do**   ▷ To check fault in the NLCA registers
12.   **If**$(S_1 = \varphi_L^i(S_0))$ and $(S_2 = \varphi_L^{2i}(S_0))$ **break**
13.   **end For**
14. $j \leftarrow i$ ▷ Fault occurs in j-th NLCA register
15. **If**$(i = 16)$
16.   double-byte faults occur
17. **else Return** j

---

6   Conclusion

In this paper, the S-boxes based on synthetic nonlinear cellular automata have been studied. The S-boxes are constructed using CA Rule 90, Rule 150, and Rule 86, having non-linearity injections. A design scheme has been proposed to prevent byte-fault in S-boxes at the cost of hardware and memory redundancy.

References

1. Boneh, D., DeMillo, R.A., Lipton, R.J.: On the importance of checking crypto-graphic protocols for faults (extended abstract). In: Fumy, W. (ed.) EUROCRYPT 1997. LNCS, vol. 1233, pp. 37–51. Springer, Heidelberg (1997). https://doi.org/10.1007/3-540-69053-0_4
2. Bousselam, K., Natale, G.D., Flottes, M., Rouzeyre, B.: On countermeasures against fault attacks on the advanced encryption standard. In: Joye, M., Tunstall, M. (eds.) Fault Analysis in Cryptography. Information Security and Cryptography, pp. 89–108. Springer, Heidelberg (2012). https://doi.org/10.1007/978-3-642-29656-7_6
3. Carlet, C.: S-boxes, Boolean functions and codes for the resistance of block ciphers to cryptographic attacks, with or without side channels. In: Chakraborty, R.S., Schwabe, P., Solworth, J. (eds.) SPACE 2015. LNCS, vol. 9354, pp. 151–171. Springer, Cham (2015). https://doi.org/10.1007/978-3-319-24126-5_10

4. Cattell, K., Muzio, J.C.: Synthesis of one-dimensional linear hybrid cellular automata. IEEE Trans. CAD Integr. Circ. Syst. **15**(3), 325–335 (1996). https://dx.doi.org/10.1109/43.489103
5. Chaudhuri, P.P., Roy Chowdhury, D., Nandi, S., Chattopadhyay, S.: Additive Cellular Automata: Theory and Applications. IEEE Computer Society Press (1997)
6. Cusick, T.W., Stanica, P.: Cryptographic Boolean Functions and Applications. Academic Press (2009)
7. Daemen, J., Rijmen, V.: The Design of Rijndael: AES - The Advanced Encryption Standard. Information Security and Cryptography, Springer, Heidelberg (2002). https://doi.org/10.1007/978-3-662-04722-4
8. Ghoshal, A., Sadhukhan, R., Patranabis, S., Datta, N., Picek, S., Mukhopadhyay, D.: Lightweight and side-channel secure 4 × 4 S-boxes from cellular automata rules. IACR Trans. Symmetric Cryptol. **2018**(3), 311–334 (2018). https://doi.org/10.13154/tosc.v2018.i3.311-334
9. Heys, H.M.: A tutorial on linear and differential cryptanalysis. Cryptologia **26**(3), 189–221 (2002). https://doi.org/10.1080/0161-110291890885
10. Maiti, S., Chowdhury, D.R.: Design of fault-resilient S-boxes for AES-like block ciphers. Cryptogr. Commun. **13**(1), 71–100 (2020). https://doi.org/10.1007/s12095-020-00452-0
11. Mariot, L., Picek, S., Leporati, A., Jakobovic, D.: Cellular automata based S-boxes. Cryptogr. Commun. **11**(1), 41–62 (2018). https://doi.org/10.1007/s12095-018-0311-8
12. Mukhopadhyay, D.: An improved fault based attack of the advanced encryption standard. In: Preneel, B. (ed.) AFRICACRYPT 2009. LNCS, vol. 5580, pp. 421–434. Springer, Heidelberg (2009). https://doi.org/10.1007/978-3-642-02384-2_26
13. Picek, S., Mariot, L., Yang, B., Jakobovic, D., Mentens, N.: Design of S-boxes defined with cellular automata rules. In: Proceedings of the Computing Frontiers Conference, CF 2017, Siena, Italy, 15–17 May 2017, pp. 409–414 (2017). https://doi.acm.org/10.1145/3075564.3079069
14. Saha, D., Mukhopadhyay, D., Roy Chowdhury, D.: A diagonal fault attack on the advanced encryption standard. IACR Cryptology ePrint Archive 2009, 581 (2009). https://eprint.iacr.org/2009/581
15. Schmidt, J., Medwed, M.: Countermeasures for symmetric key ciphers. In: Joye, M., Tunstall, M. (eds.) Fault Analysis in Cryptography. Information Security and Cryptography, pp. 73–87. Springer, Heidelberg (2012). https://doi.org/10.1007/978-3-642-29656-7_5
16. Tunstall, M., Mukhopadhyay, D., Ali, S.: Differential fault analysis of the advanced encryption standard using a single fault. In: Ardagna, C.A., Zhou, J. (eds.) WISTP 2011. LNCS, vol. 6633, pp. 224–233. Springer, Heidelberg (2011). https://doi.org/10.1007/978-3-642-21040-2_15
17. Tupsamudre, H., Bisht, S., Mukhopadhyay, D.: Destroying fault invariant with randomization. In: Batina, L., Robshaw, M. (eds.) CHES 2014. LNCS, vol. 8731, pp. 93–111. Springer, Heidelberg (2014). https://doi.org/10.1007/978-3-662-44709-3_6
18. Wolfram, S.: Cryptography with cellular automata. In: Williams, H.C. (ed.) CRYPTO 1985. LNCS, vol. 218, pp. 429–432. Springer, Heidelberg (1986). https://doi.org/10.1007/3-540-39799-X_32
19. Wolfram, S.: Random sequence generation by cellular automata. Adv. Appl. Math. **7**, 123–169 (1986)

Privacy Preserving of Two Local Data Sites Using Global Random Forest Classification

Latha Gadepaka[1]([✉]) and Bapi Raju Surampudi[1,2]

[1] School of Computer and Information Sciences, University of Hyderabad,
Hyderabad, India
latha.gadepaka@gmail.com
[2] Cognitive Science Lab, International Institute of Information Technology,
Hyderabad, India

Abstract. In the rapidly growing computing world, the data is being generated every minute, and it has been a big challenge to manage and maintain privacy of the data when it is required to share among different locations. In this regard the privacy preserving data mining is playing a major role to design and develop the methods and models to preserve privacy of data in data owners perspectives, when ever the necessity of exchanging the information between multiple parties to be done. There has been lot of research going on in the field of computational intelligence, machine learning and soft computing domains and some good number of algorithms and secured models are being developed by the researchers. We have worked on the random forest classification as the best example model to preserve privacy of two parties when a combined classification to be done in order to build a privacy preserving global random forest classifier. The process has two phases from local random forest to global random forest. The aim was to build a final global random forest by aggregating local random forests of local or individual parties based on voting between parties. In this work there are two proposed algorithms for horizontal and vertical partitioning of data Horizontal-PPGRF and Vertical-PPGRF. Both were performing well in building PPGRF without disclosing the input information of any party to each other. The ensemble learning is applied through random forest classifier to build a secured global random forest of two parties.

Keywords: Random forest · Classification · Privacy preserving · Data partitioning · Ensemble learning

1 Introduction

Most data mining techniques are specified to acquire knowledge from highly quantified databases, while most of the information generated is already available for access, and some times distributed among multiple environments under different authority, which makes violating privacy at the time of obtaining data.

© The Author(s), under exclusive license to Springer Nature Switzerland AG 2022
S. Joshi et al. (Eds.): SpacSec 2021, CCIS 1599, pp. 117–129, 2022.
https://doi.org/10.1007/978-3-031-15784-4_10

This situation may lead to some misuse difficulties as there is always a threat of identifying specific information about an individual, resulting in major loss of privacy which is the serious issue to be addressed. For example U.S Department of defence banned all data-mining tasks including research and development deeply concerning growing problem of violating an individual's privacy as per Data-Mining Moratorium Act [11]. Hence the importance of Privacy Preserving Data Mining has been increased to enable these types of situations aiming for privacy protection while extracting private details of an individual [5].

2   Privacy Preserving

Privacy preserving is an important task to solve serious privacy issues. Privacy Preserving Data Mining (PPDM) applied through various data mining techniques provide many privacy preserving methods [1,11]. Methods like Data Swapping, Data Perturbation, Noise addition, oblivious transfer, data anonymity, and many other methods follow different ways of private computations to produce final results without effecting on privacy of an individual, while exchanging their own information among multiple parties [7,9]. These methods worked well in assuring privacy. Our main motivation was to use a neural network to preserve privacy while data is distributed among multiple parties to gain combined results same as secure multi party computing [8].

3   Data Partitioning

A data set can be divided and shared to a particular data mining model, in order to gain combined results in small amount of communication time. There are good number of partitioning methods available like horizontal, vertical, and arbitrary partitioning [6] etc., among them we discuss two basic ways of partitioning mostly used by many data mining applications. If we define a data set D = (E, I) where E is set of entities for whom information is collected, and I is the set of features, that is collected. Assume that there are n number of parties from $P_1, P_2,....P_n$, then a data set D is partitioned into k number of data sets from $D_1, D_2, ... D_k$ and each partition is denoted as $D_1 = (E_1, I_1).....,D_n = (E_n, I_n)$ respectively.

- **Horizontal Partitioning:** It assumes parties from different locations extract same set of features I_n for dissimilar set of entities E_n, that means a data set is divided into n partitions where each partition holds set of horizontal records (rows).
- **Vertical Partitioning:** It assumes that parties from different locations collect dissimilar set of feature I_n for the same set of entities E_n, which means a data set is divided into n where each partition holds set of vertical records (columns).

4   Ensemble Learning

Ensemble Learning method also called as learning from multiple classifier systems consists number of base learners usually generated from training data by a base learning algorithm to train multiple learners to solve the same problem. It constructs a set of learners and combine them. The generalization ability of an ensemble is much stronger than that of base learners. Ensemble methods are able to boost learning ability and performance of weak learners (base learners) (Fig. 1).

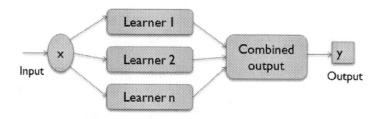

Fig. 1. Ensemble learning network

4.1 Bootstrap Aggregating - Bagging

Bagging is the bootstrap aggregating, which is a Machine learning ensemble meta-algorithm, designed to improve stability and accuracy of machine learning algorithms mostly used in statistical classification and regression. It also reduces variance and helps to avoid over fitting of data. It is usually applied to decision tree classification but can be used for type of method or algorithm (Fig. 2).

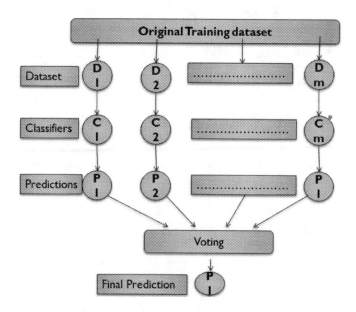

Fig. 2. Bagging ensemble learning process

A bootstrap ensemble method creates individuals for its ensemble by training each member network on a random redistribution of the original training set. Patterns may be duplicated in the member training set and not all the patterns in the original training set occur in the member training set.

4.2   Random Forest Classification

A Random forest classification method used for building 'n' number of decision trees and combine these trees together for getting an accurate and stable prediction results". The random forest is constructed through the ensemble of decision trees, where a forest of decision trees is created. The method used ensemble learning with bagging process to build a random forest. The main idea of bagging process is gather individual learning models and group them in order to boost the overall result. The random forest can be used for both classification and regression problems, that helps in developing more number of machine learning models for various application domains like privacy preserving and distributed computing and cloud computing etc. Random Forest classification is a supervised learning algorithm that creates decision trees on data samples and then gets prediction from each of them and finally selects best solution by voting [10].

Why Random Forest? Because of the random feature selection in Random Forest, trees are more independent of each other compared to normal bagging which results in better predictive performance. Random Forest is faster than bagging because tree learns only from subset of features. General Random forest classification algorithm is given below [4].

Algorithm 1. Random Forest Classification Algorithm

Input: Records R, attributes A, class attribute c, randomization parameter s, tree depth δ, number of trees o.
Output: An Ensemble of o decision trees.
For $k \leftarrow 1$ to o Do
$R \leftarrow$ randomly select $n=|R|$ records out of R with replacement
$tree^k \leftarrow$ Recursive_Random_Tree (R,A,c,s,δ)
End
return $\{tree^1, tree^2,.....tree^o\}$

---

5   Privacy Preserving Global Random Forest Classification-Horizontal

Privacy preserving Random Forest classification adopts the perturbation based approach to preserve privacy while constructing number of decision trees in Random forest. The data is horizontally partitioned and distributed to the parties to be joined in random forest classification. The proposed algorithm repeatedly executes a C4.5 algorithm to generate decision trees from subsets, then aggregates them and finds the final ensemble of Random forest without violating privacy of parties. For this problem the referral work taken from [3] and modified the stages as per the requirements to build a privacy preserving global random forest classifier. The privacy preserving algorithm of building a global random forest from all the local random forests of local parties is presented here.

Algorithm 2. Privacy Preserving Global Random Forest Classification-Horizontal

---

Partitioning: Dataset D_n, partitioned horizontally
Initialize: $D(P_1) = \{d_i, d_i + 1, ...d_s\}$, $D(P_2) = \{d_j, d_j + 1....k\}$.
Input: Records R, attributes A, class attribute c, randomization parameter s, tree depth δ, number of trees o.
begin:
Step 1: *Building Local Decision Trees:*
Party P_1 builds decision trees $t_i = DTC4.5(d_i)$ For each $d_i \in (d_i, ...d_s)$.
Party P_2 builds decision trees $t_j = DTC4.5(d_j)$ For each $d_j \in (d_j, ...d_k)$.
Step 2: *Building Local Random forests:*
Party 1 builds $LRF_1 = Unique(t_i)$
Party 2 builds $LRF_2 = Unique(t_j)$
Step 3: *Aggregation:* Initial Global Random Forest-1
$IGRF_1 = Unique(LRF_1, LRF_2)$.
Step 4: *Local Voting:* on left out trees in P_1 and P_2
Party 1 builds $LRF_{1A} = Majclass(t_i)$
Party 2 builds $LRF_{2B} = Majclass(t_j)$
Step 5: *Append:* Initial Global Random Forest-2
$IGRF_2 = Mejclass(LRF_{1A}, LRF_{2B})$.
Step 6: *Final global random forest:*
$HFGRF = AGGR(IGRF_1, IGRF_2)$
End

Here Privacy preserving is achieved by hiding original datasets at local level, and with the secured way of sending only the classified data of the local parties to the aggregation [2]. Each party performs independent voting at their local levels in the process of building a final global random forest. In this entire process, the only information that is commonly shared or known to all the parties is Initial and Global Random forest and the final global random forest. Hence the objective of preserving privacy in random tree classification has been successfully achieved.

5.1   Process of Horizontal-PPGRF Algorithm

The complete process of privacy preserving random forest classification is presented in process flow diagram followed by steps involved in detail given below (Fig. 3).

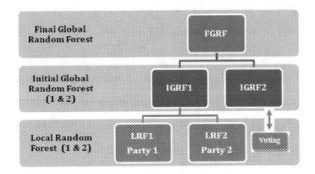

Fig. 3. The process flow of privacy preserving global random forest classification-horizontal

1. *Local Random Forest Construction:* For each party, subsets of their own dataset are selected randomly to generate decision trees and based on these subsets a local Random Forest is generated by the local parties at their own sites, then sends to the Ensemble Aggregation.
2. *Secured Ensemble Aggregation:* The Ensemble aggregation will receive the ensembles from the local parties and securely aggregate them into one ensemble after removing redundancies and constructs an initial Global Random Forest.
3. *Local Voting:* Local vote manager receives the initial global random forest and specifies or vote for the majority of class at their site and sends the updated initial global random forest back to the other parties.
4. *Final Global Random Forest:* After receiving votes from all the parties, the last party receives the voted initial global random forest and joins all the voted trees of local random forests to form final ensemble of decision trees i.e., the Final Global Random Forest.

6   Privacy Preserving Global Random Forest Classification - Vertical

Privacy preserving Global Random Forest classification for vertical data distribution adopts three levels of privacy preserving, (a) to preserve privacy while constructing number of decision trees in Random forest, (b) aggregating the local random forests of local decision trees, and (c) Voting on local random forests for the final aggregation. Algorithm proposed for Random Forest Classification for privacy preserving of vertically distributed data is given below.

Algorithm 3. Privacy Preserving Global Random Forest Classification-Vertical

Vertical Partitioning: of given dataset $D(n) = \{d_i, d_i + 1, d_j, d_j + 1, ...d_n\}$,
Party-1 holds $D(P_1) = \{d_i, ...d_n\}$, attribute set $(A_i) = \{a_i, a_i + 1, ...a_j\}$
Party-2 holds $D(P_2) = \{d_i, ...d_n\}$ attribute set $(A_j) = \{a_j, a_j + 1....k\}$
Input: Records R, attributes A, class attribute c, randomization parameter s, tree depth δ, number of trees o.
Begin: For Parties $P_1 \& P_2$
Step 1: *Building Local Decision Trees:*
Party P_1 builds decision trees $t_i = DTC4.5(d_i)$ For each $d_i \in (d_i, ...d_s)$.
Party P_2 builds decision trees $t_j = DTC4.5(d_j)$ For each $d_j \in (d_j, ...d_k)$.
Step 2: *Building Local Random forests:*
Party 1 builds $LRF_1 = Unique(t_i)$
Party 2 builds $LRF_2 = Unique(t_j)$
Step 3: *Aggregation:* Initial Global Random Forest-1
$IGRF_1 = Unique(LRF_1, LRF_2)$.
Step 4: *Local Voting:* on unique trees in LRF_1 and LRF_2 of P_1 and P_2
Party 1 builds $LRF_{1A} = Unique(Majclass(t_i))$
Party 2 builds $LRF_{2B} = Uique(Majclass(t_j))$
Step 5: *Append:* Initial Global Random Forest-2
$IGRF_2 = Unique(LRF_{1A}, LRF_{2B})$.
Step 6: *Final Global Random Forest:*
$VFGRF = AGGR(IGRF_1, IGRF_2)$
End

The proposed algorithm iteratively executes a C4.5 algorithm at local parties to generate private decision trees, then aggregates them to build the ensemble of local random forests by selecting unique trees from all generated trees. Party 1 builds LRF-1 and party 2 builds LRF-2, then after ensemble aggregation the privacy preserving algorithm builds an initial global random forest from LRF-1 and LRF-2 of local parties. In final stage the voting is done at local parties based on the majority of class from classified trees of party 1 and party 2. A final global random forest (FGRF-Vertical) will be constructed.

6.1   Process of Vertical-PPGRF Classification

The complete process of privacy preserving random forest classification is presented in process flow diagram, followed by steps involved for building privacy preserving Global Random Forest, when data is vertically distributed. The diagram shows how patries independantly builds local random forests and how ensemble aggregation is performed to build IGRF-1, IGRF-2 and Final Global Random Forest, using Vertical-PPGRF method (Fig. 4).

1. Distributing the data vertically between multiple parties.
2. Building Local Random Forests (LRF-1 & LRF-2) by parties 1 and 2.
3. Aggregating the local random forests using ensemble aggregation.
4. Building the Initial Global Random Forest-1.

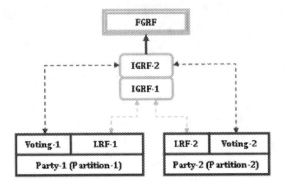

Fig. 4. Process flow of privacy preserving global random forest classification-vertical

5. Voting on classified trees and building new LRF-1A and LRF-2B with majority class.
6. Aggregating LRF-1A and LRF-2B and building the Initial Global Random forest-2.
7. Finally aggregation of IGRF-1 and IGRF-2 will be performed and Final Global Random Forest (V-FGRF) is constructed.

7   Experiments and Results

The experiments are carried out for iris, glass datasets in python (anaconda environment). The results are produced for Horizontal-PPGRF and Vertical-PPGRF classification methods. In process of building a final global random forest there are three main privacy preserving phases to follow to build IGRF-1, IGRF-2 and FGRF for each dataset. each party generates specified number of decision tress in random forest (between 10 to 100 threshold), limiting tree depth to 5 (this can be varied for larger datasets). The attribute selection in decision trees is done by measuring entropy values.

7.1   Results of Horizontal-PPGRF

In First Phase, the process starts with partitioning the dataset into two horizontal partitions and will be distributed to two parties (p1 and p2). Then for each partition, generates specified number of decision tress in random forest. Then from generated decision trees, all unique decision trees are picked to form local random forests for two parties (Party 1 builds LRF1 and Party 2 builds LRF2). Now aggregating all the uniquely classified decisions trees in LRF-1 and LRF-2 to build an Initial global random forest-1 (IGRF-1). In next phase of computations local parties performs voting on miss classified trees and generates IGRF-2 by appending trees with majority class. The results are given in following tables for Iris data set. Now according the proposed algorithm a final global random forest is to be constructed by performing voting on initial global random forests (IGRF-1 & IGRF-2) generated by both the parties. In last phase, the final aggregation of IGRF-1 and IGRF-2 takes place to build The final global random forest (FGRF) (Tables 1 and 2).

Table 1. IGRF-1 and IGRF-2 in horizontal-PPGRF for Iris dataset

Trees	LRF-1	LRF-2	IGRF-1	Voting-1	Voting-2	IGRF-2
10	8	10	18	1	0	1
20	11	20	31	4	0	4
30	13	30	43	4	0	4
40	13	39	52	6	1	7
50	17	45	62	7	5	12
60	18	59	77	9	1	10
70	14	36	50	4	12	16
80	22	59	81	10	7	17
90	17	73	90	5	10	15
100	22	81	103	9	9	18

Table 2. Final global random forest of Horizontal-PPGRF for Iris dataset

IGRF-1	IGRF-2	H-FGRF
18	1	19
31	4	35
43	4	47
52	7	59
62	12	74
77	10	87
50	16	66
81	17	98
90	15	105
103	18	121

7.2   Privacy Analysis of Horizontal-PPGRF

The privacy analysis is explained in view of three main phases involved in the Horizontal-PPGRF method as follows (Table 3).

Table 3. IGRF-1 and IGRF-2 of seeds data set in Horizontal-PPGRF

Trees	LRF-1	LRF-2	IGRF-1	Voting-1	Voting-2	IGRF-2
10	9	4	**13**	1	1	**2**
20	12	13	**25**	4	3	**7**
30	30	19	**49**	0	3	**3**
40	32	22	**54**	4	7	**11**
50	47	27	**74**	1	9	**10**
60	58	30	**88**	2	11	**13**
70	61	42	**103**	4	9	**13**
80	73	46	**119**	4	12	**16**
90	77	40	**117**	8	17	**25**
100	80	52	**132**	11	14	**25**

- *Local level privacy:* Local privacy is the major priority as parties have sensitive information at local level while building a global random forest. In proposed method no party directly share the raw data or the original attribute values to the other party, other than the resulting local random forest. Hence there will not be any privacy loss of an independent party. Result of privacy metric $priv_{PIC}$ (percentage incorrectly classified) derives the level of privacy at local level. In this case if incorrectly classified percentage of a party is high than the privacy level is high. The percentage is high for Horizontal-PPGRF and proved that the privacy is high.
- *Aggregation level privacy:* The privacy level must be high at this phase because, the aggregation is performed on the information shares by parties. Information or the results are produced by both the parties for the aggregation of LRF-1 and LRF-2 for building IGRF. Hence the level of privacy is the major concern and as per the results of privacy metric conditional mutual information $priv_{CMI}$ given the better privacy level (High) and shown that the aggregation level privacy is well preserved.
- *Global level privacy:* The final phase of building Global random forest must assure the global privacy, that means once parties shares their local level results and expects a secured outcome at global level. anyhow the voting is performed by local parties at their local level and will share only voted trees to the IGRF-1 and IGRF-2 for global aggregation. Hence the privacy is well preserved because of the secured aggregation without privacy violation. In this case also the privacy metric result has given the high privacy based on the cumulative entropy $priv_{CUE}$ value of both parties falls in high privacy range.

7.3   Results of Vertical-PPGRF

For each vertical partition, generates specified number of decision tress (10 to 100) limiting tree depth to 5. Constructs LRF-1 and LRF-2 considering all unique trees from the generated decision trees. Then the algorithm generates an Initial Global Random Forest (IGRF-1) by aggregation of all the unique trees from LRF-1 and LRF-2. Then all the unique decision trees with majority class from both parties to be selected through voting process, which results the two local random forests LRF-1A and LRF-2B from both parties. Then by aggregating and selecting unique trees from both parties, an Initial Global random Forest-2 (IGRF-2) will be constructed as shown in following table. Now in last phase of the process a final global random forest is to be constructed by performing voting on initial global random forests (IGRF-1 & IGRF-2) generated by both the parties. The final aggregation of IGRF-1 and IGRF-2 takes place to build The final global random forest (FGRF-Vertical) which is the final global random forest constructed using privacy preserving random forest classification for vertical data distribution. In vertical case of iris dataset the party-2 returns the IGRF-2 as the final global random forest. The resulting table of Privacy Preserving Global Random Forest (FGRF-Vertical) is given below (Tables 4 and 5).

Table 4. IGRF-1 and IGRF-2 of vertical-PPGRF for Iris data set

Trees	LRF1	LRF2	IGRF1	Voting-1	Voting-2	IGRF2
10	10	10	20	9	8	17
20	20	20	40	8	15	23
30	30	30	60	17	19	36
40	40	40	80	20	22	42
50	50	50	100	23	34	57
60	60	60	120	26	28	54
70	70	70	140	33	55	88
80	80	80	160	43	23	66
90	90	90	180	44	42	86
100	100	100	200	56	88	114

Table 5. Final global Random Forest in vertical-PPGRF for Iris data set

No. of trees	IGRF1	IGRF2	V-FGRF
10	20	17	17
20	40	23	23
30	60	36	36
40	80	42	42
50	100	57	57
60	120	54	54
70	140	88	88
80	160	66	66
90	180	86	86
100	200	114	114

7.4   Privacy Analysis of Vertical-PPGRF

Privacy analysis is explained with the help of privacy measures in view of three main phases of Vertical-PPGRF method as given below

- **Local level privacy:** In vertical partitioning case, the Local level privacy of independent parties is more important as parties have sensitive information at their level while building a global random forest. The proposed method gives independent path to each party to share the raw data or original values to the other party. Hence there will not be any privacy loss of information of an independent party. Result of privacy metric $priv_{PIC}$ (percentage incorrectly classified) derives the privacy of a party at local level with respect to the individual classification percentage. If incorrectly classified percentage of a party is high, then the privacy level is said to be high. The Vertical-PPGRF method shows the high privacy level, hence the privacy is considered as well maintained.
- **Aggregation level privacy:** Privacy level in this intermediate phase must be high because of the aggregation of the information shared by parties. The results are produced by both the parties for the aggregation of LRF-1 and LRF-2 for building IGRF-1 and IGRF-2, hence a high level privacy is to be assured. As per the results of privacy metric used for this case, conditional mutual information $priv_{CMI}$ has given the better privacy level (High) and proved that the privacy is well preserved.
- **Global level privacy:** In process of building a final Global random forest, the global level privacy of parties must be assured by the model, because parties expect a secured outcome at global level after sharing local information. Though the voting is performed by local parties at their local level, they share voted trees to build the IGRF-1 and IGRF-2, hence the privacy is to be well maintained. The metric cumulative entropy $priv_{CUE}$ is used for this phase, that has given the high privacy.

8   Summary and Conclusions

The work titled Privacy Preserving Global Random Forest Classification, presented the method of building a global random forest by aggregating two local random forests of two local parties by a secured voting procedure. The paper has proposed algorithms for horizontal and vertical data distributions between parties to for building random forests. The ensemble aggregation is the privacy preserving phase where the voting happens at each party separately, then the aggregation of decision trees will be done based on the majority of voting on the classes. The results were presented for both horizontal and vertical versions of Privacy Preserving Global Random Forest classification.

9   Future Scope

The same work can be applied for more number of parties and for other ways of data partitioning. We have plan to build a secure global random forest classifier (learning model) which can be applied for other privacy preserving techniques like perturbation and randomization etc. We may undertake work to modify the present system for the large scale data sets mainly to focus on medical and financial applications where the data privacy is given the most priority.

References

1. Agrawal, R., Srikant, R.: Privacy-preserving data mining. SIGMOD Rec. **29**(2), 439–450 (2000). https://doi.org/10.1145/335191.335438, http://doi.acm.org/10.11 45/335191.335438

2. Alabdulkarim, A., Al-Rodhaan, M., Tian, Y., Al-Dhelaan, A.: A privacy-preserving algorithm for clinical decision-support systems using random forest. CMC Comput. Mater. Continua **58**, 585–601 (2019)

3. Alabdulkarim, A., Al-Rodhaan, M., Tian, Y., Al-Dhelaan, A.: A privacy-preserving algorithm for clinical decision-support systems using random forest. Comput. Mater. Continua **58**(3), 585–601 (2019). https://doi.org/10.32604/cmc.2019.05637, http://www.techscience.com/cmc/v58n3/23030

4. Archer, K.J., Kimes, R.V.: Empirical characterization of random forest variable importance measures. Comput. Stat. Data Anal. **52**(4), 2249–2260 (2008)

5. Clifton, C., Kantarcioglu, M., Vaidya, J., Lin, X., Zhu, M.: Tools for privacy preserving distributed data mining. ACM SIGKDD Explor. **4**(2) (2002). http://www.cs.purdue.edu/homes/clifton/DistDM/kddexp.pdf

6. Jagannathan, G., Wright, R.N.: Privacy-preserving distributed k-means clustering over arbitrarily partitioned data. In: Proceedings of the Eleventh ACM SIGKDD International Conference on Knowledge Discovery in Data Mining, KDD 2005, pp. 593–599. ACM, New York (2005). https://doi.org/10.1145/1081870.1081942, http://doi.acm.org/10.1145/1081870.1081942

7. Kargupta, H., Das, K., Liu, K.: Multi-party, privacy-preserving distributed data mining using a game theoretic framework. In: Proceedings of the 11th European Conference on Principles and Practice of Knowledge Discovery in Databases(PKDD), Warsaw, Poland, pp. 523–531 (2007). http://www.springerlink.com/content/a61l028j53pl8476/

8. Lindell, Y., Pinkas, B.: Secure multiparty computation for privacy-preserving data mining. J. Priv. Confidentiality **1**(1), 5 (2009)

9. Strehl, A., Ghosh, J.: Cluster ensembles–a knowledge reuse framework for combining multiple partitions. J. Mach. Learn. Res. **3**, 583–617 (2003)

10. Szucs, G.: Decision trees and random forest for privacy-preserving data mining. In: Research and Development in E-Business through Service-Oriented Solutions, pp. 71–90. IGI Global (2013)

11. Vaidya, J., Clifton, C.W., Zhu, Y.M.: Privacy Preserving Data Mining, vol. 19. Springer, Heidelberg (2006)

Privacy Preserving and Secured Clustering of Distributed Data Using Self Organizing Map

Latha Gadepaka[1]([✉]) and Bapi Raju Surampudi[1,2]

[1] Computational Intelligence Lab, School of Computer and Information Sciences, University of Hyderabad, Hyderabad, India
latha.gadepaka@gmail.com
[2] Cognitive Science Lab, International Institute of Information Technology, Hyderabad, Hyderabad, India

Abstract. Preserving privacy of data in data mining domain has been a challenging objective to achieve. There has been lot of progress in applying secure algorithms in order to achieve privacy preserving of sensitive information. In distributed data mining perspective, there is necessity to share the information among the different parties aiming for combined outcomes. Privacy preserving methods and algorithms helps in preserving privacy of data when it is compulsory to share the information between the collaborated parties to perform various data mining operations like Classification and Clustering. It is always important to address the privacy issues of an individual when the data is shared among different parties to achieve a common goal. It is observed that there has been great development in addressing the privacy issues and designing privacy preserving algorithms applied to achieve a secured model. Adopting neural network learning for privacy preserving of data has became very much promising approach. In this paper we adopt self organizing map (SOM) neural network trained in order to preserve the privacy of data of two different parties, in combined environment to perform combined clustering. We present two novel algorithms to preserve privacy of horizontally and vertically partitioned data while combined clustering is performed using SOM. We apply perturbation of data and training the SOM for horizontal partitioning and Cryptography based solutions for vertical partitioning. The proposed algorithms, Horizontal-PPSOM and Vertical-PPSOM are novel contributions in this paper and all the experiments for both algorithms shows good results with an assured privacy level.

Keywords: Privacy · Cryptography · Perturbation · Partitioning · SMC · SOM clustering · ElGamal

1 Introduction

Privacy: The Privacy has many definitions and it is especially seen through privacy concerns of individually identifiable data. The privacy of this sensitive data

© The Author(s), under exclusive license to Springer Nature Switzerland AG 2022
S. Joshi et al. (Eds.): SpacSec 2021, CCIS 1599, pp. 130–143, 2022.
https://doi.org/10.1007/978-3-031-15784-4_11

can be defined as the "protection from an unauthorized intrusion [10]". If any individual user has granted authorization to use the data of any data owner for a particular data mining task then there will not be any privacy threat or issue. The privacy is said to be violated when any sensitive or private information of and individual is disclosed without any authority for any unauthorized purpose. Most of the privacy issues of data are viewed in two ways at the time of data disclosure.

- Data is protected form disclosure: Limiting the ability to infer the values from results or even to control the results.
- Indirect disclosure of data: disclosing the data indirectly without violating privacy.

Privacy Preserving: The Privacy preserving is the objective of preserving Privacy of sensitive data of an individual, when it is to be shared or distributed among multiple parties in order to get combined results [10]. There are an increased number of methods in Data mining and Information security community that are addressing privacy and security issues and providing solutions. Privacy issues mostly being addressed while extracting or exchanging of data from multiple databases [1]. If the data is partitioned and shared among two or more parties, then "any one of the multiple parties should know nothing other than its own input and an output". The knowledge that can be learned about inputs of other party is that could be obtained or derived only from the output itself [8]. The main aim of the data mining approaches is to develop generalized knowledge, rather than identify information about an individual. There is always an issue of privacy violation when data is to be shared between two or more parties, hence the main aim of privacy preserving data mining algorithms to address such situations and to ensure that the knowledge present in the data must be protected from unauthorized disclosure.

2   Background and Related Work

There are good number of techniques and methods in privacy preserving data mining to preserve privacy like data perturbation methods, oblivious polynomial transfer methods, data anonymization methods, random response methods and also some cryptography based methods. There is also a larger scope of secure computational methods adopted in producing the combined results without effecting the privacy of a data owner while exchanging their information among multiple parties. As per the literature survey, we observed that the research on privacy preserving methods applied using neural networks domain are very few like Multilayer perceptron learning (MLP), Back-Propagation (BPN) and Self organizing map (SOM) etc. Cihan Kaleli and Huseyin polat presented efficient algorithms for Privacy preserving SOM clustering in their two papers, "Privacy preserving SOM based recommendations on horizontally distributed data" [6], and "SOM-based recommendations with privacy on multi-party vertically distributed data" [5]. They used collaborative filtering in SOM to improve privacy level of multiple parties to form combined clusters without violating the privacy. But as per our observation SOM clustering used in their work doesn't follow any specific privacy method at the input level, which is the major source of data loss. In this paper we adopt perturbation based method for horizontal partitioning while giving inputs to the combined model. For vertical data partitioning approach we adopted cryptography based methods to preserve privacy using SOM, motivated from the work presented in the paper titled "Privacy preserving back-propagation neural network learning" [3] proposed by T Cheng and S Zhong. They presented Privacy preserving two party distributed back-propagation training algorithm to securely compute the outputs in a Back propagation neural network. We also noticed that, there was no method that addressed privacy concerns at each level of data sharing, like input level, model level (process level) and output level, which we address and explain in this paper.

2.1 Data Partitioning

There are some data partitioning methods to partition the data set into multiple number of partitions as per the usage of the privacy preserving model. Based on the parties to be involved in the secure model to implement a privacy preserving method the data set will be divided into number of sub data sets and shared to the other parties. Among many partitioning methods we focused on horizontal and vertical partitioning methods in this work. If we define a data set $D = (E, I)$ where E is an entity set and I is the feature set then the horizontal and vertical partitioning methods are defined as follows.

– **Horizontal Partitioning:** data site holds same feature sets or same type of information related to different entities.
– **Vertical Partitioning:** data sites holds different feature sets or different information for the same set of entities.

2.2 Data Perturbing

Perturbation method is used to perturb the sensitive or private data values by adding some random noise to the original value and the perturbed data is shared to other parties instead of original data, which helps in preserving privacy while a combined output is to be securely computed [10]. If $X = x$ be an attribute of an individual, x is the original value and r is a random number taken from a normal distribution with mean '0' and variance '1', then instead of original value of input x data owner gives perturbed value $x + r$ to the data miner.

2.3 Secure Multiparty Computing

If two or more parties are involved in computing combined results, then privacy issues must be considered for each individual party and the privacy preserving model should ensure the privacy of any of all the parties while producing the secured results. Secure multiparty computing(SMC) refers to the secure computation of a result with multiple inputs where two or more parties are involved in giving inputs and producing combined outputs [9,10]. The main aim of SMC approach is without violating data privacy of an individual party, the expected result is produced. YAO's protocol [11] is used in SMC method where Sum or Product of numbers are computed at individual parties using a secure MOD function, until the final output has been computed by the first party where the process has been started. Privacy preserving data mining methods using SMC provides well secured solutions and most of the cryptography based solutions are considered as SMC solutions (Fig. 1).

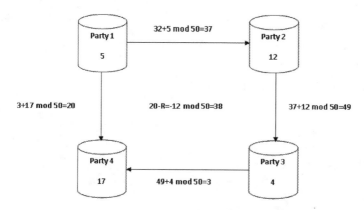

Fig. 1. Computing secure sum using secure multiparty computing

2.4   Clustering Using Self Organizing Map

SOM is self supervised learning model in neural networks where data brought into smaller levels of groups with similarity in their features that are specified by clustering approach [7]. SOM clustering follows the competitive learning, where all the output neurons compete among themselves to be activated (to win), and as a result only one neuron is activated at any a time, and this activated neuron is called the winner neuron [4], for which the weights are updated along with its neighbor neurons.

3   Perturbation Based Privacy Preserving Clustering Using SOM: Horizontal-PPSOM

In this proposed method first the data set is horizontally partitioned and each party (two parties) holds only few rows (half) of an entire data set. In next step the perturbation based approach of exchanging information between parties where the required information is shared among parties in a perturbed manner takes place. In this method any information to be shared to another party will be shared only after perturbing the data. Perturbation based privacy preserving SOM algorithm is given below.

Algorithm 1. Horizontal PPSOM Algorithm

Data Partition: The input data set is partitioned into equal number of horizontal partitions (two in our case).

Data Perturbation: Perturbing the values of data set by adding random noise 'r' through a random distribution to each input 'x'.

Initialization: Initializing random weights and required inputs for SOM clustering.

Repeat:

For all training samples $\langle \{x_A, x_B\} \rangle$

Step 1: *Competition Phase:*

(1.a) ForEach output layer node o_i

Party A computes $\sum_{j \leq m_A} \left(x_j - w_{ij}^o \right)^2$

Party B computes $\sum_{m_A \leq j \leq m_A + m_B} \left(x_j - w_{ij}^o \right)^2$.

m_A and m_B refer to nodes of Parties A and B, respectively.

(1.b) Party A and B jointly compute output for each output layer node o_i,

$$o_i = o_{i1} + o_{i2} = \sqrt{\sum_j \left(x_j - w_{ij}^o \right)^2}.$$

o_{i1} belongs to Party A and o_{i2} belongs to Party B

(1.c) Declaring Winner Neuron:

ForEach output layer node o_i

Winner Neuron $i = argmin(o_1, ..., o_l)$

i with least Euclidean distance among all l output neurons.

Step 2: *Co-Operation & Weight Updation:*

(2.a) ForEach output layer weight w_{ij}^o

$h_{j,i}$ is the neighborhood function centered around winning neuron i that is computed by Party A and Party B depending on which party holds input pattern x_j.

If $j \leq m_A$ then   A holds the input attribute x_j

A computes $w_{ij}^o \leftarrow w_{ij}^o + \eta h_{j,i}(x_j - w_{ij}^o)$.

If $m_A < j \leq m_A + m_B$ then   B holds input attribute x_j

B computes $w_{ij}^o \leftarrow w_{ij}^o + \eta h_{j,i}(x_j - w_{ij}^o)$.

Until (Termination Condition)

3.1   Process of Horizontal-PPSOM Algorithm

Horizontal PPSOM Algorithm represents perturbation based privacy preserving SOM and follows initial steps to perturb data items to be protected from direct disclosure of the information to other parties involved in the process. The process of Horizontal-PPSOM algorithm presented below (Fig. 2).

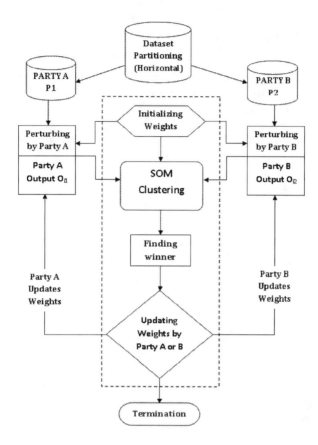

Fig. 2. Perturbation based privacy preserving clustering process

- Data Partitioning: Partitioning the data set horizontally and distribute to predefined number of parties
- Data Perturbing: Add some random noise generated from a normal distribution to the specified data items of which privacy to be preserved in data set, then form a new data set to train with perturbed values in place of original values.
- Initializing: Initialize all random weights and required input parameters for SOM clustering.
- SOM Training: Train all the samples located at each party, find the winner neuron depending on minimum euclidean distance between nodes at each party.

– Updating Weights: Modify weights of winner neuron and its neighbor neurons, then re initialize weights to the network and repeat until all rows of each partition at each party mapped to clusters.
– Termination: Terminate when all data entries of all parties are mapped to any of the clusters.

4   Cryptography Based Privacy Preserving Clustering Using SOM: Vertical-PPSOM

The vertically partitioned data set holds only few attributes and at the same time each party holds only few values of an entire record. The process of combining attributes from each party to form a full record for further computations must follow strong security methods. The privacy must be preserved while parties exchange information to each other for necessary calculations. Our privacy preserving Vertical-PPSOM Algorithm is given below.

Algorithm 2. Privacy Preserving Vertical-PPSOM Algorithm

Initialize: all weights to small random numbers and make them known to both parties.
Repeat:
For All: $\langle\{x_A, x_B\}\rangle$
Step 1: *Competition stage:*
(1.a) For Each output layer node o_i
Party A computes
$\sum_{j \leq m_A} \left(x_j - w_{ij}^o\right)^2$
Party B computes
$\sum_{m_A \leq j \leq m_A + m_B} \left(x_j - w_{ij}^o\right)^2$.
m_A belongs to Party A and m_B belongs to Party B.
(1.b) Party A and B jointly compute the combined output
for each output layer node o_i:
$o_i = o_{i1} + o_{i2} = \sqrt{\sum_j \left(x_j - w_{ij}^o\right)^2}$.
(1.c) Winner neuron i:
$i = argmin(o_1, ..., o_l)$.
Step 2: *Cooperation & weight updation:*
For Each output layer weight w_{ij}^o
Neighborhood function $h_{j,i}$ centered around winning neuron i is computed by both parties based on which party holds the input pattern x_j.
If $j \leq m_A$ then A holds the input and computes
$w_{ij}^o \leftarrow w_{ij}^o + \eta h_{j,i}(x_j - w_{ij}^o)$.
If $m_A < j \leq m_A + m_B$ then B holds input and computes
$w_{ij}^o \leftarrow w_{ij}^o + \eta h_{j,i}(x_j - w_{ij}^o)$.
Until(termination condition)

The proposed Vertical-PPSOM algorithm follows vertical partitioning of data set and consists of a security module, used to compute the square root of sum of two numbers in a secured manner. Input for Vertical-PPSOM algorithm is $\langle\{x_A, x_B\}\rangle$ where x_A is the share of party A and x_B is the share of party B. Output is set of connection weights $\{w_{ij}^o \mid \forall j \in \{1, 2, ..., a\}, \forall i \in \{1, 2, ..., b\}\}$.

4.1 Process of Vertical-PPSOM Algorithm

The main idea of Vertical PPSOM algorithm is to secure each step of Non Privacy Preserving SOM algorithm comprises of two main stages, Competitive Stage and Cooperation Stage which include Weight Updating Stage where parties secretly share their individual shares or outputs at each stage. The process of our Vertical PPSOM algorithm is explained in below given steps followed by a diagram.

1. Initializing: Initializes all the weights and other required input parameters
2. Data Partitioning: Vertically Partition the data set into predefined number of vertical partitions and distribute between two parties A & B
3. Competitive Stage: Individual shares or outputs are computed at Party A & B then winner neuron is declared depending on the euclidean distance equation of algorithm, after outputs are Combined using Secure Sum Algorithm. In this step neither the input data from the other party nor the intermediate results can be revealed.
4. Cooperative & Weight Updating Stage: Party A & B update their weights privately using neighborhood function, depending on which party holds winner neuron and it's related input.
    – Here to hide the intermediate results such as values of output layer nodes, two parties randomly share each of their results so that neither of two parties can infer the original data.
    – "randomly share", means each party holds a random number and the sum of the two random numbers equals the intermediate result.
    – Learning process can still securely carry on to produce the correct learning results even with intermediate results randomly shared among two parties.
5. Re Initialize updated weights and Repeat the process of Vertical-PPSOM until all data samples located at each party are mapped into any cluster.
6. Terminate the process of Clustering (Fig. 3).

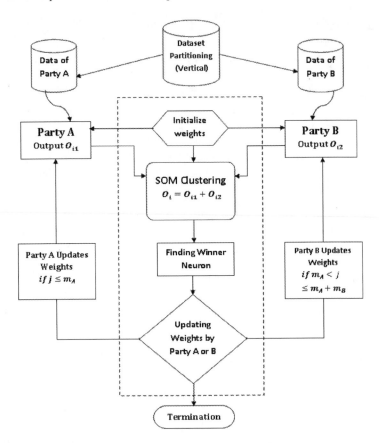

Fig. 3. Process of cryptography based privacy preserving in SOM

5   Experiments and Results

All the experiments are undertaken for both Horizontal-PPSOM and Vertical-PPSOM algorithms on 4 different data sets that are taken from UCI machine Learning Repository [2]. Both the proposed algorithms are implemented in MATLAB R2013a and compiled with the help of SOM toolbox. The results are shown for 200 epochs, weights are initialized as uniformly random values in the range $[-0.1, 0.1]$ and Learning rate η is taken as 0.1 for all the experiments of non privacy preserving SOM and PPSOM methods. The results are presented for privacy preserving SOM compared with non privacy preserving SOM drawn for two data sets (Iris, Seeds). The results of Horizontal-PPSOM and Vertical-PPSOM are presented in below given diagrams (Figs. 4, 5, 6 and 7).

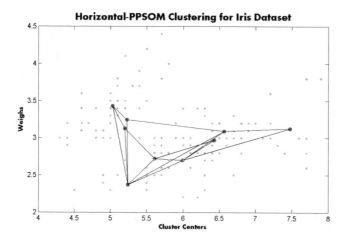

Fig. 4. Horizontal-PPSOM clustering for Iris dataset

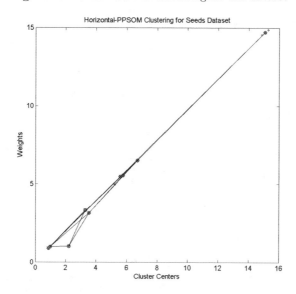

Fig. 5. Horizontal-PPSOM clustering for Seeds dataset

5.1 Privacy Analysis of Horizontal-PPSOM

The privacy in Horizontal-PPSOM is analyzed using the metric results given below, and privacy issues or concerns are explained in view of privacy violation aspects.

- **Input level privacy:** *If a party tries to learn target party's input data:* This is the major attack can be happened in any distributed model. The Horizontal PPSOM algorithm gives the better privacy level measured using privacy metric *priv_NVAR*. When a data set is horizontally partitioned, all

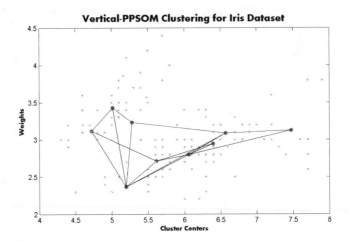

Fig. 6. Vertical-PPSOM clustering for Iris dataset

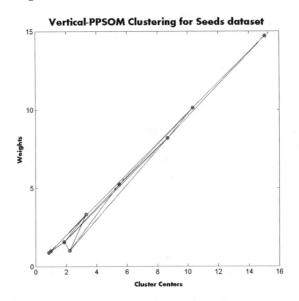

Fig. 7. Vertical-PPSOM clustering for Seeds dataset

the entities and class labels are known to all the parties other than the real values of the samples residing at one party to other party. If one party tries to attack on other's input data then the main privacy preserving method used in our Horizontal PPSOM is Perturbation of the input values before giving them to the next level computations in the model. Hence we prove that when the data is perturbed no party can try to learn or rebuild the original input values given by the owner party. This is applied for all the parties involved in the model aiming for combined result. The privacy level is proved high when the normalized variance between original and perturbed data is high.

- **Process level privacy:** *If any party tries to retrieve intermediate outcomes:* This attack can be happened when any party is curious to know the process of computing intermediate outputs of an other party. A party may eager to know the inputs of other party based on intermediate outputs or the weights came from the other party. We prove that there is no way of determining exact values of the inputs even though the intermediate outputs and weight values are known by the other party, because any party gives the output O_{ij} using its own perturbed input values and randomly generated weights. Hence There is no chance of knowing the exact input values even the other party knows the intermediate output values of the other party. In same way the weights come from one party to other are the updated weights after completion of computing the output at that party. Hence the exact weights used by one party to other cant be known.
- **Output level privacy:** *If any party tries to predict inputs from the combined output:* This can be done by any party involved in the combined model. We assure the privacy in Horizontal PPSOM at output level by proving the that any perturbed value at input level can't be reconstructed from the combined output, because of the privacy preserved at input and level and the process level. By any chance if a party tries to learn all the intermediate values and mimics as owner to replicate any of the input and weight values, even then there is no chance of coming up with exact values, because of input level perturbation and regular weight vector modification.

5.2 Privacy Analysis of Vertical PPSOM

Privacy in Vertical PPSOM is explained with respect to the privacy concerns at the expected privacy violation aspects.

- **Input level privacy:** *If a party tries to learn target party's input data:* This is the important aspect of preserving privacy in vertical partitioning algorithms. Only few features/values present at each party and it is always a big challenge when it comes to combine the input and compute combined results in vertical data distribution. The Vertical PPSOM algorithm gives the better privacy assurance compared to the other existing PPSOM algorithms. When a data set is vertically partitioned, all the entities and class labels are unknown to all the parties other than the real values of the features residing at each party. If one party tries to attack on other's input data then the cryptography based privacy preserving algorithm assures the privacy of input having used encrypted form of sharing inputs to other party. Vertical PPSOM is assuring the privacy of the input values, before giving them to the next level computations in the model. Hence we prove that when the data is encrypted and distributed, then no party can try to learn or rebuild the original input values given by the owner party. This is applied for all the parties involved in the model aiming for combined results.

- **Process level privacy:** *If any party tries to retrieve intermediate outcomes:* This attack can be happened when any party is curious to know the process of computing intermediate outputs of an other party. A party may eager to know the inputs of other party based on intermediate outputs or the weights came from the other party. We prove that there is no way of determining exact values of the inputs even though the intermediate outputs and weight values are known by the other party, because any party gives the output O_{ij} using its own encrypted input values and randomly generated weights. Hence There is no chance of knowing the exact input values even the other party knows the intermediate output values of the other party. In same way the weights come from one party to other are the updated weights after completion of computing the output at that party. Hence the exact weights used by one party to other cant be known.
- **Output level privacy:** *If any party tries to predict inputs from the combined output:* This can be done by any party involved in the combined model. We assure the privacy in Vertical PPSOM at output level by proving the that any perturbed value at input level can't be reconstructed from the combined output, because of the privacy preserved at input and level and the process level. By any chance if a party tries to learn all the intermediate values and mimics as owner to replicate any of the input and weight values, even then there is no chance of coming up with exact values, because of input level perturbation and regular weight vector modification.

6   Summary

We presented Privacy preserving SOM Clustering methods and algorithms for both perturbation based approach and cryptography based approach over horizontally and vertically distributed data among multiple parties. Horizontal PPSOM and Vertical PPSOM are two major algorithms we implemented and presented in this paper. In both horizontal and vertical versions of SOM clustering, our methods are adopted for perturbation based and cryptography based solutions respectively. Most of the privacy issues make accuracy losses but with our proposed algorithms we could acquire better accuracy with an assured privacy of an individual and with less overhead in communicating to each party.

7   Conclusions

We modified the original SOM algorithm to present Horizontal PPSOM and Vertical PPSOM algorithms for both horizontal and vertical versions. The main aim of our algorithms is to securely construct clusters using SOM between two different parties without violating their privacy, with less communication overhead at the time of encryption and decryption of messages from both parties. We conclude that both perturbation based method and cryptography based methods we implemented in our algorithms for clustering in privacy preserving SOM provides the better privacy in distributed environment.

8 Future Scope

Our further investigations are aimed for increased number of parties for other ways of data partitioning among N number of parties as the current use of information retrieval in general is rapidly growing, where we apply the same scenario for other neural network models and data mining techniques. We also aiming to build a full secure neural network model for clustering, later which can also be extended for other data mining techniques. Privacy is an important issue to be addressed in order to provide security specifically in distributed databases.

References

1. Agrawal, R., Srikant, R.: Privacy-preserving data mining. SIGMOD Rec. **29**(2), 439–450 (2000). https://doi.org/10.1145/335191.335438
2. Blake, C.L., Merz, C.J.: UCI repository of machine learning databases. University of California, Department of Information and Computer Science (1998)
3. Chen, T., Zhong, S.: Privacy-preserving backpropagation neural network learning. IEEE Trans. Neural Netw. **20**(10), 1554–1564 (2009). https://doi.org/10.1109/TNN.2009.2026902
4. Haykin, S.: Neural Networks: A Comprehensive Foundation, 2nd edn. Prentice Hall PTR, Upper Saddle River (1998)
5. Kaleli, C., Polat, H.: SOM-based recommendations with privacy on multi-party vertically distributed data. J. Oper. Res. Soc. **63**(6), 826–838 (2012). https://doi.org/10.1057/jors.2011.76
6. Kaleli, C., Polat, H.: Privacy-preserving SOM-based recommendations on horizontally distributed data. Knowl.-Based Syst. **33**, 124–135 (2012)
7. Kohonen, T., Oja, E., Simula, O., Visa, A., Kangas, J.: Engineering applications of the self-organizing map. Proc. IEEE **84**(10), 1358–1384 (1996)
8. Lin, X., Clifton, C., Zhu, M.: Privacy preserving clustering with distributed EM mixture modeling. Knowledge and Information Systems (to appear)
9. Lindell, Y., Pinkas, B.: Secure multiparty computation for privacy-preserving data mining. J. Priv. Confidentiality **1**(1), 5 (2009)
10. Vaidya, J., Clifton, C.W., Zhu, Y.M.: Privacy Preserving Data Mining, vol. 19. Springer, Heidelberg (2006)
11. Yao, A.C.: Protocols for secure computations. In: Proceedings of the 23rd Annual Symposium on Foundations of Computer Science, pp. 160–164 (1982)

Implementation of Intrusion Detection Systems in Distributed Architecture

Dhrumil Malani[1], Jimit Modi[1], Siddharth Lilani[1], Yukta Desai[1],
and Ritesh Dhanare[2(✉)] 🆔

[1] Information Technology SVKM's NMIMS MPSTME, Shirpur, India
{dhrumil.malani47,jimit.modi49,siddharth.lilani44,
yukta.desai23}@nmims.edu.in
[2] Department of Information Technology, SVKM's NMIMS MPSTME, Shirpur, India
ritesh.dhanare@nmims.edu

Abstract. Safety of information systems is paramount for all organizations that work on a network. Attackers and hackers take pleasure in capitalizing on opportunities to intrude into distributed networks. Organizations across the world are aware about this but due to the unavailability of an unerring system they remain vulnerable to attacks. Enhancing the existing system used to tackle intrusions in a distributed network would reduce risk very significantly. The problem of false positive and false negative results is highly prevalent in existing distributed intrusions detection systems that need to be handled. It is the need of the hour to work on intrusion detection systems in a distributed network with the aim of increasing efficiency which is only possible by reducing the number of false positive and negative results.

Keywords: Distributed network · Intrusion · Hacking · Data protection · Privacy · Information security · Network security · Distributed intrusion detection systems

1 Introduction

With the increase in computer technologies and advancement in cloud infrastructure, the security of data is major issue faced by the clients using the corresponding platforms and services. To cater to the following problem, intrusion detection and prevention systems are proposed, purpose being defying the illegitimate entities gaining unauthorized access to the system and notify the responsible entity about any activity found malicious.

With proliferation of extended cloud platforms and heterogeneous networks, a major portion of data of user is on cloud [11], which may be distributed across various geographic locations or servers. Here, the security of confidential information of user is of utmost importance. Also, the vulnerabilities to exploit increase for unauthorized entities. To properly counter the problem, the Intrusion Detection Systems (IDS) in such kind of environment must be efficient enough to protect the integrity of whole distributed environment [12].

© The Author(s), under exclusive license to Springer Nature Switzerland AG 2022
S. Joshi et al. (Eds.): SpacSec 2021, CCIS 1599, pp. 144–155, 2022.
https://doi.org/10.1007/978-3-031-15784-4_12

The Distributed Intrusion Detection System (DIDS) caters to multiple host nodes present in the network in master-slave configuration. The intrusion detection algorithm must be functional on all the corresponding nodes working independently. The actions are monitored in each host node (slave) and analyzed to be normal or suspicious, the report is sent over to the admin (master). The slave nodes have its own intrusion detection mechanism which accounts for the major advantage to this system over a centrally located IDS for such environment.

2 Literature Review

Before getting to intrusion detection, it was imperative for us to understand cyber security and cyber-attacks. Kutub Thakur et al. [2] describes how cyber security has been used interchangeably for information security, where later considers the role of the human in the security process while former consider this as an additional dimension and also, focus person has a potential target. To address the issue of cyber security, various frameworks and models have been developed. Kutub Thakur et al. review these models along with their limitations and review the past techniques used to mitigate these threats [1].

Cloud Computing is the preferred choice of every IT organization since it provides flexible and pay-peruse based services to its users. However, the security and privacy are a major hurdle in its success because of its open and distributed architecture that is vulnerable to intruders. Intrusion Detection System (IDS) is the most used mechanism to detect attacks on cloud. Yasir Mehmood et al. [3] provide an overview of different intrusions in cloud. It analyzes some existing cloud-based intrusion detection systems (IDS) with respect to their type, positioning, detection time, detection technique, data source and attacks they can detect. The analysis also provides limitations of each technique to evaluate whether they fulfill the security requirements of cloud computing environment or not [1].

Adriano Mauro Cansian et al. [4] present a new attack signature model to be applied on network-based intrusion detection systems engines. The proposed AISF (ACME Intrusion Signature Format) model is built upon XML technology and works on intrusion signatures handling and analysis, from storage to manipulation. This model made the process of storing and analyzing information about intrusion signatures for further use by IDS less difficult [1].

Ahmed Patel et al. [5] have reviewed intrusion detection and prevention systems used in cloud computing environments. It says that the traditional Intrusion Detection and Prevention Systems (IDPS) are largely inefficient to be deployed in cloud computing environments due to their openness and specific essence. The paper surveys, explores and informs researchers about the latest developed IDPSs and alarm management techniques by providing a comprehensive taxonomy and investigating possible solutions to detect and prevent intrusions in cloud computing systems. Ahmed Patel et al. identify a list of germane requirements and four concepts of autonomic computing self-management, ontology, risk management, and fuzzy theory are leveraged to satisfy these requirements [1].

Manish Kumar et al. [6] have proposed a distributed intrusion detection system using block chain and cloud computing. It says that Host Intrusion Detection System (HIDS) helps to detect unauthorized use, abnormal and malicious activities on the host, whereas Network Intrusion Detection System (NIDS) helps to detect attacks and intrusion on networks. Development in many other technologies and newly emerging techniques always opens the doors of opportunity to add a sharp edge to IDS and to make it more robust and reliable [1].

3   Architecture of the System

Organizations encompassing multiple departments fall under the belt of the ones using a distributed network. Network Intrusion Detection Systems can be deployed at every system or network that falls under the distributed network.

These distributed intrusion detection systems are tasked with the generation of log files and letting alarms go off in case of malicious activity detection. These alarms carry informative data and logs which are useful for all other systems which are a part of the network. The system explained above forms the crux of the distributed intrusion detection system we have developed. The entire system is orchestrated and managed by a central administrator who is responsible to take any action deemed necessary in a situation. It plays a vital role in maintaining the database of attacks and various malicious activities which have ever occurred. The central administrator facilitates monitoring of the network and instant and persistent threat analysis. Figure 1 showcases the developed system's architecture. Attackers and intruders don't rely on fixed attack patterns so the signatures of attacks keep on varying and security devices cannot detect their activity. For this very reason, it has become imperative for security devices to undergo patching and tuning processes to recognize attacks [15]. The central administrator or master node (as regarded in the Fig. 1) is dependent on alerts which are sent to it as alarm logs by intrusion detection systems at each geographically different centers of the organization. These intrusion detection systems act as slave nodes and are regarded so in further sections of this research work. As per our study, a Decision Tree classifier model or a K-Means classifier model can be used to classify the activity of an obscure user as normal or malicious on the basis of analysis of some selected features of data generated on intrusions. Our developed algorithm is deployed on each slave node's IDS to detect any hostile activity to defend the network from attacks of a similar capacity in future.

4   Design

The Master-Slave configuration in terms of software illustrates an association between a worker services which bows to a master service. According to the Jenkins documentation, this particular association is also referred as Master-Agent configuration.

Responsibilities of Jenkins master are as follow and is also pictured in the Fig. 2 [7]:

1.   To provide the web User Interface (UI)
2.   It collects job and configuration data and stores it on the disk.
3.   It also has the capability to execute jobs on its own system.
4.   It instructs and configures various jobs to be executed on slave nodes.

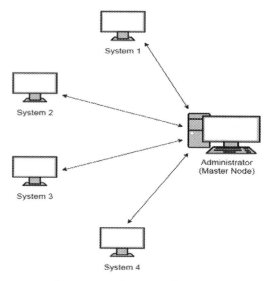

Fig. 1. Architecture of the system

The main objective behind using Jenkins slaves is the execution of various designed jobs. These jobs incorporate discrete work; the corresponding tasks to be performed are listed by Jenkins master.

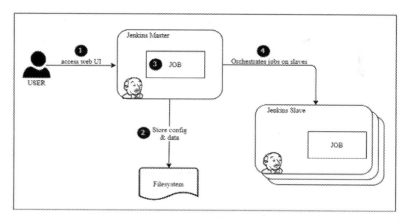

Fig. 2. Responsibilities of Jenkins master

4.1 Discrete Target Environments

Initially Jobs are performed on the Jenkins slaves each job requires a discrete target environment, the following feature is available on Jenkins master [13]. The discrete target environments may be as follow:

- Discrete processing units (CPU) and memory requirements.
- Discrete operating environments which can be available on different Operating Systems (OS).
- Discrete tools and libraries.

To fulfill the requirements, the jobs are executed in separate containers relieving some load on Jenkins Master.

4.2   Jenkins in Amazon Elastic Container Services (ECS)

Jenkins master is preferred to be executed over AWS Elastic Container Service (ECS) as it yields:

- High availability of Jenkins instances.
- Resolute storage facility for job data and Jenkins configuration.
- Gives secure access incorporating various security groups and proper encryption.
- Provides environments utilizing cloud formations that can be cloned.

The Fig. 3 [8] portrays environment –

1. Jenkins gets executed straightforward in ECS and its accessibility is secure through the internet using HTTPS aided by a load balancing mechanism (Application Load Balancer).
2. The integrity of environment is preserved aided by rules designed for security groups.
3. ECS task with attachment of EFS volume incorporates a very resolute storage facility.
4. Optimum availability is incorporated by commissioning automatic failover. This is due to various availability zones in ECS service.

4.3   Executing Slaves of Jenkins with ECS

To get to know about the whole process of execution, here we have portrayed the process from the activation of the job and its execution on the slave node of Jenkins. The Fig. 3 explains the process and the brief description is as follows [9]:

1. Master node of the Jenkins initiates the job.
2. Jenkins Master put across with the Amazon Web Service ECS API and the invocation command is passed on to ECS Task on the slave.
3. AWS commences the ECS task given by the slave node.
4. Slave node pings the master to pass on the process steps and the execution takes place.

For optimum output i.e., multiple number of availability zones for maximized availability to counter the problem of zone getting down. In correspondence to this, Jenkins slave can be designed on multiple availability zones as shown in the Fig. 4 [9].

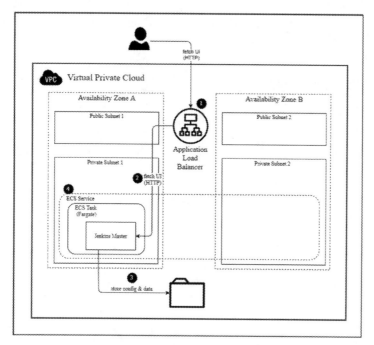

Fig. 3. Environment on collaboration of Jenkins and AWS ECS

4.4 Interaction Between AWS ECS and Jenkins Master

Cloud being the concept of Jenkins, designer gets aid from configure clouds Web User Interface (UI) and can establish connection among the modules. In cloud environment Jenkins can execute jobs on respective slave nodes. To use AWS ECS on Jenkins, amazon-ECS Jenkins plugin need to be added and configured.

1. Adding Amazon-ECS Plugin in Jenkins platform.
2. Configuration of this plugin must be correctly completed.
3. Proper AWS permissions pertaining to creation of tasks must be given to Jenkins.

4.5 Interaction Between Jenkins Master and Jenkins Slave

After establishing a communication link between master and slave. Slave sends a wakeup call to master. Jenkins Slave then waits for the instructions from master to proceed with the tasks which will be assigned by the master. Jenkins makes use of technology which is referred as Java Network Launch Protocol (JNLP) [14], allowing the master to execute anything as per the resources accessible to slave.

The general interacting procedure is as follow:

1. Once the slave is active, it is responsible to start up the master.
2. After master is up, it provides slave with set of instructions to be performed related to tasks.

3. These instructions are executed by slave i.e., execution of a Jenkins Job.

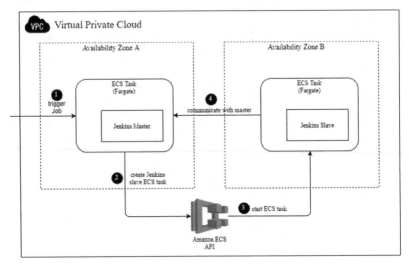

Fig. 4. Process of execution of jobs

5   Algorithms

5.1   Module 1 (Importing Libraries and Display Settings)

– import matplotlib, matplotlib.pyplot, pandas, numpy and sklearn ignore warnings
– set max columns display limit as none
– set the print threshold as 100000000
– set the precision as 3
– set axes label size as 14
– set xtick label size as 12
– set ytick label size as 12

Import matplotlib, matplotlib.pyplot, pandas, numpy and sklearn and ignore warnings. We set max columns display limit as none, the print threshold as 100000000 and the precision as 3. We set axes label size as 14, xtick label size as 12 and ytick label size as 12.

5.2   Module 2 (Loading Data and Viewing Data)

– read the Train_data.csv
– read the Test_data.csv
– print the shape of training data
– print the shape of test data

Read the Train_data.csv and the Test_data.csv and print their shapes.

5.3 Module 3 (Descriptive Analysis of Data)

– describe the training data for statistical analysis
– print number of outbound commands for training data
– print number of outbound commands for test data
– drop the column "number of outbound commands" for training data (due to redundancy)
– drop the column "number of outbound commands" for test data (due to redundancy)
– print the number of normal and anomaly counts in training data

Describe the training data for statistical analysis and print number of outbound commands for training data and test data. Then drop the columns "number of outbound commands" for training data and the column "number of outbound commands" for test data (due to redundancy). Then print the number of normal and anomaly counts in training data.

5.4 Module 4 (Scaling Numerical Attributes)

– select column names of data of types int and float from training data
– scale training data using fit transform function
– scale test data using fit transform function
– generate a dataframe for transformed training data
– generate a dataframe for transformed test data

Select column names of data of type's int and float from training data and scale training and testing data using fit transform function. Then generate a dataframe each for transformed training data and transformed test data.

5.5 Module 5 (Encoding Categorical Attributes)

– extract categorical attributes from training data
– extract categorical attributes from test data
– apply encoding transform to training data
– apply encoding transform to test data
– separate targeted columns from encoded training data
– generate a dataframe to be used for evaluation

Extract categorical attributes from training data and test data and apply encoding transform to training data and test data. Then separate targeted columns from encoded training data and generate a dataframe to be used for evaluation.

5.6 Module 6 (Feature Selection)

– set importance threshold as 3
– calculate importance for each column in the dataframe importances

- sort importance values in the dataframe
- set plotting size as 11*4
- plot a bar graph for importances
- set the x label as Features
- set the y label as Importance
- set the title as "Importance of Features Bar Graph"
- display the legend
- show the bar plot
- set the number of features to select as 15
- fit the data as per random forest classifier
- insert the selected features in feature_map
- print the selected features

Set importance threshold as 3 and calculate importance for each column in the dataframe importances. We then sort importance values in the dataframe. The plotting size is set as 11*4. A bar graph is plot for importances. We set the x label as Features, the y label as Importance and the title as "Importance of Features Bar Graph".

Display the legend and show the bar plot. The number of features to select is set as 15. We fit the data as per random forest classifier and insert the selected features in feature_map to print the selected features.

5.7   Module 7 (Dataset Partitioning)

- randomly split training and test datasets into subsets

Randomly split training and test datasets into subsets.

5.8   Module 8 (Fitting Models)

- create a decision tree classifier keeping entropy as the criterion
- use this cassifier to fit the training data

Create a decision tree classifier keeping entropy as the criterion and use this classifier to fit the training data.

5.9   Module 9 (Evaluating Models)

- calculate score on training data evaluation
- calculate accuracy on training data evaluation
- generate confusion matrix on training data evaluation
- generate classification report on training data evaluation
- print cross validation mean score for DTC
- print model accuracy for DTC
- print confusion matrix for DTC
- print classification report for DTC

We calculate score on training data evaluation, and we calculate accuracy on training data evaluation. We generate confusion matrix on training data evaluation and classification report on training data evaluation. We print cross validation mean score for DTC, model accuracy for DTC, confusion matrix for DTC and classification report for DTC.

5.10   Module 10 (Validating Models)

- calculate accuracy on test data evaluation
- generate confusion matrix on test data evaluation
- generate classification report on test data evaluation
- print cross validation mean score for DTC
- print model accuracy for DTC
- print confusion matrix for DTC
- print classification report for DTC

We calculate accuracy on test data evaluation and generate confusion matrix on test data evaluation and generate classification report on test data evaluation. We then print cross validation mean score, model accuracy, confusion matrix and print classification report for DTC.

5.11   Module 11 (Predicting Values)

- generate the prediction dataframe
- convert the dataframe to list
- write the list of output class values to a new csv file "output_1.csv" under the column name "THREAT".

We finally generate the prediction dataframe and convert it to a list and write the list of output class values to a new csv file "output_1.csv" under the column name "THREAT".

According to the algorithm, the best suited model for testing was found to be Decision Tree Classifier Model having been more accurate then K Nearest Neighbors Classifier Model with the accuracy of 99.47%. These models were evaluated on the training data set containing more than 20000 data entries. The output of testing these models on test data set is shown in the Table 1. These results are concluded using feature selection (Module 6), and the importance of each feature is calculated upon its numerical value in the data set which is portrayed in the Fig. 5 [10].

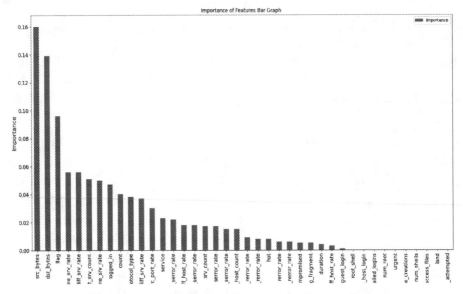

Fig. 5. Output of importance of features using feature selection

Table 1. Output on testing two models

Model	True positive	False positive	False negative	True negative	Model accuracy
Decision tree classifier model	3483	15	25	4035	99.47%
K nearest neighbors classifier model	3458	40	23	4037	99.17%

6 Conclusions

With Decision Tree Classification Model having maximum accuracy, the menace of unauthorized actions is negligible and will not get through unnoticed. In addition, machine learning algorithm can also be incorporated to analyze the similar kind of suspicious actions in order to react in a quicker manner. Machine learning algorithms will be more useful in future due to the advancement and exponential growth of the cloud platform and increase in variety of attacks by unwanted entities in multiple ways.

References

1. Malani, D., Modi, J., Lilani, S., Desai, Y., Dhanare, R.: Intrusion detection systems for distributed environment. In: 2021 Third International Conference on Intelligent Communication Technologies and Virtual Mobile Networks (ICICV), Tirunelveli, India, pp. 98–103 (2021).https://doi.org/10.1109/ICICV50876.2021.9388377

2. Thakur, K., Qiu, M., Gai, K., Ali, M.L.: An investigation on cyber security threats and security models. In: 2015 IEEE 2nd International Conference on Cyber Security and Cloud Computing, New York, NY, pp. 307–311 (2015). https://doi.org/10.1109/CSCloud.2015.71
3. Mehmood, Y., Shibli, M.A., Habiba, U., Masood, R.: Intrusion detection system in cloud computing: challenges and opportunities. In: 2013 2nd National Conference on Information Assurance (NCIA), Rawalpindi, pp. 59–66 (2013). https://doi.org/10.1109/NCIA.2013.672 5325
4. Cansian, M., da Silva, A.R.A., de Souza, M.: An attack signature model to computer security intrusion detection. In: MILCOM 2002. Proceedings, Anaheim, CA, USA, vol. 2, pp. 1368–1373 (2002). https://doi.org/10.1109/MILCOM.2002.1179680
5. Patel, A., Taghavi, M., Bakhtiyari, K., JuNior, J.C.: An intrusion detection and prevention system in cloud computing: a systematic review. J. Netw. Comput. Appl. **36**(1), 25–41 (2013)
6. Kumar, M., Singh, A.K.: Distributed intrusion detection system using blockchain and cloud computing infrastructure. In: 2020 4th International Conference on Trends in Electronics and Informatics (ICOEI) (48184), Tirunelveli, India, pp. 248–252 (2020). https://doi.org/10.1109/ ICOEI48184.2020.9142954
7. Berthier, R., Sanders, W.H., Khurana, H.: Intrusion detection for advanced metering infrastructures: Requirements and architectural directions. In: 2010 First IEEE International Conference on Smart Grid Communications, pp. 350–355. IEEE, October 2010
8. Singh, S., Shendre, O., Gujar, N., Agarwal, H., Singh, R.: Intrusion detection system and its variations. IJRAR- Int. J. Res. Anal. Rev. (IJRAR) **6**(2), 87–90 (2019)
9. Wang, Z.Q., Wang, H.Q., Zhao, Q., Zhang, R.J.: Research on distributed intrusion detection system. In: 2006 International Conference on Machine Learning and Cybernetics, pp. 181–184. IEEE, August 2006
10. Snapp, S.R., Smaha, S.E., Teal, D.M., Grance, T.: The DIDS (Distributed Intrusion Detection System) Prototype. In: USENIX Summer 1992 Technical Conference (USENIX Summer 1992 Technical Conference) (1992)
11. Wang, H., Zhou, H.: The research of intrusion detection system in cloud computing environment. In: Jin, David, Lin, Sally (eds.) Advances in Multimedia, Software Engineering and Computing Vol.1, pp. 45–49. Springer Berlin Heidelberg, Berlin, Heidelberg (2012). https:// doi.org/10.1007/978-3-642-25989-0_8
12. Snapp, S.R., Mukherjee, B., Levitt, K.N.: Detecting intrusions through attack signature analysis (No. UCRL-JC-108515; CONF- 9108194–4). Lawrence Livermore National Lab, CA (United States) (1991)
13. Liao, H.J., Lin, C.H., Lin, Y.C., Tung, K.Y.: Intrusion detection system: a comprehensive review. J. Netw. Comput. Appl. **36**(1), 16–24 (2013)
14. Liu, J., et al.: Toward security monitoring of industrial cyber-physical systems via hierarchically distributed intrusion detection. Expert Syst. Appl. 113578 (2020)
15. Li, W.: A genetic algorithm approach to network intrusion detection. SANS Institute (2004)

Practical Phase Shift Model for RIS-Assisted D2D Communication Systems

Samuel Jia Sheng Lee[(⊠)] and Choo W. R. Chiong[iD]

Curtin University Malaysia, CDT 250, 98009 Miri, Malaysia
700022062@student.curtin.edu.my, raymond.ccw@curtin.edu.my

Abstract. Device-to-Device (D2D) communications, a promising spectrum and energy-effective solution, have been developed alongside the evolution of the communication system. To exploit fully D2D communications, the major flaw that needs to be taken care of is the interference between D2D link and cellular link, as both links share the same spectrum. Many optimization techniques were proposed in the light of this problem, and one of them being Reconfigurable Intelligent Surface (RIS). Interference can be mitigated by adjusting phase shift to achieve desired beam steering. Unlike any other optimization method, RIS tackles the problem of interference by manipulating the signal path. In this paper, we study a RIS-assisted D2D single cell where multiple D2D links share the same spectrum with one cellular link. For practicality, a practical phase shift model is adapted to study the capability of the system, and this is often being ignored in many existing works. We proposed a phase shift optimization using local search technique upon the aforementioned practical model. Simulation results show that the RIS-assisted D2D networks proof to be effective by maximizing the sum rate of the system.

Keywords: Device-to-device communications · Discrete phase shifts · Reconfigurable intelligent surface

1 Introduction

As the fifth generation (5G) wireless technology is being generalized as the new standard of communication system throughout the globe, it is observed that the increasing demand of data services is inevitable. Every aspect of the communication system has been optimized by the researchers from different field of studies to keep up with the ever-increasing demand. Mobile devices especially smartphones, are no longer common only to the adults but also to the teenagers due to its capability and affordable price. With the drastic increase in performance on the mobile devices, various Internet of Things applications such as virtual reality, augmented reality and mixed reality emerged and require a more novel network architectures. In addition to that, the massive advancement of space technology in recent years has proven that space tourism will be realised sooner

© The Author(s), under exclusive license to Springer Nature Switzerland AG 2022
S. Joshi et al. (Eds.): SpacSec 2021, CCIS 1599, pp. 156–170, 2022.
https://doi.org/10.1007/978-3-031-15784-4_13

or later and telecommunication technology must also keep up with the advancement to allow communication in space. Thus, the need for the communication system to be optimized is demanded to keep up with the advancement of the technology.

Looking at the evolution of mobile communication system in the past, the communication system has been improving in terms of network capacity, data rates, and coverage. Drastic improvements can be seen from the first generation (1G) which provided only voice services to the current 5G, that provides wireless world wide web. Frequency Division Multiplexing was introduced to provide Analog Mobile Phone Service (AMPS) in the 1980s as 1G; 2G then showed an improvement in data rates from 2.8 Kbps to 64 Kbps with Code Division Multiple Access (CDMA) and IS-95; 2.5G which sits in between the second and third generation introduced General Packet Radio Services (GPRS) and Enhanced Data Rate for GSM Evolution (EDGE) along with the capable data rates up to 200 Kbps. Moving on to 3G which included technologies such as Wideband Code Division Multiple Access (WCDMA), High Speed Uplink/Downlink Packet Access (HSUPA/HSDPA), supported data rates up to 2 Mbps. 4G then achieved an even higher data rates along with technologies such as Mobile Worldwide Interoperability for Microwave Access (WiMAX) and Long Term Evolution Advanced (LTE-A) which introduced Device-to-Device (D2D) communication. Coming to the 5G era in which we are living in, D2D communication continues to be essential to the system while more advanced technologies are being introduced to further improve the data rates of the communication system and Beam Division Multiple Access (BMDA) being one of them [1].

D2D communication system, being one of the key technology for 5G and the future generation has drawn the attention of the researchers due to its capability of creating link with the user equipment (UE) that are physically close to one another, directly bypassing the need of transmitting to the base station (BS) then to the UE. The novel technology of the D2D communication provides better spectral efficiency and network capacity in the cellular network. However, there are still areas where D2D communication are lacking and needed to be developed so that the system is more mature for further deployment in more real world scenario. One of the challenges of implementing D2D communication is the occurrence of interference. Interference can be problematic while enabling D2D links with cellular links in the network as it could severely impact the system performance and even the battery life of the user device. To counter the problem, various optimization techniques had been proposed by researchers such as radio resource allocation technique, power control technique, joint power control and radio resource allocation techniques and so on [2,3]. The mentioned optimization methods tackled the problem of interference by alleviating the interference to its best at the receiving and sending end of the system. To further mitigate the interference in the system, Reconfigurable Intelligent Surface (RIS) has attracted attention to be an alternative to further optimize the system from the perspective of signal propagation. RIS technology is capable of aiding not just D2D communication, but also mmWave systems which has high penetration loss, multicell networks to avoid inter-cell interference, and many other networks such as simultaneous wireless information and power transfer (SWIPT), non-orthogonal multiple access (NOMA), multicast networks, cognitive radio networks and so on [4].

In this paper we investigate the performance of RIS-assisted D2D communication in a single cell uplink RIS-assisted heterogeneous network. The goal is to mitigate the interference through the approach of maximizing the achievable sum rate of the system while being bound to the Quality of Service (QoS) constraints. A practical optimization method is adapted from [5] and [24] for the RIS-assisted D2D communication using phase shift optimization to deal with the problem of interference.

The contributions of this paper are listed as below.

- We create an uplink RIS-assisted heterogeneous network as the system model where a cellular link and multiple D2D links share the same spectrum while RIS aims to minimize the interference.
- We formulate the sum rate maximization problem and went on optimising the phase shift of each RIS element using the local search approach based upon a practical phase shift model for practical results.
- We compare the system performance with various benchmarks to prove the effectiveness of this optimization approach.

The remaining of the paper is structured as follows. Section 2 covers the related work that had been done regarding the interference mitigation in D2D communication. In Sect. 3, the system model that is being used for investigation of system performance is presented. According to the description of the system model, we formulate the sum rate optimization problem and the practical phase shift optimization in Sect. 4. In Sect. 5, the simulation result is presented along with the performance evaluation by comparing it with other benchmarks.

2   Related Works

2.1   D2D Communication

A futuristic solution for applications involving high data rate has been demanded since 4G was introduced. Research on interference mitigation problem of D2D communication had been carried out since then from different areas. In [2] and [3] the authors studied the D2D networks and presented a bird-eye view on the problems, challenges and possible alternatives for the development of D2D communication. Ghazanfar et al. studied the interference mitigation in D2D communication underlaying cellular network and listed the challenges in interference mitigation such as device discovery, mode selection, radio resource management, modification to cellular network architecture, security in D2D and mobility management [3]. Authors in [6] proved that multiple D2D links ensure successful communication while guaranteeing links reliability with the existing cellular link and went on proposing a centralized power control technique which is more superior than the distributed power control algorithm.

Tackling the challenge of interference mitigation, Lee et al. in [7] proposed a resource allocation algorithm for cooperative D2D communication by obtaining the optimal spectrum and power allocation based upon the outage probability constraint. Yang et al. in [8] proposed a novel distributed power control policy based on the cost function designed using mean-field game (MFG) to analyse an ultra-dense D2D network instead of the traditional game models in [7]. Taking one step further with the optimization method, authors in [9] proposed a joint optimization of both resource allocation and power management with radio access network (RAN) scheme to optimize the D2D network with multiple service providers. In [10] the author proposed an algorithm of similar approach but through the preference values of D2D pairs and cellular users, and utilize the readings for optimal channel allocation. Moreover, in [11], the author investigated the D2D underlaid massive MIMO system and optimize the system with power control, specifically path-following algorithm, while assuming only imperfect channel state information (CSI) is available. In [12] proposed a pilot allocation and power optimization method for Massive MIMO underlaid with D2D communications to improve the throughput. However, it is worth noting that all of the works above cannot manipulate the propagation of the signal but only alleviate the interference to its best at the receiving or sending end of the system.

2.2   RIS-Assisted Communication

RIS technology had brought in new possibility for D2D communication in interference mitigation as it consists of only low-cost reflecting elements yet is able to achieve high spectral and energy efficiency. Some related works by researchers on the technology had been done to make RIS a mature technology to be deployable. Regarding the placement of RIS, authors in [13] studied the optimal position for further utilizing RIS by formulating an algorithm optimizing the RIS placement to better maximizing the cell coverage of the network. Different from the previous work which employed the RIS for coverage extension, the proposed coverage maximization algorithm maximizes the cell coverage. The authors from the simulated result of the coverage maximization algorithm concluded that the optimum placement of RIS should be between the base station, specifically facing vertically to the direction of the base station to maximum cell coverage. It is worth noting that the research was only on cellular network where only one base station and one user equipment were considered. There are also some works investigating the mm-Wave networks with RIS deployed. Based upon the transmission beam footprint, the decision of whether the optimal location is to be located nearer to the transmitter or the receiver was made [14,15]. Research on optimal placement of RIS in D2D underlaid wireless communication is still yet to be discovered. Furthermore, since the data rate and system performance are affected by the phase shift values of the RIS, authors in [16] investigated the consequences of limited phase shifts on the data rate particularly in uplink RIS assisted communication system. From the results obtained, it is observed that the bigger the size of the RIS, the lesser the number of required phase shift.

In addition, authors in [17] proposed a two approaches maximizing the phase shift and power within a wireless system as an energy efficient RIS-aided wireless system.

Apart from that, the capability of RIS is also being tested by Zeng et al. in [18], where the authors proposed that RIS can be implemented not only as a reflective platform, but also transmissive and even hybrid, which means it can do both reflect and transmit the signals. From the results obtained, the reflective or transmissive type outperforms the hybrid when the base station and the user equipment are far away from the RIS. However, the hybrid type performs better than the others in situation where the number of RIS elements surpass the derived threshold. Following that, the authors in [19] introduced a hybrid RIS-empowered and Decode-and-Forward Relaying system which combines both technology of RIS and relay. Instead of comparing both technology which many researchers had done, the authors proved that the relay is capable of enhancing the performance of RIS-assisted communication system.

Furthermore, instead of the fixing the position of RIS, authors in [20] explained the potential of combining the technology of RIS with Unmanned Aerial Vehicle (UAV). In [21], the author extended the application to Terahertz Communications by optimizing the UAV's trajectory together with other optimization method such as phase shift of RIS, the Thz sub-band allocation and power control. Authors in [22] proposed an UAV-assisted and RIS supported relaying system to maintain the Age of Information (AoI) of remote Internet of Things wireless network. It is suggested that UAV-assisted RIS can be applied together with D2D communication to further extend the cell coverage with the combination of both technology. Last but not least, Holographic MIMO surfaces (HMIMOS) another kind of RIS was proposed by Huang et al. [23] presented the technology of RIS on Holographic MIMO surfaces (HMIMOS) and outlined the opportunities and challenges for the implementation of HMIMOS enabled wireless communications.

3   System Model

3.1   System Description

In this project we consider the uplink single-cell RIS-assisted diverse network with multiple D2D pairs and a cellular pair. As shown in Fig. 1, RIS is implemented to mitigate the interference of D2D communication. Due to its reconfigurable characteristics, the RIS acts as a reflector to reflect signals towards the intended direction with directional beams through the reflective channel between the transmitter and receiver. Hence, the BS can receive both the direct signals from the cellular user and the reflected signals from the RIS. In addition to that, D D2D links which share the same spectrum as the cellular user are included in the system model. Similarly, the receiver of the D2D pairs can receive both direct signals and reflected signals. It is noteworthy that cross-tier interference among the links are inevitable in the presented system model because both links share the same frequency band. To encapsulate the details, the system model

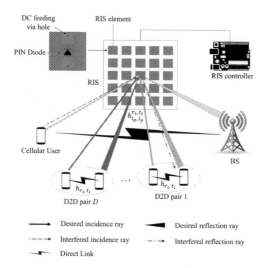

Fig. 1. System model of uplink RIS-assisted diverse network

includes a total of $D+1$ links, denoted as the set $\mathbf{L} = \{1, 2, ..., D, D+1\}$. The transmitters and receivers of link i in the system model are denoted as t_i and r_i respectively where $i \in \mathbf{L}$.

The RIS in the system model is a uniform planar array with $N \times N$ elements and each element has a voltage-controlled PIN diode with ON/OFF states which allows independent phase shift tuning of individual element in real-time. Thus, according to the regulation voltage, a phase shift value will be assigned to the RIS elements and thereby achieving the manipulation of the propagation environment to mitigate the interference. For the reflective coefficient of the RIS element, we adapt the practical phase shift model in [24], $q_{l_z,l_y} = \beta_{l_z,l_y}(\theta_{l_z,l_y})e^{j\theta_{l_z,l_y}}$ denoting the amplitude and the phase shift respectively, with $\theta_{l_z,l_y} \in [-\pi, \pi)$ and $1 \leq l_z, l_y \leq N$, where $\beta_{l_z,l_y}(\theta_{l_z,l_y})$ can be expressed as

$$\beta_{l_z,l_y}(\theta_{l_z,l_y}) = (1 - \beta_{min})(\frac{sin(\theta_{l_z,l_y} - \phi) + 1}{2})^\alpha + \beta_{min}. \tag{1}$$

The constants, β_{min}, minimum amplitude; α, controlling factor of the function curve steepness; and ϕ, the horizontal distance between $-\pi/2$ and β_{min}, should all greater than zero. When $\beta_{min} = 1$ or $\alpha = 0$, the reflective coefficient will be identical to the ideal phase shift model with unity amplitude.

Regarding the communication channels, the two types of channels namely reflective channel through the RIS and direct channel which is from the transmitter to receiver directly without passing through the RIS. The following paper symbolize the reflective channel from t_i to r_i through the RIS element $\{l_z, l_y\}$ as $h^{r_i,t_i}_{l_z,l_y}$, while the direct channel from transmitter t_i to r_i is denoted as h_{r_i,t_i}. It is noteworthy that the CSI is assumed to be known perfectly to the transmitter and thereby not affecting the phase shift design in the following sections.

3.2   Interference Analysis

To analyse the interference of the system, we first derive the received signal of link i by receiver r_i. The received signal includes both the signal from transmitter of the same link t_i and the signal reflected by the RIS. Due to the aforementioned cross-tier interference, all signals from the co-channels are included as the superposed interference and the received signal s_{r_i} can be expressed as

$$
\begin{aligned}
s_{r_i} = \; & \left(h_{r_i,t_i} + \sum_{l_z,l_y} h^{r_i,t_i}_{l_z,l_y} q_{l_z,l_y}\right)\sqrt{p_i}\, s_{t_i} \\
& + \sum_{j\in\mathbf{L},j\neq i}\left(h_{r_i,t_j} + \sum_{l_z,l_y} h^{r_i,t_j}_{l_z,l_y} q_{l_z,l_y}\right)\sqrt{p_j}\, s_{t_j} + w_{r_i}.
\end{aligned}
\tag{2}
$$

The unit-power transmitted symbol from transmitter t_i is denoted by s_{t_i}, while p_i indicates the transmission power of link I. w_{r_i} is the Gaussian white noise from $\mathcal{CN}(0,\sigma^2)$. To simplify the expression of the received signal, the following matrices are defined.

$$
\mathbf{F} = \sum_{l_z,l_y} q_{l_z,l_y}\mathbf{H}_{l_z,l_y}.
\tag{3}
$$

$\mathbf{H}_{l_z,l_y}$, a channel matrix of $(D+1)\times(D+1)$, consists of the reflective channel between all the transmitters and receivers through RIS, $\{h^{r_i,t_j}_{l_z,l_y}, 1\leq i,j\leq D+1\}$. The matrix F_{r_i,t_j} in the following section refers to the j-th row and i-th column of the matrix $\mathbf{F}$. Likewise, $\mathbf{H}^L$ having the same dimension as the previous matrix, is the matrix of direct channel, $\{h_{r_i,t_j}, 1\leq i,j\leq D+1\}$. $H^L_{r_i,t_j}$ represents the element in the j-th row and i-th column of matrix $\mathbf{H}^L$. With the above definition, s_{r_i} can be simplified as

$$
s_{r_i} = (H^L_{r_i,t_i} + F_{r_i,t_i})\sqrt{p_i}\, s_{t_i} + \sum_{j\in\mathbf{L},j\neq i}(H^L_{r_i,t_j} + F_{r_i,t_j})\sqrt{p_j}\, s_{t_j} + w_{r_i}.
\tag{4}
$$

Consequently, with the simplified formula, the SINR from the received signal by the link $i\in\mathbf{L}$ can be expressed as

$$
\varGamma_{r_i} = \frac{|\mathbf{H}^L_{r_i,t_i} + \mathbf{F}_{r_i,t_i}|^2 p_i}{\displaystyle\sum_{j\in\mathbf{L},j\neq i}|\mathbf{H}^L_{r_i,t_i} + \mathbf{F}_{r_i,t_j}|^2 p_j + \sigma^2}
\tag{5}
$$

The corresponding transmission rate then can be expressed as below based upon the Shannon's capacity formula.

$$
R_{r_i} = \log_2\left(1 + \frac{|\mathbf{H}^L_{r_i,t_i} + \mathbf{F}_{r_i,t_i}|^2 p_i}{\displaystyle\sum_{j\in\mathbf{L},j\neq i}|\mathbf{H}^L_{r_i,t_i} + \mathbf{F}_{r_i,t_j}|^2 p_j + \sigma^2}\right)
\tag{6}
$$

4 Practical Phase Shift Model

According to the system model presented above, the following section aims to formulate optimization problem to obtain the optimal solution.

4.1 Sum Rate Maximization Problem Formulation

The objective of the optimization is to maximize the achievable sum rate of the system. Maximum power transmission is being used while optimizing to minimize the complexity of the algorithm. Therefore, the optimization variable is the phase shift values of all RIS elements. All phase shift values are noted as a set $\Theta = \{\theta_{l_z,l_y}, 1 \leq l_z, l_y \leq N\}$, and the optimization problem can be expressed as

$$\max_{\Theta} \sum_{i=1}^{D+1} R_{r_i}$$

$$
\begin{aligned}
s.t. \quad &(a) \quad \Gamma_{r_i} \geq \gamma_{min}, \forall i = 1, 2, \ldots, D+1, \\
&(b) \quad q_{l_z,l_y} = \beta_{l_z,l_y}(\theta_{l_z,l_y})e^{j\theta_{l_z,l_y}}, \\
&\qquad -\pi \leq \theta_{l_z,l_y} \leq \pi, 1 \leq l_z, l_y \leq N.
\end{aligned}
\tag{7}
$$

Constraint (a) of the optimization problem is to ensure the QoS by making sure the minimum SINR requirement is met. For constraint (b), it is worth noting that since we are taking into consideration the practical phase shift model, therefore, the amplitude response, $\beta_{l_z,l_y}(\theta_{l_z,l_y})$ will not be ideal.

4.2 Practical Phase Shift Optimization

The sum rate optimization problem is tackled with a practical phase shift optimization. In the optimization problem, the power and the link channels are the variables in the optimization problem. To maximize the achievable sum rate, we apply maximum power transmission and optimize only the phase shift with the practical phase shift model that has been mentioned. Since the ideal environment cannot be achieved in practical world, it is helpful to know the capability of the system by building the optimization technique upon the practical phase shift model to obtain accurate results. During the optimization, the phase shift values of each element are optimized while fixing the other N^2+1 phase shift values until the optimum phase shift values of that particular RIS element, θ_{l_z,l_y}, is obtained while obeying the constraints in 7(a). The obtained value is then defined as $\theta^*_{l_z,l_y}$ and being used to update the next RIS element and repeat until all the RIS elements are completely optimized.

5 Performance Evaluation

In this section, a comparison of the proposed practical optimization with some other benchmark algorithms are made to estimate the effectiveness of the proposed algorithm and to study the impact of different variables of the system towards its performance.

5.1 Simulation Setup

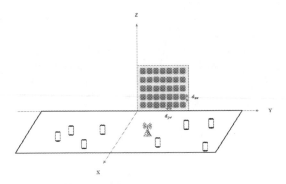

Fig. 2. Cartesian coordinate of simulation setup

In the simulation, the position of the RIS, transmitters, and receivers greatly affect the channel models. Therefore, we first introduce a three dimensional Cartesian coordinate system to present the position of each of the elements. In Fig. 2, the RIS is located at the Y-Z plane with the bottom left corner at the origin. The spacing in between RIS elements from the y-axis is, $d_{ye} = 0.005\,\mathrm{m}$, and from the z-axis, $d_{ze} = 0.005\,\mathrm{m}$. The location of the RIS element is noted from its top right corner, i.e., $L_{\{l_z,l_y\}} = \{0, l_y d_{ye}, l_z d_{ze}\}$. Furthermore, as shown in Fig. 2, the area of deployment of the BS, cellular user, and D2D users are distributed within the X-Y plane with each corner being $(0, -100, 0)$, $(0, 100, 0)$, $(100, 100, 0)$, $(100, -100, 0)$ respectively. In addition to that, all D2D pairs are distributed uniformly with maximum distance between two D2D users being 10 m in the rectangular area, while the BS and cellular user are located on both sides of semi-axis of X with a distance of 10 m. The coordinates of each receivers and transmitters are as follow, $L_{r_i} = \{r_{ix}, r_{iy}, 0\}$ and $L_{t_i} = \{t_{ix}, t_{iy}, 0\}$. Therefore, the distance from the element t_i to element $\{l_z, l_y\}$ is denoted as $DS_{t_i}^{l_z,l_y}$, while the distance from $\{l_z, l_y\}$ to r_i is noted as $DS_{l_z,l_y}^{r_i}$. The distance of both can be obtained as shown below.

$$DS_{t_i}^{l_z,l_y} = \sqrt{(t_{ix})^2 + (t_{iy} - l_y d_{ye})^2 + (-l_z d_{ze})^2} \tag{8}$$

$$DS_{l_z,l_y}^{r_i} = \sqrt{(r_{ix})^2 + (r_{iy} - l_y d_{ye})^2 + (-l_z d_{ze})^2} \tag{9}$$

For the channel model, the reflective channel of the setup is modeled as a Rician channel which includes both Line-of-Sight (LoS) and Non-LoS (NLoS). The reflective channel can be expressed as follows,

$$h_{l_z,l_y}^{r_i,t_i} = \sqrt{\frac{\beta}{1+\beta}}\tilde{h}_{l_z,l_y}^{r_i,t_i} + \sqrt{\frac{1}{1+\beta}}\hat{h}_{l_z,l_y}^{r_i,t_i} \tag{10}$$

where β is the Rician factor with value of 4, $\tilde{h}_{l_z,l_y}^{r_i,t_i}$ is the LoS component, and $\hat{h}_{l_z,l_y}^{r_i,t_i}$ is the NLoS component of the reflective channel. The LoS and NLoS components are derived as

$$\tilde{h}_{l_z,l_y}^{r_i,t_i} = \sqrt{\beta_0(DS_{t_i}^{l_z,l_y} \cdot DS_{l_z,l_y}^{r_i})^{-\alpha}}e^{-j\theta'}, \tag{11}$$

$$\hat{h}_{l_z,l_y}^{r_i,t_i} = \sqrt{\beta_0(DS_{t_i}^{l_z,l_y} \cdot DS_{l_z,l_y}^{r_i})^{-\alpha'}}\hat{h}_{NLoS,l_z,l_y}^{r_i,t_i}. \tag{12}$$

In the LoS component, $\beta_0 = -61.3849$ dB is the channel gain at a distance of 1 m, θ' is random variable in $[0, 2\pi]$, and α is the path loss exponent. For the NLoS component, α' denotes the path loss exponent in NLoS case while $\hat{h}_{NLoS,l_z,l_y}^{r_i,t_i}$ $\mathcal{CN}(0,1)$ is the small-scale fading.

On the other hand, the direct channel can be expressed as

$$h_{r_i,t_i} = h_i\sqrt{\beta_0(DS_{t_i}^{r_i})^{-\alpha}}, \tag{13}$$

where h_i is the small-scale fading which obeys Nakagami-m_i fading with parameters $\{m_i, \Omega_i\} = \{3, 1/3\}$. $(DS_{t_i}^{r_i})^{-\alpha}$ is the large-scale path loss and the distance between t_i and r_i which is obtained through the coordinates from the receiver, r_i, and transmitter, t_i.

Lastly we include some basic parameter settings for the simulation. The path loss exponent, $\alpha = 2.5$ in the LoS and $\alpha' = 3.6$ in the NLoS for large scale fading. Moreover, millimeter-wave (mm-Wave) with center frequency of 28 GHz is used for simulation. The mm-Wave noise power spectral density, σ^2 is -134 dBm/MHz. The transmission power $p_i = 23$ dBm, while the minimum SINR $\gamma_{min} = 5$ dB for all users. Regarding the practical reflective coefficient of RIS, since the power loss is not affected much by the parameter α, we fix the variable $\beta_{min} = 1.6$ in the simulation. The basic parameters are as presented above, unless specified later.

As for comparison of the optimization algorithm, a few scenarios are used to compare the performance of the proposed algorithm.

- **Ideal Phase Shift (IPS):** Ideal phase shift algorithm is achieved by setting $\beta_{min} = 1$ and the same local search is used to optimize the phase shift values of each RIS element. The ideal phase shift is used as a benchmark to investigate the upper bound of the optimization technique.
- **Random Phase Shift (RPS):** Random phase shift values are chosen for θ_{l_z,l_y} while keeping the transmission power the same as the proposed algorithm. It is noted that ideal reflective coefficient model is used in this algorithm.
- **Without-RIS:** RIS is not deployed and thus receiver can only receive the signal directly from the transmitter at the same transmission power through direct channels.

5.2 Performance Evaluation

In Fig. 3, $N = 5$, the sum rate changes as the number of D2D links increases from 1 to 6. The IPS is observed to produce the highest sum rate with the ideal phase shift model. All schemes increase steadily with the number of D2D links that are present. The gap between the proposed algorithm and the IPS algorithm, which is the upper bound, is small and shows a significant gap between RPS and Without-RIS, which proves the effectiveness of the phase shift optimization. RPS scheme although performs better than without-RIS in the beginning, the gap between the achievable system sum rate of RPS gradually becomes smaller and perform the same as the number of D2D links increase. In general, when the number of D2D links is 5, the proposed algorithm degrades from the upper bound by 2%, and performs better than RPS algorithm and Without-RIS by 10.8% and 11.2% respectively.

In Fig. 4, the D2D links are set to 3 and we plot the achievable sum rates against the number of RIS element, N. From the results obtained, it is observed that the proposed algorithm performs slightly worse than the IPS algorithm, but the increase in number of RIS elements optimized the system sum rate only to a certain extent and starts to degrade. From the results shown, all three algorithms that utilize the RIS had similar behavior in performance where the sum rate reaches its peak at $N = 4$ and starting to degrade after that. This could be due to the increase in interference occurrence without proper interference mitigation technique. Therefore, as the RIS elements increase, the interference from the other RIS elements also increase and thus degrades the performance. At $N = 4$, where the achievable sum rate peaked, the gap between the proposed algorithm with the IPS, RPS, and without-RIS are 3.1%, 10.3%, and 16.4% respectively.

Figure 5 is the graph of achievable sum rate against the RIS position. In this scenario, D2D links are set to 3 and $N = 4$. To study the effect on sum rate due to the deployment location of RIS, nine positions in the Y-Z plane were chosen which are $(0, -100, 0)$, $(0, -75, 0)$, $(0, -50, 0)$, $(0, -25, 0)$, $(0, 0, 0)$, $(0, 25, 0)$, $(0, 50, 0)$, $(0, 75, 0)$, and $(0, 100, 0)$. We put into comparison the proposed algorithm with Without-RIS algorithm to study the difference in performance. From the results obtained, when RIS is located at -100 and 100, where the sum rate is the lowest, the proposed algorithm still performs slightly better than Without-RIS. Other than that, the significant improvement in sum rate at the origin unarguably proves that the system sum rate is sensitive to the RIS position. As all the users in the simulation environment is uniformly distributed, the closer the RIS gets to the users, the more significant the improvement in the system sum rate will be.

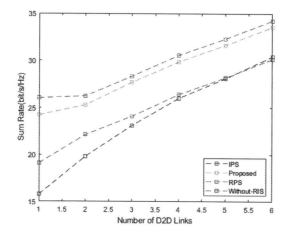

Fig. 3. Sum rate vs number of D2D links

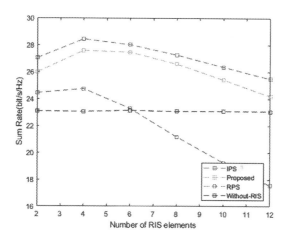

Fig. 4. Sum rate vs number of RIS elements N

In Fig. 6, we investigate the impact of minimum SINR to the system sum rate. We set D2D links to 3, $N = 4$, and the γ_{min} varies from 2 to 14 dB, then compare all fours schemes. It is worth mentioning that the proposed algorithm maximize the system sum rate while ensuring the QoS by maintaining the SINR, thus the increase of γ_{min} limits the achievable sum rate. The results shown is as expected with all four schemes showing a downward trend as the γ_{min} increases. Among all four schemes, IPS performs the best, following by proposed algorithm, RPS, and Without RIS. The gap between the achievable sum rate of proposed algorithm at $\gamma_{min} = 14$ with IPS is 4.5%, RPS being 10.9% and Without-RIS, 20.7%.

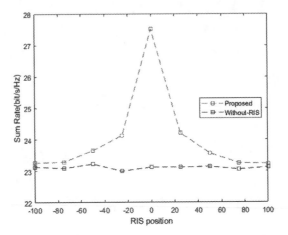

Fig. 5. Sum rate vs RIS position

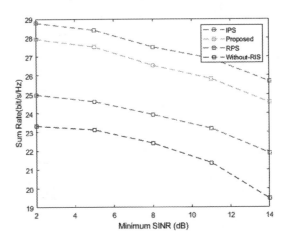

Fig. 6. Sum rate vs minimum SINR

6   Conclusion

In this paper, we considered an uplink RIS-assisted D2D communication along
with the interference analysis of D2D network. A practical phase shift optimization method is designed and proposed as an alternative to mitigate the
interference of the system and maximize the achievable sum rate while ensuring
the QoS. The numerical results have proven that the proposed algorithm performs only slightly worse than the ideal environment, represented by the IPS
algorithm and improve the sum rate significantly compared to RPS algorithm
and Without-RIS. In the future work, further optimization can be implemented
upon the established works as the numerical results to study the effect of number of RIS elements obtained convey a degradation in performance after reaching

the peak. It is suggested that the mitigation of interference is not sufficient and other variables such as the transmission power can be optimized with power allocation algorithm to further maximize the achievable sum rate and mitigate the interference of the system.

References

1. Nadeem, L., et al.: Integration of D2D, network slicing, and MEC in 5G cellular networks: survey and challenges. IEEE Access **9**, 37590–37612 (2021). https://doi.org/10.1109/ACCESS.2021.3063104
2. Ansari, R.I., et al.: 5G D2D networks: techniques, challenges, and future prospects. IEEE Syst. J. **71**, 3970–3984 (2018)
3. Safdar, G.A., Ur-Rehman, M., Muhammad, M., Imran, M.A., Tafazolli, R.: Interference mitigation in D2D communication underlaying LTE-A network. IEEE Access **4**, 7967–7987 (2016)
4. Pan, C., et al.: Reconfigurable intelligent surfaces for 6G systems: principles, applications, and research directions. IEEE Commun. Mag. **59**(6), 14–20 (2021). https://doi.org/10.1109/MCOM.001.2001076
5. Wu, Q., Zhang, R.: Beamforming optimization for intelligent reflecting surface with discrete phase shifts. In: 2019 IEEE International Conference on Acoustics, Speech and Signal Processing (ICASSP), ICASSP 2019, pp. 7830–7833, April 2019
6. Li, X., Chen, G., Wang, Y., Gu, X.: Research on power control algorithm for 6G oriented D2D communication. In: International Conference on Electronic Information Engineering and Computer Science (EIECS), vol. 2021, pp. 144–147 (2021). https://doi.org/10.1109/EIECS53707.2021.9588073
7. Lee, J., Lee, J.H.: Performance analysis and resource allocation for cooperative D2D communication in cellular networks with multiple D2D pairs. IEEE Commun. Lett. **23**, 909–912 (2019)
8. Yang, C., Li, J., Semasinghe, P., Hossain, E., Perlaza, S.M., Han, Z.: Distributed interference and energy-aware power control for ultra-dense D2D networks: a mean field game. IEEE Trans. Wirel. Commun. **16**, 1205–1207 (2017)
9. Lai, W.-K., Wang, Y.-C., Lei, H.-B.: Joint resource and power management for D2D communication across multiple service providers. IEEE Syst. J. https://doi.org/10.1109/JSYST.2021.3116940
10. Liu, S., Wu, Y., Li, L., Liu, X., Xu, W.: A two-stage energy-efficient approach for joint power control and channel allocation in D2D communication. IEEE Access **7**, 16940–16950 (2019)
11. Qiao, X., Zhang, Y., Zhou, M., Yang, L., Zhu, H.: Downlink achievable rate of D2D underlaid cell-free massive MIMO systems with low-resolution DACs. IEEE Syst. J. https://doi.org/10.1109/JSYST.2021.3098926
12. Nie, X., Zhao, F.: Pilot allocation and power optimization of massive MIMO cellular networks with underlaid D2D communications. IEEE Internet Things J. **8**(20), 15317–15333 (2021)
13. Zeng, S., Zhang, H., Di, B., Han, Z., Song, L.: Reconfigurable Intelligent Surface (RIS) assisted wireless coverage extension: RIS orientation and location optimization. IEEE Commun. Lett. **25**, 269–273 (2020)
14. Ghatak, G.: On the placement of intelligent surfaces for RSSI-based ranging in mm-Wave networks. IEEE Commun. Lett. **25**(6), 2043–2047 (2021)

15. Ntontin, K., Boulogeorgos, A.-A.A., Selimis, D.G., Lazarakis, F.I., Alexiou, A., Chatzinotas, S.: Reconfigurable intelligent surface optimal placement in millimeter-wave networks. IEEE Open J. Commun. Soc. **2**, 704–718 (2021)
16. Zhang, H., Di, B., Song, L., Han, Z.: Reconfigurable intelligent surfaces assisted communications with limited phase shifts: how many phase shifts are enough? IEEE Trans. Veh. Technol. **69**, 4498–4502 (2020)
17. Huang, C., Zappone, A., Alexandropoulos, G.C., Debbah, M., Yuen, C.: Reconfigurable intelligent surfaces for energy efficiency in wireless communication. IEEE Trans. Wirel. Commun. **18**(8), 4157–4170 (2019)
18. Zeng, S., et al.: Reconfigurable intelligent surfaces in 6G: reflective, transmissive, or both. IEEE Commun. Lett. **25**(6), 2063–2067 (2021)
19. Yildirim, I., Kilinc, F., Basar, E., Alexandropoulos, G.C.: Hybrid RIS-empowered reflection and decode-and-forward relaying for coverage extension. IEEE Commun. Lett. **25**(5), 1692–1696 (2021)
20. Kisseleff, S., Martins, W.A., Al-Hraishawi, H., Chatzinotas, S., Ottersten, B.: Reconfigurable intelligent surfaces for smart cities: research challenges and opportunities. IEEE Open J. Commun. Soc. **1**, 1781–1797 (2020)
21. Pan, Y., Wang, K., Pan, C., Zhu, H., Wang, J.: UAV-assisted and intelligent reflecting surfaces-supported terahertz communications. IEEE Wirel. Commun. Lett. **10**(6), 1256–1260 (2021)
22. Shokry, M., Elhattab, M., Assi, C., Sharafeddine, S., Ghrayeb, A.: Optimizing age of information through aerial reconfigurable intelligent surfaces: a deep reinforcement learning approach. IEEE Wirel. Commun. Lett. **70**(4), 3978–3983 (2021)
23. Huang, C., et al.: Holographic MIMO surfaces for 6G wireless networks: opportunities, challenges, and trends. IEEE Wirel. Commun. **27**(5), 118–125 (2020)
24. Abeywickrama, S., Zhang, R., Wu, Q., Yuen, C.: Intelligent reflecting surface: practical phase shift model and beamforming optimization. IEEE Trans. Commun. **68**(9), 5849–5863 (2020). https://doi.org/10.1109/TCOMM.2020.3001125

Recent Trend of Transform Domain Image Steganography Technique for Secret Sharing

Jyoti Khandelwal[1]([⊠]), Vijay Kumar Sharma[2], Jaya Krishna Raguru[2], and Hemlata Goyal[2]

[1] Department of CCE, School of Computing and Information Technology, Manipal University , Jaipur, India
jyoti.khandelwal19@gmail.com
[2] Department of CSE, School of Computing and Information Technology, Manipal University , Jaipur, India
{jaya.krishna,hemlata.goyal}@jaipur.manipal.edu

Abstract. The security of information is one of the most important attributes to be available when the secret information passes between two parties. Many techniques like watermarking, cryptography and steganography used for this purpose. Cryptography changes the position of original information or scramble the original information, but it reveals the existence of secret information. The hiding the data behind any other object is steganography characteristic. Information hiding characteristic make the steganography more popular as compare to cryptography process. In this paper transform domain-based steganography process are discussed. The main focus in transform domain steganography is the wavelet family; paper includes detail information about different wavelet used in steganography process. The procedure is investigated and contended in the provisions of its payload limit i.e., the capacity to conceal data, how much data can be covered up, and its robustness.

Keywords: Transform domain · DWT · Curvelet transform · Tetrolet transform

1 Introduction

Digital data transmission over the internet is the most popular source to share secrete information now days. Advanced medium has acquired a lot of significance nowadays and is turning into the dependable mechanism for the exchange of data. With the improvement and induction of web to everybody, it has become simpler and conceivable to copy and to disseminate the computerized data misguidedly. Carefully communicated information can be unimaginative with no deficiency of information and its quality too, which is a major issue to the security, credibility and ownership to the proprietor of the information [1].

From history of numerous years, individuals have been attempting to foster best in class procedures for secret correspondence. The three strategies related to security systems are interlaced; steganography, watermarking and cryptography. Both the procedures of cryptography and steganography used for treatment of data and information to

© The Author(s), under exclusive license to Springer Nature Switzerland AG 2022
S. Joshi et al. (Eds.): SpacSec 2021, CCIS 1599, pp. 171–185, 2022.
https://doi.org/10.1007/978-3-031-15784-4_14

encode and cover them exclusively. Both the systems are extensively known and used. Steganography covers the presence of information however cryptography calculates a message with the objective that it can't be seen. In explicit cases, sending the code information draws the thought, while the hidden information doesn't. The foundation of a stenographical mixed structure can be assessed through key parts like intangibility and breaking point. Impalpability shows the difficulty to choose the mysterious message. The other measure limit shows the best proportion of secret message or data that can be concealed securely, and strength, which implies that how fine the steganography system counterattacks the extraction of introduced data. The structure of steganography is displayed in Fig. 1, according to the steganography subdivision; four main categories play important role with their special characteristics. The most common and oldest techniques come in spatial domain categories. Least significant bit replacement and matching are the most popular methods in this category. The spatial domain is easy to use but it has also had drawbacks in information security upcoming techniques like frequency domain, spread spectrum, and other feature extraction techniques strengthen the security of data in image steganography.

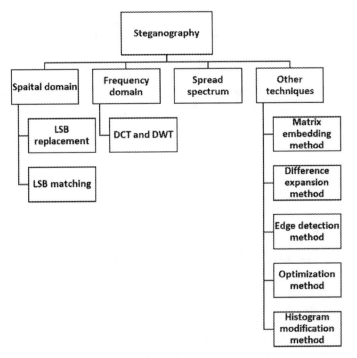

Fig. 1. Flowchart of steganography techniques.

The paper is subdivided in sections: Sect. 2 contains the introduction about transform domain, Sect. 3 contains wavelet family introduction, and Sect. 4 include the conclusion of the transform domain techniques.

2 Literature Survey on Transform Domain Techniques

The image steganography used transform domain method very frequently; in transform domain method first step is to transform the cover image into different domain. In the second step transformed coefficients used to hide the secret information. The transform domain transformed back into spatial domain to get stego image. The main characteristic of transform domain is use of signal processing operations. There are different kind of transform domain method are available, let's look into them one by one.

2.1 Discrete Cosine Transform

One of the main current conversations in picture improvement is the Discrete Cosine Transform (DCT) strategy. A DCT is another well-known strategy utilized in light of the fact that it is quick and powerful. The essential capacity of DCT is to change signals from the spatial portrayal into the frequency portrayal [2]. Many fields those are not related to the scientific field also use the DCT for their application development common applications are picture editing, picture formation. One of the important applications in the field of DSP is video conferencing. The DCT is used in change for data pressure. DCT is an even change, which has a fair course of action of reason work [3].

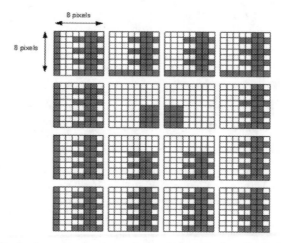

Fig. 2. Segment of an image in 8 × 8 pixel blocks using DCT.

See Fig. 2, if the image contains red, green and blue components then at the time of sampling they are divided in blocks. In 8 × 8 pixel array starts at the upper right at (0, 0) and finish at the lower right at (7, 7). At the point (x, y) the data value is $f(x, y)$. Here x and y represent the coordinate in image blocks.

2.2 Discrete Wavelet Transform

The digital images use DWT, there are many DWTs are available. According to the properties of wavelet application appropriate wavelet are selected from DWT family.

The essential work design of DWT is deterioration picture in 4 sub-groups named as: LL, HL, LH and HH. The LL sub band contains the main components of the picture. So according to the image embedding requirement sub band are used to store the secret information. There are many types of wavelets are available let's take a look in Sect. 3 how they are work and how they are different to each other [4].

2.3 Discrete Fourier Transform

In the field of advanced sign preparing discrete fourier transform (DFT) is very important tool. In image steganography DFT can be used in three possible ways. First, by using the DFT signal's frequency spectrum calculation which is directly examine the encoded frequency, phase, and amplitude of the image sinusoids signal. Second, DFT able to discover a framework's motivation reaction and framework's recurrence reaction, as well as the other way around. Third, DFT help in more elaborate signals intermediate steps. The DFT is exceptionally helpful symmetrical changes and have been viewed as the critical advances for signal handling in symmetrical recurrence division multiplexing correspondence frameworks [5].

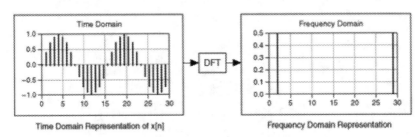

Fig. 3. Transform DFT data from time domain to the frequency domain.

According to the Fig. 3, if DFT apply on N tests of time-space the outcome likewise is of length N tests, yet the data it contains is of the frequency domain representation.

3 Wavelet Family

3.1 Haar Wavelet

Haar wavelet is the oldest wavelet in wavelet family, the simplicity of the haar wavelet makes it more popular. It is also known as symmetric wavelet in mathematical operation it is known as haar transform. The haar transform give a generalized model for all other wavelet transform. In mathematics, haar create sequence of rescaled square shapes. The main advantage of using haar is simplicity, speed, memory efficiency and disadvantage is that it is in contiguous [6].

Figure 4 show the haar transform, consider transforming the single seismic trace. The trace consists two zones, a weak zone on the left side, and a strong zone on the right side.

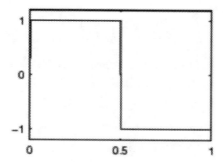

Fig. 4. Haar wavelet.

3.2 Daubechies Wavelet

Daubechies wavelets are the most notable wavelets. They address the foundations of wavelet signal getting ready and are used in various applications. These are similarly called Maxflat wavelets as their repeat responses have most noteworthy equity at frequencies 0 and π. Daubechies and haar wavelet are almost similar the main contrast between them comprises in how these scaling signs and wavelets are characterized. The debaucheries family wavelet knows with name dbN see (Fig. 5), where db is surname and N is the order of wavelet [6].

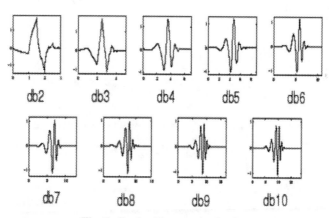

Fig. 5. Daubechies wavelet family.

3.3 Coiflets

Coiflets designed by Ingrid Daubechies, at the request of Ronal Coifman, to have scaling function with vanishing moments. It means the Coiflet wavelet can use the wavelet with the greater number of vanishing moments for analysis resulting in a sparse representation. The reconstruction part needs smoother wavelet support. The Coiflets family wavelet knows with name coifN see (Fig. 6), where coif is surname and N is the order of wavelet [7].

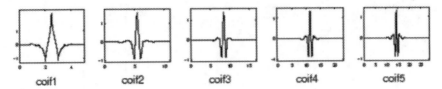

Fig. 6. Coiflets wavelet family.

3.4 Symlet

Symlet wavelets are the changed variation of Daubechies wavelets with extended balance. They are similarly estimations and moderately maintained wavelets The scaling channels utilized are close immediate stage channels and the effect of Symlet is practically same as those of the Daubechies wavelets. The Symlet wavelet and scaling activity for demands are as show below in Fig. 7:

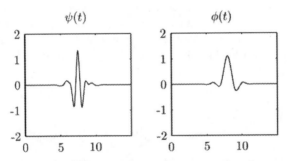

Fig. 7. Symlet wavelet function and scaling functions.

The Symlet wavelets are otherwise called Daubechies' smallest disproportionate wavelets however they are more symmetric.

3.5 Biorthogonal Wavelet

In image and signal reconstruction linearity is the important aspect. The biorthogonal wavelet gives more control over image reconstruction than an orthogonal wavelet. The image is reconstructed similar with the help of filters impulse response. The reverse biorthogonal wavelet constructed with the help of pair of biorthogonal wavelets [8].

The resulting spline biorthogonal wavelets for ($p = 4, \hat{p} = 4$) is illustrated in Fig. 8.

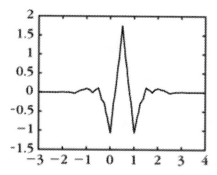

Fig. 8. Biorthogonal wavelet.

3.6 Reverse Biorthogonal Wavelet

The reverse biorthogonal wavelet otherwise called rbio, it is a sort of wavelet which is corresponded to a wavelet change. It isn't basically symmetrical yet using reverse biorthogonal wavelet, gives an open door in arranging in any system appear differently in relation to even wavelets, for case, the possibility in fostering the symmetric wavelet limits [9].

3.7 Meyer Wavelet

Meyer wavelet is a classic wavelet, it has many good properties. The haar and daubechies wavelet are support orthogonal wavelets but with the help of meyer wavelet they are able to reconstruct perfect image quality. This is achieved due to the properties of meyer wavelet like induction vastly, perfection, lessens quickly and its range is limited, meyer wavelet is gainful to mathematical ascertain, so it applies generally in designing majors [10].

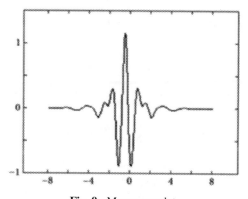

Fig. 9. Meyer wavelet.

Figure 9, shown the meyer wavelet, its smoothness, sufficient decay, vanishing mean and oscillatory behavior with diverse oscillation scan can be seen from the figure.

3.8 Curvelet Transform

The curvelet transform is analysis tool which is used in multiscale geometric objects. The objects include the curve inside of it. The curvelet development motive is to improve the traditional transformations work on curves and edges. The best result of curvelet came if the image contains the curves. The previous research on curvelet proof that the curvelet small scale coefficient better than wavelet's high frequency coefficients. The curvelet implement in image steganography by two methods:

(i)   Using Wrapping Method.
(ii) Using Fast Fourier Transformation algorithm (FFT).

The recommended technique for curvelet varies by the spatial lattice decision. The job of spatial network decision is too used the decipher curvelet coefficients at each scale and point. The result of both methods is in form of curvelet coefficient table. The coefficient table listed the curvelet coefficient according to the spatial location, angle and scaling factor [11]. Type of Curvelet Transform:

Continuous-Time Curvelet Transform. The Curvelet work on two-measurement information type like picture. The hub of these two measurements addresses spatial variable and recurrence space variable x, ω separately. Recurrence space has two polar directions r and θ [12]. The curvelet change characterized in two windows these windows notice the materialness conditions. The windows know as spiral window $\{W(r)\}$, and precise window $\{V(t)\}$. The mathematical representation of this window is:

$$\sum_{j=-\infty}^{\infty} W^2\left(2^j r\right) = 1, r \in \left(\frac{3}{4}, \frac{3}{2}\right),$$ (1)

$$\sum_{j=-\infty}^{\infty} V^2(t-l) = 1, t \in \left(-\frac{1}{2}, \frac{1}{2}\right).$$ (2)

The radial window and angular window support the polar "wedge", represented as U_j. The representation of U_j in fourier domain is:

$$U_j(r, \theta) = 2^{-3j/4} W\left(2^{-j}r\right) V\left(\frac{2^{\lfloor j/2 \rfloor}\theta}{2\pi}\right)$$ (3)

Figure 10, induced tiling of the frequency plane and spatial cartesian grid associated with a given scale and orientation.

Fast Discrete Curvelet Transform via Wrapping. The wrapping based curvelet is the new innovation in the field of curvelet change. The wrapping based curvelet change is a multiscale pyramid; the pyramid contains many sub groups. The sub groups are arranged on various sizes of various directions and positions in the recurrence space. The 2D picture is utilized in wrapping of fourier examples as information. The picture cluster is as cartesian exhibit f [m, n], where the scope of m lies between 0 to M and n lie between 0 to N. Here, the M and N are the elements of the cluster [11].

$$c^D\left(j, l, k_1, k_2\right) = \sum_{\substack{0 \leq m < M \\ 0 \leq n < N}} f[m, n]\phi^D_{j,l,k_1,k_2}[m, n]$$ (4)

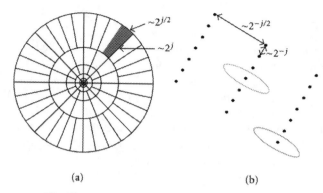

(a)   (b)

Fig. 10. Curvelet tiling of space and frequency [2].

According to the Eq. (4), the output collected in to the curvelet coefficients $c^D(j, l, k_1, k_2)$ indexed by scale j, an orientation l and spatial location parameters k_1 and k_2.

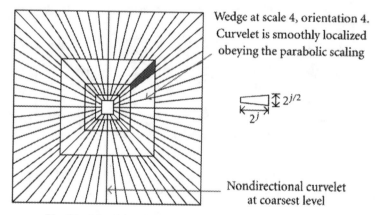

Wedge at scale 4, orientation 4. Curvelet is smoothly localized obeying the parabolic scaling

Nondirectional curvelet at coarsest level

Fig. 11. 5-level fast discrete curvelet transform via wrapping.

Figure 11, illustrates the whole image represented in spectral domain in the form of rectangular frequency tiling by combining all frequency responses of curvelets at different scales and orientation.

3.9 Tetrolet Transform

The tetrolet transform work on the basic structure of Haar filter. The Haar filter divided the 2D image in four blocks according to the low pass and high pass filter. The size of the block in Haar is 2×2 square, but in tetrolet the image divided in 4×4 blocks in horizontal and vertical direction. The block is not overlapping each other because the image is also not overlap. Each block divided fit for another block available in the subdivision [13]. Sometime the size of image not able to divide in four parts in that case tetrolet transform uses the zero-padding [14]. There are five shapes see (Fig. 12) available to represent the tetrolet transform they are named as:

1. Square-O-Type
2. Rectangle-I-Type
3. T-Type
4. S-Type
5. L-type

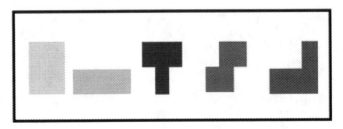

Fig. 12. 5-shapes of the tetrominores [15].

After the locating work of tetrominores, the pixels of 4×4 blocks are rearranged according to TT rules see (Fig. 13). The image is reform by the tetrominores with the help of haar wavelet transform.

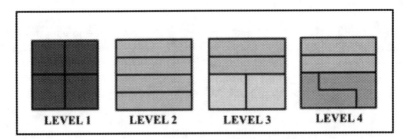

Fig. 13. A combination of tetrominores for a 4×4 pixel block [15].

The decomposition of the tetrolet complete in four steps, the steps are as follows [16]:

1. Divide the 2D image into 4 × 4 blocks.
2. For each block find the sparsest tetrolet representation.
3. Low and high pass coefficients rearrange into 2 × 2 block into every subdivide block.
4. The high- pass part or tetrolet coefficients store.

Repeat step 1 to 4 to the low-pass image.

4   Wavelet Selection

Selection of correct wavelet depend upon different wavelets analysis tests. Different wavelet properties also show impact on wavelet selection such as orthogonality, compact support, symmetry, and vanishing moment. The wavelet family with its properties presented in the following Table 1.

Table 1. The wavelet family with its properties.

Wavelet family	Wavelet Member	Orthogonal	Compact Support	Filters Length	Support Width	Vanishing moment
Haar	'haar'	Yes	Yes	2	1.0	1
Db	'db1', 'd45'	Yes	Yes	$2N$	$2N - 1$	N
Coif	'coif1', 'coif5'	Yes	Yes	$6N$	$6N - 1$	$2N$
Sym	'sym1', 'sym45'	Yes	Yes	$2N$	$2N - 1$	N
Bior	biorNd, Nr	Yes	Yes	$\max(2Nr, 2Nd) + 2$	$2N + 1$ for rec., $2Nd + 1$ for dec.	Nr
Rbio	rbiorNd,Nr	No	Yes	$\max(2Nd, 2Nr) + 2$	$2N + 1$ for rec., $2Nr + 1$ for dec.	Nr
dmey	'dmey'	-	-	-	-	-

Were Nr, Nd, and N are the orders: r for reconstruction and d for decomposition [17].

5 Comparative Study Between DCT, DWT, and DFT

The 32 × 32 binary image resolutions used as an secret. This image will embed on image with 65536 total pixel amount, since 1 pixel of binary image will embed on 8 × 8 image sub-block. Figure 14(a) is used as a secret image and Fig. 14(b) as a cover image.

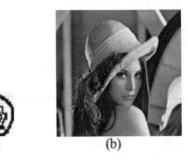

(a)   (b)

Fig. 14. (a) Secrete image, (b) Cover image [18].

Table 2 shows the results of embedding secrete image to the Low Frequency (LF), Middle Frequency MF, and Highest Frequency (HF) of cover image.

Table 2. PSNR results of image watermark in DCT, DFT, and DWT [18].

Freq: Embed Pixel Coordinate	DCT PSNR (dB)	DFT PSNR (dB)	DWT PSNR (dB)
LF: [w0, h1]	40, 24	32, 2	33, 78
MF: [w3, h3]	39, 96	35,18	33,87(HL) 33, 87(LH)
HF: [w7, h7]	40, 82	32,18	33, 87

6 Comparative Study Between Daubechies and Cofilet Wavelet

The properties of different wavelet discuss in Table 1, according to the properties Daubechies and Confilet wavelet have many similarities but the vanishing point of Confilet is more than Daubechies wavelet. In this section, the results are obtained at 3rd level of decomposition [19]. The MATLAB tool is used to obtain the results. The result analyzed on Mean Square Error (MSE), Peak Signal to Noise Ratio (PSNR), and Signal to Noise Ratio (SNR) factors. Here, two images taken for result analysis as shown in Fig. 15 (a-b).

Table 3, clearly represent the Coiflet wavelet give better result for both images. The selection of correct wavelet gives better result on different comparison factors. The graphical representation of result show in Fig. 16, and Fig. 17.

(a)   **(b)**

Fig. 15. (a) Lena image (b) Barbara image.

Table 3. Result comparison between Daubechies and Coiflet wavelet filters [19].

Image	Daubechies Wavelet			Coiflet Wavelet		
	MSE	PSNR	SNR	MSE	PSNR	SNR
LENA	19.8668	80.9348	26.7019	17.3779	82.2733	27.3232
BARBARA	301.7555	53.7291	17.1073	266.9607	54.9543	17.6704

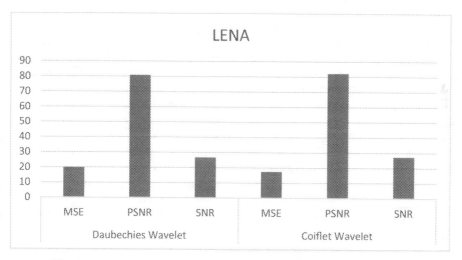

Fig. 16. Comparison between Daubechies and Coiflet result on Lena image.

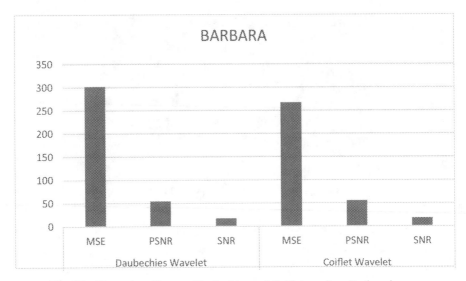

Fig. 17. Comparison between Daubechies and Coiflet result on Barbara image.

7 Conclusion

In this paper, we have surveyed a transform domain image steganography technique, which is used for texture retrieval of image. This work is based on the adaptability of transform domain according to image geometry in frequency domain. The main focus of this paper is on wavelet method for image steganography, according to the study haar wavelet is the oldest one which create base for other wavelet techniques. The older wavelet is very easy to use because they break the image in four squares according to the low and high pass filters but this structure also makes them common. The curvelet and tetrolet wavelet introduce new feature in the traditional wavelet family. Curvelet give better results if your image contains the curves because the curvelet work on angular concept, at the same place on the off chance that we talk about the tetrolet, tetramines adjusts as indicated by picture math. In this way, there is no need of taking explicit bearings, rather picture calculation is thought about. We trust that this study will assist analysts with choosing the best calculation and component extraction techniques to meet their necessities.

References

1. Sharma, N., Batra, U.: A review on spatial domain technique based on image steganography. In: 2017 International Conference on Computing and Communication Technologies for Smart Nation (IC3TSN), Gurgaon, India, pp. 24–27. IEEE (2017)
2. Azani Mustafa, W., et al.: Image enhancement based on discrete cosine transforms (DCT) and discrete wavelet transform (DWT): a review. In: IOP Conference Series: Materials Science and Engineering, Bogor, Indonesia, pp. 1–10. IOP Publishing (2019)
3. Raid, A.M., Khedr, W.M., El-dosuky, M.A., Wesam, A.: JPEG image compression using discrete cosine transform - a survey. Int. J. Comput. Sci. Eng. Surv. **5**(2), 39–47 (2014)

4. Hemalatha, S., Dinesh Acharay, U., Renuka, A., Priya, R.: A secure color image steganography in transform domain. Int. J. Cryptogr. Inf. Secur. **3**(1), 17–24 (2013)
5. Zhou, J.: Realization of discrete fourier transform and inverse discrete fourier transform on one single multimode interference coupler. IEEE Photonics Technol. Lett. **23**, 302–304 (2011)
6. Sharda, S., Budhiraja, S.: Performance analysis of image steganography based on DWT and Arnold transform. Int. J. Comput. Appl. **69**, 46–50 (2013)
7. Kaur, S., Rani, V.: Designing an efficient image encryption-compression system using a new HAAR, SYMLET and COIFLET wavelet transform. Int. J. Comput. Appl. **129**(15), 1–6 (2015)
8. Shaker, A.N.: Comparison between orthogonal and bi-orthogonal wavelets. J. Southwest Jiaotong Univ. **55**(2), 1–10 (2020)
9. Abidin, Z.Z., Manaf, M., Shibhgatullah, A.S.: Experimental approach on thresholding using reverse biorthogonal wavelet decomposition for eye image. In: 2013 IEEE International Conference on Signal and Image Processing Applications, Melaka, Malaysia, pp. 349–353. IEEE (2013)
10. Zhang, X., Deng, C., Han, Y.: The image space of meyer wavelet transform. In: Proceedings of 2013 2nd International Conference on Measurement, Information and Control, Harbin, pp. 1136–1139. IEEE (2013)
11. Mostafa, H., Fouad, A., Sami, G.: A hybrid curvelet transform and genetic algorithm for image steganography. Int. J. Adv. Comput. Sci. Appl. **8**(8), 328–336 (2017)
12. Alzubi, S., Islam, N., Abbod, M.: Multiresolution analysis using wavelet, ridgelet, and curvelet transforms for medical image segmentation. Int. J. Biomed. Imaging **2011**(2011), 1–18 (2011)
13. Liu, S., Huang, X., Zhang, D., Yan, Q., Du, X., Fang, F.: Stationary tetrolet transform: an improved algorithm for tetrolet transform. J. Phys: Conf. Ser. **1069**(1), 1–8 (2018)
14. Ceylan, M.: Performance comparison of tetrolet transform and wavelet-based transforms for medical image denoising. Int. J. Intell. Syst. Appl. Eng. **5**(4), 222–231 (2017)
15. Rajeshkumar, N., Yuvaraj, D., Manikandan, G., Balakrishnan, R., Karthikeyan, B., Raajan, N.R.: Secret image communication scheme based on visual cryptography and tetrolet tiling patterns. Comput. Mater. Continua **65**(2), 1283–1301 (2020)
16. Indra, P.: Tetrolet transform based efficient breast cancer classification system. In: Second International Conference on Current Trends in Engineering and Technology - ICCTET, Coimbatore, India, pp. 579–583. IEEE (2014)
17. Achmamad, A., Jbari, A.: A comparative study of wavelet families for electromyography signal classification based on discrete wavelet transform. Bull. Electr. Eng. Inform. **9**(4), 1420–1429 (2020)
18. Asmara, R.A., Agustina, R.: Comparison of Discrete Cosine Transforms (DCT), Discrete Fourier Transforms (DFT), and Discrete Wavelet Transforms (DWT) in Digital Image Watermarking. Int. J. Adv. Comput. Sci. Appl. **8**(2), 245–249 (2017). https://doi.org/10.14569/IJACSA.2017.080232
19. Abhinav, D., Swatilekha, M.: Comparative analysis of Coieflet and Daubechies wavelets using global threshold for image denoising. Int. J. Adv. Eng. Technol. **6**(5), 2247–2252 (2013)

Design of a High Efficiency Access Control and Authentication Analysis Model for Cloud Deployments Using Pattern Analysis

Anagha Raich[(✉)] and Vijay Gadicha

G. H. Raisoni University, Amravati, India
Anagha.raich@gmail.com, vijay.gadicha@raisoni.net

Abstract. Cloud deployments face large scale attacks due to improper access control and authentication vulnerabilities. This allows attackers to inject improper information into the cloud application, thereby degrading its performance. Attackers inject various attacks, into the cloud deployments, which allows them to access the system even after attacks are removed from application layer. In order to detect and mitigate these attacks, a wide variety of application layer algorithms are designed. These algorithms determine request type via analysis & sanitization of user inputs, which makes them resilient to a wide variety of attacks. But access control & authorization attacks are still persistent with cyber networks, and cannot be detected & mitigated only via input request analysis. In order to remove this limitation, the underlying text proposes a pattern analysis engine for mitigation of cloud access control and authentication vulnerabilities. This engine creates a virtual firewall for all access & authorization requests; and applies multiple pattern analysis models for each user input. The proposed model was deployed on a private cloud, and results were compared in terms of accuracy of authorization, attack detection, delay of authorization check, delay of access control check, accuracy of access control check, and accuracy of user input-based attacks. It was observed that the proposed model is able to identify improper authorization, and improper access control attacks. It was observed that the proposed model has better accuracy with moderate delay of detection when compared with various other models.

Keywords: Pattern analysis · Authentication · Access control · Attacks · Accuracy

1 Introduction

Authentication and access control are two of the most important aspects for any cloud deployment. The former decides which user must be allowed into the system, while the later controls which parts of the cloud must be given access to the authenticated user. In order to perform this task, a multitude of algorithmic models must be designed and connected in tandem. These models include, but are not limited to, entity-based authentication, hardware-based authentication, kernel-level access control, page-level access control, attribute-based access control, etc. A typical implementation that deploys

© The Author(s), under exclusive license to Springer Nature Switzerland AG 2022
S. Joshi et al. (Eds.): SpacSec 2021, CCIS 1599, pp. 186–200, 2022.
https://doi.org/10.1007/978-3-031-15784-4_15

these models at application layer can be observed from Fig. 1, wherein 4 different types of requests are shown,

- Login page access request
- Login request using credentials
- Access request for allowed resources
- Access request for restricted resources

In this model, requests sent by a client can be categorized into the given 4 types, and each of these requests has a separate response from the server. The login page access request searches for presence of an authentication point in the system. If the login page is available, then server responds with HTTP OK (response code 200) response. If it is not present, then a HTTP Not Found (response code 500) is sent to the client. Once login page access is given to a requesting client, then login requests can be sent by them using various authentication mechanisms that include, email & password, phone number, social login, OAuth login, etc. These login requests (R2) are handled by the central layer, and based on cloud-side rules, a cluster of cookies are created by the server, and sent to the client. The client is expected to send these cookies for authentication with each consecutive access request.

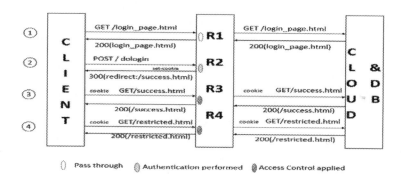

Fig. 1. A typical application-level authentication and access control implementation

Upon authentication, the client sends access control requests to cloud along with said cookies. The cloud checks these requests, and depending upon a permission model, grants or revokes access to certain pages & in-page operations. A wide variety of models are designed for performing these access control & authentication tasks. Survey of these models can be observed from the next section, wherein various nuances, advantages, limitations, and improvement recommendations are discussed. From this survey it is observed that, most of the reviewed state-of-the-art models work by analysis of user requests, and then use a request-response model for identification and mitigation of attacks. This approach is able to detect direct attacks on the system, but is unable to avoid elastic attacks, wherein attackers use tampered cookies, and invalid sessions for accessing restricted server zones. To remove this drawback, Sect. 3 proposes design of a pattern analysis engine for mitigation of cloud access control and authentication vulnerabilities. This design description is followed by result evaluation and comparison with various state-of-the art methods, wherein parameters like accuracy, and delay of operation are evaluated & compared. Finally, this text concludes with some interesting observations about the proposed model, and recommends methods to further improve its performance.

2 Literature Review

Estimating authentication and access control attacks requires design of multiple request checking and validation models, which must work in tandem in order to detect and mitigate these attacks. For instance, the work in [1] proposes an immutable, transparent, traceable and distributed blockchain model that uses trust access authentication. This model reduces number of attacks during authentication, and can track improper post authentication user behavior in order to improve system security. The proposed model uses proof of correctness (PoC), and performs all consensus with the help of verifier nodes that have high trust levels. This work can be combined with [2], wherein a Multidimensional access control model is defined. This model uses collaborative authentication, via User Type Approval (UTA), and combines it with differentiated service security for access control. The model showcases high accuracy, and moderate delay of authentication and access control when compared with state-of-the-art models. These protocols can be tested for vulnerability analysis using the work in [3], wherein various test models are executed for the system, and its security performance is estimated. This system is able to identify security vulnerabilities in a wide variety of environments, including Internet of Things (IoT) as discussed in [4]. The proposed model in [4] utilizes elliptic curve cryptography (ECC) and combines it with key agreement protocol for incorporating access control and highly secure authentication. This work can be improved using biometric authentication frameworks as suggested in [5], wherein Telecare Medicine Information System (TMIS) is used as an application. The biometric model has an accuracy of over 95%, which is moderately secure, and can be used for household security systems. This model can be combined with the work in [6], wherein identity-based signatures are used for access authentication in IPv6 Networks. The proposed model is applied to vehicular networks, but can be used virtually for any real time cloud deployment. The model in [6] provides a good access control mechanism, but can be improved in terms of authentication via the work in [7], wherein multifactor authentication models are described. These models include username & password combination, email & password combination, phone number & OTP combination, etc. Which allows cloud deployments to validate users via standard mechanisms of authentication. Similar models are proposed in [8–12], wherein trust based authentication, multimodal biometric authentication, practically unclonable functions (PUFs), environment aware zero-effort two-factor authentication scheme, and fuzzy vector signature are proposed to provide high security authentication via user input pattern matching.

High performance authentication models can also be observed from [13–16] wherein natural authentication models using hand & finger movements, blockchain based authentication models using high traceability, mutual authentication for constraint-oriented networks, and two-way communication schemes for software defined optical networks are discussed. These models can be combined with the work in [17–20] for providing finer access control and finer authentication via an attribute level scheme using blockchains, data aggregation via access control mechanisms, dynamic keystroke analysis, and key agreement schemes.

An application of these models on electronic healthcare record (EHR) management can be observed from [21], wherein a sensitive and energetic access control model is described. This model is able to improve overall efficiency of access control and authentication via node-level input checking, and filtering. The security of this model can be further improved using the work in [22–25]. These schemes include three factor user-controlled single sign-on, dynamic highly reconfigurable trusted user grouping model via attributes and metagraphs theory, conditional privacy preserving authentication model for side channel attack removal, and various other security architectures are discussed. Mathematical transforms such as Phase Truncated Fourier Transform (PTFT) can also be used for cancellable biometric authentication as discussed in [26], wherein accuracy of authentication is very high. Application of these models can be observed from [27–30], wherein secure cloud messaging, unlimited health care services via blockchain, secure group communications, and ontology data for access control are described. Similar models for authentication and access control that utilize secret sharing, and location-based authentication with access control can also be observed from [31, 32]. These models aim at improving security via accessing and analyzing user inputs using multiple Directives. Summary of various authentication and access control mechanisms can also be observed from [33], wherein analysis of these models based on threats and tokens is described. Image Fusion & Two-Share Cryptography is proposed in [34] to generate Strong Password. Based on relatively large image collection, short repeating cycles could be avoided. Compared to other methods, this requires human-interaction and careful selection of images.

Summary and Discussion

It can be observed that a very limited number of approaches have been for momentary analysis for access control, and most of them depend on rule-based analysis of user inputs. Moreover, the reviewed approaches do not provide a momentary analysis model that can be used for high efficiency authentication & access control. Motivated by this observation, the proposed approach uses pattern analysis engine for mitigation of cloud access control and authentication vulnerabilities in cyber networks, and is described in the next section.

3 Proposed Pattern Analysis Engine for Mitigation of Cloud Access Control and Authentication Vulnerabilities in Cyber Networks

As observed from the literature, designing a high efficiency authentication and access control engine for cloud deployments is done using various techniques that depend upon user input analysis. Based on this analysis, Directives are developed that allow the system to categorize input requests into malicious and normal. But these Directives do not perform momentary pattern analysis on user input, which limits their capabilities to detect improper authentications & access control requests. In order to add momentary pattern analysis on user requests, this section proposes an engine that performs this task. This engine is made up of three major models, each of which are described in different sub-sections. These models perform the following tasks,

- Directive for header-level authentication
- Momentary pattern analysis engine for header-level access checking
- High efficiency logging engine for future IP tracing and attack mitigation

Each of these models are then combined together, and used as headers on cloud deployments. The reason for placing these models on cloud headers is to pre-process requests before they run through the cloud deployment. Initially all requests are passed through the directive for header-level authentication, design of which can be observed from Sect. 3.1 of this text. All authenticated requests are given to momentary pattern analysis engine for header-level access checking, design of which can be observed from Sect. 3.2 of this text. Finally, all requests that are identified to be malicious are given to a high efficiency logging engine, design of which can be observed from Sect. 3.3 of this text.

3.1 Directive for Header-Level Authentication

Every incoming request is given to a header-level authentication engine. This engine is executed before the user can access any other part of the cloud deployment. Design of this engine can be described using the following steps,

Each user is asked for a username/password combination, or email/password combination, or phone/OTP combination, or social login, or OAuth login.

Algorithm for Header-Level Authentication

Required: Each user input (username, password, email, phone, OTP, etc.) is passed through the following checks,

Ensure: Input should not content hypertext marks, quotes, double slash.

1. **Procedure: Authentication**
2. Let P be each input string from header level.
3. For each P input string check the following

- Does the user input consist of any hypertext markups, single quotes ('), double slash signs (--), scripting constants or regular expression, non-displaying character, input encoding

4. If any of the conditions is true, then that particular character is marked, and replaced with blanks. This incident is reported via logging engine with the following details,

- Attack Type: SQLi or XSS
- IP Address of user
- Time stamp

5. The compare the input string P with the database entries, and if they match stored credentials, then login request is passed.
6. For each passed login request, a session is started on the server with given user's credentials. These credentials include, user's ID, email, phone number, username, etc. depending upon the provided information. ID of this session is stored on the browser using secure hashing algorithm 256 (SHA256)
7. For each invalid request, incident is reported via logging engine with the following details,

   - Attack Type: Invalid Authentication
   - IP Address of user
   - Time stamp
   - Authentication information used for login

It is required by the browser to pass stored hash value with every consecutive request in order to access any cloud service. Processing of this hash value-to-session mapping is described in the next section of this text.

3.2 Momentary Pattern Analysis Engine for Header-Level Access Checking

Once a user has logged into the system, and a hash value is stored on their browser, then momentary pattern analysis engine is activated. This engine uses the following 2 database relationships,

- Non encapsulated access pages by the admin
- Read, write, and modify access given to these pages on a per user basis

Using these relationships, a header-level momentary analysis engine is activated, which works as follows,

- For each client request, all the request variables (GET, POST, PUT, and DELETE) are scanned.
- Each of these variables are setup by internal cloud page designs, wherein a mapping as observed from Table 1 is done,

Table 1. Variable to action mapping

Request type	Variable name	Page name	Action on cloud
POST	btnInsert	Health Record	Write

- Let, the user passed session hash be H_{pass}
- If, $H_{pass} \in Server_{session}$, then access control is checked, else user is logged out of the system and incident is reported via logging engine with the following details,

  - Attack Type: Invalid Authentication
  - IP Address of user
  - Time stamp
  - All request variables and their values

- Once authenticated, the following Table 2 is generated on a per request basis,

Table 2. Generated table for each request

UID	Req type	Variable name	Page name	Sanitized value
1	POST	btnInsert	Health record	abcd

- Table 1 and 2 are matched, and based on page name, request type, and variable name.
- If there is no matching, then incident is reported via logging engine with the following details,

  - Attack Type: Invalid Access
  - IP Address of user
  - Time stamp
  - Page name
  - All request variables and their values

- If a match is found, then database rules are checked, and user access parameters are evaluated. Based on these parameters, the following conditions are possible,

  - Request for write on this page, and write on this page is granted
  - Request for read on this page, and read on this page is granted
  - Request for view on this page, and view on this page is granted
  - Request for write on this page, and write on this page is NOT granted
  - Request for read on this page, and read on this page is NOT granted
  - Request for view on this page, and view on this page is NOT granted

- If any of the granted conditions are satisfied, then user request is processed normally using sanitized input values.
- If any of the NOT granted conditions are satisfied, then incident is reported via logging engine with the following details,

- Attack Type: Invalid Access
- IP Address of user
- Time stamp
- Page name
- All request variables and their values

• Each incident report is checked, and following momentary identity is evaluated for the given user ID,

$$T_{valid} = (\frac{\sum_{T=t_1}^{t_2} R_{invalid_T}}{\sum_{T=t_1}^{t_2} R_{valid_T}}) \dots (1)$$

where, T_{valid} is momentary validity when checked between time instances t_1 & t_2, while $R_{invalid_T}$ and R_{valid_T} are number of invalid & valid requests passed during this momentary interval.

• If $T_{valid} > 0.1$, then over 10% of all requests are invalid. In such a case, user is logged out, the IP from which login was done is blocked, and incident is reported via logging engine with the following details,

- Attack Type: Invalid Momentary Access
- IP Address of user
- Time stamp
- Page name
- All request variables and their values

Using this process, every access request is tracked using momentary pattern analysis. After momentary analysis, a high efficiency logging engine is designed. As already indicated, this engine is integrated into both momentary analysis and authentication validation engines. Design of this engine can be observed from the next sub-section.

3.3 High Efficiency Logging Engine for Future IP Tracing and Attack Mitigation

The high efficiency logging engine is based on a graph database, wherein relationships between IP addresses, their sessions, and their improper activity are tracked. This engine uses the following format as indicated in Table 3, for storing data, and then represents this data in a graph format as observed from Fig. 2.

Table 3. Data storage design for the high efficiency logging engine

UID	IP	Attack Type	Timestamp	Page Name
Req. Vars	Req. Var. Vals	Auth. Info	Prev. Page Name	Meta Data

Using this storage design, any type of event can be logged for a given user, and for the given IP. These events are represented using a graph format, as observed from Fig. 2 as follows,

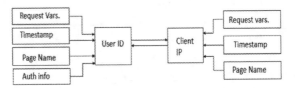

Fig. 2. Per-user and per-IP basis

In Fig. 2, an analysis engine is able to track number of invalid authorizations, and access control requests are sent by the attacker. This assists in future risk mitigation from the given IP and from the given User ID (as they are linked via this graph). In most cases, requests from the particular IP or UID are blocked, and access is restricted to the entire cloud deployment. Based on these designs, result evaluation for the proposed model, and various state-of-the-art access control & authentication models is done. This analysis, and comparison can be observed from the next section.

4 Results Analysis and Comparison

Using the proposed design, various attacks are performed on the cloud deployment. This cloud deployment uses an electronic health care record (EHR) maintenance model, that works using the following rules,

- Users can sign-up using a unique username, and password. They are also needed to upload a photo identification file for future checking purposes.
- Each user can upload their own healthcare records, view them, and modify them.
- Users can check number of doctors present in the system, and allow them to view certain records as per requirement.
- Doctors can view these records, and perform diagnosis.
- Admin account can grant access to users for other pages depending upon requirement.

Using this system design, the following scenarios were simulated,

- A large number of authentication requests were given to the system.
- After login, access control attacks are performed using the following conditions,

  - Access to pages not meant for user operation.
  - Uploading EHR for other users which are not logged in from the current browser.
  - Viewing EHRs of other users.

Total 50 million requests were sent to the system, and performance was measured using accuracy of authorization attack detection, delay of authorization check, delay of access control check, accuracy of access control check, and accuracy of user input-based attacks. Each of these parameters along with their respective values were tabulated, and visualized for different access control & authorization models. For instance, accuracy of authorization attack detection (A3D) can be observed from Table 4 as follows, (Fig. 3)

Table 4. Accuracy of authorization attack detection for different models

Num. requests	A3D (%) [2]	A3D (%) [21]	A3D (%) Proposed
1k	98.5	98.51	100
10k	98.4	98.43	99.99
25M	99.49	99.53	99.98

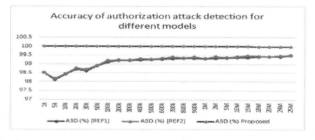

Fig. 3. Accuracy of authorization attack detection for different models

Based on this analysis, it can be observed that the proposed model has better authorization attack accuracy when compared with models proposed in [2], and [21], thereby showcasing its superior performance. Similar observations were made for delay of authorization check (DAC), and can be observed from Table 5 as follows, (Fig. 4)

Table 5. Delay of authorization attack detection for different models

Num. requests	DAC (ms) [2]	DAC (ms) [21]	DAC (ms) Proposed
1k	10.15228	10.15125	2
50k	310.4146	310.3832	61.40614
25M	1430.295	1429.72	284.6569

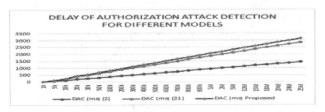

Fig. 4. Delay of authorization attack detection for different models

Based on this analysis, it can be observed that the proposed model showcases 35% reduction in delay when compared with models proposed in [2], and [21]. This is due to the light weight sanitization and session hashed based authorization process followed by the model, thereby showcasing its superior performance. Similar observations were made for accuracy of access control check (A2C2), and can be observed from Table 6 as follows, (Fig. 5)

Table 6. Accuracy of access control detection for different models

Num. requests	A2C2 (%) [2]	A2C2 (%) [21]	A2C2 (%) Proposed
1k	53.25	55.26	98.44
10k	58.2	52.22	98.73
25M	51.75	52.77	98.22

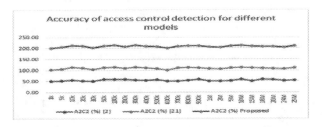

Fig. 5. Accuracy of access control detection for different models

As per analysis, based on this analysis, it can be observed that the proposed model has 35% better access control detection accuracy when compared with models proposed in [2], and [21]. Thereby showcasing its superior performance under a large number of requests. Similar observations were made for delay of access control check (DAC2), and can be observed from Table 7 as follows, (Fig. 6)

Table 7. Delay of access control check detection for different models

Num. requests	DAC2 (ms) [2]	DAC2 (ms) [21]	DAC2 (ms) Proposed
1k	5.41	5.71	1.97
700k	400.35	445.05	146.63
25M	754.41	754.39	279.3

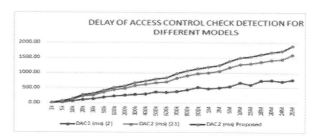

Fig. 6. Delay of access control check detection for different models

Based on this analysis, it can be observed that the proposed model showcases 40% reduction in delay when compared with models proposed in [2], and [21]. This is due to the light-weight pattern analysis for access control check process followed by the model, thereby showcasing its superior performance. Similar observations were made for accuracy of user attack (AUA), which includes SQL injection, access control & cookie hijacking, and can be observed from Table 8 as follows, (Fig. 7)

Table 8. Accuracy of user attack detection for different models

Num. requests	AUA (%) [2]	AUA (%) [21]	AUA (%) Proposed
1k	99.42	98.93	99.18
700k	99.62	99.12	99.37
25M	99.2	98.71	98.96

Based on this analysis, it can be observed that the proposed model has similar performance for user attack detection accuracy when compared with models proposed in [2], and [21], thereby making it deployable for real time cloud environments.

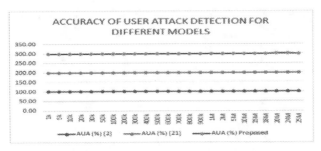

Fig. 7. Accuracy of user attack detection for different models

5 Conclusion

The proposed light weight momentary pattern analysis engine for detection of access control and authentication attacks is based on IP tracing, User ID tracking and rule checking. These operations are combined with momentary evaluation of requests, and their pattern matching with administrator led access control, which enables the underlying model to remove complex authorization and access control steps as used conventionally. This results in a high speed, and high accuracy, engine that is resilient against improper authentication, invalid access, and user level attacks. The proposed model is able to showcase over 35% improvement in terms of access control attack detection performance, and reduce delay by over 40% when compared with state-of-the-art models. The performance for user level attacks is very high, and comparable with existing models, thereby making the proposed model high deployable on real time clouds.

References

1. Cai, T., Yang, Z., Chen, W., Zheng, Z., Yu, Y.: A blockchain-assisted trust access authentication system for solid. IEEE Access **8**, 71605–71616 (2020)
2. Ai, Z., Liu, Y., Chang, L., Lin, F., Song, F.: A smart collaborative authentication framework for multi-dimensional fine-grained control. IEEE Access **8**, 8101–8113 (2020)
3. Alhaidary, M., et al.: Vulnerability analysis for the authentication protocols in trusted computing platforms and a proposed enhancement of the OffPAD protocol. IEEE Access **6**, 6071–6081 (2018)
4. Das, A.K., Wazid, M., Yannam, A.R., Rodrigues, J.J.P.C., Park, Y.: Provably secure ECC-based device access control and key agreement protocol for IoT environment. IEEE Access **7**, 55382–55397 (2019)
5. Mehmood, Z., Ghani, A., Chen, G., Alghamdi, A.S.: Authentication and secure key management in e-health services: a robust and efficient protocol using biometrics. IEEE Access **7**, 113385–113397 (2019)
6. Gao, T., Deng, X., Wang, Y., Kong, X.: PAAS: PMIPv6 access authentication scheme based on identity-based signature in VANETs. IEEE Access **6**, 37480–37492 (2018)
7. Maciej, B., Imed, E.F., Kurkowski, M.: Multifactor authentication protocol in a mobile environment. IEEE Access **7**, 157185–157199 (2019)
8. Chaudhry, S.A., Yahya, K., Al-Turjman, F., Yang, M.-H.: A secure and reliable device access control scheme for IoT based sensor cloud systems. IEEE Access **8**, 139244–139254 (2020)

9. Zhang, X., Cheng, D., Jia, P., Dai, Y., Xu, X.: An efficient android-based multimodal biometric authentication system with face and voice. IEEE Access **8**, 102757–102772 (2020)

10. Zhao, J., et al.: A secure biometrics and PUFs-based authentication scheme with key agreement for multi-server environments. IEEE Access **8**, 45292–45303 (2020)

11. AlQahtani, A.A.S., Alamleh, H., Gourd, J.: 0EISUA: zero effort indoor secure user authentication. IEEE Access **8**, 79069–79078 (2020)

12. Seo, M., Hwang, J.Y., Lee, D.H., Kim, S., Kim, S., Park, J.H.: Fuzzy vector signature and its application to privacy-preserving authentication. IEEE Access **7**, 69892–69906 (2019)

13. Wang, H., Chen, T., Liu, X., Chen, J.: Exploring the hand and finger-issued behaviors toward natural authentication. IEEE Access **8**, 55815–55825 (2020)

14. Mudhar, J.K., Kalra, S., Malhotra, J.: An efficient blockchain based authentication scheme to secure fog enabled IoT devices. In: 2020 Indo – Taiwan 2nd International Conference on Computing, Analytics and Networks (Indo-Taiwan ICAN), pp. 75–80 (2020)

15. Adil, M., et al.: MAC-AODV based mutual authentication scheme for constraint oriented networks. IEEE Access **8**, 44459–44469 (2020)

16. Tang, Y., Liu, T., He, X., Yu, J., Qin, P.: A lightweight two-way authentication scheme between communication nodes for software defined optical access network. IEEE Access **7**, 133248–133256 (2019)

17. Ding, S., Cao, J., Li, C., Fan, K., Li, H.: A novel attribute-based access control scheme using blockchain for IoT. IEEE Access **7**, 38431–38441 (2019)

18. Jasim, A.A., et al.: Secure and energy-efficient data aggregation method based on an access control model. IEEE Access **7**, 164327–164343 (2019)

19. Saini, B.S., et al.: A three-step authentication model for mobile phone user using keystroke dynamics. IEEE Access **8**, 125909–125922 (2020)

20. Lyu, Q., Zheng, N., Liu, H., Gao, C., Chen, S., Liu, J.: Remotely access "my" smart home in private: an anti-tracking authentication and key agreement scheme. IEEE Access **7**, 41835–41851 (2019)

21. Riad, K., Hamza, R., Yan, H.: Sensitive and energetic IoT access control for managing cloud electronic health records. IEEE Access **7**, 86384–86393 (2019)

22. Hsu, C.-L., Le, T.-V., Hsieh, M.-C., Tsai, K.-Y., Lu, C.-F., Lin, T.-W.: Three-factor UCSSO scheme with fast authentication and privacy protection for telecare medicine information systems. IEEE Access **8**, 196553–196566 (2020)

23. Hou, Y., Garg, S., Hui, L., Jayakody, D.N.K., Jin, R., Hossain, M.S.: A data security enhanced access control mechanism in mobile edge computing. IEEE Access **8**, 136119–136130 (2020)

24. Alshudukhi, J.S., Mohammed, B.A., Al-Mekhlafi, Z.G.: An efficient conditional privacy-preserving authentication scheme for the prevention of side-channel attacks in vehicular ad hoc networks. IEEE Access **8**, 226624–226636 (2020)

25. Park, C.-S., Nam, H.-M.: Security architecture and protocols for secure MQTT-SN. IEEE Access **8**, 226422–226436 (2020)

26. Alarifi, A., Amoon, M., Aly, M.H., El-Shafai, W.: Optical PTFT asymmetric cryptosystem-based secure and efficient cancelable biometric recognition system. IEEE Access **8**, 221246–221268 (2020)

27. Al Sibahee, M.A., et al.: Lightweight secure message delivery for E2E S2S communication in the IoT-cloud system. IEEE Access **8**, 218331–218347 (2020)

28. Indumathi, J., et al.: Block chain based internet of medical things for uninterrupted, ubiquitous, user-friendly, unflappable, unblemished, unlimited health care services (BC IoMT U6 HCS). IEEE Access **8**, 216856–216872 (2020)

29. Kumar, V, Kumar, R, Pandey, SK. A secure and robust group key distribution and authentication protocol with efficient rekey mechanism for dynamic access control in secure group communications. Int J Commun Syst. 2020; 33:e4465.

30. Kiran, G.M., Nalini, N.: Enhanced security-aware technique and ontology data access control in cloud computing. Int. J. Commun. Syst. **33**, e4554 (2020)
31. Tiwari, D., Chaturvedi, G.K., Gangadharan, G.R.: ACDAS: authenticated controlled data access and sharing scheme for cloud storage. Int. J. Commun. Syst. **32**, e4072 (2019)
32. Yuan, H., Maple, C., Lu, Y., Watson, T.: Peer-assisted location authentication and access control for wireless networks. Internet Technol. Lett. **2**, e71 (2019)
33. Boonkrong, S.: Authentication and access control: practical cryptography methods and tools (2021). https://doi.org/10.1007/978-1-4842-6570-3
34. Gadicha, V.B., Alvi, A.S.: A review towards enhancing authentication scheme using image fusion and multishared cryptography. In: IEEE ICCSP 2015 Conference, p. 4 (2015)

A Study on Cyber Security in Various Critical IT Infrastructure Organizational Sectors: Challenges and Solutions

Sachin Kumar Sharma[1,2]([⊠]) [ID], Arjun Singh[1,2]([⊠]) [ID],
and Manoj Kumar Bohra[1,2]([⊠]) [ID]

[1] Department of Computer and Communication Engineering, Jaipur, India
sachin_43721@yahoo.com, {arjun.singh,
manojkumar.bohra}@jaipur.manipal.edu
[2] Department of Computer and Communication Engineering, Manipal University Jaipur, Jaipur,
India

Abstract. In today's digital era, information is becoming important assset for the various organizations. The production of data and information is moving on electronic platforms and replacing traditional paper based methods. The integration of computer and communication capabilities in traditional business activities, the probability of threat of cyber insecurity is increasing. The threat of data leakage due to different known and unknown vulnerabilities, insiders, lack of knowledge etc. are becoming challenges for every organization, specially for critical IT infrastructure.

This paper analyses a cyber-crime perspective and the range of various cyber-attacks experienced by various critical IT infrastructure such as Banking, Finance & Insurance Government, Defense, Power & Energy, Telecom, Health, Transport and Strategic & Public Enterprises. Moreover, this literature review also identifies role of nodal agencies of cyber security and various cyber security framework to protect the information stored in computer resources.

Keywords: Cyber security · Cyber insecurity · Critical IT infrastructure · Cyber attack · Cyber warfare · Cyber insurance · Personal sensitive data or information · Cyber security framework

1 Introduction

In current time organizations, body corporate & various governments have become largely dependent on IT infrastructure and digital platforms. Cyber-attacks become more popular among cyber criminals and more disastrous as use of digital technology increases. Cyber-attacks are becoming popular and increases day by day because these type of attacks are cheaper, very appropriate, fast and less dangerous to attacker than other type of physical attacks. Cyber criminals require little expenditure like a computer/mobile with s/w tools and an Internet connection. There are no geographic boundaries of electronic data exchange. Law of every country regarding cyber security

© The Author(s), under exclusive license to Springer Nature Switzerland AG 2022
S. Joshi et al. (Eds.): SpacSec 2021, CCIS 1599, pp. 201–212, 2022.
https://doi.org/10.1007/978-3-031-15784-4_16

and cyber-crimes are different in nature. It is also difficult to identify, detect and controls over cyber criminals due to anonymous and complex nature of the Internet [1]. Cyber threats are increasing on Critical IT Infrastructures (CIIs) of various organizations that can affect lives of human beings [2]. It is becoming important to prevent loss of customers as well as to protect organisational reputation. For this, IT assets must be protected from various cyber threats. It is very essential for all the organizations that to know about the baseline cyber security.

There has been a huge paradigm shift in Information and communication technology (ICT) of each business sector [3]. The current era or industries which are also popular as Industry 4.0 is based on Internet of Things (IoT), Cloud Computing, Machine Learning and Artificial Intelligence. These technologies are increasing the automation, fast communication, self-monitoring, and production with less human intervention. More dependency on computer technology attracts the cyber risks and threats.

The objective of this paper to discuss about the current cyber security issues in various business domains especially Critical IT Infrastructure. In this paper, the requirement of cyber security in current digital technology based organizations has been identified in eight different domains which belong to critical IT infrastructure (CIIs).

2   Related Work

Cyber Security is becoming necessity of Information and communication technology (ICT) domain to combat with cyber-attacks. To secure the IT assets of the organization from various threats. Cyber Security is the group of activities that focuses on defending the computer resource from unauthorized/illegal access, change, interruption, revelation, alteration or destruction through technology, processes and practices to ensure the preservation of confidentiality, integrity and availability.

As per IT act of India, "Critical Information Infrastructure is any computer resource, the incapacitation or destruction of which, shall have debilitating impact on national security, economy, public health or safety." The National Critical Information Infrastructure Protection Centre (NCIIPC) is the nodal agency for issue guidelines to secure the Critical IT Infrastructure. As per NCIIPC, following sectors comes under Critical IT Infrastructure sector:

- Banking, Finance & Insurance
- Government
- Defense
- Power & Energy
- Telecom
- Health
- Transport
- Strategic & Public Enterprises

The related work by different researchers In following Critical IT infrastructure Sectors are as follows:

2.1 Cyber Security in Banking, Finance and Insurance Sector

Internet banking has become a very popular banking medium these days. The wallet has been become e-wallet. Money is moving in form of electronic means from one person to another person. The cyber-attacks set a challenge for Internet banking and E-commerce organizations [4]. Today Banking and financial industries are working as Fintech Industries. The Banks and financial institutes are adopting best cyber security processes and practices through guidelines issued by regulatory bodies like Reserve Bank of India (RBI), National Payments Corporation of India (NPCI), Securities and Exchange Board of India (SEBI), National Bank for Agriculture and Rural Development (NABARD), The Unique Identification Authority of India (UIDAI), and Insurance Regulatory and Development Authority of India (IRDAI) [5]. In addition to it, Payment card industries are also complying the various IT security standards like Payment Card Industry Data Security Standard (PCI-DSS). After the adoption of all the procedures and best practices of IT Security, Banking and finance sector is facing cyber security threats. Phishing and social engineering attacks on individual personal data and information like Bank Account No., PIN, CVV, Passwords are targets of cybercriminals. Financial frauds are still now a severe challenge due to the lack of control on security breaches, loopholes, and awareness in society [6]. Phishing is an attack where the cyber-criminal creates the forged link of a genuine webpage to dupe a user to obtain their personal Information. It is a social engineering attack using various techniques to convince the user to disclose their personal information [7]. Cyber- criminals uses phishing with different methods to lure the online users. In addition to it, due to increasing cyber issues, Cyber insurance is becoming a rapidly developing sector which appeals more attention of business organizations to deal with residual risks related to cyber security [8] (Table 1).

Table 1. Key findings related to Cyber Security in Banking, Finance & Insurance Sector

Authors	Findings	Reference
Alghazo et al.	i. Internet Banking Facts ii. Cyber Security Challenges in Internet Banking iii. Increasing use of electronic banking	[4]
Dubey et al.	i. Internet banking allows users to use banking facility Anytime, Anywhere ii. Cyber Frauds Awareness through various mediums iii. Core Banking platforms have been moved to new electronic methods	[6]
Gupta et al.	i. Thorough analysis of Phishing and social engineering attacks ii. Modus operendi of social engineering attacks iii. Tabnabbing Attack using link to lure user	[7]

(continued)

Table 1. (*continued*)

Authors	Findings	Reference
Marotta, Angelica et al.	i. Necessity of Cyber Insurance ii. Residual Cyber Risks iii. Risk Management through Cyber Insurance iv. Challenges of Cyber Insurance Market	[8]

2.2 Cyber Security in Government Sector

Various Governments have also faced the cyber security related attacks on government Information and communication technology (ICT) Infrastructure. E-Governance is becoming the platform of service delivery to the citizens and increased the transparency in public dealings by the governments [9]. Web portals and applications of the governments are key target of cyber criminals. Distributed Denial of Service Attacks, Website defamation, Brute Force Attack, Man in the Middle Attacks, weak encryption, help from service providers etc. are the key challenges for the government officials. In recent years, Governments have reported increasing numbers of cyber-attacks on Government IT Infrastructure. Therefore, cyber-security is on high priority for the Government and Its officials [10] (Table 2).

Table 2. Key findings related to Cyber Security in Government Sector

Authors	Findings	Reference
Tripathi et al.	i. E-Governance Issues ii. E-Governance and its benefits. Fast Delivery of the services, transparency etc.	[9]
Kim et al.	i Increased no. of cyber-attacks on government IT infrastructure ii. Cyber Frauds Awareness through various mediums	[10]

2.3 Cyber Security in Defense

The use of computer and communication technology in defence sector is becoming very critical in for security of any country. Preparation, Storage & transfer of top secret/confidential information using computer resource are to be considered as very critical aspect [11]. Dependency of information communication technology for upgradation and advancement of the weapons with new feature of artificial intelligence, cyber surveillance & reconnaissance/information gathering systems, global positioning system (GPS) along with increasing volume of critical data and information have necessitated the usage of reliable and updated cyber security solutions for the defence industry [12].

Malware issues, weak encryption, Distributed Denial of Service (DDoS) Attack, Website Defamation, Misinformation, Fake news, Fake accounts, Recruitment of personals for cyber terrorism using social media are common cyber issues which can affect sovereignty and integrity of any country [13]. Today, combating with cyber warfare is also becoming an emerging challenge for defence sector [14] (Table 3).

Table 3. Key findings related to Cyber Security in Defence

Authors	Findings	Reference
Egloff et al.	i. Cyber Intrusion ii. Public Attribution Framework iii. Public attribution – as part of a strategy iv. Cyber Surveillance	[11]
Broeders et al.	i. American Computer Fraud and Abuse Act (CFAA) ii. Active Cyber Defense iii. Honeypots iv. Distributed Denial of Service attack[DDoS] v. Cyber Terrorism	[12]
Tagarev et al.	i. Cyber Security Policy Formulation ii. Cyber Crisis Management Plan iii. Hybrid Threats iv. Information Communication Technology (ICT) Defense	[13]
Katagiri et al.	i. Cyber war in 21st century ii. Cyber Warfare & Proxy War	[14]

2.4 Cyber Security in Power and Energy

Smart Grids & Virtual Power Plant, As its name infers that advancement of computer technology also impacted power and energy sector. Information and real time critical data related to distribution, transmission, grid monitoring, load balancing, environmental parameters, sensors etc. is controlling by the IT assets in the field of power energy [15]. The next generation power and energy system will integrate the traditional electrical system with information communication technology to enhance the connectivity, automation and communication of the different power and energy network equipment [16]. Supervisory control and data acquisition (SCADA) is also playing very important role for controlling large power and energy systems like grids, pipeline, distribution and communication centres over a network like internet or intranet. Use of computer technology creates a larger attack surface for cyber criminals [17]. Vulnerabilities in the operation technology which is based on Information communication technology may arise critical cyber threats to power and energy system [18] (Table 4).

Table 4. Key findings related to Cyber Security in Power & Energy Sectors

Author	Findings	Reference
Venkatachary et al.	i. Cyber security issues in power sector ii. Virtual Power Plants iii. Smart Grids iv. Data and controls related to distribution, communication, Load balancing etc.	[15]
Tan et al.	i. Cyber security of smart grids ii. Smart grid architecture and methodology Issues	[16]
Hossain et al.	i. Cyber security for large demographic sectors like power & energy ii. SCADA iii. Cyber Security for SCADA iv. SCADA on WAN and Internet	[17]
Krause et al.	i. Device and application security ii. Network Security iii. Policies, Procedures, and Awareness iv. Monitoring and controlling smart grids	[18]

2.5 Cyber Security in Telecom

Our all e-activities like sending text, searching content, watching videos, accessing social media, digital payments, live streaming etc. is becoming possible due to the IT infrastructure behind the telecom service providers [19]. A number of core telecommunication services are still uses the outdated and vulnerable protocols like SS7 (Signalling System No. 7). Since 2014, SMS based traffic using the SS7 protocol can be intercepted [20]. SS7 protocol has become one of the critical cyber threats to the telecom industry including banking. Malicious actors can easily intercept 2 factor authentications (2FA) and can hack the accounts of users. Outdated and vulnerable computer resource is the key cyber threat for telecom industry [21] (Table 5).

2.6 Cyber Security in Health Sector

In today's scenario, The healthcare system can be seen as a cyber-physical system where physical systems are connected with each other using computer technologies to interact with each other to perform required function [22]. Digital healthcare technology is increasing exponentially and creates huge market of electronic health care delivery. Nowadays, Internet of things (IoT) devices are also becoming part of healthcare. About 50 billion device are networked together to share data and information [23].

However, there are lots of challenges of security of personal and sensitive information stored in healthcare IT Infrastructure. Increased connectivity to internet or digital devices has exposed medical devices to new cyber threats and risks. Health sector is an attractive target for cybercriminals because it is a vulnerable platform of personal sensitive data or

Table 5. Key findings related to Cyber Security in Telecom Sector

Author	Findings	Reference
Adel et al.	i. Cyber Security case study for telecom sector ii. Role of telecom sector in digital transfomation iii. Cyber security issues in telecom sector	[19]
Welch et al.	i. Weaknesses of SS7 ii. Exploiting the weaknesses of SS7	[20]
Hossain et al.	i. Exploitation of SS7 protocol vulnerabilities ii. One-time-password interception iii. 2 factor authentication exploitation iv. SMS interception	[21]

information and it is not adequately secure. Breach in IT Infrastructure of health sector is critical to safety of patient also [24]. The breaches in health sector have put privacy of patient at a critical risk [25] (Table 6).

Table 6. Key findings related to Cyber Security in Health Sector

Author	Findings	Reference
Dogaru et al.	i. Cyber Physical System ii. Health Insurance Portability and Accountability Act iii. Cyber Threats to Patient data	[22]
Strielkina et al.	i. IoT Devices in Medical care ii. Information sharing using IoT Devices iii. Statistics of IoT Devices using in the Medical Field	[23]
Coventry et al.	i. Cyber Technology in health care ii. Medical Instruments controlled by digital infrastructure iv. Exchange of Medical data & information v. Personal & Sensitive data	[24]
Mahler et al.	i. Breaches in Medical Data ii. Malware like Ransomware iii. Outdated protocol iv. Unpatched technology	[25]

2.7 Cyber Security in Transport

The convergence of information technology (IT) and operation technology (OT) has brought significant changes in passenger facilities like online reservations, reliability & security in travel, increased operational efficiency, and capacity management in the transport sector. Almost every domain of transport like Railway, Aviation, Shipping & Highways are using information technology for transparent services to their clients [26].

Screening of passengers, Passenger Information System, Schedules & Timing, Announcement, Fare collection, automated cards, food facilities etc. are based on Information technology. Safety and security is also key concern in rapid transport system.

However, there have been various cyber issues which are affecting the various transportation system like disruption to transport control systems, unauthorized access to toll booths, tampering in electronic cards, Interruption in fare collection, viral of fake information, Denial of service attack on online reservation portals, E-Mail Hacking, Phishing, Data Diddling issues in web portals by insiders etc. [27]. In the era of Smart City, underground rapid metro railway stations are also adopting advanced Information Technology [28]. Technological developments towards vehicle automation like GPS navigation, anti-lock braking systems (ABS), auto pilot are well-known examples in automobile sector. Vulnerability and loophole may cause serious issues for human life. Therefore, these vehicles must be developed to combat with such cyber threats and equipped with adequate defensive measures [29] (Table 7).

Table 7. Key findings related to Cyber Security in Transport Sector

Author	Findings	Reference
Ervural et al.	i. Significant changes in passenger facilities using ICT Infrastructure ii. Capacity management using Information Technology iii. Cyber Security Challenges in Web and mobile applications of transport	[26]
Kour et al.	i. Cyber Attacks on transport facilities ii. Tampering in electronic cards, Interruption in fare collection & viral of fake information issues iii. Automation in railways using information communication technology	[27]
Kertis et al.	i. Improving the cyber security in Smart City Concept ii. Issues in rapid transport system iii. Real Time Monitoring through Technology based automation	[28]
Yağdereli et al.	i. Technological Development in Automatic vehicles ii. GPS and Satellite Navigation iii. Anti-lock braking systems iv. Defencing capabilities for Autonomous vehicles	[29]

2.8 Cyber Security in Strategic and Public Enterprises

Similar to private sector, Strategic & Public Enterprises like public sector undertaking (PSU) are also facing various cyber-attacks. Phishing, malware issues like ransomware, stolen personal sensitive data, illegal cryptomining, supply chain attack, email frauds, cyber espionage, cybersquatting etc. are common issues to Strategic & Public Enterprises

[30]. Cyber technology is one of the graver threats to the national security along with biological and nuclear threats [31] (Table 8).

Table 8. Key findings related to Strategic & Public Enterprises

Author	Key findings	Reference
Andreasson et al.	i. Internet facing cyber attacks ii. Cryptomining iii. Cyber security issues in public sector iv. Supply chain attack	[30]
Cavelty et al.	i. National cyber security issues ii.Biological threats and nuclear threats iii. Cyber Security: a top priority in the future	[31]

3 Challenges

In this section we will discuss regarding challenges or open issues identified in Sect. 2 related to cyber security in various sectors. Following are the challenges and open issues identified:

a) The research papers are domain specific, not provide the general view of cyber security.
b) The research papers do not cover various legal mandate & International Standards.
c) The latest trends are developing new threat models for various critical IT infrastructure sectors.
d) The coordination with the various nodal agencies in case of cyber incident is missing.
e) Defence strategies as per guidelines and various cyber security frameworks against cyber threats are missing.
f) For verification of compliances like cyber security audit, adoption of Information Security Management System (ISMS) of cyber security etc. are missing.

4 Motivation

The research related work evidenced that cyber security is key concern for each organization. Paper based methods have converted in Digital/Electronics Methods, Organizations are dependent on technology. As per research review evidences, motivation to explore the solutions for various enterprises to enhance cyber security posture are:

a) To identify the loopholes and vulnerabilities in the Information Communication Technology.
b) To develop a baseline methodology of cyber security activities.
c) To identify Basic ICT controls to Enhance Cyber Security Posture.
d) To reduce the probability of cyber-attacks.
e) To maintain legal and regulatory bodies requirements.

5 Conclusion

Cyber-attacks are affecting every sector in these days. An organization with functional cyber security strategies must be structured to combat the cyber threats. Unpatched devices, outdated protocols, weak encryption, unmanaged IT security Access controls, malware threats like ransomware, lack of awareness are main causes for cyber security of critical IT infrastructure. A methodology of active cyber security practice & controls must be implemented across the entire cyber physical systems of the organization with the help of their IT team and other important stakeholders [32].

The organization must frame well documented information security policies which is approved by the management and communicated to all employees and stakeholders of the organization. The information security policy must be reviewed on regular interview [33]. The management of the organization shall assign the responsibilities of information security in the organization. In case of critical IT Infrastructure in India, The designation of Chief Information Security Officer (CISO) must be available in the organization [34]. The organization must also prepare a cyber-crisis management plan, which will helpful in case of invocation of incident. It is part of Disaster recovery and business continuity planning. The Organization must perform third party comprehensive IT security Audit of computer resource periodically or as and when the system is upgraded [35].

The organizations must follow the guidelines, advisories, whitepapers and vulnerability notes issued by nodal agencies like Indian Computer Emergency Response Team (CERT-In) & National Critical Information Infrastructure Protection Centre (NCIIPC). Along with it, organization must follow cyber security standards and frameworks issued by the National Institute of Standards and Technology (NIST), Information Security Management System (ISMS) Standards [36].

References

1. Andreea, B.: Cyber-attacks – trends, patterns and security countermeasures. In: 7th International Conference On Financial Criminology, Wadham College, Oxford, United Kingdom, pp. 13–14 (2015)
2. Mantzana, V., Georgiou, E., Gazi, A., Gkotsis, I., Chasiotis, I., Eftychidis, G.: Towards a global CIs' cyber-physical security management and joint coordination approach. In: Abie, H., Ranise, S., Verderame, L., Cambiaso, E., Ugarelli, R., Giunta, G., Praça, I., Battisti, F. (eds.) CPS4CIP 2020. LNCS, vol. 12618, pp. 155–170. Springer, Cham (2021). https://doi.org/10.1007/978-3-030-69781-5_11
3. Jhanjhi, N.Z., Humayun, M., Almuayqil, S.N.: Cyber security and privacy issues in industrial internet of things. Comput. Syst. Sci. Eng. 37(3), 361–380 (2021)
4. Alghazo, J.M., Kazmi, Z., Latif, G.: Cyber security analysis of internet banking in emerging countries: user and bank perspectives. In: 4th IEEE International Conference on Engineering Technologies and Applied Sciences (ICETAS). IEEE (2017)
5. Financial Regulators in India. https://dea.gov.in/business/financial-regulators. Accessed 29 Oct 2021
6. Dubey, R., Manna, A.: E-banking frauds and fraud risk management. Tactful Manag. Res. J. (2017)
7. Gupta, S., Abhishek, S., Akanksha, K.: A literature survey on social engineering attacks: phishing attack. In: International Conference on Computing, Communication and Automation (ICCCA). IEEE (2016)

8. Marotta, A., et al.: Cyber-insurance survey. Comput. Sci. Rev. **24**, 35–61 (2017)
9. Tripathi, A., Bhawana, P.: E-governance challenges and cloud benefits. In: IEEE International Conference on Computer Science and Automation Engineering, vol. 1. IEEE (2011)
10. Kim, J.: Cyber-security in government: reducing the risk. Comput. Fraud Secur. 8–11 (2017)
11. Egloff, F.J., Smeets, M.: Publicly attributing cyber attacks: a framework. J. Strateg. Stud. 1–32 (2021)
12. Broeders, D.: Private active cyber defense and (international) cyber security—pushing the line?. J. Cybersecurity **7**(1) (2021)
13. Tagarev, T.: Academic ICT research for defence and security. In: Atanassov, K.T. (ed.) Research in Computer Science in the Bulgarian Academy of Sciences. SCI, vol. 934, pp. 471–491. Springer, Cham (2021). https://doi.org/10.1007/978-3-030-72284-5_21
14. Katagiri, N.: Cyber countermeasures for democracies at war. In: Conduct of War in the 21st Century. Routledge, 116–127 (2021)
15. Venkatachary, S.K., Alagappan, A., Andrews, L.J.B.: Cybersecurity challenges in energy sector (virtual power plants) - can edge computing principles be applied to enhance security? Energy Inf. **4**(1), 1–21 (2021). https://doi.org/10.1186/s42162-021-00139-7
16. Le, T.D.: Smart grid cybersecurity experimentation: architecture and methodology. Inf. Sci. (2021)
17. Hossain, N., et al.: Cyber security risk assessment method for SCADA system. Inf. Secur. J. Glob. Perspect. 1–12 (2021)
18. Krause, T., et al.: Cybersecurity in power grids: challenges and opportunities. arXiv preprint https://doi.org/10.48550/arXiv.2105.00013 (2021)
19. Adel, A., Sarwar, D., Hosseinian-Far, A.: Transformation of cybersecurity posture in IT telecommunication: a case study of a telecom operator. In: Jahankhani, H., Jamal, A., Lawson, S. (eds.) Cybersecurity, Privacy and Freedom Protection in the Connected World. ASTSA, pp. 441–457. Springer, Cham (2021). https://doi.org/10.1007/978-3-030-68534-8_28
20. Welch, B.: Exploiting the weaknesses of SS7. Netw. Secur. 17–19 (2017)
21. Holtmanns, S., Oliver, I.: SMS and one-time-password interception in LTE networks. In: 2017 IEEE International Conference on Communications (ICC). IEEE (2017)
22. Dogaru, D.I., Dumitrache, I.: Cyber security in healthcare networks. In: E-Health and Bioengineering Conference (EHB). IEEE (2017)
23. Strielkina, A., et al.: Cybersecurity of healthcare IoT-based systems: regulation and case-oriented assessment. In: IEEE 9th International Conference on Dependable Systems, Services and Technologies (DESSERT). IEEE (2018)
24. Coventry, L., Branley, D.: Cybersecurity in healthcare: a narrative review of trends, threats and ways forward. Maturitas **113**, 48–52 (2018)
25. Mahler, T., et al.: Know your enemy: characteristics of cyber-attacks on medical imaging devices. arXiv preprint arXiv:1801.05583 (2018)
26. Ervural, B.C., Ervural, B.: Overview of cyber security in the industry 4.0 Era. In: Industry 4.0: managing the digital transformation. Springer, Cham, pp. 267–284 (2018).https://doi.org/10.1007/978-3-319-57870-5_16
27. Kour, R., et al.: eMaintenance in railways: issues and challenges in cybersecurity. Proc. Inst. Mech. Eng. Part F J. Rail Rapid Transit. **233**(10), 1012–1022 (2019)
28. Kertis, T., Prochazkova, D.: Cyber security of underground railway system operation. In: Smart City Symposium Prague (SCSP). IEEE (2017)
29. Yağdereli, E., Gemci, C., Aktaş, A.Z.: A study on cyber-security of autonomous and unmanned vehicles. J. Defense Model. Simul. **12**(4), 369–381 (2015)
30. Andreasson, K.J.: Cybersecurity: Public Sector Threats and Responses. Taylor & Francis (2011)
31. Cavelty, M.D.: Cyber-Security. The Routledge Handbook of New Security Studies. Routledge, 166–174 (2010)

32. Hovav, A., Gnizy, I., Han, J.: The effects of cyber regulations and security policies on organizational outcomes: a knowledge management perspective. Eur. J. Inf. Syst. 1–19 (2021)
33. ISO/IEC 27001:2013: Information technology—security techniques—information security management systems—requirements. https://www.iso.org/standard/54534.html. Accessed 29 Oct 2021
34. The suggested roles responsibilities of the Chief Information Security Officer (CISO) in critical IT infrastructure. https://nciipc.gov.in/documents/Roles_Responsibilities-CISO.pdf. Accessed 29 Oct 2021
35. Information Technology (Reasonable security practices and procedures and sensitive personal data or information) Rules (2011). https://www.meity.gov.in/writereaddata/files/GSR313E_1 0511%281%29_0.pdf. Accessed 29 Oct 2021
36. The National Institute of Standards and Technology. https://www.nist.gov. Accessed 29 Oct 2021

Short-Delay Multipath Errors in NavIC Signals for Stationary Receivers

Kartik Tiwari[1], A. Althaf[2], and Hari Hablani[2]([✉])

[1] Ashoka University, Delhi-NCR, India
kartik.tiwari_ug22@ashoka.edu.in
[2] Indian Institute of Technology, Indore, India
{phd1601121012,hbhablani}@iiti.ac.in

Abstract. This paper presents, in part, a tutorial overview of the code phase error and carrier phase error caused by a single reflected path and an iterative algorithm to determine the root of the well-known multipath-affected discriminator function. The algorithm is then applied to determine the code error and carrier phase error in GPS signals in a single reflected path environment, and is validated by comparing the results with the known results. The algorithm is further used to determine and illustrate single-path errors in NavIC (Navigation with Indian Constellation) signals for the first time in the literature. The NavIC errors differ significantly from the GPS errors because of the limited and slow traverses of the elevation and azimuth angles of the three geostationary and four geosynchronous NavIC satellites signals to a stationary receiver on the ground. NavIC multipath errors of a real receiver on the ground for both L5 and S1 frequencies are presented. The multipath errors of the two frequencies differ greatly because the S1 wavelength (0.12 m) is nearly half of the L5 wavelength (0.25 m) and, therefore, the S1 multipath error frequencies are nearly twice of the L5 multipath error frequencies. The real multipath errors differ from the ideal single-path ground reflection errors because, in reality, the diffractors may be multiple comprising both horizontal and vertical, and the reflections vary with time due to both elevation and azimuth of the satellite signals, causing substantial disorder in errors.

Keywords: NavIC · Multipath · Navigation · Signal

1 Introduction

It is possible for receivers to receive direct navigation signals from satellites affected by delayed, reflected signals. Such reflections can be caused by objects surrounding the receivers like high-rise buildings, satellite dishes on the terraces in urban settings, or ground diffractors. Multipath error can lead to loss of accuracy in the position, velocity and time estimates using the navigation satellites

This research was supported by Space Applications Center, Indian Space Research Organization as a part of NGP-17 project. *Manuscript presented at the 72nd International Astronautical Congress, Dubai, 2021-10-28. Copyright by IAF.*

© The Author(s), under exclusive license to Springer Nature Switzerland AG 2022
S. Joshi et al. (Eds.): SpacSec 2021, CCIS 1599, pp. 213–238, 2022.
https://doi.org/10.1007/978-3-031-15784-4_17

such as NavIC (Navigation with Indian Constellation). Multipath errors are well understood for the GPS signals. This document discusses our attempts to identify and understand multipath error for NavIC frequencies.

The paper is organized as follows. Sections 2–6 provide a tutorial on short-delay multipath errors. Section 2 illustrates the ideal, triangle autocorrelation function – a central element of the delay lock loop. Section 3 presents the formulation and illustration of maximum phase error and fading and enhancement of the direct signal caused by a single reflected signal. Section 4 outlines the early and late correlators and illustrates the ideal discriminator functions for wide and narrow correlators. Section 5 illustrates the distortion of the triangle autocorrelation function by a single reflected signal, which causes errors in determination of the root of the discriminator function. The nonlinear, coupled equations of the code phase errors and carrier phase errors caused by a single-path reflection and an iterative algorithm to solve them are presented in Sect. 6. The algorithm is applied to GPS signals in Sect. 7 and results are compared with the known code phase and carrier phase errors for validation of the software. The validated algorithm is applied to the NavIC signals of L5 and S1 frequency bands. Section 8 summarizes the equations of code phase multipath error envelopes and non-zero mean errors, and illustrates them for NavIC signals. Section 9 presents a case study of real multipath errors in the NavIC signals using an Accord receiver and an antenna. Relationships of the additional reflected path length with elevation and azimuth angles of the signal, and thus time, are summarized. Frequency bandwidth of the reflected signal and its influence on the accuracy specifications of Doppler shift is explored. Real multipath errors of NavIC signals and their relationship with the elevation and azimuth angles of the satellites are presented. Section 10 concludes the paper.

2   Code Auto-correlation - No Multipath Error

The receiver maintains an exact replica of the code that it receives from a particular navigation satellite signal and measures the relative time delay between the satellite code and the receiver replica. This delay is then used to calculate the receiver distance to that satellite. Once the distances to at least four such navigation satellites are known, the receiver proceeds to solve a set of four equations that yield the position of the receiver and its clock bias with the NavIC or GNSS system time reference. A principal element of this measurement process is the determination of correlation between the received signal and the receiver-generated signal, implemented in a delay lock loop (DLL) in the receiver.

2.1   Satellite Psuedorandom Code

The satellite code is a pseudo-random code of 1023 (equivalently, $2^{10} - 1$) chips repeating every millisecond. This implies that each chip pulse width is $(1/1023)$ ms $= 0.9775 \, \mu s \approx 1 \, \mu s$. The satellite code is multiplied with receiver's replica of the code and averaged as explained in [2]. At zero time delay estimation error ($\Delta\tau = 0$), the normalized value of the correlation is equal to 1. This value of 1, or the peak, is what the autocorrelation algorithm seeks.

EXAMPLE 1: Auto correlation Code [1]

Suppose the carrier code is $(+1, -1, -1, +1, -1)$ and the receiver's replica being correlated is $(+1, -1, +1, -1, -1)$. The product of each term then becomes $(+1, +1, -1, -1, +1)$. Taking the sum of all bits and dividing the sum by 5 gives us the value 0.2 instead of 1 which we would get if the two codes were the same. Therefore, the receiver replica code is not for this satellite and the receiver will look for a signal for which the correlation is 1.

2.2   Delay Lock Loop

As mentioned previously, at zero delay estimation error ($\Delta\tau = 0$), the normalized auto-correlation value becomes 1. For an uncorrupted signal, this is the highest possible value of the output of an auto-correlation function. A receiver, thus, tries to find this auto-correlation peak in order to measure the time delay. Delay Lock Loops are used for this process. *Misra and Enge* [2] in Chapter 10 describe a basic DLL as the following:

> ... the delay lock loop correlates the received Signal with a slightly early replica of the Signal and a slightly late replica of the signal. When locked to the received Signal, the early correlator samples the peak of the correlation function on the rising edge, and the late correlator samples the peak on the falling edge.

In the delay lock loop, a navigation signal affected by its reflected signal does not produce the expected ideal correlation triangle between a direct satellite signal and the receiver-generated pure pseudo-random code. The ideal correlation triangle is shown in Fig. 1 while perturbed correlation triangles will be shown in Sect. 5.

Because of perturbation in the correlation triangle, the discriminator function – the early correlator triangle minus the late correlator triangle – is distorted and its root does not yield the correct value of the signal arrival delay. The delay estimation error, in nanoseconds, thus caused by the reflected signal is the multipath error, and it is illustrated in Sect. 6 (also see [8]).

The algorithm and the software we developed is first validated by comparing our multipath error results for GPS with the results in the literature. The software then is used to generate the multipath error results for the NavIC signals.

2.3   Autocorrelation Function

Autocorrelation is a function of the unknown signal time delay τ. Denoting its estimate as τ^*, the residual estimation error is denoted $\Delta\tau$. So, the autocorrelation as a function of $\Delta\tau$ is [Chapter 9, 2]

$$R(\Delta\tau) = \begin{cases} \frac{\Delta\tau}{T_C} + 1 & \text{if } -T_C < \Delta\tau < 0 \\ 1 - \frac{\Delta\tau}{T_C} & \text{if } 0 < \Delta\tau < T_C \\ 0 & \text{otherwise} \end{cases} \tag{1}$$

where T_C (chip pulse width) is equal to 0.9775 μs. As demonstrated in Fig. 1, the autocorrelation function has a sharp and distinct peak when $\Delta\tau = 0$.

Since this paper deals exclusively with the multipath error, $\Delta\tau$ in this paper represents the delay of the multipath relative to the direct signal, denoted $\Delta\tau_M$ in *Misra-Enge* [2].

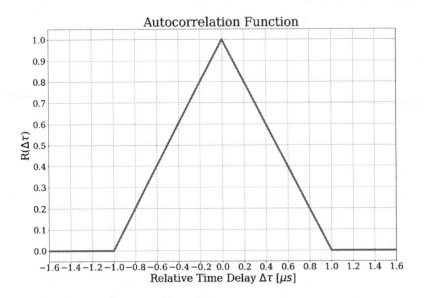

Fig. 1. Uncorrupted autocorrelation peak with its peak at $\Delta\tau = 0$

3   Phase and Amplitude Errors Caused by Single Reflected Signal

Suppose $\Delta\tau_M$ denotes the extra time a reflected signal takes to reach the receiver antenna relative to the direct signal from a satellite. The reflecting surface may be the ground supporting the antenna or may be a wall in the neighborhood, reflecting the navigation signal, and the reflected signal traverses an extra distance Δl relative to the direct signal. Clearly, $\Delta l = c\Delta\tau_M$, where c is the speed of light. Δl would depend on the direct signal elevation and azimuth angle of the reflector relative to the signal. See more about it in Sect. 8.

Doherty et al. [3] analyzed signal strength variation in the presence of reflected signals, determined the maximum perturbation in the phase of the signal before entering the receiver software and the code phase error caused by the reflected signal. Because of their fundamental importance, signal strength variation and phase perturbations are summarized below. Denote (see Fig. 2).

V_D = Directly received signal voltage
V_R = Reflected signal voltage
R = Resultant voltage
θ_m = Phase difference between directly received and reflected signal.

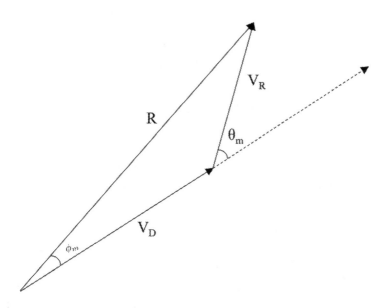

Fig. 2. An illustration of the vectorial addition of reflected signal and direct signal to form the resultant composite signal

As mentioned earlier, the resultant signal is a vector sum of the direct signal and reflected signal. This is illustrated in the Fig. 2. From Fig. 2, *Hofman-Wellenhof et al.* [10] show that the change in the phase angle of the direct carrier signal due to the reflected signal is

$$\tan \phi_m = \frac{(V_R/V_D)\sin\theta_m}{1 + (V_R/V_D)\cos\theta_m} \tag{2}$$

The zero-slope condition of $\tan \phi_m$ with respect to θ_m gives the following θ_m^* for maximum $\tan \phi_m$

$$\frac{d}{d\theta_m}\left[\frac{\sin\theta_m}{1 + (V_R/V_D)\cos\theta_m}\right] = 0 \tag{3}$$

$$\implies \theta_m^* = \cos^{-1}\left(-\frac{V_R}{V_D}\right)$$

Substituting $\cos \theta_m^*$ and the corresponding $\sin \theta_m^*$, the maximum perturbation in the carrier phase, denoted $\phi_{m_{max}}$, caused by the reflected signal reaching the antenna is found to be

$$\tan \phi_{m_{max}} = \frac{(V_R/V_D)}{\sqrt{1 - (V_R/V_D)^2}} \tag{4}$$

which, more simply, is

$$\phi_{m_{max}} = \sin^{-1}(V_R/V_D) \tag{5}$$

Direct signal is enhanced, or constructively interfered, when the reflected signal is in sync (in phase, θ_m in Fig. 2 equals zero) with the direct signal. The maximally enhanced signal, then, normalized with its direct value is, in dB,

$$E_m = 20 \log_{10}(V_D + V_R)/V_D$$
$$= 20 \log_{10}(1 + \sin \phi_{m_{max}})$$

(E for enhanced). Similarly, when the reflected signal and the direct signal are out of phase (θ_m in Fig. 2 equals 180°), the direct signal is destructively interfered and it experiences a fade. The maximally faded signal, normalized with V_D, is then, in dB

$$F_m = 20 \log_{10}(V_D - V_R)/V_D$$
$$= 20 \log_{10}(1 - \sin \phi_{m_{max}})$$

(F for faded). The total variation in signal is the sum of max fade and max enhancement. These relations are demonstrated in Fig. 3, following [3]. As in [3], Fig. 3 is used by picking a value of V_D/V_R in decibels from the x-axis and finding its corresponding value of $\phi_{m_{max}}$ on the y-axis. From there, look for the corresponding values of max fade, max enhancement and total variation in the signal strength, all on the x-axis for the $\phi_{m_{max}}$ specified.

4   Discriminator Function (Without Multipath Error)

A discriminator function is defined as the difference between early correlator and late correlator averages. The shape of the discriminator function is primarily influenced by the correlator spacing τ_d, written also as dT_C when normalized with the code chip width T_C. We shall later see how this correlator spacing mitigates the effect of the delayed reflected signal and curbs the multipath error.

The early (S_E) correlator and late (S_L) correlator samples in a discriminator function $D_c()$ are discussed in [2], Section 10.5, and are defined as

$$S_E(\Delta\tau) = \sqrt{C}R(\Delta\tau - \tau_d/2) \tag{6}$$

$$S_L(\Delta\tau) = \sqrt{C}R(\Delta\tau + \tau_d/2) \tag{7}$$

where C is the signal power, $\tau_d = T_C$ for wide correlators and $\tau_d < T_C$ for a narrow correlators and $R()$ is the autocorrelation function. The discriminator function $D_c()$ is defined as -

$$D_c(\Delta\tau) = S_E(\Delta\tau) - S_L(\Delta\tau) \tag{8}$$

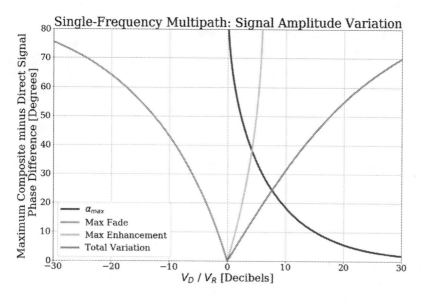

Fig. 3. Single frequency carrier phase error and signal amplitude effects due to multipath

EXAMPLE 2: $V_D/V_R = 20\text{dB}$

This is an extreme example of nearly no reflection since $V_D/V_R = 10^{20/20} = 10$,

$$V_R/V_D = 0.1 = \sin(\phi_{m_{max}}) \implies \phi_{m_{max}} = 5.74^\circ$$

The Max Fade F_m becomes

$$F_m = 20\log_{10}(1 - \sin\phi_{m_{max}}) = 20\log_{10}(1 - 0.1)$$
$$F_m = 20\log_{10}(0.9) = -0.92\text{dB}$$

The Max Enhancement E_m is

$$E_m = 20\log_{10}(1 + \sin\phi_{m_{max}}) = 20\log_{10}(1 + 0.1)$$
$$E_m = 20\log_{10}(1.1) = 0.83\text{dB}$$

E_m and F_m concur with Fig. 3. The signal strength varies from +0.27 dB to -0.28 dB, and the total variation is 1.75 dB.

It passes through the discriminator function passes through the origin where the delay estimation error $\Delta\tau$ is zero. These are shown in Fig. 4 for $\tau_d = T_C$, $0.5T_C$ and $0.1T_C$. As demonstrated in Fig. 4, in the absence of multipath, the function

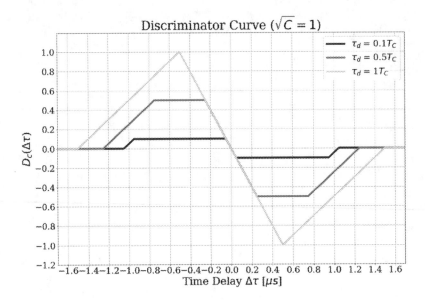

Fig. 4. Discriminator function curves for three different correlator spacing (τ_d = $0.1T_C, 0.5T_C, 1T_C$)

is zero at the origin, and its slope at the origin is independent of τ_d, though the apex of its triangle is truncated and its base shrinks progressively as τ_d lowers from $1T_C$ to $0.1T_C$. The results shown in Fig. 4 are of course not new. They are widely available in the literature, but they are shown here to lend confidence to the subsequent multipath errors for the NavIC frequencies.

5   Autocorrelation Function Perturbed by Multipath

When a direct signal is blended with a reflected signal, its triangle autocorrelation with the receiver-generated pure pseudo-random code is distorted, as explained in [2], Sec. 10.7. The reflected signal travels a greater distance and, hence, always arrives after the direct ray. However, it interacts constructively or destructively according to its relative phase with the direct signal, causing it to fade or enhance as illustrated earlier in Sect. 3. The relative phase angle of the reflected signal from the direct signal varies from 0 to 360°.

The reflected signal can cause the correlation peak to rise if it arrives in phase with the direct signal as demonstrated in Fig. 5 where the composite peak is slightly higher than the autocorrelation peak of the direct ray. Similarly, if the reflected signal arrives out of phase, the multipath signal interferes destructively with the direct ray and lowers the peak as demonstrated in Fig. 6. In Fig. 5 and 6, $\Delta\tau_M$ is the multipath delay relative to the direct signal, and α is the multipath ratio V_R/V_D.

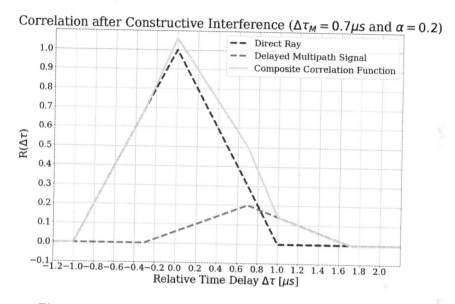

Fig. 5. Autocorrelation peak perturbed due to constructive interference

To calculate the delayed multipath autocorrelation function illustrated in Figs. 5 and 6, a function called $R_m()$ is defined that takes in a range of values for the delay estimation error $\Delta\tau$ (the same for direct ray and reflected ray), the time delay $\Delta\tau_M$ of the reflected signal relative to direct signal and multipath-to-signal amplitude ratio α. Using these parameters, and the autocorrelation function $R()$ defined by Eq. (1) previously, the autocorrelation function for reflected signal can be modelled as -

$$R_m(\Delta\tau) = \alpha R(\Delta\tau + \Delta\tau_M) \tag{9}$$

A threshold is defined for the multipath delay $\Delta\tau_M$ which distinguishes a short-delay multipath from a long-delay. Ref. [2] explains in Sec 10.7.1 that

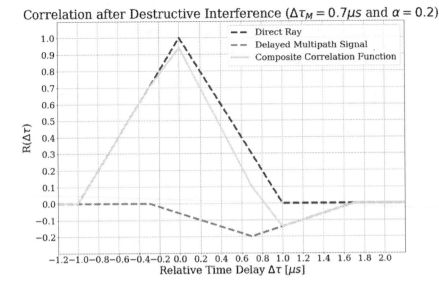

Fig. 6. Autocorrelation peak perturbed due to destructive interference

'No errors exist when the rising edge of the delayed peak does not touch the late correlator sample'. Mathematically, the condition of long-delay multipath is expressed by the inequality

$$\Delta\tau_M \geq T_C + \frac{\tau_d}{2} \tag{10}$$

where recall that τ_d is the correlator spacing, equal to dT_C. A long delay multipath is demonstrated in Fig. 7 for $\Delta\tau_M = 1.6\,\mu s$ and $\tau_d = T_C$ or $d = 1$ and $T_C = 1\,\mu s$. In such cases, there is no effect of multipath on null tracking.

6   Multipath-Affected Discriminator Function

Since discriminator function is dependant on the autocorrelation function and - as we just observed - autocorrelation function gets perturbed by multipath, the discriminator function also gets affected by the presence of multipath. This is made clear by Fig. 8 which demonstrates how the discriminator function for same input parameters can differ when the multipath-to-signal ratio α becomes non-zero.

Braasch and Graass [4] developed a model of a discriminator function $D_c()$ affected by a single reflected signal. It is defined using the following two nonlinear equations -

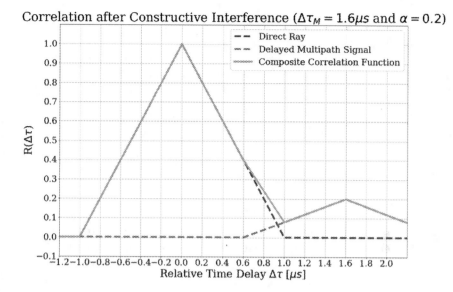

Fig. 7. Composite autocorrelation peak unchanged by a long-delay multipath (for wide correlator)

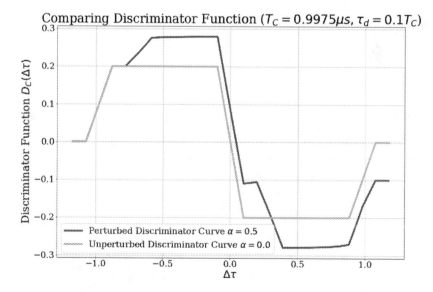

Fig. 8. Perturbation of the discriminator function and the resulting pseudorange error caused by a multipath using a narrow correlator

Discriminator Function:

$$D_c(\tau) = [R(\tau + \tau_d) - R(\tau - \tau_d)]\cos\phi_m +$$
$$\alpha[R(\tau + \tau_d - \Delta\tau_M) - (\tau - \tau_d - \Delta\tau_M)]\cos(\theta_m - \phi_m) \qquad = 0 \qquad (11)$$

where the multipath-caused carrier phase tracking error (same as the one calculated by Eq. (2) using a different approach) is defined as

$$\phi_m(\tau) = \tan^{-1}\left(\frac{\alpha R(\tau - \Delta\tau_M)\sin\theta_m}{R(\tau) + \alpha R(\tau - \Delta\tau_M)\cos\theta_m}\right) \qquad (12)$$

and relative phase of the multipath signal, θ_m, is related to the signal frequency and $\Delta\tau_M$ thus:

$$\theta_m = 2\pi\Delta\tau_M f \qquad (13)$$

An algorithm was developed to solve (11) and (12) to determine the code delay estimation error τ (the same as $\Delta\tau$ used earlier) for a reflected signal time delay $\Delta\tau_M$ relative to the direct signal and the corresponding phase delay θ_m of the multipath relative to the direct signal. Henceforth, the solution to (11) and (12) i.e. the value of τ satisfying $D_c(\tau) = 0$ for ϕ_m defined by (12) would be referred to as τ^*.

Our objective is to solve the two non-linear functional Eqs. (11) and (12) for τ and ϕ_m at a given multipath delay $\Delta\tau_M$ and the phase θ_m. We do this iteratively in an algorithm as explained below.

1. Assign $\Delta\tau_M$ the first value from a specified range $[\Delta\tau_M]$. $\Delta\tau_M$ is the additional traversal time of the reflected signal to arrive at the receiver antenna relative to the direct signal.
2. Compute the corresponding $\theta_m(\Delta\tau_M)$ with Eq. (13).
3. Assign τ the first value from a specified range $[\tau]$ (in our case $[\tau] = [-0.1T_C, 0.1T_C]$).
4. Using τ and $\theta_m(\Delta\tau_M)$, compute $\phi_m(\tau)$.
5. Plug in the calculated value of $\phi_m(\tau)$ in the expression for $D_c(\tau)$ and evaluate the complete expression.
6. Check if $D_c(\tau) = 0$ (or its approximation to the desired limit of zero).
7. If **YES** then:
   (a) Store the value of τ (call this τ^*) and $\phi_m(\tau^*)$ for the corresponding $\Delta\tau_M$ in the memory.
   (b) Assign $\Delta\tau_M$ the next value in the range $[\Delta\tau_M]$.
   (c) Move to Step 2 and repeat for all values in $[\Delta\tau_M]$.
   (d) Thus repeat for all values in $[\Delta\tau_M]$
8. If **NO** then:
   (a) Assign τ the next value from the range $[\tau]$.
   (b) Mov e to Step 4 and repeat.

By the time the algorithm has iterated through all values of $\Delta\tau_M$, it should have a range of corresponding code tracking error τ^* and carrier tracking error $\phi_m(\tau^*)$ stored in the memory.

7   Single-Reflection Errors of GPS and NavIC Signals: Illustrations

7.1   GPS Signal L1 Results for Validation

The above algorithm generated Fig. 9 for the GPS L1 frequency $f = 1575.42$ MHz with a narrow correlator spacing $\tau_d = 0.1T_C$, and the multipath ratio $\alpha = 0.6$. The upper and lower bounds in red in Fig. 9 correspond to maximum and minimum code tracking error. This envelope is discussed in greater detail in Sect. 8. In Fig. 9 we observe that the negative peaks of the code error are even greater in magnitude than the multipath delays that cause them. Also, as is well known, the errors are non-sinusoidal with a growing negative bias. These results agree with those in [4].

To compare our results with *Brodin* [5], the code tracking error τ^* nanoseconds needed to be converted to degrees. This is done as follows. A code chip pulse width is $T_C = 0.9775\,\mu s$ and it is equivalent to one wavelength i.e. $360°$. Hence, the wavelength of each chip is

$$\lambda_{code} = c \times T_C = 299.79246\,\text{m}/\mu s \times 0.9775\,\mu s = 293.05\,\text{m}$$

Therefore, the code wave is $360°/293.05\,\text{m} = 1.23$ degrees per meter. Further, the initial multipath delay $\Delta\tau_M$ relative to the direct signal was 300 ns i.e. 89.91 m or ~90 m. Over a multipath phase change of $360°$, the multipath delay changes by c/f where f is frequency of the signal. In the case of GPS L1 signal, a phase change of $360°$ corresponds to 0.19 m. Since, $0.19\,\text{m} \ll 89.91\,\text{m}$, the multipath delay is assumed to be constant and the relative phase is varied independently in Fig. 10. The range for code tracking error ($\pm 12°$) in our calculations differ from the calculations presented in *Brodin* [5] ($\pm 9°$). This is likely due to a mismatch in one of the constant parameters that is used in the calculation.

The results in Fig. 10, unlike those in Fig. 9, are symmetric about the x-axis because these are for $\tau_d = 0.1T_C$, $\alpha = 0.5$, and the initial multipath delay $\Delta\tau_M = 300$ ns. The code delay estimation error plateaus at the multipath delay [4] (as explained further in Sect. 8)

$$\Delta\tau_{M plateau} = (1 + \alpha)\tau_d$$

For the parameters just stated, $\Delta\tau_{M plateau} = 75$ ns, whereas the results in Fig. 10 are for $\Delta\tau_M = 300$ ns. For these parameters, the code delay estimation error oscillates between its equal positive and negative limits, though the error is positive for a longer part of the period than it is negative in one multipath phase cycle.

7.2   Multipath Errors for NavIC Signal

The above algorithm was applied to NavIC signals, and the results are shown in Figs. 11, 12 and 13. The central frequency of NavIC L5 band is $f_{L5} = 1176.45$ MHz and for S-band is $f_S = 2492.02$ MHz. The corresponding wavelengths are

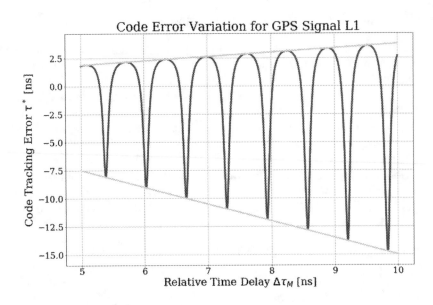

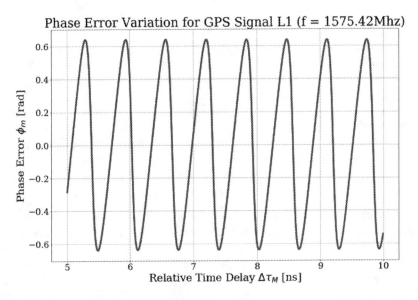

Fig. 9. Code error and phase error oscillations in GPS Signal L1 versus reflected wave time delay for the multipath amplitude ratio of 0.6

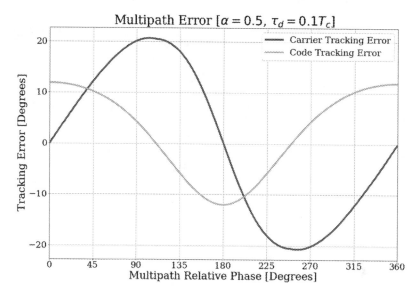

Fig. 10. Code and Carrier Error variation across one period of multipath relative phase (initial $\Delta\tau_M = 300$ ns)

0.255 m and 0.120 m, respectively. Because the wavelength of NavIC L5 (0.255 m) is longer than that of the GPS L1 (0.19 m), the multipath oscillations periods are longer and the oscillations are slower in Fig. 11 than those for GPS in Fig. 9. On the other hand, since the S-band wavelength 0.12 m is nearly half of the L5 wavelength, the multipath oscillations for the S-band in Fig. 13 are twice as many as that for the L5 signals in Fig. 11. We also see that the negative peaks of the code errors are greater in magnitude than the positive peaks, as is typical with the multipath errors, and the envelopes cradle the errors as expected. The code delay estimation errors in nanoseconds in the above figures is converted to meters easily by recalling that 1 ns = 0.3 m.

8   Multipath Error Envelopes

As mentioned earlier, the multipath error oscillates between a positive limit and negative limit as the phase of the reflected signal varies relative to the direct signal with the continuous change in the satellite elevation angle. *van Nee* presented these upper and lower bounds – the multipath error envelopes – in [12], and they are illustrated here to gain familiarity with them and then to draw them for the NavIC multipath errors in Figs. 11, 12 and 13. The upper bound of the envelope is caused by the constructive interference and the lower bound by the destructive interference. These two bounds constitute the multipath error envelopes (Fig. 14).

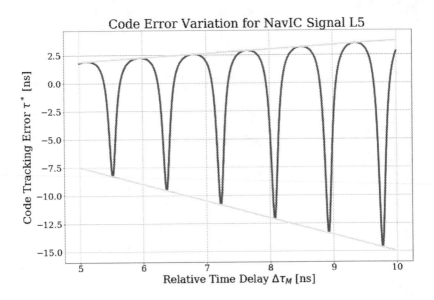

Fig. 11. Code error oscillations for NavIC L5 frequency

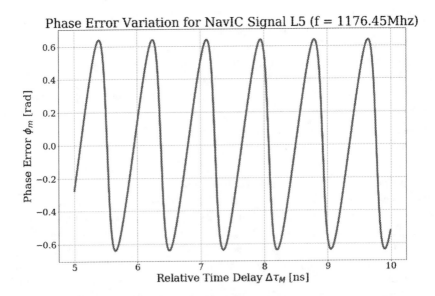

Fig. 12. Phase error oscillations for NavIC L5 frequency

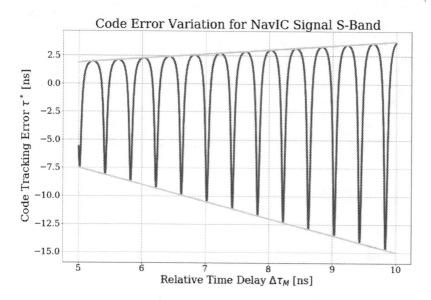

Fig. 13. Code error oscillations for NavIC S-Band frequency

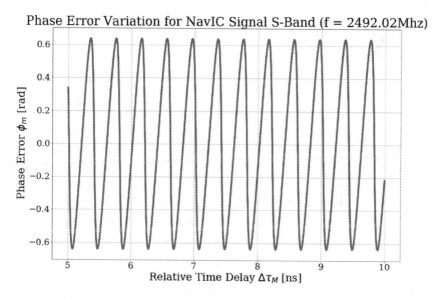

Fig. 14. Phase error oscillations for NavIC S-Band frequency

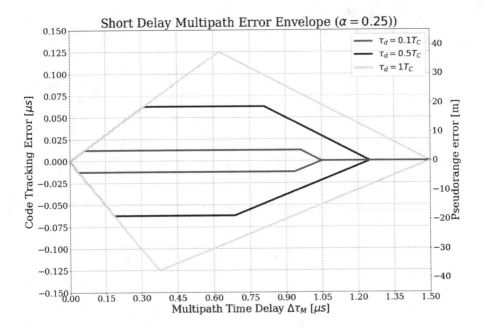

Fig. 15. Multipath error envelopes for three different correlator spacing ($\tau_d = 0.1T_C, 0.5T_C, 1T_C$)

To calculate the upper bound of the code multipath error, τ_{max}^*, two constants are defined [12]:

$$a = \tau_d \left(\frac{1 + \alpha}{2} \right)$$

$$b = T_C - \tau_d \left(\frac{1 - \alpha}{2} \right)$$

These constants parametrize the piece-wise function for the multipath error envelope -

$$\tau_{max}^* = \begin{cases} \frac{\alpha \Delta \tau_M}{1+\alpha} & \text{if } 0 \leq \Delta \tau_M < a \\ \frac{\alpha \tau_d}{2} & \text{if } a \leq \Delta \tau_M \leq b \\ \frac{\alpha}{2-\alpha}(T_c + \tau_d/2 - \Delta \tau_M) & \text{if } b < \Delta \tau_M \leq T_c + \tau_d/2 \\ 0 & \text{if } \Delta \tau_M > T_c + \tau_d/2 \end{cases} \quad (14)$$

To calculate the lower bound τ_{min}^* caused by the destructive interference, all instances of α in (14) are replaced by $-\alpha$. Plotting the two bounds together gives us Fig. 15 where the code delay estimation error is presented in both microseconds and distance (1 ns $\approx$ 0.3 m). These results are indeed the same as in Fig. 10.23 [2], where the multipath amplitude is 12 dB ($10^{-12/20} = 0.25 = \alpha$) below the amplitude of the direct ray. The effect of τ_d in Fig. 15 is discussed next.

8.1 Effect of Correlator Spacing

Figure 15 shows that a narrower correlator spacing (1 T_C to 0.5 T_C to 0.1 T_C) de-escalates the code delay estimation error envelope. The error envelope is not symmetric about the x-axis as we saw earlier in Figs. 9, 11 and 13 and now in Fig. 15. Even though the positive and negative limits are numerically equal, the negative error reaches its limit faster than the positive error, thus causing asymmetric oscillatory errors with a time varying bias. Ref. [12] shows that for $\tau_d < T_C$, when the multipath delay exceeds $(1+\alpha)\tau_d/2$, the code delay estimation error reaches its limits on both sides positive and negative. Additional features of the envelope seen in Fig. 15 are well known, so they are not discussed further.

8.2 Effect of Multipath-to-Signal Amplitude Ratio

Surfaces with poor reflective qualities attenuate the incident signals, and result in a low value of multipath-to-direct amplitude ratio α. This ratio depends also on the multipath rejection properties of the receiver antenna. The effect of multipath-to-direct amplitude ratio on the code delay estimation error is portrayed in Fig. 16 for $\tau_d = T_C$. The lower is the reflection coefficient, α, the lesser is the multipath-caused code delay error, as we see the shrinking envelopes in Fig. 16 with the reduction in α. In case of no reflections, $\alpha = 0$.

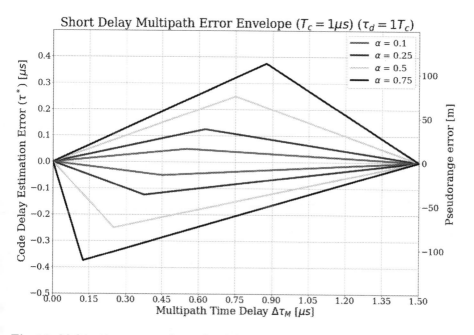

Fig. 16. Multipath error envelopes for different multipath-to-direct amplitude ratio ($\alpha = 0.1, 0.25, 0.5, 0.75$)

8.3   Mean Error

As evident from the envelopes in Figs. 15 and 16 and also from Figs. 10, 11, 12 and 13, even though the positive and negative plateaus of the envelope are quantitatively equal, the signals take different durations of multipath delays to reach those plateaus. Hence the error envelopes are asymmetric about the x-axis. This means that the multipath-caused mean error vs. $\Delta\tau_M$ is nonzero. *Breivik et al.* [7] discuss this non-zero bias error for a correlator-spacing $\tau_d = T_C$. For a given path difference $\Delta l = c\Delta\tau_M$ between a direct signal and its reflected signal, the bias ϵ_M (in meters) is

$$\epsilon_M = -c\Delta\tau_M \left(\frac{\alpha^2}{1 - \alpha^2} \right) \tag{15}$$

for

$$\Delta\tau_M \leq \frac{1 - \alpha}{2}\tau_d$$

Figure 17 depicts a magnified initial region of the short-delay multipath error in Fig. 16 and the code delay estimation error bias for the multipath ratios $= 0.1$ and 0.25. The results show that the bias increases with α and the additional distance a reflected signal traverses.

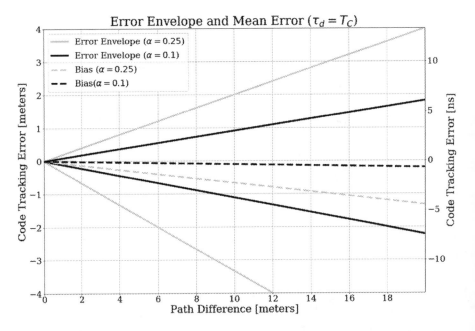

Fig. 17. Multipath error envelopes and the associated bias for different multipath-to-signal amplitude ratios ($\alpha = 0.2, 0.5$)

9   NavIC Multipath Errors of a Stationary Receiver - A Case Study

In the preceding sections, we have explored the relationship between the extra time $\Delta\tau_M$ the reflected signal takes to reach the antenna relative to the direct signal, and the code phase and carrier phase errors, but we have not shown what determines $\Delta\tau_M$. Indeed, if $\Delta\tau_M$ is fixed, then the code and carrier phase errors will be constant. So we will now investigate the dependence of $\Delta\tau_M$ on the physical time t and the types of the reflectors.

Hofman-Wellenhof et al. [10] show that the extra path length of a signal from a satellite at an elevation angle el, reflected from the ground and reaching the receiver antenna at a height h in the extra time $\Delta\tau_M$ relative to the direct signal is

$$\Delta l(t) = c\Delta\tau_M = 2h \sin el(t) \tag{16}$$

For a vertical reflector at a normal distance h from the antenna, with the normal at an azimuth angle az relative to the satellite signal, the reflected signal travels the extra length [3]

$$\Delta l(t) = 2h \cos el \cos az \tag{17}$$

In both cases the corresponding phase angle θ_m of the reflected signal relative to the direct signal, used in the preceding sections, at the antenna will be

$$\theta_m = 2\pi f \Delta\tau_M - \phi_R = 2\pi f(\Delta l/c) - \phi_R \tag{18}$$

where ϕ_R is the change in the phase angle (180°) due to the reflection. The above variables ($\Delta\tau_M, \Delta l$ and θ_m) vary with time as elevation and azimuth angles of the satellite signals change. These variations in the case of the 24-h NavIC satellites for an Accord receiver [11] are illustrated in a sky plot Fig. 18 at IIT Gandhinagar and in Fig. 19 as a function of time over 24 hrs from 5:00 AM to the next day 5:00 AM at IIT Indore. The azimuth and elevation angles vary greatly but slowly for the geosynchronous satellites in the inclined orbits (GSO) and much less for the essentially equatorial geostationary orbits (GEO). Also, for the GSO satellites the range of variation of azimuth is greater than that of the elevation angles. The significance of this will become apparent below.

9.1   Frequency Bandwidth of the Reflected Signals

As the elevation and azimuth angles of the satellite signals change, the extra length of a single reflected signal changes. For a horizontal reflector, the rate of change is

$$\dot{\Delta l} = 2h \cos(el)\dot{el} \tag{19}$$

and for a vertical reflector the rate is

$$\dot{\Delta l} = -2h[\cos(el)\sin(az)\dot{az} + \cos(az)\sin(el)\dot{el}] \tag{20}$$

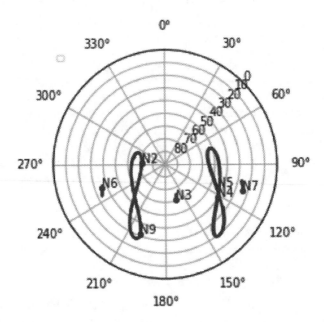

Fig. 18. Variations in the case of the 24-h NavIC satellites for Accord receiver at IIT Gandhinagar as a sky plot

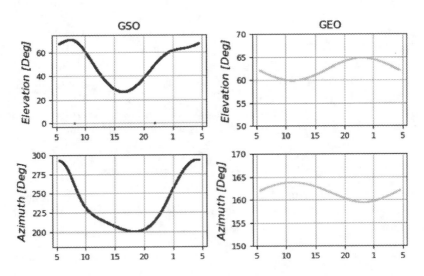

Fig. 19. Variations in the case of the 24-h NavIC satellites for Accord receivers at IIT Indore as a function of time

and the corresponding rate of change of the relative multipath phase angle is

$$\dot{\theta}_m = 2\pi f_M = 2\pi \frac{\dot{\Delta l}}{\lambda} \tag{21}$$

as shown in [16] for horizontal reflectors.

van Nee [6,12] calls f_M the fading bandwidth and called to attention the receiver position uncertainty caused by the multipath error and therefore its potential influence on the search of the correct frequency bin in the delay lock loop for signal acquisition.

9.2 Accord Receiver Doppler Shift Accuracy Specification

As van Nee [6,12] noted, Smith and Graves [13] determined that for the 12-h GPS satellites a 1m receiver position error could cause a 1 mHz Doppler frequency error if the earth's rotation rate is ignored and 1.38 mHz if it is not. For the 24-h NavIC satellites, Althaf et al. [14] showed that for an antenna of 2m height a ground reflection of a NavIC GSO satellite signal causes a Doppler shift of 0 to ± 1.6 mHz, so the shortest period of the Doppler shift is 625 s, or $\sim$10 min. The equations of f_M shown above reveal that a vertical reflector will cause greater Doppler shift than a horizontal reflector because both azimuth and elevation angles vary for a vertical reflector whereas only elevation angle varies for a horizontal reflector. The related numerical results for a vertical reflector are not available, but the f_M of the NavIC signals may rise up to no more than 10 mHz (0.01 Hz) and the shortest period would be $\sim$100 s.

The Accord receiver antenna's multipath rejection ratio, though not known, is discussed in [9] and is expected to be between 10 dB (3.2) to 34 dB (50.1). Also, the Accord receiver's velocity accuracy is specified to be 0.2 m/s (1σ), which is equal to 0.8 Hz (1σ) for L5 signal (wavelength 0.255 m) and 1.67 Hz (1σ) for the S signal (wavelength 0.12 m). Assuming that an average PDOP (position dilution of precision) of the NavIC signals is 4, the expected frequency error jitter in the range rate observables for L5 would be 0.8 Hz/PDOP = 0.2 Hz (1σ) and similarly for the S signal, 0.4 Hz (1σ). So, we anticipate that the RSS of the frequency jitter caused by thermal noise and multipath error will be less than these specifications. A related illustration is shown below.

9.3 Real Multipath Errors in NavIC Signals: Illustration

An example of the receiver multipath error and the corresponding profiles of the elevation angles versus local time from 9:30 PM to 5:30 AM for 8 h are shown in Fig. 20 for six NavIC satellites for L5 frequency in the left column and S frequency in the right column. These errors are real, obtained from the dual-frequency code phase and carrier phase observables using the well-known formula with twice the iono delay term removed [14] but the ambiguity and noise not removed. Also, the receiver antenna is in the Workshop Building with several potential reflectors in the surroundings, and therefore the reflected signals may have a general Rayleigh distribution.

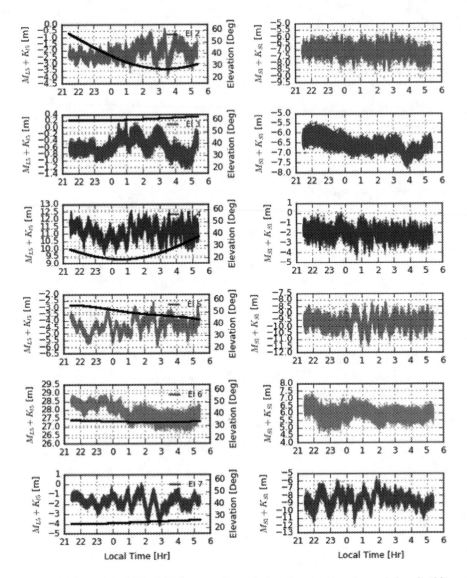

Fig. 20. Multipath in L5 and S1 frequencies and elevation vs. time in workshop building – March 12, 2021

As commented above, the multipath error frequencies vary in Fig. 20 during the eight hours shown since the six signal elevation angles and azimuth angles vary as typified in Figs. 18 and 19 for a GEO satellite and a GSO satellite. Because the satellites are spread out in the constellation, the six elevation and azimuth angle profiles and their rates are varied and the slow frequencies and the fast frequencies are randomly scattered in time. Since the S wavelength (0.12 m) is nearly half of the L5 wavelength (0.255 m), the S-multipath frequencies are twice the L5 multipath frequencies, as we observe in the left and right columns of Fig. 20.

The left column results in Fig. 20 is for the L5 frequency and the right column is for the S frequency. In the left top plot, the low-frequency (not the noise) oscillations are the slowest, with a period of ~40 min, and the trough-to-peak ~4 m when the elevation angle is near its minimum value, ~27°, and its rate of change is slow – zero or nearly zero, because then the multipath oscillation frequency f_M is ~0. As the elevation angle increases to ~60°, the oscillations speed up and amplitudes lower down.

In the left top-fourth plot in Fig. 20, when the elevation angle approaches its peak, 55° and its slope nears zero, the oscillations slow down, with a period of ~1 h and trough-to-peak ~2 m. In the left top-fifth plot for a GEO satellite, the elevation angle changes little, so the elevation rate is nearly zero, and therefore the multipath error is highly noisy with smaller amplitudes and slow oscillations, ~1 m, with a drifting bias as expected.

As stated above, the S1 frequency multipath errors in the right column are twice as fast as the L5 multipath error in the left column. The trough-to-peak amplitudes in both frequencies are about the same for all satellites except for the last one in the left-bottom plot where the trough-to-peak amplitude is ~6 m.

Figure 20 is not over a 12-h period, so complete ranges of the elevation angles of the satellites are not covered, and therefore we do not have a full spectrum of the multipath errors in these plots. Also, as shown in the analysis, the multipath error depends also on the relative azimuth angle of the reflector and its rate, but the azimuth angles are not shown here, so our comments here are not complete.

The multipath errors are mixed with the receiver noise and fixed ambiguities, and they need to be separated using the receiver delay lock loop, phase lock loop and frequency lock loop parameters and performance characteristics, as Braasch has demonstrated in [15].

The accuracy of the Accord receiver position estimate is stated to be 10 m (1 σ) without SBAS [Space-Based Augmentation System] and 6 m (1 σ) with SBAS [12]. A SBAS provides corrections for the navigation satellites position errors, satellite clock errors and ionospheric delays. The NavIC signals provide these corrections, similar to the GAGAN system for civil aviation services. With typical multipath error illustrated in Fig. 20, the receiver's position estimation accuracies are shown in [9] and the Accord receiver meets its specifications well.

10 Conclusion

The paper presents an overview of the code phase and career phase errors caused by a single reflected path, and illustrates them for the first time for NavIC signals in both frequencies L5 and S1. Real multipath errors are also illustrated for a NavIC receiver site at IIT Indore campus for both signal frequencies L5 and S1, and the causes of their substantial differences are identified. If no special efforts are made in the receiver or its antenna design and in the antenna's installation at any ground location, short-delay multipath errors of several meters are inevitable. Since these errors are non-sinusoidal, oscillatory with nonzero mean and long periods, they hinder accurate estimation of carrier phase ambiguities and thus high-accuracy positioning. Further, unlike other errors, multipath errors compound with between-receiver differencing and between-satellite differencing, so they preclude high-accuracy relative navigation for a stationary baseline as well. For this reason, several investigators have attempted in the past to estimate the multipath errors using their relationship with the C/N0 of the signal and compensate for them. However, Bilich et al. [16] have expressed their concerns over the extraordinary effort required for this estimation and yet relatively small returns in their mitigation. For this reason, it seems more cost-effective to use instead high-accuracy receivers with choke ring antennas for essentially a complete removal of the multipath error.

Acknowledgment. We are grateful to Space Application Centre, Indian Space Research Organisation for supporting this study as part of the NGP-17 project.

References

1. Blewitt, G.: Basics of GPS technique: observation equations. Geodetic Appl. GPS (1997)
2. Misra, P., Enge, P.: Global Positioning System: Signals, Measurements and Performance (1997)
3. Doherty, P.H., Bishop, G.J., Klobuchar, J.A.: Multipath effects on the determination of absolute ionospheric time delay from GPS. Radio Science
4. Braasch, M.S., van Graas, F.: Mitigation of Multipath in DGPS Ground Reference Stations (1992)
5. Brodin, G.: GNSS Code and Carrier Tracking in the Presence of Multipath (1996)
6. van Nee, R.D.J.: GPS Multipath and Satellite Interference (1992)
7. Breivik, K., Enge, P., Forssell, B., Kee, C., Walter, T.: Detection and Estimation of Multipath Error in GPS Pseudorange Measurements Using Signal-to-Noise Ratio in a Stationary Single-frequency Receiver (1996)
8. Parkinson, B.W., Spilker, J.J., Jr. (eds.): Global Positioning System: Theory and Applications, vol. 1, chapter 14. Multipath Effects, pp. 547–568
9. Althaf, A., Hablani, H.: NavIC signals multipath analysis, estimation and mitigation for high-accuracy positioning. ION ITM GNSS 2878–2895 (2020)
10. Hofmann-Wellenhof, B., Lichtenegger, H., Wasle, E.: GNSS - Global Navigation Satellite Systems. Springer, Heidelberg (2008)
11. IRNSS-GPS-GLONASS-GAGAN Receiver Brochure, Accord Software & Systems Private Ltd., Rev. 1.1, January 2016
12. van Nee, R.D.J.: Multipath effects on GPS code phase measurements. ION GPS 915–924 (1991)
13. Smith, C.A., Graves, K.W.: Sensitivity of GPS acquisition to initial data uncertainties. Navigation: J. ION **31**, 220–232 (1984)
14. Althaf, A., Hablani, H.: Assessment of errors in NavIC observables for stationary receivers. Navigation: J. ION 347–364 (2020)
15. Braasch, M.S.: Isolation of GPS multipath and receiver tracking errors. ION NTM 511–521 (1994)
16. Bilich, A., Larson, K.M., Axelrad, P.: Modeling GPS phase multipath with SNR: case study from the Salar de Uyuni, Boliva. J. Geophys. Res. **113**, B04401 (2008)

Point Clouds Object Classification Using Part-Based Capsule Network

Jonathan Then Sien Phang$^{(\boxtimes)}$ (iD) and King Hann Lim (iD)

Curtin University Malaysia, CDT 250, 98009 Miri, Sarawak, Malaysia
`jonathanpts@postgrad.curtin.edu.my`

Abstract. Point cloud object classification task has become trending due to crucial applications of depth sensors in fields such as autonomous robotic navigation and semantic environment learning. With recent advancement in machine learning algorithms, more research efforts have been invested in achieving efficient and feasible depth information processing. In this paper, a novel part-to-whole capsule network is proposed to learn point cloud objects through parts feature reasoning. To efficiently obtain the part features, the local parts are segmented using a neural likelihood estimator network and encoded into part capsules. Through dynamic routing algorithm, the network learns to determine the existence of an object class via parts voting. A reconstruction loss is incorporated to the proposed network to further enhance the learnt object class feature. Lastly, the proposed network is evaluated using classification rate and compared to several pioneering existing works.

Keywords: Point clouds · Object classification · Capsule neural network · Neural Likelihood Estimation

1 Introduction

Three dimensional (3D) object recognition is crucial in the recent advancement of autonomous robotic applications [1] and semantic environment learning from depth sensors [2,3]. The use of artificial neural networks (ANN) to learn semantic 3D learning such as object detection, object classification, and 3D mapping are benefited from data-driven learning on depth perception from real-world environment. Several popular 3D data representation are depth-map (RGB-D) and point clouds [4], where RGB-D is a data format of a RGB image coupled with a depth-map and point cloud is a sparse data point sampled from an object surface [5]. Comparatively, representation of 3D object in point cloud could preserve richer spatial and geometric information than RGB-D due to its sparsity and non-grid structure. However, the process of dealing with point clouds efficiently possesses a set of challenges, such as points permutation invariant and sparsity of data points [6]. In general, three learning models are used to learn and encode 3D point clouds for classification, i.e. point-based model, graph-based model, and capsule-based model.

© The Author(s), under exclusive license to Springer Nature Switzerland AG 2022
S. Joshi et al. (Eds.): SpacSec 2021, CCIS 1599, pp. 239–247, 2022.
https://doi.org/10.1007/978-3-031-15784-4_18

Point-based models [7, 8] are the early works that implemented deep learning network for efficient point clouds learning. PointNet [6] is one of the pioneering work that devised a shared MLP-based network to directly process raw input point clouds. The network is modeled based on Hausdorff distance and universal approximation theorem. In addition, with implementation of max pooling in PointNet, the network is permutation invariance toward input point clouds. In its incremental work, PointNet++ [9] implemented recursive PointNet to achieve local feature grouping using farthest point sampling as guidance. In converse to PointNet, where it only encode global features, PointNet++ aggregate the local features relative to the encoded global features. Therefore, PointNet++ is able to learn better than PointNet.

As point-based models are more emphasized on point-wise learning and extra steps are required to aggregate the local features, graph-based models [10–12] learn the set of point clouds by drawing a directed graph of each point, i.e. vertices and edges. Benefited from directed graph, such model is able to aggregate local information directly in a sparse data environment. In addition, by aggregating hierarchical of directed graphs, a coarse graph can be produced to group the local features as a global feature. In one of the early graph-based model, Valsesia et al. [10] proposed a graph neural network to synthesize object shapes. An adjacency matrix is calculated by using the directed graph features of each vertex in each graph convolution layer. Despite its superior results, the calculation of the adjacency matrix requires quadratic computation complexity and consumes a lot of memory. In DGCNN [13], a graph is dynamically constructed on each local point cloud and projected into high dimensional feature space for network learning. Multiple variants of DGCNN [14–16] are devised to improve its performance while reducing the model size.

Distinct from the existing works that learn by extracting most significant features and aggregate them from local to global level, capsule network is proposed to enforce part-to-whole learning of an object. For an instance, capsule network in [17] implemented equally strided convolution layers to extract local part features of an object in 2D images. Following that, Dynamic Routing algorithm as a soft clustering algorithm is devised to cluster the extracted part features into an object capsules, where each object capsule contains object specific features. The latter, Hinton et al. [18] proposed Expectation-Maximization (EM) routing algorithm to enhance the soft clustering step. Despite initial implementations of capsule network are on 2D images, Zhao et al. [19] proposed a capsule network to learn point cloud objects. The method implemented replicas capsule encoders and Dynamic Routing algorithm to obtain latent capsules that represents the point cloud object. While other capsule networks [20, 21] incorporated pose estimation in the model to achieve pose equivariance during inference, which can generalize to novel viewpoints on input point clouds.

Inspired by part-to-whole relationship learning in capsule networks [17, 19–21], a capsule network is proposed for part-based point clouds learning. To motivate and demonstrate the benefit from enforced part-to-whole learning of a capsule network, the proposed network utilizes segmented parts from input point clouds for parts reasoning to learn point cloud object. Intuitively, the parts reasoning is essentially driven by the Dynamic Routing algorithm that allow voting on existence of point cloud object by parts. This is mainly achieved by searching for maximum response of a part feature corresponding to a object class capsule using operation such as dot product. Next, in order to consistently segments parts from input point clouds, a Neural Likelihood Estimation (NLE) [22] is implemented to estimate the likelihood parameters of input point clouds and local parts of input point clouds are segmented using the estimated likelihood parameters. Each segmented parts are encoded using a graph-based encoder into part capsules. Subsequently, a capsule network is implemented to learn object by agreement on object via parts voting. A reconstruction loss is incorporated to regularize the learnt class capsule features. In the experiment, the proposed network is evaluated using classification rate and compared to several pioneering existing works.

2   Part-Based Capsule Network

The proposed network shown in Fig. 1 comprises two stages (a) Parts segmentation for part segments identification from the input point cloud using a NLE network, and (b) Part-to-whole relationship learning using capsule network with Dynamic Routing algorithm.

2.1   Parts Segmentation

In contrary to 2D images where each pixel is ordered in grid space, a point cloud $S_1 = \{x_n \in \mathbb{R}^3\}_{n=1}^N$, with N number of points, is commonly presented in sparse

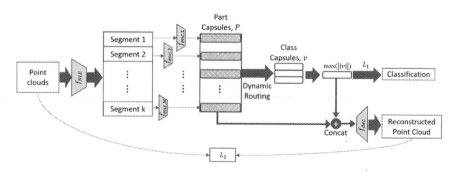

Fig. 1. A point clouds objects classification model is proposed using neural likelihood estimation (NLE) network and a standard capsule network. Local parts are segmented from input point cloud based on estimated likelihood parameters from NLE network. The segmented parts are subsequently encoded into vector form of part capsules. Dynamic routing algorithm is implemented to route the part capsules into respective class capsule. The routed class capsule are optimized using a joint loss consisted margin loss, L_1 and Chamfer distance, L_2.

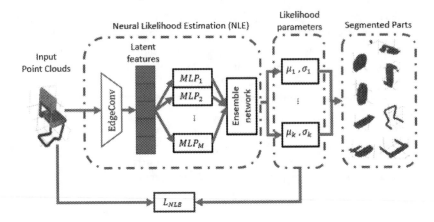

Fig. 2. The NLE network comprises an EdgeConv layer and an Ensemble MLP layers to estimate its point cloud's mean and variance for local parts extraction using Gaussian maximum likelihood as an guiding objective function.

and un-ordered grid-less space. In order to segment parts from a point cloud, one can implement a clustering technique, i.e. k-clustering to obtain patches of point cloud that represent local parts. However, such technique requires high number of iterations to converge on each cluster. In addition, each initialization of k-clustering is randomized, resulting the acquired local parts are random in each network feed-forward. To overcome this, a neural likelihood estimator (NLE) network is proposed to consistently segment local parts from an input point cloud.

Figure 2 shows the proposed NLE network denoted by $f_{NLE} : S_1 \mapsto Q$. It comprises a latent feature embedding network and an ensemble MLPs that decodes M likelihood parameters $Q = [q_1, ...q_M]$ of the input point cloud. Within the NLE, a graph-based encoder, Edgeconv [13] is adopted as features encoder network to encode the global latent features of input point cloud. Following that, an ensemble network consisted M MLPs and a projection shared MLP are implemented to decode individual likelihood parameter i.e. $q_m = [\mu_m, \sigma_m]$, where $\mu_m \in \mathbb{R}^3$ and $\sigma_m \in \mathbb{R}^3$ are the mean and variance. By obtaining the likelihood parameters of input point cloud, k nearest points belong to each likelihood parameter is selected to form a local part point cloud $p_m \in \mathbb{R}^{k \times 3}$, where $k = \frac{N}{M}$, resulting an aggregated local parts of $P = [p_1, ...p_M]$.

2.2   Part-to-Whole Learning

Once the locally segmented parts of input point clouds are obtained in the first stage, these segments are fed into a capsule network for part-to-whole relationship learning using a vector representation. In this implementation, the proposed capsule network comprises two main layers, i.e. parts capsules layer and class capsules layer. To obtain the part capsules $u = \{u_m \in \mathbb{R}^d\}_{m=1}^M$, where

d is the dimension size of a part capsule, a list of independent encoder modules, $[f_{enc,1}, \ldots, f_{enc,M}]$ is implemented to encode individual part features. Each encoder module comprises an EdgeConv layer and a MLP projection layer, such that $f_{enc,m} : P_m \mapsto u_m$. Therefore, a part capsule mainly holds the latent features of each local part in the form of response vector.

Subsequently, the class capsules $v = \{v_c \in \mathbb{R}^{d'}\}_{c=1}^{C}$, where d' is the dimension of a class capsule and C is the number of class, are responsible in containing features of each object class category. Different from standard perceptron operation, a routing algorithm [17] is implemented to operate and propagate the lower-level features to higher-level features. The operation can be viewed as a soft clustering step in voting each part capsule (lower-level features) into respective class capsule (higher-level features). For detailed algorithm flow of the dynamic algorithm, please refer to [17].

As each class capsule represent a class category, the selection of class capsule to classify a point cloud is obtained by choosing the class capsule with most significant magnitude $\max(||v||)$. To further optimize the part capsules and latent features of selected class capsule, they are concatenated to reconstruct an output point cloud $S_2 = \{y_n \in \mathbb{R}^3\}_{n=1}^{N}$. For the reconstruction step, a decoder network [23] denoted as $f_{dec} : \max(||v||) \mapsto S_2$ is implemented to output a reconstructed point cloud.

2.3 Objective Functions

The optimization of the proposed network is conducted independently in the first stage and second stage. For an instance, the NLE is optimized in prior to the capsule network, using Gaussian Maximum Likelihood as the objective function derived in Eq. (1). This is to ensure the NLE is as generalized as possible and the part-to-whole learning is not dependent on the NLE.

$$\mathcal{L}_{NLE}(S_1, Q_m) = -\ln\left[\sum_{n=1}^{N}\prod_{m=1}^{M}\mathcal{N}(x_n|\mu_m, \Sigma_m)\right], \tag{1}$$

where,

$$\mathcal{N}(x_n|\mu_m, \Sigma_m) = \frac{1}{(2\pi)^{\frac{3}{2}}|\Sigma_m|^{\frac{1}{2}}}e^{-\frac{1}{2}(x_n-\mu_m)^T\Sigma_m^{-1}(x_n-\mu_m)}. \tag{2}$$

On the other hand, the optimization of capsule network in second stage is using a joint-loss objective function L_{cap}, where $L_{cap} = L_1 + L_2$. The first term of the joint-loss L_1 is the margin loss derived in Eq. (3) implemented in capsule network [17] and the second term L_2 is Chamfer distance (CD) [7,24] that measure the reconstruction quality of reconstructed point cloud and is derived in Eq. (4).

$$L_1 = T_c\max(0, m^+ - ||v_c||)^2 + \lambda(1 - T_c)\max(0, ||v_c|| - m^-)^2 \tag{3}$$

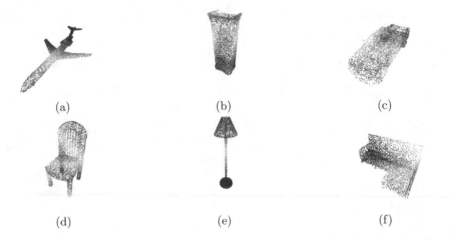

Fig. 3. Visualization of dataset samples from Modelnet10, ModelNet40, and ShapeNet-Core13: (a) Airplane, (b) Cabinet, (c) Car, (d) Chair, (e) Lamp, (f) Sofa.

where T_c is the targeted class and $T_c = 1$ if the object class exist. The margins $m^+ = 0.9$, $m^- = 0.1$, and the regularizing term is set $\lambda = 0.5$.

$$L_2(S_1, S_2) = \frac{1}{|S_1|} \sum_{x \in S_1} \min_{y \in S_2} ||x - y||_2^2$$
$$+ \frac{1}{|S_2|} \sum_{y \in S_2} \min_{x \in S_1} ||x - y||_2^2, \quad (4)$$

3   Result and Discussions

The proposed network is evaluated using two benchmark 3D datasets, i.e. ModelNet10, ModelNet40 [25] and ShapeNetCore13 [26] dataset. The ModelNet10 is a subset of ModelNet40 which contain 10 categories of labelled CAD object models with 3991 training and 908 testing data. On the other hand, ShapeNet-Core13 is a subset of the full ShapeNetCore55 dataset, covering 13 common object categories of labelled CAD object models with 31,772 training and 7,956 testing data. The visualization of point cloud samples, i.e. airplane, cabinet, car, chair, lamp, and sofa are shown in Fig. 3. The hyper-parameters used in this implementation are $M = 16$ and $N = 2048$. The proposed network is developed on Pytorch 1.9.0 using mixed precision network parameter. Batch size of 64 and learning rate 1×10^{-3} are used for network optimization.

Table 1 shows the classification performance of proposed network and existing works on ModelNet10, ModelNet40, and ShapeNetCore13 to evaluate point clouds object learning capability. Despite using significantly less number of network parameters, the proposed network achieved on-par classification rate with 92.9% on ModelNet10, 88.9% on ModelNet40 and 94.1% on ShapeNetCore13.

Table 1. Network parameters comparison on the benchmark dataset ModelNet10, ModelNet40, and ShapeNetCore13 in classification rate (%).

Method	#param	ModelNet10	ModelNet40	ShapeNetCore13
PointNet [6]	3.5M	92.7	89.4	94.5
PointNet++ [9]	1.5M	–	89.2	–
DGCNN [13]	1.8M	94.5	91.5	95.1
3DPointCapsule [19]	69.2M	92.4	89.3	93.9
Zhao et al. [21]	0.4M	–	85.3	–
Ours	0.38M	92.8	88.9	94.1

Notably, the proposed network is approximately 182 folds smaller than 3DPoint-Capsule while having similar classification performance.

To make a difference compared to existing works, the proposed network segments local parts of the input point clouds for parts reasoning through agreement via Dynamic Routing algorithm [17] to vote on an object. Essentially, the agreement to vote is achieved by searching most significant response of part capsules corresponding to an object capsule based on a dot-product operation. In contrary, most existing works rely on extending the dimension of latent features of the input point clouds to draw the most significant features. Although, DGCNN outperformed all networks with an adequate network parameters, the added stacks of EdgeConv made the network computation extensive due to the search for neighbourhood points on each layer.

While the closely related work 3DPointCapsule implemented 1024 replicas of point cloud encoder to search for significant parts, it similarly implemented Dynamic Routing algorithm to vote on its lower level capsules corresponding to its higher level capsule. However, due to high numbers of replicated encoder, the network parameter is drastically increased. In contrast, the proposed network utilizes 16 segmented parts to encode into 16 part capsules, comparing to 1024 primary capsules in 3DPointCapsule. Hence, this justifies the efficacy of object learning through agreement on segmented parts compared to parts searching by network where it sees fit.

4   Conclusion

In this paper, a capsule network with enforced part-to-whole relationship is proposed for point clouds learning. The network comprises two stages, i.e. (a) a Neural Likelihood Estimator network is proposed to segment local part of input point cloud; (b) a standard capsule network is implemented to learn the reasoning of an object's existence using the agreement on parts voting through dynamic routing algorithm. The proposed network showed an adequate point clouds object learning capability evaluated on classification performance compared to exiting works despite having significantly less network parameter. It achieved testing classification accuracy of 92.8% in ModelNet10 and 94.1% in ShapeNetCore13. In current state of the proposed network, the network is mainly designed to establish part-to-whole learning for point clouds object learning. In future work, pose features can be incorporated into the capsule network to achieve equivariance towards various input transformation.

References

1. Arnold, E., Al-Jarrah, O.Y., Dianati, M., Fallah, S., Oxtoby, D., Mouzakitis, A.: A survey on 3D object detection methods for autonomous driving applications. IEEE Trans. Intell. Transp. Syst. **20**(10), 3782–3795 (2019)
2. Guo, Y., Wang, H., Hu, Q., Liu, H., Liu, L., Bennamoun, M.: Deep learning for 3D point clouds: a survey. arXiv preprint arXiv:1912.12033 (2019)
3. Hu, Q., Yang, B., Khalid, S., Xiao, W., Trigoni, N., Markham, A.: Towards semantic segmentation of urban-scale 3D point clouds: a dataset, benchmarks and challenges. In: Proceedings of the IEEE/CVF Conference on Computer Vision and Pattern Recognition, pp. 4977–4987 (2021)
4. Phang, J.T.S., Lim, K.H., Chiong, R.C.W.: A review of three dimensional reconstruction techniques. Multimed. Tools Appl. **80**(12), 17879–17891 (2021). https://doi.org/10.1007/s11042-021-10605-9
5. Yi, L., Gong, B., Funkhouser, T.: Complete & label: a domain adaptation approach to semantic segmentation of lidar point clouds. In: Proceedings of the IEEE/CVF Conference on Computer Vision and Pattern Recognition, pp. 15363–15373 (2021)
6. Qi, C.R., Su, H., Mo, K., Guibas, L.J.: PointNet: deep learning on point sets for 3D classification and segmentation. In: Proceedings of the IEEE Conference on Computer Vision and Pattern Recognition, pp. 652–660 (2017)
7. Yuan, W., Khot, T., Held, D., Mertz, C., Hebert, M.: PCN: point completion network. In: 2018 International Conference on 3D Vision (3DV), pp. 728–737. IEEE (2018)
8. Huang, Z., Yu, Y., Xu, J., Ni, F., Le, X.: PF-Net: point fractal network for 3D point cloud completion. In: Proceedings of the IEEE/CVF Conference on Computer Vision and Pattern Recognition, pp. 7662–7670 (2020)
9. Qi, C.R., Yi, L., Su, H., Guibas, L.J.: PointNet++: deep hierarchical feature learning on point sets in a metric space. arXiv preprint arXiv:1706.02413 (2017)
10. Valsesia, D., Fracastoro, G., Magli, E.: Learning localized generative models for 3D point clouds via graph convolution. In: International Conference on Learning Representations (2018)
11. Shu, D.W., Park, S.W., Kwon, J.: 3D point cloud generative adversarial network based on tree structured graph convolutions. In: Proceedings of the IEEE/CVF International Conference on Computer Vision, pp. 3859–3868 (2019)
12. Xu, M., Ding, R., Zhao, H., Qi, X.: PAConv: position adaptive convolution with dynamic kernel assembling on point clouds. In: Proceedings of the IEEE/CVF Conference on Computer Vision and Pattern Recognition, pp. 3173–3182 (2021)
13. Wang, Y., Sun, Y., Liu, Z., Sarma, S.E., Bronstein, M.M., Solomon, J.M.: Dynamic graph CNN for learning on point clouds. ACM Trans. Graph. (TOG) **38**(5), 1–12 (2019)
14. Zhang, K., Hao, M., Wang, J., de Silva, C.W., Fu, C.: Linked dynamic graph CNN: learning on point cloud via linking hierarchical features. arXiv preprint arXiv:1904.10014 (2019)

15. Wang, K., Chen, K., Jia, K.: Deep cascade generation on point sets. In: IJCAI, vol. 2, p. 4 (2019)
16. Hassani, K., Haley, M.: Unsupervised multi-task feature learning on point clouds. In: Proceedings of the IEEE/CVF International Conference on Computer Vision, pp. 8160–8171 (2019)
17. Sabour, S., Frosst, N., Hinton, G.E.: Dynamic routing between capsules. arXiv preprint arXiv:1710.09829 (2017)
18. Hinton, G.E., Sabour, S., Frosst, N.: Matrix capsules with EM routing. In: International Conference on Learning Representations (2018)
19. Zhao, Y., Birdal, T., Deng, H., Tombari, F.: 3D point capsule networks. In: Proceedings of the IEEE/CVF Conference on Computer Vision and Pattern Recognition, pp. 1009–1018 (2019)
20. Srivastava, N., Goh, H., Salakhutdinov, R.: Geometric capsule autoencoders for 3D point clouds. arXiv preprint arXiv:1912.03310 (2019)
21. Zhao, Y., Birdal, T., Lenssen, J.E., Menegatti, E., Guibas, L., Tombari, F.: Quaternion equivariant capsule networks for 3D point clouds. In: Vedaldi, A., Bischof, H., Brox, T., Frahm, J.-M. (eds.) ECCV 2020. LNCS, vol. 12346, pp. 1–19. Springer, Cham (2020). https://doi.org/10.1007/978-3-030-58452-8_1
22. Papamakarios, G.: Neural density estimation and likelihood-free inference. arXiv preprint arXiv:1910.13233 (2019)
23. Groueix, T., Fisher, M., Kim, V.G., Russell, B.C., Aubry, M.: A papier-mâché approach to learning 3D surface generation. In: Proceedings of the IEEE Conference on Computer Vision and Pattern Recognition, pp. 216–224 (2018)
24. Liu, M., Sheng, L., Yang, S., Shao, J., Hu, S.M.: Morphing and sampling network for dense point cloud completion. In: Proceedings of the AAAI Conference on Artificial Intelligence, vol. 34, pp. 11596–11603 (2020)
25. Wu, Z., et al.: 3D ShapeNets: a deep representation for volumetric shapes. In: Proceedings of the IEEE Conference on Computer Vision and Pattern Recognition, pp. 1912–1920 (2015)
26. Chang, A.X., et al.: ShapeNet: an information-rich 3D model repository. arXiv preprint arXiv:1512.03012 (2015)

Study of Various Attacks Over Images Transferred Optically Through Communication Channel

Anshika Malsaria[✉] and Pankaj Vyas

Manipal University Jaipur, Jaipur, India
{anshika.malsaria,pankaj.vyas}@jaipur.manipal.edu

Abstract. On the basis of double random phase encoding (DRPE), we present an improved picture encryption technique in this work. In order to protect images from being compromised, a secure picture encryption system with a large key domain and low quantization error must be developed, as previously stated. DRPE, the second lens is unable to offer any security contribution, and it is always feasible to compute the FT to offset this operation if one knows the final cipher-image. This is regarded to be one of the most important components of the DRPE system. A variety of attacks on DRPE-type encryption schemes have been developed in recent years. This optical technology and traditional cryptography are being compared in an attempt to acquire a better knowledge of the system and overcome the attack susceptibility of DRPE systems. In order to avoid some of the current issues in traditional cryptosystems and prevent the comfortable realization of the cipher-image in the transform domain, a safe image encryption symmetric method must be designed and implemented.

Keywords: Symmetric · Transform · Domain · Cipher · Image

1 Introduction

Optical cryptosystems, which offer advantages over discrete mathematics-based encryption but have disadvantages as well, have been widely explored [1]. For example, optical encryption techniques may be used to encrypt the information about an item while simultaneously collecting the picture of the object. Furthermore, optical encryption may be accomplished by the use of ultrahigh-speed parallel computing. The double random phase encoding (DRPE) optical cryptosystem is a straightforward and straightforward optical cryptosystem. It has been used to a variety of kinds, including fractional DRPE, Fresnel DRPE, color image DRPE, generalized model of DRPE, incoherent DRPE, and phase-only DRPE. DRPE is a cryptography method that uses a symmetric key. The optical setup for DRPE consists of a 4-f correlate and two random phase masks, one in the spatial plane and the other in the Fourier plane, respectively. It is utilized as a symmetric key picture of the system, and it is put in the Fourier plane to do this. When it comes to cryptography, the symmetric key is unique, but the phase key images of DRPE contain some redundancy between the encryption and decryption operations, respectively.

© The Author(s), under exclusive license to Springer Nature Switzerland AG 2022
S. Joshi et al. (Eds.): SpacSec 2021, CCIS 1599, pp. 248–262, 2022.
https://doi.org/10.1007/978-3-031-15784-4_19

Even if the DRPE key contains some incorrect phase values, the plaintext pattern may be retrieved with acceptable noise using the DRPE algorithm. As a result, in DRPE, a plaintext pattern may be obtained by using several keys. As a result, it is critical to understand the relationship between these keys and all key patterns QNN, which is defined by the picture size, N × N pixels, and phase quantization level, Q. The properties of all phase keys were investigated using small images (e.g., 3 × 3 pixels) and a small number of phase quantization levels (e.g., four levels) in studies based on key-space analysis [2]. Small images (e.g., 3 × 3 pixels) and a small number of phase quantization levels (e.g., four levels) were used in research findings based on key-space analysis. Furthermore, utilizing key-length analysis, the characteristics of big phase key pictures (e.g., 512 × 512 pixels) were evaluated using a statistical technique based on a statistical method.

A number of assaults, including the cypher text-only attack (COA), the known-plaintext attack (KPA), and the chosen-plaintext attack (CPA) [3], have been demonstrated to be vulnerable to DRPE. In the KPA, a key is calculated by comparing a known plaintext-cipher text combination with a newly estimated key. For cryptanalysis, the Fourier iterative phase retrieval technique has been employed successfully. Using the KPA, the phase key is estimated by performing iterative calculations in both the spatial and Fourier planes, respectively. The amplitude components in the spatial and Fourier planes, which correspond to the known plaintext picture and the Fourier amplitude of the known cypher text image, respectively, are the constraint requirements for phase retrieval in the spatial and Fourier planes. We previously discovered that the single phase of the KPA could only decode the previously known cypher text image. In that work [4], we utilized a multi-valued picture with non-zero pixel values as the known plaintext images for the KPA, and the KPA was able to detect the image. We were unable to decrypt unknown cypher text pictures using the estimated key, but we were successful in decrypting the known cypher text images using the estimated key. The singular key is the phase key picture that has the singular quality in this study, and it is labelled as such. Whether or whether the single key will be able to decipher all of the unknown cypher text pictures is still up in the air. Cypher text images are composed of a plaintext picture and a random phase mask in the spatial plane, which are the characteristics of the image. By varying these settings, we were able to create a variety of cypher text pictures, which we then tested for decryption using the single key.

2 Technique for Double Random Phase Encoding

DRPE is one of the well-known and effective classical optical image encryption techniques established by Refregier and Javidi [5], and it has been used successfully in a number of applications. In the case of DRPE, the goal is to encode the plain image by converting it into stationary white noise, which is referred to as the cypher image. This is accomplished by applying statistically independent two random phase diffusers (masks) in the 4f system, one in the input plane and another in the Fourier plane. Figures 1(a) and 1(b) depict the schematic 4f configuration of encryption and decryption in DRPE based on the Fourier domain, where $R_1(x, y)$ and $R_2(x, y)$ are two RPMs or diffusers.

With signal encryption, the RPM in the input plane makes the signal white but non-stationary, while the RPM in the Fourier plane keeps the signal white but makes it stationary. It also has the property of being an autocorrelation function.

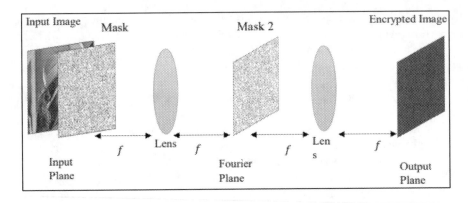

(a).

(b).

Fig. 1. (a) Optical setup of 4*f* based encryption system (b) Optical setup of 4*f* based decryption system

3   Types of Attacks on DRPE

Known plaintext attack, the attacker has access to pairs of known plaintexts and their associated cypher texts, which he can use to his advantage. In order to decode any more communications, he must either guess the secret key (or a set of secret keys) or create a method that would allow him to decrypt anything further messages. Generally speaking, this technique is regarded to be quite effective, especially if the number of pairings is not excessive. This attack scenario is more realistic than the plaintext attack scenario that was picked. The probable word approach, which is a popular technique to solve classical simple substitution or transposition cyphers and is an example of a known-plaintext attack, is an example of a known-plaintext assault [6].

Chosen-plaintext attack, in which case the attacker has the flexibility to pick plaintexts and read their associated encryptions, known as cypher texts. Although this assault is believed to be less feasible than the well-known plaintext attack, it is nonetheless considered to be a highly hazardous one. The fact that the cypher is sensitive to a known plaintext assault does not imply that it is also vulnerable to a selected plaintext attack, but it does not imply the inverse. With public key cryptography, when the encryption key is made publicly available and attackers may encrypt whatever plaintext they choose, chosen-plaintext assaults become highly significant.

Cypher text-only attacks Attack models for cryptanalysis that presume that the attacker has only passive capability to listen in on encrypted communication are known as cypher text-only attacks. While the attacker does not have access to the plaintext before to encryption, in all realistic cypher text-only assaults, the attacker retains some knowledge of the plaintext after the encryption has been completed. For example, the attacker may be familiar with the language in which the plaintext has been written. Additional to this, standard protocol data and messages are frequently included in the plaintext of many deployed systems, making them susceptible to guessing and knowledge-based attacks when used in conjunction with cypher text-only attacks on these systems. As a result, in order to accomplish their aim, attackers may rely on specific redundancy assumptions about the plaintexts. This scenario is the weakest in terms of the attacker's capabilities, and as a result, it is the most applicable in real-world applications.

Brute Force Attack (BFA), the attacker attempts to identify the key by attempting each and every conceivable combination of letters and numbers. If the key is 8 bits in length, the number of potential keys is $2^8 = 256$, which is the maximum number of keys. The attacker is aware of both the ciphertext and the method; he is now attempting to decrypt the message using each of the 256 keys one at a time. If the key is too lengthy, it would take an extremely long time to execute the attack.

Statistical attacks take use of statistical flaws in a cryptosystem, such as the inability to generate really random numbers or floating-point mistakes produced by the central processing unit.

Analytic Attack an algebraic cryptographic assault is a mathematical manipulation that seeks to make the cryptographic method less difficult by the use of algebraic equations. Upon successful completion of this assault, the attacker will be able to rapidly determine how the plain text is transformed to the cyphered text [7].

Differential Attack The attack is based largely on the fact that a specific input/output difference pattern happens only for certain values of inputs, which allows it to be successful. Typically, the attack is performed to the non-linear components in the same way as it would be done to a solid component (usually they are in fact look-up tables or S-boxes). Following the intended output difference (between two chosen or existing plaintext inputs) leads to the identification of potential key values. For example, if a differential of $1 => 1$ (implying that a difference in the least significant bit (LSB) of the input gives rise to an output difference in the LSB) occurs with a probability of 4/256 (as is possible with the non-linear function in the AES cypher, for example), then that differential is only possible for 4 values (or 2 pairs) of inputs. Consider the following scenario: we have a non-linear function whose key is XOR'ed before evaluation, and the values that enable the differential are 2, 3, and 4, 5. If an attacker sends in the values 6, 7, and sees the proper output difference, it implies that the key is either 6 K = 2, or 6 K = 4, which means that the key K is either 2 or 4 respectively [8].

4   Encryption Schemes Related on DRPE Utilizing Different Transforms

Optical encryption methods depend primarily on physical keys and optical processing is essentially two-dimensional and conducts parallel processing. In addition to the high speed, optics offers numerous benefits and multiple degrees of freedom helpful for data encoding. The security of DRPE, and also the key space available, was becoming a primary cause of anxiety. In turn, this paved the door for many other researchers to develop alternative optical image encryption schemes that were inspired by DRPE, in order to increase safe encryption capabilities by increasing the size of the security keys and decreasing background noise. As a result, many different variations of DRPE, such as fractional Fourier transform [9], Fresnel transform [10], gyrator transform [11], linear canonical transforms (LCT), fractional cosine transform (FrCT) [12], Hartley transform (HT) [13], fractional Mellin transform (FrMT) [14], fractional wavelet transform (FrWT), and others, were proposed, each These additional keys serve as a supplementary parameter, posing further challenges for attackers in their quest to discover the source of the information. Various approaches make use of LCTs, which are a three-parameter family of linear integral transforms that are used in some applications. The primary goal of creating such systems or procedures is to increase the security, adaptability, and user-friendliness of the system or method. In order to combat these dangers, we must develop new security measures. The discipline of optics has completely transformed the defense, medicinal, and broadcasting systems. For the delivery and storage of multimedia and data, optical data storage has emerged as a potential option. Blue ray discs and compact discs, in particular, may be used to randomly access the material that has been placed on them. The widespread use of these devices contributed to the widespread acceptance of optical technology. The government sector has invested money in the advancement of "Cryptography equipment".

4.1   Fractional Fourier Transform Based on DRPE

The Fourier transform is a generalized variant of this transform. In essence, it is an extension of the classical Fourier transform as well as a temporal frequency distribution. In comparison to the standard Fourier transform, this transformation is more versatile. The order of transformations varies between 0 and 1. As a result of the use of this transform, the key space of FRFT-based systems is increased, making them more secured. When used at order, the fractional Fourier transform (FFT) [14, 15] is an integral operator that translates a given function $f(x)$ onto a function $G^\alpha(u)$ [16, 17]

$$G^\alpha(u) = \int_{-\infty}^{+\infty} f(x)K_\alpha(x, u)Dx \tag{1}$$

In such case the kernel of the FrFT is described this way:

$$K_\alpha(x, u) = \frac{\exp\{\frac{\pi}{4}sgn(\emptyset) - \frac{\emptyset}{2})}{\sqrt{|\sin(\emptyset)|}}\exp\{i\pi\left[u^2 + x^2\right]cot\emptyset - 2uxcsc\emptyset] \tag{2}$$

where $\emptyset = \frac{\pi}{2}\alpha$

Where K_α is kernel of the FrFT and $\emptyset$ is a *sgn* work. The reverse FrFT compares to the FrFT at fractional request $-\alpha$. The FrFT administrator is added substance regarding the fractional request, $\mathcal{F}^\alpha \mathcal{F}^\beta = \mathcal{F}^{\alpha+\beta}$ FrFT is the principal request of FT with $\alpha = 1$. The FT is a direct transformation permitting a sign initially caught in the space area to be successfully turned through $\frac{\pi}{2}$ radian and projected into the symmetrical exceptional recurrence area. While in FrFT is a straight transformation that turns the sign through a subjective point into the blended recurrence space. The point of turn in stage space is relative to a request α of FrFT [18]. The FrFT has a periodicity of 4 regarding the fractional request α. The speculation of normal FT to the FrFT doesn't accompany an extra computational expense. The FT transform is supplanted by FrFT in straightforward DRPE strategy. The significant element here changed is the fractional request α, which expands the vital space and further improves the security. It is an extra level of opportunity in both xaxis and y-pivot to further develop security and power to dazzle unscrambling assault [19]. The FrFT utilized in DRPE to encrypt the picture with an additional level of opportunity can be introduced here numerically. Let a unique picture $I(x, y)$ that will be encrypted is increased first by RPM $R_1(x, y)$ and is then engendered in FrFT area with fractional request α. The complex-esteemed got is

$$\{u, v\} = F_\gamma FT^\alpha [I(x, y)XR_1(x, y) \tag{3}$$

The got optical wavefront $G(u, v)$ is adjusted by another RPM $R_2(u, v)$ with fractional request β in opposite FrFT.

$$E\{\mu, v\} = F_\gamma FT^{-\beta}[G(u, v)XR_2(u, v) \tag{4}$$

The encrypted picture $E(\mu, v)$ is gotten and can be communicated via an uncertain channel. The mathematical execution of FrFT has been concentrated in (H. M. Özaktas et al. 1996). The first picture must be decoded with all right keys and fractional orders. The quantity of boundaries for the key space is R_1, R_2, α, β which is enormous when contrasted with regular DRPE. Hennelly and Sheridan [20] presented an encryption plot by arbitrary moving in the FrFT space. Further, they looked into various FrFT based optical encryption strategies and performed heartiness trial of the encryption frameworks as for misalignment and visually impaired unscrambling. Further, a few examinations on encryption strategies and its applications in this FrFT area have been talked about.

4.2 Fresnel Transform Based on DRPE

In Fresnel transform based picture encryption method frequency, spread distance, and testing boundaries go about as extra keys for encryption and unscrambling. In 1999, Matoba and Javidi gave an encryption plot dependent on FrT utilizing irregular keys which added the third measurement to the RPMs by moving the RPM away from the Fourier plane. The FrT of an information picture $I(x, y)$ at a proliferation distance z, when it is enlightened by a plane influx of frequency λ can be numerically processed through Fresnel Kirchhoff recipe as

$$F_Z(u, v) = FrT_{\lambda, z}\{I(x, y)\} = \int_{-\infty}^{+\infty} \int_{-\infty}^{+\infty} f(x, y)h_{\lambda, z}(u, v, x, y)dxdy \tag{5}$$

where the administrator $FrT_{\lambda,z}$ indicates the Fresnel transform with boundaries λ and z, and $h_{\lambda,z}$ is the kernel of the transform provided by

$$FrT_{\lambda,z1}\{FrT_{\lambda,z2}f(x)\} = FrT_{\lambda,z1+z2}\{f(x)\} \tag{6}$$

A property of the FrT is

$$G\{\mu, v) = FrFT^{\lambda,z1}[I(x,y)XR_1(x,y) \tag{7}$$

z_1 and z_2 are addressed as two distance boundaries or proliferation removes and are chosen by the size of the gap to fulfill the Fresnel estimation. The circulations of complicated sufficiency in the neighboring planes are controlled by an FrT as for z_1, z_2 and λ. In 2004, Situ and Zhang [21] presented an adaptable and smaller method of optical DRPE in FrT. When contrasted with DRPE dependent on FT, FrT is focal point less which limits the equipment necessity and is simpler to execute. Each FrT can be identified with an FrFT of some request followed by fitting amplification and extra quadratic stage increase. The proliferation distances z_1, z_2, frequency λ go about as an extra keys and broaden the vital space in encryption and decoding which further improves the security for example FrT gives an additional level of opportunity. The optical arrangement of FrT is displayed in Fig. 2 where it has input plane, transform plane and yield plane. In the info plane, the information picture $I(x,y)$ is diffused with RPM $R_1(x,y)$ and spreads a distance z_1 in FrT space.

$$E\{\mu, v) = FrFT^{\lambda,z2}[G(u,v)XR_2(u,v) \tag{8}$$

The yield $G(u,v)$ acquired is diffused with second stage RPM $R_2(x,y)$ put in transform plane and proliferates a distance z_2 again in the FrT space to get the encrypted image.

The quantity of boundaries for the key area is R_1, R_2, z_1, z_2 and λ which is enormous when contrasted with traditional DRPE.

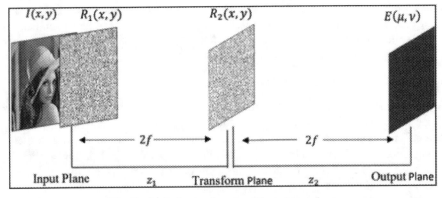

Fig. 2. Optical setup based on Fresnel transform

5 Defiance of DRPE Against Attacks

Cryptanalysis of DRPE based frameworks stood out since the security of the encryption framework has consistently been a significant concern. The assault calculations have been examined and show the DRPE weaknesses. In the writing it has been demonstrated that the first twofold arbitrary stage encryption plan and frameworks dependent on DRPE have imperfections because of the straight attributes of optical transformations as plaintext, key and cipher text has a useful relationship which makes it a direct encryption framework. Because of this innate linearity, DRPE based image encryption plans are defenseless against certain assaults. The assaults are applied to customary DRPE are basically: CCA [22], CPA [23], KPA, and COA [24] to investigate the weakness. It is likewise expected that a similar stage just veils are utilized for encoding distinctive information images. Carnicer et al. in 2005 detailed first that DRPE is powerless against CCA and can recuperate keys productively. In 2006, Gopinathan [25] likewise explored KPA on DRPE and demonstrated keys can be recuperated by utilizing the heuristic calculation. In 2006, Peng [23] planned CPA and KPA on DRPE utilizing PRA. Creators expressed that a strategy for CPA on focal point less DRPE in the FrT. An aggressor can get to two encryption keys with the assistance of the motivation capacities as picked plaintexts where unscrambling measure is lossless. In 2007, Tang et al. planned a COA strategy by assessing plaintext's help and expressed this assault requires considerably less asset than different kinds of assault. The most perilous assault was the point at which one of the creators tracked down the key by utilizing just two known images. So later it was recommended to utilize enormous size keys for encryption and not to rehash the equivalent keys for encrypting distinctive plain images. In 2007, Frauel [26] concentrated on many assaults against DRPE and exhibited that beast power assault on the keys utilized in DRPE is unreasonable, even subsequent to attempting to decrease the quantity of mixes for rearrangements yet it vulnerable to CPA and KPA. In 2007, Monaghan [27] introduced a key-space investigation of the DRPE method and exhibited that few self-assertive keys can unscramble a picked encrypted image in their framework. In 2009, Qin and Peng concentrated on a strategy for KPA on DRPE in the FrFT because of its straight nature. By this assailant can get to two encryption stage keys with the assistance of the PRA in the FrFT area and can get the two FrFT request keys by utilizing a comprehensive inquiry.

In 2012, He et al. introduced a crossover two-venture assault plot that consolidates the CPA and KPA calculations to obtain the mystery keys of the optical cryptosystem dependent on a twofold arbitrary stage plentifulness encoding (DRPAE) strategy. In 2015, Liu et al. [28] showed that DRPE is powerless against COA where an assailant can recover the comparing plaintext from the main code text under certain condition. It depends on a half and half iterative stage recovery (HIPR) calculation that joins different stage recovery calculations. In 2017, Li [29] showed DPRE procedure is powerless against the COA and with the factual ergodic property of the dot; the plaintext or plain image can be recuperated from the code text or code image alone attributable to the way that their energy unearthly thickness capacities are indistinguishable. Qin and He [30] concentrated on optical cryptanalysis of DRPE plots and showed that because of the linearity property of their encryption transformations, plans are helpless against CPA,

KPA. Creators effectively break encryption plans with the assistance of a specific amount of plaintext-figure text (P, C) sets.

6 A Scheme of Asymmetric Image Encryption Based on DRPE

The reliability of this technique suffers as a result of its symmetric and linear nature, as it is vulnerable to a wide range of attacks, including chosen plain image attacks, chosen cypher image attacks, known plain image attacks, and cypher image only attacks [22], as well as a number of practical issues, including key distribution and management [23]. In order to address these difficulties, the asymmetric key cryptosystem was developed, which employs a public and private key pair for encryption and decryption, respectively. For the purposes of this cryptosystem, phase truncated part (PT) refers to the use of only random amplitude mask as the public key for encrypting an image at the sender side, and the amplitude truncated part (AT) refers to the use of only random phase mask to serve as the private key for decrypting an image at the receiver side. This phase mask factor provides nonlinearity into the cryptosystem, making it more resistant to common conventional attacks such as the well-known plain image attack. The proposed technique, despite the fact that it collects some specified images such as grey scale and binary images and generates their corresponding encrypted images, makes it difficult for the cryptanalyst to correctly decrypt an encrypted image because the cube root involved adds nonlinearity to the path in which the encrypted image is decrypted. Uneven image encryption conspire dependent on DRPE can be performed through stage truncation and through EMD to deliver non-straight nature in DRPE. DRPE plans talked about above were before presented with the idea of the symmetric key where a similar mystery key is utilized for encryption and decoding. DRPE based cryptosystems are straight and are helpless against certain assaults. To deliver the nonlinear nature in the DRPE plan, Qin and Peng in 2010 planned lopsided plan dependent on non-straight PTFT where encryption keys vary from decoding keys. The abundances' part is held to acquire figure image and stage part it shortened and held for unscrambling. In PTFT encryption plot the encryption keys are viewed as open and decoding key viewed as private. Accordingly, for decoding the data aggressor realizes the public key yet requires the private key to unscramble the data. This PTFT was likewise acquainted with take care of one of the issues of key conveyance yet later it was not viewed as "hilter kilter" as the encryption and decoding key pair are not freely produced by the collector. Many plans explored in the above areas were subsequently changed with a PTFT plan to make it resistant to assaults [31] Plan depends on the Diffie-Hellman convention, in which the key can be traded with high security and permits two clients to trade a mysterious key over an uncertain channel with no earlier insider facts. The hilter kilter plan can be numerically explained. Let the first image $I(x, y)$ that will be encrypted is increased first by RPM $R_1(x, y)$ and is then FT. Just the stage shortened part (PT) for example abundances part is taken forward and stage complex part for example abundances shortened (AT) part is held as the decoding key DK_1.

$$G\{u, v\} = PT\big[FT\big[I(x, y)XR_1(x, y)\big]\big] \tag{9}$$

$$DK_1 = AT[FT\big[I(x, y)XR_1(x, y)\big]] \tag{10}$$

where $PT[.]$ is the stage truncation administrator, AT $[.]$ is sufficiency truncation admin-istrator? The got optical wavefront $G(u, v)$ is regulated by $R_2(u, v)$ in IFT space where abundances part is taken ahead to acquire the encrypted information $E(\mu, v)$ and stage difficult part is held as the decryption key DK_2

$$E\{\mu, v\} = PT[FT[G(u, v)XR_2(u, v)]] \tag{11}$$

$$DK_2 = AT[FT[G(u, v)XR_2(u, v)]] \tag{12}$$

The encrypted image $E(\mu, v)$ acquired is get and can be sent through an unreliable channel. R_1 and R_2 are two public keys utilized for encryption and are not needed at the hour of decryption. DK_1 and DK_2 are two private keys utilized for unscrambling the encrypted image. With wrong decryption keys, the data isn't recuperated. The flow graph of encryption and decryption measure for deviated cryptosystem is displayed in Figs. 3(a, b).

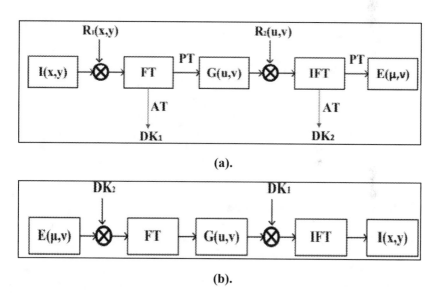

(a).

(b).

Fig.3. (a) Flow graph of asymmetric encryption technique (b) Flow graph of asymmetric decryption technique

7 Measures to Remove Attacks on DRPE in Future

In the following scenario, each of these assaults may be resisted by utilizing secure operating modes that have been adopted from classical encryption techniques and applied to the circumstance. With the DRPE technology, we may adapt a variety of various modes for optical implementation, which is particularly useful. ECB is a kind of DRPE that is commonly seen. In light of its reversibility, the CBC algorithm will only provide a rudimentary level of security. In the face of all dangers, CFB displays a very high degree of security. The use of CFB to foil approximation decryption efforts that require only a single plaintext–cipher text pair results in error propagation for genuine optical system decryptors as a result of equipping them with CFB. While it is possible that OFB is not totally secure against all attacks at this moment, it does not appear to enable any error propagation for the legal decrypter to take place. Because it is important to do a proper calculation of f1 while operating in the OFB mode in order to prevent the propagation of errors, this phase should be carried out using digital optics or digital electronics in particular. There must be great caution given while creating a particularly efficient optical implementation for the irreversible function f1 in CFB and OFB to guarantee that the function is not reversed. DRPE cannot be used as a cryptographic hash function because it is sensitive to phase retrieval techniques, which is possible for the most efficient nonlinear operation in analogue optics (square law detection). As previously stated, DRPE cannot be used as a cryptographic hash function because it is sensitive to phase retrieval techniques [22]. The cryptanalysis shows that to limit the dangers, it is recommendable to acquaint non-direct tasks with optical encryption frameworks. Customary DRPE likewise experienced key administration and transmission issues as RPMs that should be safely moved to the collector for unscrambling is of the same size of code image so the plain-image can be remade appropriately. Transmission and key administration issues became intriguing for specialists. A portion of the creators discovered the arrangement by utilizing bedlam-based image rearranging can be used to defeat these issues. There have been various upgrades to the DRPE including further developing security, lessening commotion, eliminating outline issue, giving validation, and so forth are as yet in measure. The security of the optical encryption framework is as yet under dynamic examination. Upgrades to the DRPE framework have been constantly revealed.

8   DRPE Schemes of Image Scrambling

Scrambling has the potential to disrupt the strong connection that exists between neighboring pixels. The random sequences created by chaotic systems are sorted in a number of picture encryption methods, and then the locations of the image pixels are reorganized with a set of index numbers. However, merely translating the index into the cipher text picture pixels one by one may result in certain fixed spots being overlooked. Also mentioned is the fact that the periodicity and inefficiency of standard permutation design may not be sufficient to fulfil the security standards [32]. As a result, it is important to do more research into scrambling tactics. Shahna presented a permutation approach that works on both the pixel and bit levels, complicating the encryption process while also achieving high-performance random permutation [33]. Xian created a fractal sorting matrix to disrupt the components in the plaintext picture and applied it to the plaintext image. The disordered sorting matrix could be produced from an initial block in a flexible manner and could be made to any size; it was also safer in picture encryption. To make the scrambling procedure more difficult, Wang divided the plaintext picture into four sub-blocks and applied varying degrees of Arnold transform to each of the sub-blocks. In addition, an effective diffusion algorithm has the potential to alter the statistical law of pixel values. Gong used chaotic sequences to XOR the compressed plaintext directly, which was a breakthrough [34]. Because the decryption among unrelated pixels would not influence each other, it is possible that the image will be partly disclosed. As a result, Mirzaei proposed a novel diffusion approach for the cryptosystem, in which the plaintext picture was divided into four sub images and then reassembled. In the process of the following sub image pixel, each encrypted pixel of the preceding sub image was involved. Sheela used a combination of two-level diffusion operations and the pixels transform in an image encryption system to conceal the statistical nature of plaintext more successfully than previous methods did. When processing each pixel in the first diffusion level, two points were used, one for each pixel's location in the chaos matrix, and the second diffusion level was addressed by the previously ciphered pixel [35].

8.1 The Arnold Transform (*ArT*)

In an investigation of ergodic hypothesis, *ArT* was examined by Arnold [36]. *ArT* revises the pixels of the image $I(x, y)$ for a $M \times M$ size by changing the situation of the pixels haphazardly. The situation of the pixel (x, y) changes to (x', y') subsequent to utilizing *ArT* to an image. The *ArT* can be numerically communicated as

$$ArT_M : \begin{pmatrix} x' \\ y' \end{pmatrix} = \begin{pmatrix} 1 & 1 \\ 1 & 2 \end{pmatrix} \begin{pmatrix} x \\ y \end{pmatrix} (modM)(x, y) \in M \tag{13}$$

where directions of pixel before revamp are addressed by (x, y) and directions of a pixel after improvement are addressed by (x', y') and the modulus after division activity is addressed by mod. It is otherwise called occasional transform. The image changes or get mixed after some number of cycles and returns after a specific number of emphases. The time frame þ of *ArT* is numerically communicated as

$$peroid = \min\{\omega : [ArT\{I(x, y), M\}]^{\omega} = f(x, y)\} \tag{14}$$

where least worth is meant by min and the quantity of cycles is meant by a positive whole number ω. *ArT* of an image $I(x, y)$ can be portrayed as

$$ArT(I(x, y), M) = \{(v, (x', y'))|(x', y')^T\} \tag{15}$$

$$= \begin{pmatrix} 1 & 1 \\ 1 & 2 \end{pmatrix}(x, y)^T (modM) \tag{16}$$

The worth at every pixel (x, y) for an image $I(x, y)$ is meant by v in the above articulation. T characterizes the translate of (x, y). *ArT* is applied to the 2-D image preparing. The image is mixed utilizing *ArT* for ω cycles and the mixed image can be recuperated to the first image by applying reverse *ArT* for m (= þ – ω)emphases. Hence, both intermittent scrambling transform þ and number of cycle's ω are keys to decode the first image. The scrambling time of *ArT* is related with the size of image M, not really set in stone qualities for certain cases are 96 for 128×128 and 192 for 256×256 individually. The quantity of emphases is a security boundary which assumes a significant part in encryption for giving security from the aggressor. For recuperating or remaking the first image, the recipient should know the right worth of various emphases applied at the sender side. ArT is a non-direct strategy and was read to address the issue of low security in straight image encryption plot [37]. For scrambling the image in DRPE $4f$ framework ArT is applied twice, first to the info image and afterward to the halfway image.

9 Conclusion

This is an era of rapid technical advancement. Almost all forms of useful data communication took occur through the use of a public network, which was widely available. In this study, we have examined optical image encryption methods in further detail. We have examined DRPE optical image encryption methods, as well as the performance of these technologies. In this study, we have explored the idea of optical encryption modes and examined the thing in light of existing attacks. Although we have only taken into account DRPE as a single attack vector. Every encryption method is unique in that it is separated from the others. SPM upgrades the security and eliminates the weakness by balancing the period of the code image acquired in the wake of applying two RPMs in GT and IGT area. The plan likewise furnished multi-overlap security with the utilization of ArT, GT, RPM and, SPM. This comprises the enormous number of security boundaries for decryption which thus brings about extra key space. The plan was checked against many assaults and has been broke down by contrasting and other image encryption plans, results acquired affirm the triple concealing accomplishes better execution as far as impediment, clamor, key affectability and so forth.

References

1. Javidi, B., Carnicer, A., et al.: Roadmap on optical security. J. Opt. **18**(8) (2016). Article 083001
2. Monaghan, D.S., Gopinathan, U., Naughton, T.J., Sheridan, J.T.: Key-space analysis of double random phase encryption technique. Appl. Opt. **46**(26), 6641–6647 (2007). https://doi.org/10.1364/AO.46.006641
3. Carnicer, A., et al.: Vulnerability to chosen-cypher text attacks of optical encryption schemes based on double random phase keys. Opt. Lett. **30**(13), 1644–1646 (2005). https://doi.org/10.1364/OL.30.001644
4. Nakano, K., Takeda, M., Suzuki, H., Yamaguchi, M.: Security analysis of phase-only DRPE based on known-plaintext attack using multiple known plaintext–ciphertext pairs. Appl. Opt. **53**(28), 6435–6443 (2014)
5. Refregier, P., Javidi, B.: Optical image encryption based on input plane and Fourier plane random encoding. Opt. Lett. **20**(7), 767–769 (1995)
6. Kong, D., Shen, X., Xu, Q., Xin, W., Guo, H.: Multiple-image encryption scheme based on cascaded fractional Fourier transform. Appl. Opt. **52**(12), 2619–2625 (2013)
7. Zhu, B., Liu, S., Ran, Q.: Optical image encryption based on multifractional Fourier transforms. Opt. Lett. **25**(16), 1159–1161 (2000)
8. Biham, E., Shamir, A.: Differential Cryptanalysis of the Data Encryption Standard. Springer (1993). ISBN 0-387-97930-1, ISBN 3-540-97930-1

9. Alieva, T., Bastiaans, M.J., Calvo, M.L.: Fractional transforms in optical information processing. EURASIP J. Adv. Signal Process. **2005**(10), 1–22 (2005). https://doi.org/10.1155/ASP.2005.1498

10. Hennelly, B.M., Sheridan, J.T.: Generalizing, optimizing, and inventing numerical algorithms for the fractional Fourier, Fresnel, and linear canonical transforms. J. Opt. Soc. Am. A **22**(5), 917–927 (2005)

11. Rodrigo, J.A., Alieva, T., Calvo, M.L.: Gyrator transform: properties and applications. Opt. Express **15**(5), 2190–2203 (2007)

12. Wu, J., Zhang, L., Zhou, N.: Image encryption based on the multiple-order discrete fractional cosine transform. Opt. Commun. **283**(9), 1720–1725 (2010)

13. Chen, L., Zhao, D.: Optical image encryption with Hartley transforms. Opt. Lett. **31**(23), 3438–3440 (2006)

14. Zhou, N., Wang, Y., Gong, L.: Novel optical image encryption scheme based on fractional Mellin transform. Opt. Commun. **284**(13), 3234–3242 (2011)

15. Hua, J., Liu, L., Li, G.: Extended fractional Fourier transforms. J. Opt. Soc. Am. A **14**(12), 3316–3322 (1997)

16. Ozaktas, H.M., Zalevsky, Z., Kutay, M.A.: The Fractional Fourier Transform: with Applications in Optics and Signal Processing, 6th edn. Wiley, Chichester (2001)

17. Unnikrishnan, G., Joseph, J., Singh, K.: Optical encryption by double-random phase encoding in the fractional Fourier domain. Opt. Lett. **25**(12), 887–889 (2000)

18. Lizarazo, Z., Moreno, Y.M.T.: Encryption for security using optical fractional Fourier transform. In: 5th Iberoamerican Meeting on Optics and 8th Latin American Meeting on Optics, Lasers, and Their Applications, vol. 5622, pp. 1328–1334 (2004)

19. Nishchal, N.K., Unnikrishnan, G., Joseph, J., Singh, K.: Optical encryption using a localized fractional Fourier transform. Opt. Eng. **42**(12), 3566–3572 (2003)

20. Hennelly, B.M., Sheridan, J.T.: Image encryption and the fractional Fourier transform. Optik **114**(6), 251–265 (2003)

21. Situ, G., Zhang, J.: Double random-phase encoding in the Fresnel domain. Opt. Lett. **29**(14), 1584–1586 (2004)

22. Carnicer, A., Montes-Usategui, M., Arcos, S., Juvells, I.: Vulnerability to chosen cypher text attacks of optical encryption schemes based on double random phase keys. Opt. Lett. **30**(13), 1644–1646 (2005)

23. Peng, X., Wei, H., Zhang, P.: Chosen-plaintext attack on lensless double-random phase encoding in the Fresnel domain. Opt. Lett. **31**(22), 3261–3263 (2006)

24. Zhang, C., Liao, M., He, W., Peng, X.: Cipher text-only attack on a joint transform correlator encryption system. Opt. Express **21**(23), 28523–28530 (2013)

25. Gopinathan, U., Monaghan, D.S., Naughton, T.J., Sheridan, J.T.: A known-plaintext heuristic attack on the Fourier plane encryption algorithm. Opt. Express **14**(8), 3181–3186 (2006)

26. Frauel, Y., Castro, A., Naughton, T.J., Javidi, B.: Resistance of the double random phase encryption against various attacks. Opt. Express **15**(16), 10253–10265 (2007)

27. Monaghan, D.S., Gopinathan, U., Naughton, T.J., Sheridan, J.T.: Key-space analysis of double random phase encryption technique. Appl. Opt. **46**(26), 6641–6647 (2007)

28. Liu, X., Wu, J., He, W., Liao, M., Zhang, C., Peng, X.: Vulnerability to cipher text-only attack of optical encryption scheme based on double random phase encoding. Opt. Express **23**(15), 18955 (2015)

29. Li, G., Yang, W., Li, D., Situ, G.: Cypher text-only attack on the double random-phase encryption: Experimental demonstration. Opt. Express **25**(8), 8690–8697 (2017)

30. Qin, W., He, W.: Optical cryptanalysis of DRPE-based encryption systems. In: 2009 International Conference on Optical Instruments and Technology: Optoelectronic Information Security. Proceedings of SPIE, vol. 7512, p. 751203 (2009)

31. Sinha, A.: Fractional Fourier transform based key exchange for optical asymmetric key cryptography. W Trans. Comput. **7**(2), 52–56 (2008)

32. Zhang, W., Yu, H., Zhao, Y.-L., Zhu, Z.-L.: Image encryption based on three-dimensional bit matrix permutation. Signal Process. **118**, 36–50 (2016)

33. Shahna, K., Mohamed, A.: A novel image encryption scheme using both pixel level and bit level permutation with chaotic map. Appl. Soft Comput. **90**, Article ID 106162 (2020)

34. Sun, F.Y., Lu, Z.W.: Digital image encryption with chaotic map lattices. Chin. Phys. B **20**(4), 405–411 (2011)

35. Sheela, S.J., Suresh, K.V., Tandur, D.: Image encryption based on modified Henon map using hybrid chaotic shift transform. Multimed. Tools Appl. **77**(19), 25223–25251 (2018). https://doi.org/10.1007/s11042-018-5782-2

36. Arnold, M.A., Small, G.W.: Determination of physiological levels of glucose in an aqueous matrix with digitally filtered Fourier transform near-infrared spectra. Anal. Chem. **62**(14), 1457–1464 (1990)

37. Liu, S., Sheridan, J.T.: Optical encryption by combining image scrambling techniques in fractional Fourier domains. Opt. Commun. **287**, 73–80 (2013)

Satellite Image Classification Using ANN

Pratistha Mathur and Kavita[(✉)]

Manipal University Jaipur, Jaipur, India
Kavita.chaudhary@outlook.com

Abstract. Every human being is capable of recognizing patterns. There are various problems in domains like bioinformatics, data mining, document classification, image analysis, remote sensing, and speech recognition where automatic recognition is needed. The rapid growth in computing power enables the development of such applications. Remote Sensing is one of the areas where a huge amount of data is available. In this paper, we have explored the supervised and unsupervised ANN for classifying satellite images. The adaptive pattern recognition capability of ANN is used to simulate the spatial variations in the images of an object/area. Multi-layer feed-forward neural network using backpropagation learning method and self-organizing feature map (SOFM) has experimented. Experiments are implemented using MATLAB. It is hoped that this multidisciplinary work will be useful for researchers and image processing users in the field of computer science and remote sensing.

Keywords: Artificial neural network · Image processing · Supervised · Unsupervised

1 Introduction

The huge quantity of remote sensing data, obtained by the increasing number of earth observation satellites, extends the vast potential for environment-related applications in the global, regional, and local scales [1]. The data along with the new application domain extends from observing human settlements to natural resource management, from agricultural study to retort for natural disasters, from the valuation of the effect of climate change to preserving biodiversity [13]. The pattern recognition discipline provides suitable methods, the logical framework allows the development of classification and prediction techniques for the analysis of remote sensing data [2, 11]. Proceeding in this direction a general dynamic model for pattern recognition using an artificial neural network is proposed and validated. For the sake of completeness of the document and before going into the actual problem definition we introduce and describe the relevant topics, to the extent they are needed in this paper. One of the most interesting aspects of the world is that it can be made up of patterns. Remote Sensing (RS) is the technology for sampling electromagnetic radiation to attain and interpret non-immediate geospatial data, to extract the feature, object, or class data [3, 4]. To observe the earth satellite must-have remote sensors is known as remote sensing satellite. Data is collected using either passive or active remote sensing systems. Remote sensing system collects analog (e.g.,

© The Author(s), under exclusive license to Springer Nature Switzerland AG 2022
S. Joshi et al. (Eds.): SpacSec 2021, CCIS 1599, pp. 263–271, 2022.
https://doi.org/10.1007/978-3-031-15784-4_20

hardcopy aerial photography or video data) and or digital data (e.g., a matrix of brightness values obtained using a scanner, linear array). Most of the remote sensing satellites determine the energy in a very specific well-defined spectrum wavelength [12]. In the present work, we aim to employ the adaptive pattern recognition capability of ANN to simulate the temporal and spatial variations in the images of an object/area. The model shall be tested with satellite-derived remotely sensed images.

2 Materials and Methods

2.1 Study Area and Data

In the case study, we did the land cover classification so Indian Remote Sensing Satellites (IRS) data is selected. The selection of the data also depends on the cost of the data. One can get the data of India at a low cost from Indian satellites. IRS 1C/D carry three separate imaging sensors, the WiFS, the LISS, and the high-resolution panchromatic sensor. The Linear Imaging Self scanning sensor 3 (LISS 3/L3) serves the need of multispectral imagery clients [5]. LISS 3 acquires four bands (520–590, 620–680, 770–860, and 1550–1750 nm) with 23.7-m spatial resolution. To acquire the satellite data, the area of interest must be specified, which may include city, district, state, or any contiguous area.

2.2 Methods

1. **Artificial Neural Network**

   Artificial Neural Network (ANN) is a computational paradigm inspired by the information processing system found in the biological world [14]. The brain is at the core of the system which has a huge number of small processing units called "neurons". They are heavily interconnected and operate in parallel. Though each neuron individually performs some elementary transformation of the signal at a very slow speed compared to a digital/electronic device, the brain accomplishes very complex perceptual and other cognitive tasks within a very small time [6]. The study

Fig. 1. The flow of complete process

of neural networks tries to analyze and implement this computational paradigm using electronic devices.

Figure 1 briefly shows the methodology of this work. The complete process is divided into two phases, in the first phase the supervised and unsupervised classification of the satellite image is done with its accuracy assessment and in the second phase, an algorithm is applied to analyze the trends in satellite images.

2. **Image Preprocessing**

Raw data has more geometric and radiometric distortions which require corrections. The numerous required corrections are radiometric corrections and geometric corrections [7]. Radiometric corrections is a procedure that normalizes the non-uniform responses based on laboratory calculated radiometric values. In geometric corrections, the distortion is generated by the relative motion of a satellite concerning the earth, and due to earth curvature panoramic [8]. In the present study, the radiometric and geometric correction is done by the NRSA itself at the time of purchase of the data. Sample images taken for trend analysis are geo-referenced using ERDAS IMAGINE which is a professional software used for multispectral image processing.

3. **Feature Identification**

The next task is the selection of training samples based on spectral signatures. Analysis of a digital product for obtaining information on the earth surface necessitates knowledge of spectral signatures of different earth surface features, prior knowledge of the ground and subject experience. Based on this various training samples were selected. Sample pixel should be selected as a representative for each class in an area for example for agriculture data. The agriculture area appears in a red tone in view of the high infrared reflectance of vegetation in the FCC [15]. Surface water bodies are identified through their dark blue tone resulting from the absorption of infrared radiation by water [9, 10]. Training samples can be taken for vegetation, water bodies, hilly area, urban area, and others. Once the numbers of land cover types are known, the user has to provide samples for each cover type by cropping them from the digital data. Table 1 shows the characteristics of the land cover classes of LISS III images.

Examples of a few training samples are shown in Fig. 2. These samples are called Training Samples since they are used by the ANN to classify all the pixels into various cover types.

Class 1: Heavy Vegetation
Class 2: Dry Land Area
Class 3: Water bodies
Class 4: Light Vegetation.

Table 1. Characteristics of land cover classes

Land cover class	Description	Characteristic on LISS III FCC
Dense Forest	Tall dense trees	Dark red with rough texture
Sparse vegetation	Low vegetation density with the exposed ground surface	Dull red to pinkish
Agriculture	Crops	Dull red and smooth appearance
Fallow land	Agriculture fields without crops	Bluish/greenish grey with a smooth texture
Barren	Region without vegetation	Yellowish
Settlements	Town & villages block-like appearance	Bluish
Waterbody	River &lakes	Cyanish blue to blue according to a depth of water

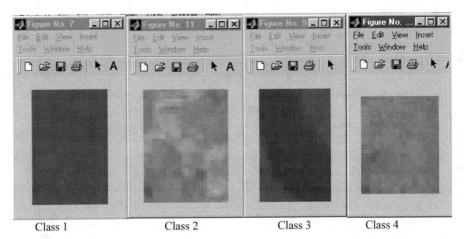

Class 1   Class 2   Class 3   Class 4

Fig. 2. Training Sites for Banasthali area images of January 2002-Supervised Classification

Features are the characteristics of the land cover type that identifies it uniquely. In one pixel, the values in three bands can be regarded as components of a 3-dimensional vector, the feature vector. An example of a feature vector (23, 78, 51) gives the DN (digital number) values for three bands. Such a vector can be plotted in a 3-dimensional space called a feature space.

We can extract different kinds of features from the satellite images like gray level mean, gray level standard deviation, statistics on co-occurrence matrices, means and variances of Gabor filtered outputs, texture, NDVI, and spatial/shape parameters like aspect ratio, convexity, solidity, roundness, and orientation of each region etc. Mean and variances are the basic features among all. Image means is always considered as one of the best features and it is true that this simple descriptor is able to discriminate various classes like clouds, sea, fields, desert, city, forest etc. (Figs. 3 and 4).

Fig. 3. Input image-March 2002

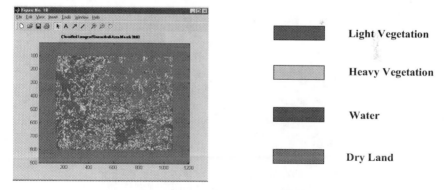

Fig. 4. Supervised classification of March 2002

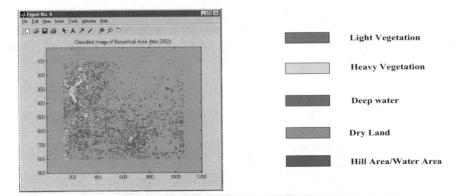

Fig. 5. Unsupervised classification of March 2002

The image of January 2003 is shown in Fig. 6. We have taken nine training classes as Crop_area, Water_body, Fallow_land1, Fallow_land 2, Fallow_land3, Fallow_land4, Open_scrub, Grazing_land and Salt_effected_area to be classified from the Satellite image (Fig. 5). The final classified images are shown in Fig. 7. Figure 9 and Fig. 10

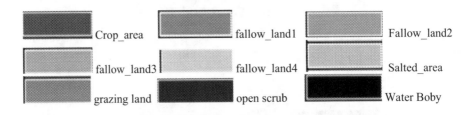

Fig. 6. FCC of January 2003

represent the supervised and unsupervised classification respectively on Jan 2003 image
(Fig. 9) (Fig. 8).

Fig. 7. FCC of February 2003

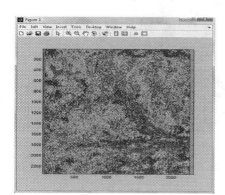 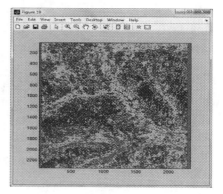

Fig. 8. Classified images of Jan 2003 using supervised classification

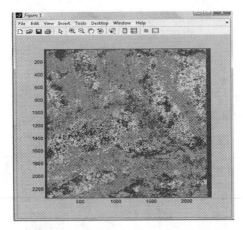

Fig. 9. Classified image of Feb 2003 using supervised classification

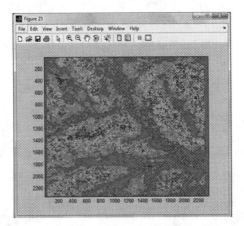

Fig. 10. Classified image of Feb 2003 using unsupervised classification

3 Conclusion

The present work model has been developed to classify the image into various classes, which illustrates the changes in the spatial patterns. In the process, the model experimented for supervised classification. Using FeedForward neural network the algorithm was developed and implemented in MATLAB. This algorithm inputs the training vector from various spatial classes. Hence features for various classes were computed and fed to the model for training. After training, simulation was done and then the model was tested on several images. Experiments were done by taking different no of classes and were verified with the ground truths. Satellite images were taken of the familiar Banasthali region since supervised classification can be done only for known regions. Unsupervised techniques are needed to study regions beyond human reach. Hence SOFM based classification method is developed for that. The accuracy of this method is also tested by comparing it with the ISODATA clustering method, which is available for unsupervised classification in ERDAS IMAGINE, a professional software used for multispectral image processing. The comparison shows the potential of using ANN (SOFM) as a tool for classification purposes, and accuracy can be increased with the increase of the number of classes and features in the model.

References:

1. Torres, P., Rodes-Blanco, M., Viana-Soto, A., Nieto, H., García, M.: The role of remote sensing for the assessment and monitoring of forest health: a systematic evidence synthesis. Forests **12**, 1134 (2021). https://doi.org/10.3390/f12081134
2. Gómez-Chova, L., Tuia, D., Moser, G., Camps-Valls, G.: Multimodal classification of remote sensing images: a review and future directions. Proc. IEEE **103**, 1560–1584 (2015). https://doi.org/10.1109/JPROC.2015.2449668
3. Virnodkar, S.S., Pachghare, V.K., Patil, V.C., Jha, S.K.: Remote sensing and machine learning for crop water stress determination in various crops: a critical review. Precision Agric. **21**(5), 1121–1155 (2020). https://doi.org/10.1007/s11119-020-09711-9
4. Darkwah, S.O., Scoville, M.D., Wang, L.K.: Geographic information systems and remote sensing applications in environmental and water resources. In: Wang, L.K., Wang, M.-H.S., Hung, Y.-T., Shammas, N.K. (eds.) Integrated Natural Resources Management, vol. 20, pp. 197–236. Springer, Cham (2021). https://doi.org/10.1007/978-3-030-55172-8_5
5. Lillesand, T., Kiefer, R.W., Chipman, J.: Remote Sensing and Image Interpretation. Wiley, Hoboken (2015)
6. Kumar, S., Suresh, L.: Fruit fly-based artificial neural network classifier with kernel-based fuzzy c-means clustering for satellite image classification. Int. J. Image Grap. **20**, 2050016 (2020). https://doi.org/10.1142/S0219467820500163
7. Jakob, S., Zimmermann, R., Gloaguen, R.: The need for accurate geometric and radiometric corrections of drone-borne hyperspectral data for mineral exploration: MEPHySTo—a toolbox for pre-processing drone-borne hyperspectral data. Remote Sens. **9**, 88 (2017). https://doi.org/10.3390/rs9010088
8. John, J., Bindu, G., Srimuruganandam, B., Wadhwa, A., Rajan, P.: Land use/land cover and land surface temperature analysis in Wayanad district, India, using satellite imagery. Ann. GIS **26**, 343–360 (2020). https://doi.org/10.1080/19475683.2020.1733662
9. Navalgund, R.R.: Remote sensing. Reson. **7**, 37–46 (2002). https://doi.org/10.1007/BF02836169
10. Gleason, C., Durand, M.: Remote sensing of river discharge: a review and a framing for the discipline. Remote Sens. **12**, 1107 (2020). https://doi.org/10.3390/rs12071107
11. Blaschke, T.: Object based image analysis for remote sensing. ISPRS J. Photogramm. Remote. Sens. **65**(1), 2–16 (2010)
12. Sanchez, J., Maria P.C.: Remote Sensing. Space Image Processing, pp. 11–44. Routledge (2018)
13. Dagar, J.C., Gangaiah, B., Gupta, S.R.: Agroforestry to sustain island and coastal agriculture in the scenario of climate change: indian perspective. In: Dagar, J.C., Gupta, S.R., Teketay, D. (eds.) Agroforestry for Degraded Landscapes, pp. 367–424. Springer, Singapore (2020). https://doi.org/10.1007/978-981-15-4136-0_13
14. Devikanniga, D., Vetrivel, K., Badrinath, N.: Review of meta-heuristic optimization based artificial neural networks and its applications. In Journal of Physics: Conference Series, vol. 1362, no. 1, p. 012074. IOP Publishing (2019)
15. Rajendran, S., et al.: WorldView-3 mapping of Tarmat deposits of the Ras Rakan Island, Northern coast of Qatar: environmental perspective. Mar. Pollut. Bull. **163**, 111988 (2021)

Power Quality Disturbance Classification Using Transformer Network

Dar Hung Chiam$^{(\boxtimes)}$ and King Hann Lim

Curtin University Malaysia, CDT 250, 98009 Miri, Sarawak, Malaysia
chiamdh@postgrad.curtin.edu.my

Abstract. The quality of power supplies has become an increasingly important subject in ensuring smooth operations of advanced instruments, especially in smart grid systems. Wide range of non-linear loads and advanced power electronics are connected to the grid causing abrupt power quality disturbances (PQD). Constant monitoring using machine intelligence can activate automate control of PQD detection and classification. In this paper, a transformer network is proposed to substitute the Long short-term memory (LSTM) network by tackling the problem of sequential processing while performing automatic time-series PQD classification. The aim of this paper is to provide a direct comparison of the multiple PQD classification performance between LSTM and transformer network. The training performance using noisy and noiseless signal are tested under several signal-to-noise ratio. In addition, three unknown noises are used to evaluate the model generalization towards noises that are not seen during training phase.

Keywords: Transformer network · Power quality disturbance · Classification · LSTM

1 Introduction

High-quality power supplies generated from clean energy [1–3] is highly required nowadays especially with the newly introduction of electric vehicles and smart grid technologies. The advancement of power electronics enables the growth of distributed energy resource networks and multiple control mechanism in power generation and distribution. However, these acceleration of technologies development [4,5] poses huge challenges in governing good quality of power distribution and hence, the focus of power quality disturbance (PQD) analysis is greatly interested [6,7]. PQD refers to the unusual transmission activity that distorts the grid performance and they can be categorized into three main types [8], i.e. transients (impulsive and oscillatory), magnitude variation (Sag, swell, interrupt), and steady-state waveform distortions (harmonics, periodic notch, flicker). These PQDs have negative impact on the lifespan of electrical and electronics instruments, particularly sensitive industrial equipment. In order to overcome the detrimental effects from PQDs, continuous monitoring and identification of

© The Author(s), under exclusive license to Springer Nature Switzerland AG 2022
S. Joshi et al. (Eds.): SpacSec 2021, CCIS 1599, pp. 272–282, 2022.
https://doi.org/10.1007/978-3-031-15784-4_21

PQDs is thus required in the distribution network to understand the underlying causes and occurrence of the disturbances.

Recently, the application of deep learning (DL) [9,10] is important in the field of PQDs detection and classification. Various DL methods are proved to be able extract salient features automatically from the input signals during the training stage [11]. Long short-term memory (LSTM) is among the most studied architecture due to the nature of single dimension and sequence related characteristics of PQD signals [12]. On the other hand, transformer network [13] is newly introduced as a superior model replacing the needs of convolutions and recurrence in the field of natural language processing [14] and automatic speech recognition [15]. The use of attention mechanism in the transformer network can highlight the generalized features from the series of input. In this paper, transformer network is proposed to extract salient sequential features from raw time-series PQD signals. Both transformer network and LSTM network are used as sequential feature extractor for the classification. Addictive white Gaussian noise (AWGN) of 20–40 dB signal to noise (SNR) levels are used for the classification performance comparison on noisy environment. Three unknown noises are introduced to further test the generalization of the proposed model.

2   Related Works

Generally, detection and classification of PQD can be categorised into three phases, signal processing, feature extraction, and classification. Signal processing phase includes data normalization and signal transformations. Some signal processing or signal transformation techniques used includes Fourier transform [16], wavelet transform [17], discrete wavelet transform [18], wavelet packet transform [19], S-transform [20], and Hilbert-Huang transform [21]. Statistical features are normally extracted [22] during the feature extraction phase. Some example of statistical features extracted includes root mean square, standard deviation, mean, minimum, maximum, kurtosis, skewness, and entropy. However, these handcrafted feature extraction methods requires professional knowledge. Feature selection layer is introduced to further improve the classification performance by selecting important features from the generated feature sets [23]. This further increases the complexity of the implementation.

Extracted features are then be fed into decision making mechanism for the classification process. Pattern recognition methods used includes support vector machine [24], decision tree [25], expert systems [26], and artificial neural network [27]. The classification performance of support vector machine and decision tree are highly dependent on the training samples used. Expert system on the other hand is having disadvantage on its high computing cost. Artificial neural network is good with its real-time process, the classification accuracy is however prone to noise. Deep neural network (DNN) has thus been studied for its advantage in automatic feature extraction with classification process [28–30].

DNN methods rely fundamentally on DL methods, which consists of multiple layers of neurons or architectures. Four layers of LSTM has been used in

[31] for the PQD classification process. The combination of convolution neural network and LSTM layers are showing good classification performance [11,32]. Transformer network has been introduced as an superior model replacing the needs of convolutions and recurrence [13]. Transformer encoder has shown good performance in speech recognition [33] and image segmentation [34]. Besides, transformer has been proof to have increased training efficiency by allowing training parallelization [35].

3   PQD Classification Using Transformer Network

Transformer network is used to extract the sequential features from time series voltage waveform. The latent feature extracted from the encoder is fed into fully connected layer for classification. The proposed transformer network utilised the encoder part from [13], with standard trainable 1-D positional encoding. The proposed model structure is shown in Fig. 1. Different from previous studies which uses 5–10 periods of signal waveform [28,36], single-period PQD waveform classification is performed.

3.1   PQD Data Generation and Sampling

PQD signals are simulated based on mathematical model as listed in Table 1. The mathematical modelling equations are similar across previous studies [29,37]. 18 classes of PQDs are generated, which includes normal class ($P0$), 9 classes of single PQDs ($P1 - P9$), and 8 classes of combined disturbances ($P10 - P17$). 200 samples are generated for each PQD classes with sampling frequency of 10 kHz. Point labelling is used where a different magnitude with more than $\pm0.005\%$ from normal extreme cases indicates the presence of disturbance. Single "stride" windowing method is performed on the simulated data. Thus, three-period waveform data generation would be suffice to cover different time-frame combinations of the signal waveform in single-period window. One-hot-encoded window labelling is then generated based on the point labelling. Data formatting and normalization is performed before passing into embedding layer. The normalization process is expressed in Eq. (1),

$$V(t) = \frac{v(t)}{\max\limits_{t \in n} v(t)}, \tag{1}$$

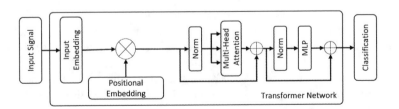

Fig. 1. Proposed transformer network for time-series PQD classification

Table 1. 18 classes of PQDs.

Label	Class Description	Label	Class Description
P0	Normal	P9	Flicker
P1	Sag	P10	Sag+Harmonics
P2	Swell	P11	Swell+Harmonics
P3	Interrupt	P12	Interrupt+Harmonics
P4	Impulse Transient	P13	Harmonics+Notch
P5	Spike	P14	Sag+Transient
P6	Harmonics	P15	Swell+Transient
P7	Oscillatory Transient	P16	Sag+Oscillatory Transient
P8	Notch	P17	Swell+Oscillatory Transient

where n represents number of windows and t represents window size. The formatted input, $V(t)$ is the normalization of magnitude $v(t)$ over maximum magnitude present in the entire data sample.

3.2   Transformer Network Architecture

The normalised single-period windowed signal will be first passed through a multilayer perceptron layer to perform 1-D input embedding, $I \in \mathbb{R}^{l \times d}$, where l is the sequence length, and d is the input dimension which is kept at $d = 1$ for the 1-D input. Position embedding is added to the input embedding to encode the sequence information. Transformer encoder block [13,38] starts by taking input and perform normalisation first before passing to multi-head attention block. Multi-Head attention block projects the normalised input, I into three vectors, Query Q, Key K, and Value V with trainable matrices, W_q, W_k, W_v as [38],

$$Q, K, V = IW_q, IW_k, IW_v. \tag{2}$$

Scaled dot-product attention is performed between query and key in Eq. (2), where K^T represents the transpose of K.

$$A = QK^T, \tag{3}$$

$$Attn(Q, K, V) = Softmax(\frac{A}{\sqrt{d_k}})V, \tag{4}$$

A single-head attention is represented by Eq. (4), where $\frac{1}{d_k}$ is a scaling factor. Multi-head attention is achieved by multiple sets of trainable matrices, $W_q^{(i)}$, $W_k^{(i)}$, $W_v^{(i)}$ as follows [38],

$$Q^{(i)}, K^{(i)}, V^{(i)} = IW_q^{(i)}, IW_k^{(i)}, IW_v^{(i)}, \tag{5}$$

$$Head^{(i)} = Attn(Q^{(i)}, K^{(i)}, V^{(i)}) \tag{6}$$

$$MultiHead(Q, K, V) = Concat(Head^{(1)}, ..., Head^{(n)})W_O \qquad (7)$$

where n represents number of heads, i is the index of the head. W_O is trainable parameter of size $\mathbb{R}^{d_k \times d}$. Multi-head attention output is then normalised again before passing through multilayer perceptron layer layer for further processing and output as encoded feature.

4 Experiment Setup

The experiments was conducted using Pytorch. A total of 1.44M samples windowed from 3600 randomly generated 3-period PQD signals are partitioned into 70% training data, 15% validation data and 15% testing data. The generated samples are based on mathematical modelling equations from previous studies [29, 37] which are discussed in Sect. 3.1. Two experiments are conducted to analyse the performance of proposed transformer network versus pure LSTM network. Transformer network is using same dimension linear embedding, where $l = 200$, and attention with 4 heads in this entire experiment. The LSTM model used on the other hand is a single layer LSTM with 100 hidden units. For comparison, both models are trained for 50 epochs. Experiment # 1 is conducted to analyse the model while training with noiseless dataset. The performance of the model are tested using noiseless dataset, and 20–40 dB SNR AWGN. Experiment # 2 on the other hand studies the model trained with randomly added 20–50 dB SNR AWGN on the training data samples. The performance of the model is first analysed under noiseless and 20–40 dB SNR AWGN. The model is further tested with three unknown noises to test if the model can be generalised to unknown noises. The three added noises are Noise #A with 15 dB SNR AWGN, Noise #B with 20–25 dB SNR positive-uniformly distributed random noise, and Noise #C with 15–30 dB SNR uniformly distributed random noise. The SNR in this experiment is calculated using equation depicted as,

$$SNR = 10 \log_{10} \frac{P_{signal}}{P_{noise}}. \qquad (8)$$

Classification accuracy is the main evaluation matrix used. The individual class's classification accuracy, Acc_n is the true positive, TP_n over the total test samples for m classes of PQD, S_j as,

$$Acc_n = \frac{TP_n}{\sum_{j=0}^{m} S_j}. \qquad (9)$$

Weighted accuracy is used to overcome the imbalanced data sample used. The weightage of each class is calculated by dividing the total number of samples of an individual class over the total number of samples. Weighted accuracy, (WAcc) can be calculated by multiplying the individual class accuracy with its weight, which can be depicted as,

$$WAcc = \sum_{j=0}^{m} W_j \times Acc_j. \qquad (10)$$

5   Experiment #1 - Training with Noiseless Dataset

In this experiment, both LSTM and transformer network are trained with noise-less data samples. The trained models are then tested using 5 group of samples, which includes noiseless samples, and AWGN with SNR levels of 20 dB, 30 dB, and 40 dB respectively. Results tabulated in Table 2 shows that the proposed transformer network is having better performance on noisy conditions, which is 55.56% compared to LSTM model with only 13.26% on 20 dB SNR level. It is also noticed that transformer network is able to achieve > 80% WAcc on above 30 dB noise level. The WAcc of LSTM model on the other hand shows significant impact on high noise condition while classify most of the noisy signals oscillatory transient (P7). Transformer network is able to achieve overall good classification performance. However, it shows weakness in some of the PQD classes such as Interrupt (P3), Harmonics+notch (P13), and Swell+oscillatory Transient (P17). A detail analysis into confusion matrix shows that P3 is having confusion with Interrupt+Harmonics (P12). It is noticed that the harmonics signals are having relatively small magnitude difference compared to the interrupt signal magnitude difference. Harmonics signal can only be recognize from magnitude difference or

Table 2. Noiseless training: classification performance comparison between LSTM network and transformer network.

Model	LSTM				Transformer			
SNR / Class	20dB	30dB	40dB	noiseless	20dB	30dB	40dB	noiseless
P0	0.00	0.00	1.33	99.83	9.38	76.62	99.74	99.95
P1	0.05	20.31	59.54	98.01	59.17	87.51	92.29	92.47
P2	0.05	11.27	54.57	98.46	76.60	94.20	96.61	96.81
P3	12.54	44.64	69.23	97.85	53.66	66.68	69.78	70.37
P4	0.00	5.50	70.32	97.33	40.28	80.44	86.90	87.58
P5	0.00	6.01	56.03	97.78	62.74	85.29	87.99	87.86
P6	0.20	31.51	84.21	99.41	79.93	97.99	99.41	99.59
P7	98.30	98.13	95.87	94.95	84.97	90.70	91.38	91.25
P8	0.39	18.28	53.50	96.83	48.41	75.67	78.55	78.45
P9	0.00	0.76	42.16	99.86	68.92	98.51	99.88	99.88
P10	3.70	60.84	91.68	96.20	80.91	88.84	89.75	90.00
P11	52.78	77.89	95.25	97.93	94.83	97.47	97.67	97.80
P12	26.74	60.65	84.23	90.70	63.91	72.83	74.44	74.35
P13	14.51	83.61	97.60	97.92	59.86	58.35	58.24	57.91
P14	13.09	57.18	92.89	94.34	65.71	74.34	74.70	74.51
P15	6.70	32.59	86.33	95.25	72.26	76.80	77.00	76.84
P16	69.36	73.09	80.28	81.25	80.72	80.65	80.74	80.91
P17	48.56	55.55	59.68	72.29	15.31	15.09	15.02	14.93
WAcc	13.26	31.84	58.36	96.42	55.56	81.39	87.71	87.84

localised pattern. On the other hand, class P13 is having confusion with harmonics (P6). While transformer has good pattern recognition in highlighting the location of the notch. However, it is having decreased performance with the weaker notch which is having smaller magnitude difference compared to the signal. Class P17 is showing confusion with class Sag+Oscillatory Transient (P16). P16 and P17 are similar in nature. When the Sag or Swell is having smaller variation as compared to the effect of oscillatory transient on the windowed signal, small magnitude difference will become the only indicator to differentiate between the two classes. As a conclusion, although transformer network perform adequate classification disregard to the noise interference, it has a weakness in identifying small magnitude changes. On the other hand, LSTM model has poor noise immunity with low classification rate at 20 dB noise level when the noisy data is not seen in the training sequence.

6   Experiment #2 - Training with Noisy Dataset

In Experiment #2, both of the models are trained using training data samples randomly polluted with 20–50 dB SNR AWGN. The results in Table 3 shows

Table 3. Noisy training: classification performance comparison between LSTM network and transformer network.

Model	LSTM				Transformer			
SNR \ Class	20dB	30dB	40dB	noiseless	20dB	30dB	40dB	noiseless
P0	96.83	99.61	99.85	99.94	88.42	99.74	99.94	99.95
P1	85.92	94.32	96.42	96.87	78.44	90.77	91.74	91.77
P2	87.82	94.80	96.81	96.99	87.10	93.91	94.50	94.58
P3	70.96	85.55	90.66	91.89	53.96	58.69	58.76	58.90
P4	49.54	81.74	90.06	91.28	46.72	68.48	71.31	71.70
P5	66.05	95.24	97.33	97.46	44.82	52.31	53.41	53.88
P6	92.83	98.70	99.18	99.27	91.78	98.48	98.77	98.77
P7	91.47	92.10	91.73	91.85	86.55	89.38	89.42	89.53
P8	72.52	94.76	97.02	96.91	38.45	49.83	52.09	52.48
P9	91.59	97.60	98.09	98.19	93.15	99.34	99.87	99.93
P10	87.63	93.95	95.09	95.24	84.16	87.81	88.12	88.17
P11	96.30	97.19	97.34	97.39	95.91	97.41	97.61	97.62
P12	59.16	77.59	87.62	89.64	65.17	69.33	68.70	68.36
P13	81.53	93.79	96.01	96.25	49.81	46.82	46.49	46.49
P14	57.29	76.68	84.85	86.33	56.62	56.78	57.21	57.13
P15	68.39	86.05	90.72	91.47	70.66	72.57	71.94	72.02
P16	73.93	74.88	75.01	75.07	77.04	77.27	77.12	77.11
P17	42.86	48.92	49.80	49.95	19.96	20.38	20.06	20.10
WAcc	82.62	91.52	93.68	94.07	76.06	82.90	83.27	83.31

Table 4. Testing classification rate in (%) with three unknown noise performance comparison.

Model	Noise					
	Train without noise			Train with noise		
	A	B	C	A	B	C
LSTM	10.36	46.85	16.28	52.42	48.34	56.69
Transformer	40.84	60.27	41.64	56.55	53.17	57.96

drastic improvement especially for the LSTM model. Training with noise exposed the models to noisy conditions during the training. LSTM model presents marvelous pattern recognition performance on "seen" noises. Transformer network shows improvement on high noise 20 dB SNR AWGN (from 55.56% to 76.06%). This improvement mainly focuses on class P0, P1, P2, which are having global features. However, it can be noticed that the classification performance on low noise conditions (40 dB SNR and noiseless) decreased. Class P3, P13, and P17 are still showing weakness, while the WAcc of other classes (P5, P8, and P14) decreased drastically. Training with noise improves the classification performance of LSTM by exposing all possible samples for the LSTM network during the training phase. Transformer network on the other hand does not show promising improvements. Training with noise does not help in improving the classification performance of the transformer network.

Experiment #2 continues with testing both models under unknown noises. Three unknown noises which are not previously exposed to the models are introduced into the test samples. Noise #A is a 15 dB SNR AWGN, Noise #B is 20–25 dB SNR of positive-uniformly distributed random noise, and Noise #C is 15–30 dB SNR uniformly distributed random noise. The performance of the model trained with and without noise are tabulated in Table 4. Training without noise results in low classification accuracy for LSTM model. Transformer network is still able to achieve > 40% accuracy for noise #A, #B and #C. Training with 20–50 dB AWGN does helps in improving the classification performance forf both of the models. However, the classification performance of LSTM does not achieve similar performance level of 82.62% even on noise #B and noise#C which are having similar noise levels. Transformer on the other hand shows more generalised performance on both trained with and without noise tests.

7 Conclusion

The performance of automatic time-series PQD classification is compared between the proposed transformer network and LSTM model. Both model are used to extract sequential feature automatically from time-series PQD signals for classification. Two experiments are conducted to test the classification performance of the two models. Experiment #1 is conducted by training the two models with noiseless PQD signals samples. Results shows that transformer network outperformed LSTM model in terms of noise immunity. Transformer network can achieve WAcc of 55.56% under 20 dB SNR AWGN test, as compared to mere 13.26% by LSTM model. This shows that transformer network is more generalised, where it can adapt to noisy conditions which is not pre-trained. However, it is also found out that transformer is having difficulty in classifying signals with small magnitude changes. In Experiment #2, both of the models are trained with randomly polluted 20–50 dB SNR AWGN. LSTM model shows great performance of 82.62% when tested with 20 dB SNR AWGN. This shows that LSTM model can perform well on pre-trained conditions. Transformer training with noise does not show overall improvement. The second part of the experiment #2 continues by testing the models with three unknown noises. Results show that transformer network is more generalised to achieve better and consistence classification performance over signal polluted with unknown noises. As a conclusion, transformer network is a more general approach compared to LSTM model. Automatic feature extraction can be done with time-series sequential feature extraction using LSTM or transformer. However, LSTM model is prone to noise and only perform well on seen conditions. Training the network with every single type of noise polluted condition is not practical. The proposed transformer network is having a more generic design which gives better performance without training with noise. However, there is still room for improvement for the transformer network to perform better. Insensitive to magnitude difference is a major concern on the transformer network. For the future work, adding more layers of attention mechanism might help improve the performance by having different levels of latent features. A combination of LSTM with transformer can also be considered.

References

1. Ackermann, T., Andersson, G., Söder, L.: Distributed generation: a definition. Electr. Power Sys. Res. **57**(3), 195–204 (2001)
2. Liang, X.: Emerging power quality challenges due to integration of renewable energy sources. IEEE Trans. Ind. Appl. **53**(2), 855–866 (2016)
3. Khalid, M.R., Alam, M.S., Sarwar, A., Asghar, M.J.: A comprehensive review on electric vehicles charging infrastructures and their impacts on power-quality of the utility grid. ETransportation **1**, 100006 (2019)
4. Luo, A., Xu, Q., Ma, F., Chen, Y.: Overview of power quality analysis and control technology for the smart grid. J. Mod. Power Syst. Clean Energy **4**(1), 1–9 (2016). https://doi.org/10.1007/s40565-016-0185-8
5. Hossain, E., Tür, M.R., Padmanaban, S., Ay, S., Khan, I.: Analysis and mitigation of power quality issues in distributed generation systems using custom power devices. IEEE Access **6**, 16816–16833 (2018)
6. Bravo-Rodríguez, J.C., Torres, F.J., Borrás, M.D.: Hybrid machine learning models for classifying power quality disturbances: a comparative study. Energies **13**(11), 2761 (2020)
7. Mishra, M.: Power quality disturbance detection and classification using signal processing and soft computing techniques: a comprehensive review. Int. Trans. Electr. Energ. Syst. **29**(8), e12008 (2019)

8. Committee, E., et al.: IEEE rEcommended Practice for Monitoring Electric Power Quality, c1–81. IEEE Std (2009)
9. Sindi, H., Nour, M., Rawa, M., Öztürk, Ş, Polat, K.: An adaptive deep learning framework to classify unknown composite power quality event using known single power quality events. Expert Syst. Appl. **178**, 115023 (2021)
10. Wang, S., Chen, H.: A novel deep learning method for the classification of power quality disturbances using deep convolutional neural network. Appl. Energy **235**, 1126–1140 (2019)
11. Rodriguez, M.A., Sotomonte, J.F., Cifuentes, J., Bueno-López, M.: Power quality disturbance classification via deep convolutional auto-encoders and stacked LSTM recurrent neural networks. In: 2020 International Conference on Smart Energy Systems and Technologies (SEST), pp. 1–6. IEEE (2020)
12. Ozcanli, A.K., Yaprakdal, F., Baysal, M.: Deep learning methods and applications for electrical power systems: a comprehensive review. Int. J. Energy Res. **44**(9), 7136–7157 (2020)
13. Vaswani, A., et al.: Attention is all you need. Adv. Neural Info. Process. Syst. **30**, 5998–6008(2017)
14. Zeyer, A., Bahar, P., Irie, K., Schlüter, R., Ney, H.: A comparison of transformer and LSTM encoder decoder models for Asr. In: 2019 IEEE Automatic Speech Recognition and Understanding Workshop (ASRU), pp. 8–15. IEEE (2019)
15. Vig, J., Belinkov, Y.: Analyzing the structure of attention in a transformer language model. arXiv preprint arXiv:1906.04284 (2019)
16. Jurado, F., Saenz, J.R.: Comparison between discrete STFT and wavelets for the analysis of power quality events. Electr. Power Syst. Res. **62**(3), 183–190 (2002)
17. De Yong, D., Bhowmik, S., Magnago, F.: An effective power quality classifier using wavelet transform and support vector machines. Expert Syst. Appl. **42**(15–16), 6075–6081 (2015)
18. Xiao, F., Lu, T., Wu, M., Ai, Q.: Maximal overlap discrete wavelet transform and deep learning for robust denoising and detection of power quality disturbance. IET Gener. Transm. Distrib. **14**(1), 140–147 (2019)
19. Karafotis, P.A., Georgilakis, P.S.: Power quality monitoring and evaluation in power systems under non-stationary conditions using wavelet packet transform. High Voltage **4**(3), 186–196 (2019)
20. Reddy, M.V., Sodhi, R.: A modified S-transform and random forests-based power quality assessment framework. IEEE Trans. Instrum. Meas. **67**(1), 78–89 (2017)
21. Li, P., Gao, J., Xu, D., Wang, C., Yang, X.: Hilbert-Huang transform with adaptive waveform matching extension and its application in power quality disturbance detection for microgrid. J. Mod. Power Syst. Clean Energy **4**(1), 19–27 (2016)
22. Khokhar, S., Zin, A.A.M., Memon, A.P., Mokhtar, A.S.: A new optimal feature selection algorithm for classification of power quality disturbances using discrete wavelet transform and probabilistic neural network. Measurement **95**, 246–259 (2017)
23. Singh, U., Singh, S.N.: Optimal feature selection via NSGA-II for power quality disturbances classification. IEEE Trans. Ind. Inf. **14**(7), 2994–3002 (2017)
24. Naderian, S., Salemnia, A.: An implementation of type-2 fuzzy kernel based support vector machine algorithm for power quality events classification. Int. Trans. Electr. Energy Syst. **27**(5), e2303 (2017)
25. Zhong, T., Zhang, S., Cai, G., Li, Y., Yang, B., Chen, Y.: Power quality disturbance recognition based on multiresolution S-transform and decision tree. IEEE Access **7**, 88380–88392 (2019)

26. Muthusamy, T.A., Ramanathan, N.: An expert system based on least mean square and neural network for classification of power system disturbances. Int. J. Futur. Revolut. Comput. Sci. Commun. **4**, 308–313 (2018)

27. Bhavani, R., Prabha, N.R.: A hybrid classifier for power quality (PQ) problems using wavelets packet transform (WPT) and artificial neural networks (ANN). In: 2017 IEEE International Conference on Intelligent Techniques in Control, Optimization and Signal Processing (INCOS), pp. 1–7. IEEE (2017)

28. Deng, Y., Jia, H., Li, P., Tong, X., Li, F.: A deep learning method based on long short term memory and sliding time window for type recognition and time location of power quality disturbance. In: 2018 Chinese Automation Congress (CAC), pp. 1764–1768. IEEE (2018)

29. Liu, H., Hussain, F., Yue, S., Yildirim, O., Yawar, S.J.: Classification of multiple power quality events via compressed deep learning. Int. Trans. Electr. Energy Syst. **29**(6), e12010 (2019)

30. Junior, W.L.R., Borges, F.A.S., Rabelo, R.D.A.L., de Lima, B.V.A., de Alencar, J.E.A.: Classification of power quality disturbances using convolutional network and long short-term memory network. In: 2019 International Joint Conference on Neural Networks (IJCNN), pp. 1–6. IEEE (2019)

31. Mohan, N., Soman, K., Vinayakumar, R.: Deep power: deep learning architectures for power quality disturbances classification. In: 2017 International Conference on Technological Advancements in Power and Energy (TAP Energy), pp. 1–6. IEEE (2017)

32. Garcia, C.I., Grasso, F., Luchetta, A., Piccirilli, M.C., Paolucci, L., Talluri, G.: A comparison of power quality disturbance detection and classification methods using CNN, LSTM and CNN-LSTM. Appl. Sci. **10**(19), 6755 (2020)

33. Liu, A.T., Li, S.W., Lee, H.Y.: Tera: self-supervised learning of transformer encoder representation for speech. IEEE/ACM Trans. Audio Speech Lang. Process. **29**, 2351–2366 (2021)

34. Chen, J., et al.: TransUNet: transformers make strong encoders for medical image segmentation. arXiv preprint arXiv:2102.04306 (2021)

35. Dong, L., Xu, S., Xu, B.: Speech-transformer: a no-recurrence sequence-to-sequence model for speech recognition. In: 2018 IEEE International Conference on Acoustics, Speech and Signal Processing (ICASSP), pp. 5884–5888. IEEE (2018)

36. Bagheri, A., Gu, I.Y., Bollen, M.H., Balouji, E.: A robust transform-domain deep convolutional network for voltage dip classification. IEEE Trans. Power Delivery **33**(6), 2794–2802 (2018)

37. Tang, Q., Qiu, W., Zhou, Y.: Classification of complex power quality disturbances using optimized S-transform and kernel SVM. IEEE Trans. Ind. Electron. **67**(11), 9715–9723 (2019)

38. Yan, H., Deng, B., Li, X., Qiu, X.: TENER: adapting transformer encoder for named entity recognition. arXiv preprint arXiv:1911.04474 (2019)

On-Orbit, Non-destructive Surface Surveillance and Inspection with Convolution Neural Network

Sanjay Lakshminarayana[1]($\boxtimes$) (iD), Shubham Bhaskar Thakare[2] (iD), and Krishna Vamshi Duddukuru[1] (iD)

[1] Department of Civil and Industrial Engineering - Aerospace Engineering Division, University of Pisa, 56126 Pisa, Tuscany, Italy
sanjaylakshminarayana@outlook.com
[2] Department of Mechanical Engineering, Wichita State University, Wichita, KS 67260, USA
sxthakare@wichitastate.edu

Abstract. In this paper, the concept for on-orbit, non-destructive Infrared survey and inspection of the surface defects on an interplanetary human module with large surface area and power capabilities, for long flight duration is derived. Automated Probe with thermal imaging camera is used to capture 2D thermal images at that position during rendezvous around the human module. Thermal imaging datasets are classified under binary classification problem and Custom CNN with TensorFlow Architecture is developed. The test accuracy obtained at initial stage of development is about 92%. Converted 2D high resolution grey thermal images are segmented to measure cracks by mapping the pixels. Upon identification of fault position, on-board crew is alerted and original designer is updated, to address the problem remotely. Thereby, an effort has been done herein to significantly reduce the crew EVA spent in survey for surface faults during mission in harsh space environment and the corresponding pre-mission training requirements.

Keywords: Extra vehicular activity · Thermal imaging · Convolution neural network - tensorflow · On orbit servicing and maintenance · Non-destructive testing · Image segmentation

1 Introduction

With the public interest, private investments in human exploration mission to moon and mars rising, the development of new techniques and artificial intelligence enabled machines suitable for manufacturing and servicing will play key role in meeting critical requirements for long term human missions. Especially for settlement missions and cargo transportation to moon, mars and beyond. Private space companies like SpaceX, Virgin galactic etc. aim to build alternate settlements and increase the access to space at public level.

© The Author(s), under exclusive license to Springer Nature Switzerland AG 2022
S. Joshi et al. (Eds.): SpacSec 2021, CCIS 1599, pp. 283–293, 2022.
https://doi.org/10.1007/978-3-031-15784-4_22

As defined in Sarafin (1995), fatigue damage is gradual degradation of material under cyclic loading conditions, causing small cracks to form in the vicinity of microscopic defect areas. European Cooperation for Space Standardization (ECSS) (2009a, 2021) underlines standard procedure for choosing the type of Non-destructive testing (NDT), based on the initial crack size, depth and shape factors. Standard tests are allocated for highest probability of crack detection and for fracture control is advised. But structural elements have defects located in worst possible areas and orientations. NDT method used to test for the defects before launching may not be successful at detecting every crack due to an upper bound on the properties of the geometry. It is also known that, Dynamic loads which vary the fracture toughness of the geometry under the action of sufficient number of cycles of amplitude tend to propagate cracks even in most adequate of environments. [1–4] If the detected cracks are within the limits for the structural design of a particular mission, it is a well-known fact that inter-planetary space travel is posed by several threats. By travelling at high speeds, the impacts of the micro meteors can initiate or lead to propagation of defects, increasing the probability of permanent damage. Shielding developed currently is suitable for small-scaled satellites, up-scaled version is expensive and impractical.

For human missions, it will be advantageous from the safety and relaunch cost point of view, to carry on board equipment that is capable of custom delivery of solutions, particularly concerning leak response. These operations not only require a specially trained crew, but also tedious procedures and require long duration training on ground before ability to perform EVA. Also, defect areas are mostly posed with additional challenge and difficulty to access with life threat to the crew. Even with tedious and expensive procedure, the effectiveness of the solution is nowhere near expected efficiency. Also, owing to lack of complete awareness of the system being repaired due to the limited human capacity, knowledge gaps between the original ground designer and the trained crew exist.

With the limited information which exists on the real time On-Orbit Upgrade and repair activities, existing models are based on the most notable repair in space history, viz, Hubble space telescope. During Hubble space program activities, astronauts received tens of months of constant training and practice at specially designed training facilities, to perform replacement and repairs to the space telescope. EVA to fix Hubble, took a handful of days with 8-hour long shifts performed by Astronauts. Exploring the possibilities of developing a model for application in real time, Hastings et.al applied Monte Carlo simulation to randomize variables for servicing scenarios to map the time and its impact on satellites reliability. Results clearly indicates that servicing albeit with a small percentage of risk is beneficial for life extension of satellite. Working proof of reliable operation due to inspection and servicing is Hubble telescope itself. However, activities performed during Hubble servicing are not completely relevant to the current day scenario, especially for human missions. In future, a deeper and more generalized architecture is required for human missions, especially of inter-planetary nature [5]. Fatigue damage is inevitable during long term missions with corresponding large surface area of the structures of various modules. It can be prevented with real time inspection for damage and to overcome the limitation of some of the standardized ground-based tests. By developing alternative solutions, without the requirement of highly skilled operator or EVA's.

The architecture proposed involves an automated probe that performs inspection of surface, directly exposed in space, without direct physical contact between the instrument and the test surface area. Infrared (IR) thermography is nondestructive testing technique which works by measuring the temperature at each point on the surface. The surface temperature is recorded and analysed with an IR Camera. The thermal camera displays the surface temperature in form of an image [6]. Using Thermal diffusion theory, the temperature profiles in and around the cracks with finite depth has already been modelled. In the image captured by the thermal camera, differences in surface temperature are observed as image gradients. The data provides an advantage over other methods with high detection probability with distinct information about defects. As applied in Yang et.al, thermal excitation provided by external source on to the surface, enables better detection of real cracks when thermal source and crack are along same direction, resulting in higher temperature gradients due to enhanced heating effect. Further, temperature profiles of deep surface cracks and shallow surface scratch has been modelled. Crack is classified for a steel plate, based entirely on surface temperature gradients formed on either side of the vicinity of crack. Results clearly indicate that Temperature gradients assist to identify the defect, as the temperature variation is high in its vicinity [4, 7].

The surface defect detection in thermal image is made possible by computer vision algorithms. Working similar to human vision, are fast, accurate in identifying and classifying the object data. Faster Region-CNN, based on Regional Proposal Network (RPN) detects cracks in an effective way compared to Region-CNN, similar architecture is employed in Yang et.al, Zemmar et al., for crack detection and analysis in steel plate and biological materials in 3D respectively. These require relatively large computing infrastructure and real-time classification of object data is difficult. You only Look Once (YOLO) architecture is extremely fast at processing multi-resolution data in real-time, outperforming R-CNN and Mobile Single Deep Neural Network (SDN) in terms of Average Precision and Detection time by a margin. YOLO algorithm is based on regression methods, considers the whole image and calculates the class probability to label the bounding boxes. Alternately, in Zhai et.al unmanned aerial vehicle (UAV) systems are being utilized for surveillance and inspection purposes during flight. CNN based on RESNET architecture employing multi-task binary classification problem has been developed. Model can detect, process and classify spatial image data in real time, with variety of defects over multiple image backgrounds. UAV can achieve fully automated surveillance, data acquisition, diagnostics and situational understanding. The architecture can easily be adopted for other applications. As discussed, YOLO is faster but CNNs adopting PythonTensor-Flow which is symbolic math library based on data-flow and differentiable programming allow for far more in-depth customisation especially for image classification applications, [7–13]. Also, during space travel, defect of every type is relevant and potentially life threatening to on-board crew. Therefore, Tensor-Flow based CNN architecture is adopted in this paper for deeper customization of Real-time image datasets at relatively lower computing cost.

2 Design of Operation

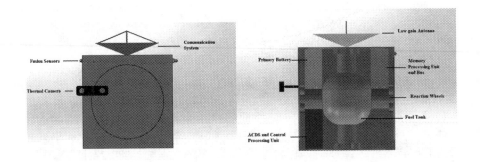

Fig. 1. 3D CAD representation of the probe

The CAD model shown in Fig. 1 represents the Probe with IR thermal imaging, which consists of emitter and receiver. Working in real time, sensors are fixed on all faces. It is used to achieve ease of operation in complex spaces. The mass of the main sub-systems included in the probe are discussed in Table 1. Even though, it is beyond scope of this paper to investigate Complete Automation of probe in terms of Navigation and Guidance, Propulsion, detailed Power budget, Communication and the operation of the instruments, Surveillance procedure assumes conditions below. During operation,

(a) Relative motion between the probe and the human module is assumed to be non-uniform. Automated probe is expected to rendezvous around the human space module at nearly constant distance to the surface assisted by imparting control force powered by an on-board propulsion system with Fusion sensors for attitude guidance. Additionally, ACDS is equipped with 6 - Reaction wheels along 3 Axes with accuracy of 4 RPM, operating at 0.2 W, on-board propulsion system is used for momentum dumping when necessary. It is required to limit variations that arise from perturbations in attitude and distance during operation of thermograph, to obtain high resolution images (without blur).

(b) To counter external noise, assuming that peak intensity of external radiation is along normal to the surface area being inspected. Probe is required to operate parallel to the surface plane of human module to block the noise.

(c) Assuming the outer surface of the human module is in thermal equilibrium with surroundings. Probe is required to incident energy on to the surface of the module, by the means of Light Source for thermal excitation to induce significant temperature difference (against background noise). The large temperature gradient improves, temperature resolution in the image data recorded by thermograph. Thermal camera operates at voltage input of 16V DC, in wavelength range of 1–14 microns with a minimum detector array size of 144 × 144 and Operating at temperature range of [50,120] K.

Table 1. Mass budget as represented in Fig. 1b

System	Component/Function	Wt in Kg
Fusion Sensors and Processing Units	Proximity sensor	0.1
	Inertia sensor	0.2
	IR sensor	0.1
	Reaction wheels	0.75
	Storage, CPU and BUS	7.5
Fuel	Control Force	35
Communication	Ground/Module/Probe	15
IR Thermography	Thermal Imaging Camera	4
	Processing Tools & Memory	4
Emitter and Receivers		2.8
Misc.		1
Total Mass Budget		70

3   Auto - Identification of Defects

The development of artificial neural network which enables to classify the thermal images with defect from the thermal image without defect, by well-known binary classification problem with Python - Tensor-Flow is presented in Sect. 3.1 and Sect. 3.2. Results are discussed in Sect. 4.

3.1   Preparing Image Data-set

There is no suitable pre-existing data-set available for this study nor a pre-trained CNN based on the presented architecture. The data obtained, consists of multiple types of defects at various developing stages as shown in Fig. 2. Private firms successfully implemented, IR Thermography to identify during early stage of defects, Cracks, Live Gas Leaks in piping as shown in Fig. 2(b), short circuits in Solar Arrays etc. Figure 2(b) represents, Spots with abnormal temperature distribution caused by Live Leakage, Cracks and Fractures at surface and sub-surface in Piping. In Fig. 2(a), 2(c) and 2(d), hot spots identify defective cell, short circuit, defect at connection points of solar panel. The idea is to collect images relevant to Space applications, Test sample of 68 was obtained from [14–21] with variety of resolution, out of which 32 samples were positive for defect. Sample size is increased with data augmentation, it is necessary to avoid over-fitting and it resulted in increasing the test accuracy result of the base-model.

  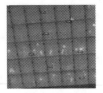 

Fig. 2. Thermal image dataset with defects

Each image is stored as Data Frame. Image with and without defects are concatenated along same axis, data frames are split further with train Test flip function [22–24]. Dataset comprised of images, with size 502 × 317. Greater than 75% of the data frame is used to train and remaining as test set with Image pixel class as binary. Because, obtained datasets were of varying size and resolution, to augment the datasets without loss of resolution, the images were sliced to 250 × 250. Standard Encoding of the thermal images are done in RGB scale. The classified Data frame is composed of 330 trained set, 338 test set images and 82 validated set.

3.2   Network Architecture and Implementation

The problem is considered as binary classification problem where in likelihood of the data belonging to either (a) With Defect assigned integer value 1 or (b) Without Defect assigned integer value 0 is predicted. A standard TensorFlow CNN implemented in [25] but of 4 layers with Max pooling with size[2 × 2], 3 fully connected layers is considered given the size of the available dataset. The input image is of dimensions (250, 250, 3), with max pool layer of stride (2, 2). The first layer is comprised of 32 Filters, rest of the 3 layers are of 64 filters. At 2nd Layer, input dimension is reduced to (121, 121, 64) and (58, 58, 64), (27, 27, 64) for 3rd and 4th layers respectively. The output of the fully connected 4th layer is passed on to SoftMax layer to normalize the classification vector. All the hidden layers use ReLu activation function, as it is very well known to decrease the likelihood of vanishing gradient problem and in this case, also for faster learning. The designed CNN is represented in Fig. 3.

3.3   Training Experiments

The training corresponds to varying three parameters, Image dataset size (D), Number of Nodes (N) and Learning Rate (I), with I = [0.001, 1], D = [25, 100]

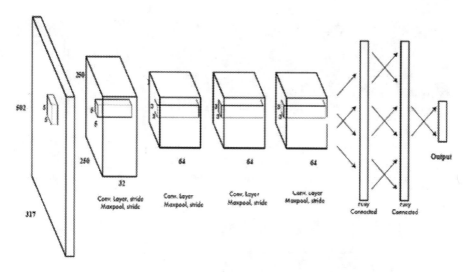

Fig. 3. 4-Layer CNN model

%, N = [16, 32, 64, 128, 256]. For each experiment, the value of accuracy for every Epoch = [100] was recorded, to identify the best model. Also, training was performed on Python IDE on a Personal Computer with 16 GB memory.

3.4 Image Segmentation

Thermal Image with Defect Fig. 4(a) is then converted from Standard RGB to grey scale, during which the quality of the image is not affected. Grey images limit the need of large storage space, the environment in which, the images captured favour their use as saturation if present, in the original image is reduced upon conversion. Also, Gray images preserve Temperature gradients of the original thermal image, In terms of proportionate gradients in gray scale. Therefore, Defect information is not lost, entirely. Gray Image is shown in Fig. 4(b). Before measuring the crack, image is enhanced by contrast stretching [9, 26–28] as shown in Fig. 4(b). Image is segmented by setting an arbitrary threshold value as the defined value and the image with segmented crack is obtained as shown in Fig. 4(c). Clearly, the Crack Width (L_C) is the ratio of the product of calibration length (C_L) and crack pixels (P_L) to the calibration pixels (C_P) as given by Eq. (1).

$$L_C = P_L * C_L/C_P \tag{1}$$

4 Result Discussion

The best value of accuracy was obtained for I = [0.001], N = [64], Epoch = 100 with D = 98% yields an accuracy of 92% with corresponding f1 score

(a)   (b)   (c)

Fig. 4. (a) High resolution thermal image identified for defect (b) Thermal image converted to gray scale (c) Segmented with multiple defects (Color figure online)

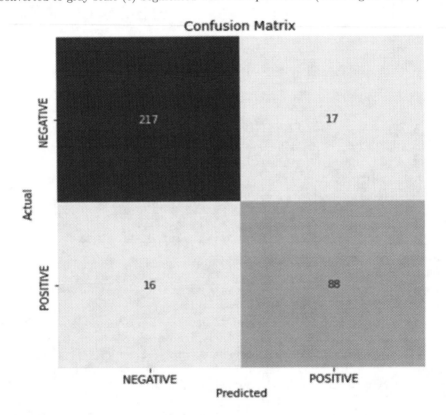

Fig. 5. Confusion matrix of CNN

obtained from Fig. 5 is 92%. Clearly the accuracy is dependent on the training image dataset and resolution of the image in the data set. By obtaining, real data from space missions, the accuracy value for CNN architecture proposed in this paper, can surpass 95% easily. It is important to bear in mind that in this paper, the prime focus is to investigate and provide a proof of concept for an automated probe based on CNN in rendezvous around human module. Equipped with thermal camera, along with Fusion sensors. A probe, capable of surveying the surface area for defects, identified by processing the thermal image data as shown in Sect. 3.1 to Sect. 3.3. Upon identification of defect, the image with defect is processed with procedure in Sect. 3.4 and On-board crew is alerted by the probe for further examination.

In Sect. 3.4, Using equation (1), the image size in Fig. 4 is arbitrarily taken to 154×176 (width $\times$ height) pixels, by taking 1 pixel = 1/100th of an Inch as reference. The Height (almost equal to the original height of the object in Fig. 4) of the major crack is maximum 14.08-inch. Also, by trial and error, threshold value for this model is best between 0.45 and 0.55.

5   Conclusion

Concept for a working On Orbit, IR- Non-Destructive for Real-time Survey and Inspection of surface defects adopting custom developed CNN has been investigated. Probe represented in Sect. 2 with completely automated sub-systems holds potential to enable better access to majority of the module surface. Fully Automated Probe configuration can be used commonly for surveillance, independently of module design and Area Spans. Probe, at about the size of micro-satellite can be launched, attached with other modules in single launch. However, operation is at cost of on-board propulsion system utilized for translation motion around module, on-board batteries charge-discharge cycle, limiting the surveillance time.

Method in Sect. 3.1, 3.2 and 3.3 provide greater adaptability and automation for survey and inspection. Section 3.4 revisits known image segmentation technique in measuring the dimension of the defect and thereby its extent. The design assists with Extra Vehicular Activity, eliminates exposure to life threatening situation for crew and results in reduction of launch and operation costs. Such operations primarily require many months of training and preparation on Earth, including tens of hours of spacewalks for detection and fixing of defects on large surface spans. The mass of the probe is kept below 100 Kg and the total wattage about 100 W. The proposed CNN model accuracy rate at defect identification and classification is best at 92%. But with real-time mission data, it is expected to reach 95% and higher. Further, Post-Processed Data can be manually implemented with CAD software tools to regenerate the 3D data and to design replacements for the defect areas by the original designer. Finally, 3D printing solutions available on-board will enable crew to implement the new design to resolve or replace the defect area, which is the only manual task requiring EVA.

Acknowledgement. We express special thanks to Dr Vinod Singh Yadav, Assistant Professor, National Institute of Technology, Uttarakhand, India. Dr Amit Kumar Bairwa, Manipal University Jaipur and Dr RoopaShree Tantri for their valuable guidance and motivation in completion of the work.

References

1. Sarafin, T.P., Larson, W.J.: Spacecraft Structures and Mechanisms-from Concept to Launch. Microcosm, Torrance (1995)
2. European Cooperation for Space Standardization (ECSS). https://ecss.nl/item/? glossary_id=1776. Accessed 6 Mar 2021
3. European Cooperation for Space Standardization (ECSS) Non-destructive testing. https://ecss.nl/standard/ecss-q-st-70-15c-non-destructive-testing/. Accessed 1 May 2021
4. Rodríguez-Martín, M., Lagüela, S., González-Aguilera, D., Martinez, J.: Prediction of depth model for cracks in steel using infrared thermography. Infrared Phys. Technol. **71**, 492–500 (2015). https://doi.org/10.1016/j.infrared.2015.06.013
5. Hastings, D.E., Joppin, C.: On-orbit upgrade and repair: the Hubble space telescope example. J. Spacecr. Rockets **43**, 614–625 (2006). https://doi.org/10.2514/1.15496
6. Speakman, J.R., Ward, S.: Infrared thermal imaging: principles and applications. Zoology-Jena- **101**, 224–232 (1998)
7. Yang, J., Wang, W., Lin, G., Li, Q., Sun, Y., & Sun, Y.: Infrared thermal imaging-based crack detection using deep learning. IEEE Access **7**, 182060–182077 (2019). https://doi.org/10.1109/access.2019.2958264
8. Zemmar, A., Lozano, A.M., Nelson, B.J.: The rise of robots in surgical environments during COVID-19. Nat. Mach. Intell. **2**, 566–572 (2020). https://doi.org/10.1038/s42256-020-00238-2
9. Santhi, B., Krishnamurthy, G., Siddharth, S., Ramakrishnan, P.K.: Automatic detection of cracks in pavements using edge detection operator. J. Theor. Appl. Inf. Technol. **36**(2), 199–205 (2012)
10. Barreira, E., de Freitas, V.P.: Evaluation of building materials using infrared thermography. Construct. Build. Mater. **21**(1), 218–224 (2007)
11. Redmon, J., Divvala, S., Girshick, R., Farhadi, A.: You only look once: unified, real-time object detection. In: 2016 IEEE Conference on Computer Vision and Pattern Recognition (CVPR). Presented at the 2016 IEEE Conference on Computer Vision and Pattern Recognition (CVPR). IEEE (2016) https://doi.org/10.1109/cvpr.2016.91
12. Li, Y., Han, Z., Xu, H., Liu, L., Li, X., Zhang, K.: YOLOv3-Lite: a lightweight crack detection network for aircraft structure based on depthwise separable convolutions. Appl. Sci. **9**, 3781 (2019). https://doi.org/10.3390/app9183781
13. Zhai, X., Liu, K., Nash, W., Castineira, D.: Smart autopilot drone system for surface surveillance and anomaly detection via customizable deep neural network. In: International Petroleum Technology Conference. OnePetro (2020). https://doi.org/10.2523/IPTC-20111-MS
14. http://tmt.co.il/product/solar-panels-thermal-visual-inspection/ . Accessed 17 Oct 2021
15. https://westerninfrared.com/problems/solar-panels/ . Accessed 17 Oct 2021
16. López-Fernández, L., Lagüela, S., Fernández, J., González-Aguilera, D.: Automatic evaluation of photovoltaic power stations from high-density RGB-T 3D point clouds. Remote Sens. **9**(6), 631 (2017). https://doi.org/10.3390/rs9060631
17. PhotoVoltaic Solutions https://kitawa.de/en/thermography-pv-systems. Accessed 17 Oct 2021
18. Thermography. https://www.murcal.com/, https://www.murcal.com/pdf20folder/15.testo_thermography_guide.pdf. Accessed 17 Oct 2021

19. Balasubramani, G., Thangavelu, V., Chinnusamy, M., Subramaniam, U., Padman-aban, S., Mihet-Popa, L.: Infrared thermography based defects testing of solar photovoltaic panel with fuzzy rule-based evaluation. Energies **13**(6), 1343 (2020). https://doi.org/10.3390/en13061343

20. Runnemalm, A. and P. Broberg.: Surface crack detection using infrared thermography and ultraviolet excitation. Quant. InfraRed Thermography, 1–7 (2014)

21. Lee, S.Y., Tama, B.A., Moon, S.J., Lee, S.: Steel surface defect diagnostics using deep convolutional neural network and class activation map. Appl. Sci. **9**(24), 5449 (2019). https://doi.org/10.3390/app9245449

22. Inoue, H.: Data augmentation by pairing samples for images classification. arXiv preprint arXiv:1801.02929 (2018)

23. Paper, D.: Scikit-learn classifier tuning from complex training sets. In: Hands-on Scikit-Learn for Machine Learning Applications, pp. 165–188. Apress, Berkeley (2020). https://doi.org/10.1007/978-1-4842-5373-1_6

24. Nelli, F.: pandas in depth: data manipulation. In: Python Data Analytics, pp. 131–165. Apress, Berkeley (2015). https://doi.org/10.1007/978-1-4842-0958-5_6

25. Han, Z., Chen, H., Liu, Y., Li, Y., Du, Y., Zhang, H.: Vision-based crack detection of asphalt pavement using deep convolutional neural network. Iran. J. Sci. Technol. Trans. Civ. Eng. **45**(3), 2047–2055 (2021). https://doi.org/10.1007/s40996-021-00668-x

26. Sternberg, S.R.: Grayscale morphology. Comput. Vision Graphics Image Process. **35**, 333–355 (1986). https://doi.org/10.1016/0734-189x(86)90004-6

27. Chen, X., Li, J., Huang, S., Cui, H., Liu, P., Sun, Q.: An automatic concrete crack-detection method fusing point clouds and images based on improved otsu's algorithm. Sensors **21**, 1581 (2021). https://doi.org/10.3390/s21051581

28. Li, S., Zhao, X.: Image-based concrete crack detection using convolutional neural network and exhaustive search technique. Adv. Civ. Eng. **2019**, 1–12 (2019). https://doi.org/10.1155/2019/6520620

Ramadan Group Transform Fundamental Properties and Some its Dualities

A. A. Soliman[1], K. R. Raslan[2], and A. M. Abdallah[3]([✉])

[1] Department of Mathematics, Faculty of Science, Arish Univeristy, AL-Arish 4511, Egypt
[2] Department of Mathematics, Faculty of Science, Al-Azhar Univeristy, Cairo, Egypt
[3] Department of Basic Science, Higher Technological Institute, 10th of Ramadan City, Egypt
ahmedabdel31@yahoo.com

Abstract. In preceding manuscript, we investigate the fundamental properties of RG transform and used to solve fractional differential equations. Also, the connection between RG transform and some useful integral transforms obtained.

Keywords: Fractional differential equations · Integral transforms · Fourier transform

1 Introduction

In recent years, new techniques for obtaining analytical solution of fractional equations were developed. In order to solve this kind of equations, an integral transform were extensively demonstrated. These transforms are used to convert fractional differential equations into algebraic equations. The main goal of integral transform is to get easier equations. The purpose of this study is to establish the relationship between RG transform and some integral transforms namely Mellin, Laplace, Fourier, Yang and ARA transform. Moreover, some fundamental properties were carefully mentioned. The plan of this discussion is as follows: Some fundamental properties of RG transform are [6–9]. In addition to, RG for fractional differential equation were illustrated. Thereafter, the relationship between RG transforms and some useful integral transforms were explained.

1.1 Some Fundamental Properties of RG Transform

Ramadan Group transform (RG) of a continuous and exponential order function $g(t)$ is defined in the set $G = \left\{ g(t) : |\exists M, m_1, m_2 > 0, \ |g(t)| < M e^{\frac{|t|}{m_i}}, \ if \ t \in (-1)^i \times [0, +\infty) \right\}$, is given by [9]

$$RG[g(t)] = K(s, u) = \int\limits_{0}^{+\infty} e^{-st} g(ut) dt; \ s, \ u > 0, \tag{1}$$

© The Author(s), under exclusive license to Springer Nature Switzerland AG 2022
S. Joshi et al. (Eds.): SpacSec 2021, CCIS 1599, pp. 294–302, 2022.
https://doi.org/10.1007/978-3-031-15784-4_23

where s and u are the transform variables. The inverse RG transform is defined in [8] (Tables 1 and 2)

$$RG^{-1}[K(s, u)] = \frac{1}{2\Pi i} \int_{a-i\infty}^{a+i\infty} e^{\frac{st}{u}} K(s, u)dt,$$

Table 1. Some useful properties of RG transform

No	Property & mathematical form
1	**Linearity** $RG\big[ag(t) + bf(t)\big] = aRG\big[g(t)\big] + bRG[f(t)]$ a, b are constants
2	**Change of scale** $RG[g(at)] = K(s, au) = \frac{1}{a}K(\frac{s}{a}, u)$
3	**Translation** $RG[g(\frac{t}{a})] = K(s, \frac{u}{a})$
4	**First shifting** $RG[e^{\pm at}g(t)] = k(s \mp au, u)$
5	**Second shifting** $RG\big[g(t - a)\big] = e^{-as}K(s, u)$
6	**Convolution** $RG[f(t) * g(t)] = \int_a^t f(t - t_1)g(t_1)dt_1$ $= vK_1(s, u)K_2(s, u)$
7	**Derivatives** $RG[f^{(n)}(t)] = \frac{s^n}{u^n} K(s, u) - \sum_{k=0}^{n-1} \frac{s^{n-k-1}}{u^{n-k}} f^{(k)}(0)$
	Integration $RG\left[\int_0^t g(v)dv\right] = \frac{u}{s}K(s, u)$

Theorem 1.1. *If $f(t)$ is defined on G then,*
$$RG[t^{b-1}E_{a,b}(ct^a)] = \frac{1}{u}\left[\frac{(\frac{s}{u})^{a-b}}{(\frac{s}{u})^a - c}\right] \text{ for } a, b > 0, \text{ where Mittag-Leffler function is}$$
given as $E_{a,b}(t) = \sum_{i=0}^{+\infty} \frac{t^k}{\Gamma(ak+1)}$.

Proof. *By definition of RG transform,* through the substitution $t = \frac{xu}{s}$. Then, we get the required result.

Table 2. RG transform of important functions

No	f(t)	RG[f(t)] = K(s, u)
1	a	$RG[a] = \frac{a}{s}$
2	t^n	$RG[t^n] = \begin{cases} \dfrac{u^n n!}{s^{n+1}}, & n = 1, 2, \ldots, \\ \dfrac{u^n \Gamma(n+1)}{s^{n+1}}, & n > 0 \end{cases}$
3	e^{at}	$RG[e^{at}] = \frac{1}{s+au}$
4	$\sin(at)$	$RG[\sin(at)] = \frac{au}{s^2 + a^2 u^2}$
5	$\cos(at)$	$RG[\cos(at)] = \frac{s}{s^2 + a^2 u^2}$
6	$\sinh(at)$	$RG[\sinh(at)] = \frac{au}{s^2 - a^2 u^2}$
7	$\cosh(at)$	$RG[\cosh(at)] = \frac{s}{s^2 - a^2 u^2}$
8	$H(t-a)$	$RG[H(t-a)] = \frac{1}{s} e^{\frac{-as}{u}}$
9	$\delta(t-a)$	$RG[\delta(t-a)] = \frac{e^{\frac{-as}{u}}}{u}$

Remark 1. Mittag-Leffler function of one variable denoted as.

$$RG[E_a(t)] = \frac{u^k \Gamma(k)}{as^{k+1} \Gamma(ak)}.$$

2   RG Application

In this section, RG transform will be used to solve certain non-homogenous fractional differential equations. One of RG transform application on fractional differential equation is Lane Emdern equation.

2.1   Fractional Lane Emdern Equation

Lane-Emden equations makes much attention to researchers due to its vast applications in many biological models, physical science and astrophysics [1].

Its form given by [1]

$$D^\alpha u(t) + \frac{2}{t} u_t(t) + G(u) = 0, \ 0 < \alpha \leq 1$$

with the initial condition $u(0) = a$, $u'(0) = b$, a, b are constants.

Example

$$D^\alpha y(t) + \frac{2}{t} y'(t) - y(6 + 4t^2) = 0, \ 0 < \alpha \leq 1 \tag{2}$$

under the initial condition $u(0) = 1$, $u'(0) = 0$.

Equation (2) is equivalent to

$$tD^\alpha y(t) + 2y'(t) - y(6t + 4t^3) = 0 \tag{3}$$

Applying the RG decomposition method [13, 14] on (2), we gain

$$u\frac{d^\alpha}{du^\alpha}K(s,u) + 2\left(\left(\frac{s}{u}\right) - \sum_{i=0}^{n} y^{(i)}(0)\right) - RG[D_n] = 0, \tag{4}$$

operating inverse RG transform on (4), we get the desired solution

$$y_0(t) = 1, \ y_1 = t^\alpha + \frac{t^{2\alpha}}{5}, \ y_1 = \frac{3t^{2\alpha}}{10} + \frac{13t^{2\alpha}}{105} + \frac{t^{4\alpha}}{90}, \dots$$

i.e.,

$$y = \sum_{i=0}^{n} y_i = 1 + t^\alpha + \frac{t^{2\alpha}}{2!} + \dots = e^{t^\alpha}.$$

3 RG Dualities

3.1 Relation to RG Transform to Fourier Transform

We recall that Fourier transform is defined as [4, 11]

$$\xi[g(t)] = \xi(s,u) = \int_{-\infty}^{+\infty} e^{-iwt} g(t)dt \tag{5}$$

Substitute $iwt = sz \Rightarrow dt = \frac{s}{iw}dz$ in Eq. (4)

$$\xi[g(t)] = \frac{s}{iw}\int_{-\infty}^{+\infty} e^{-sz} g(\frac{sz}{iw})dz = \frac{s}{iw}K(s,\frac{s}{iw}). \tag{6}$$

Also, substitute $u = 1$ in Eq. (1)

$$\xi[g(t)] = K(iw, 1). \tag{7}$$

Conversely, let $ut = z \Rightarrow dt = \frac{dz}{u}$ in Eq. (1)

$$K(s,u) = \frac{1}{u}\int_{-\infty}^{+\infty} e^{-s\frac{z}{u}} g(z)dz = \frac{1}{u}\int_{-\infty}^{+\infty} e^{-iz\frac{s}{iu}} g(z)dz = \frac{1}{u}\xi\left(\frac{s}{iu}\right). \tag{8}$$

Also, if we put $st = iwz \Rightarrow dt = \frac{iw}{s}dz$ in Eq. (1) (Table 3)

$$K(s,u) = \frac{iw}{s}\int_{-\infty}^{+\infty} e^{-iwz} g(\frac{uiw}{s}z)dz = \frac{iw}{s}\xi\left[g\left(\frac{uiw}{s}\right)\right]. \tag{9}$$

Table 3. Fourier transform of important functions

No	f(t)	$\xi[g(t)] = \xi(s, u)$
1	**a**	$\sqrt{2\pi}\, a\, \delta(w)$
2	t^n	$\frac{1}{2}\begin{pmatrix} \sqrt{2\pi}\,(-i)^n \delta^{(n)}(-w) \\ +\sqrt{2\pi}\,(-i)^n \delta^{(n)}(w) \end{pmatrix}$ for even part
3	t^n	$\frac{-i}{2}\begin{pmatrix} \sqrt{2\pi}\,(-i)^n \delta^{(n)}(w) \\ -\sqrt{2\pi}\,(-i)^n \delta^{(n)}(-w) \end{pmatrix}$ for odd part
4	e^{at}	$\sqrt{2\pi}\,\delta(w - ia)$
5	$\sin(at)$	$i\sqrt{\frac{\pi}{2}}\,\delta(w - a) - i\sqrt{\frac{\pi}{2}}\,\delta(w + a),\ a \in \mathbb{R}$
6	$\cos(at)$	$\sqrt{\frac{\pi}{2}}\,\delta(w - a) + \sqrt{\frac{\pi}{2}}\,\delta(w + a),\ a \in \mathbb{R}$
7	$\sinh(at)$	$\frac{\sqrt{2\pi}\,\delta(w-ia) - \sqrt{2\pi}\,\delta(w+ia)}{2}$
8	$\cosh(at)$	$\frac{\sqrt{2\pi}\,\delta(w-ia) + \sqrt{2\pi}\,\delta(w+ia)}{2}$

3.2 Relation to RG Transform to Yang Transform

Yang transform of the function g(t) is given by [5]

$$\Upsilon[g(t)] = \Xi(w) = \int_0^{+\infty} e^{-\frac{t}{w}} g(t)\,dt \tag{10}$$

Put $t = uz \Rightarrow dt = u\,dz$ in Eq. (9), we get

$$\Upsilon[g(t)] = \Xi(w) = u\int_0^{+\infty} e^{-\frac{uz}{w}} g(uz)\,dz = uK\left(\frac{u}{w}, u\right). \tag{11}$$

In the same way, substitute $\frac{t}{w} = sz \Rightarrow dt = sw\,dz$ in Eq. (9), we have

$$\Upsilon[g(t)] = \Xi(w) = sw\int_0^{+\infty} e^{-sz} g(swz)\,dz = swK(s, sw). \tag{12}$$

Conversely, let $ut = z \Rightarrow dt = \frac{dz}{u}$ in Eq. (1), we obtain

$$K(s, u) = RG[g(t)] = \int_0^{+\infty} e^{-\frac{sz}{u}} g(z)\,dz = \Xi\left(\frac{u}{s}\right). \tag{13}$$

Or, set $st = \frac{z}{w} \Rightarrow sdt = \frac{dz}{w}$ in Eq. (1), we gain (Table 4)

$$K(s, u) = RG[g(t)] = \frac{s}{w} \int_0^{+\infty} e^{-\frac{z}{w}} g(\frac{uz}{ws}) dz = \frac{s}{w} \Upsilon\left[g\left(\frac{u}{ws} t\right)\right].$$

Table 4. Yang transform of important functions

No	f(t)	$\Upsilon[g(t)] = \Xi(w)$
1	a	au
2	t^n	$\Upsilon[t^n] = \begin{cases} u^{n+1} n!, & n = 1, 2, \ldots, \\ u^{n+1} \Gamma(n+1), & n > 0 \end{cases}$
3	e^{at}	$\frac{u}{1-au}$
4	$\sin(at)$	$\frac{au^2}{1+a^2u^2}$
5	$\cos(at)$	$\frac{u}{1+a^2u^2}$
6	$\sinh(at)$	$\frac{au^2}{1-a^2u^2}$
7	$\cosh(at)$	$\frac{u}{1-a^2u^2}$

3.3 Relation to RG Transform and Laplace Transform

Laplace transform of the function g(t) is given by [12, 15]

$$L[g(t)] = G(s) = \int_0^{+\infty} e^{-st} g(t) dt, \ s > 0 \tag{14}$$

In particular, when $t = uz \Rightarrow dt = udz$ in Eq. (13), then

$$G(s) = u \int_0^{+\infty} e^{-suz} g(uz) dz = uK(su, u) \tag{15}$$

Also, if we put $u = 1$ in Eq. (1), we have

$$K(s, 1) = G(s). \tag{16}$$

Similarly, by putting $ut = z \Rightarrow dt = \frac{dz}{u}$ in Eq. (1), we have (Table 5)

$$K(s, u) = \frac{1}{u} \int_0^{+\infty} e^{-\frac{sz}{u}} g(z) dz = \frac{1}{u} G(\frac{s}{u}). \tag{17}$$

Table 5. Laplace transform of important functions

No	f(t)	$L[g(t)] = G(s)$
1	a	$\frac{a}{s}$
2	t^n	$L[t^n] = \begin{cases} \dfrac{n!}{s^{n+1}}, & n = 1, 2, \ldots, \\ \dfrac{\Gamma(n+1)}{s^{n+1}}, & n > 0 \end{cases}$
3	e^{at}	$\frac{1}{s-a}$
4	$\sin(at)$	$\frac{a}{s^2+a^2}$
5	$\cos(at)$	$\frac{s}{s^2+a^2}$
6	$\sinh(at)$	$\frac{a}{s^2-a^2}$
7	$\cosh(at)$	$\frac{s}{s^2-a^2}$

3.4   Relation to RG Transform and Mellin Transform

Mellin transform can be given by [3]

$$M[g(t); s] = M(s) = \int_0^{+\infty} t^{s-1} g(t) dt \tag{18}$$

It follows from Eq. (16), from the relation to Laplace and Mellin transformations [2, 16]

$$K(s, u) = \frac{1}{u} G\left(\frac{s}{u}\right) = \frac{1}{u} M(g(-\ln t))\left(\frac{s}{u}\right). \tag{19}$$

It is immediately concluded using Eq. (14), from the relation to Laplace and Mellin transformations [16] (Table 6)

$$M(g(t)) = L\left(g\left(e^{-t}\right)\right) = uRG\left[g\left(e^{-t}\right)\right]\left(\frac{u}{s}\right). \tag{20}$$

3.5   Relation to RG Transform and ARA Transform

ARA transform can be given by [10]

$$\wp_n[g(t)](s) = ARA(n, s) = s \int_0^{+\infty} t^{n-1} e^{-st} g(t) dt, \ s > 0 \tag{21}$$

By substituting n = 1 in Eq. (20)

$$K(s, u) = s\wp_1[g(ut)](s). \tag{22}$$

Table 6. Mellin transform of important functions

No	f(t)	$M[g(t); s] = M(s)$
1	**a**	$2\pi a\delta(is)$
2	t^n	$2\pi a\delta(i(s+n))$
3	e^{at}	$(-a)^s\,\Gamma(s)$
4	$\sin(at)$	$a^{-s}\sin(\frac{\pi s}{2})\Gamma(s)$
5	$\cos(at)$	$(s-1)!\,a^{-s}\cos(\frac{\pi s}{2})$
6	$\sinh(at)$	$\frac{1}{2}\Gamma(s)\left[(-t)^{-s} - t^{-s}\right]$
7	$\cosh(at)$	$\frac{1}{2}\Gamma(s)\left[(-t)^{-s} + t^{-s}\right]$

It is immediately concluded using Eqs. (1), (20) that (Table 7)

$$\wp_n[g(t)](s) = s\int_0^{+\infty} t^{n-1}e^{-st}g(t)dt = s\,RG\left[t^{n-1}g(\frac{t}{u})\right]. \tag{23}$$

Table 7. ARA transform of important functions

No	f(t)	$\wp_n[g(t)](s) = ARA(n, s)$
1	a	$\frac{a}{s^{n-1}}\Gamma(s)$
2	t^n	$\frac{\Gamma(m+n)}{s^{m+n-1}}$
3	e^{at}	$\frac{s}{(s-a)^n}\Gamma(s)$
4	$\sin(at)$	$(1 + \frac{a^2}{s^2})^{\frac{-n}{2}}s^{1-n}\sin(n\tan^{-1}(\frac{a}{s}))\Gamma(n)$
5	$\cos(at)$	$(1 + \frac{a^2}{s^2})^{\frac{-n}{2}}s^{1-n}\cos(n\tan^{-1}(\frac{a}{s}))\Gamma(n)$
6	$\sinh(at)$	$\frac{s}{2}\Gamma(n)\frac{1}{s^n}\left[\frac{1}{(1-\frac{a}{s})^n} - \frac{1}{(1+\frac{a}{s})^n}\right]$
7	$\cosh(at)$	$\frac{s}{2}\Gamma(n)\frac{1}{s^n}\left[\frac{1}{(1-\frac{a}{s})^n} + \frac{1}{(1+\frac{a}{s})^n}\right]$

4 Conclusion

The main result of this paper is to investigate fundamental properties of RG transform. Further RG transform can be used to solve fractional differential equations with variable coefficients such as Lane-Emdern Equation. The applicability of the duality between RG and other integral transforms is demonstrated using tabular presentation.

RG transform is a convenient tool for solving fractional differential equations and the connection of RG transform with any integral transform goes much deeper. Tabular presentation of the integral transforms are given with the help of mention dualities relations to visualize the importance of dualities between RG transform and mention integral transforms.

Results show that the integral transform is helpful for solving many problems of science and technology. RG transform and mention integral transforms in this manuscript are strongly related to each others. In this context RG transform has been successfully applied to fractional equations to find analytic solutions. In future, the use of these duality relations in many applications is very effective tool.

References

1. Abdel-Salama, E.A.B., Nouhb, M.I., Elkholy, E.A.: Analytical solution to the conformable fractional Lane-Emden type equations arising in astrophysics. Sci. Afr. **8**, 1–7 (2020)
2. Aggarwal, S., Bhatnagar, K.: Dualities between Laplace transform and some useful integral transforms. Int. J. Eng. Adv. Technol. **9**(1), 936–941 (2019)
3. Bertrand, J., Bertrand, P., Ovarlez, J.: The Mellin Transform. The Transforms and Applications. CRC Press Inc, France (1995)
4. Bochner, S., Chandrasekharan, K.: Fourier Transforms. Princeton University Press, London (1949)
5. Dattu, K.U.: New integral transform: fundamental properties, investigations and applications. Iaetsd J. Adv. Res. Appl. Sci. **5**(4), 534–539 (2018)
6. Ramadan, M.A., Raslan, K.R., Hadhoud, A.R., Mesrage, A.K.: A substitution method for partial differential equations using Ramadan group integral transform. Asian Res. J. Math. **7**(4), 1–10 (2017)
7. Ramadan, M.A.: The convolution of Ramadan group integral transform: theory and applications. J. Adv. Trends Basic Appl. Sci. **1**(2), 191–197 (2017)
8. Ramadan, M.A., Mesrage, A.K.: Solution of partial and integro-differential equations using the convolution of Ramadan Group transform. Asian Res. J. Math. **11**(3), 1–15 (2018)
9. Raslan, K.R., Ramadan, M.A., El-Danaf, T.S., Hadhoud, A.R.: On a new general integral transform: some properties and remarks. J. Math. Comput. Sci. **6**(1), 103–109 (2016)
10. Saadeh, R., Qazza, A., Burqan, A.A.: New integral transform: ARA transform and its properties and applications. Symmetry **12**(6), 925 (2020)
11. Salamat, K., Ilyas, N.: Dualities between Fourier sine and some useful integral transformations. J. Math. Sci. Comput. Math. **2**(4), 542–563 (2021)
12. Schiff, J.L.: Laplace Transformation. Theory and Applications. Springer, New York (1999). https://doi.org/10.1007/978-0-387-22757-3
13. Soliman, A.A., Raslan, K.R., Abdallah, A.M.: On some modified methods on fractional delay and nonlinear integro-differential equation. Sound Vibr. **55**(4), 263–279 (2021)
14. Soliman, A.A., Raslan, K.R., Abdallah, A.M.: Analysis for fractional integro-differential equation with time delay. Ital. J. Pure Appl. Math. **46**, 989–1007 (2021)
15. Spiegel, M.R.: Theory and Problems of Laplace Transforms. Schaums Outline Series, McGraw-Hill, New York (1965)
16. Zemanian, A.H.: the distributional Laplace and Mellin transformations. SIAM J. Appl. Math. **14**(1), 41–59 (1996)

Enhancing Security Mechanism in Smart Phones Using Crowdsourcing

Shivani Gupta[1]([✉])[iD], Srinivas Ravipati[1], Ranjeet Kumar[1], and V. Vani[2]

[1] Vellore Institute of Technology, Chennai, India
shivani.panchal@iiitdmj.ac.in
[2] National Institute of Technology, Puducherry, India

Abstract. Mobile phone applications today request permissions to access a large number of resources, which clients must acknowledge partially or completely during installation (e.g., on Android, on iOS) based on the application being installed in smartphones. Generally, clients, in any case, don't be able to make informed decisions about which permissions are essential for their usage. For enhanced protection, we look to use crowdsourcing to give a minimum set of permissions that will safeguard the ease of use of the application for differing clients. We have done a study on the users, in which members investigated diverse authorization sets for the well-known application.

In this paper, we proposed a crowdsourcing management framework that includes convenience scores for different clients that can be anticipated precisely, empowering reasonable suggestions. We also offer a control architecture for permission to that assists inexperienced users in making a low-risk judgement about whether to accept or deny a permission request.

Keywords: Security · Crowd sourcing · Smart phone · Mobile data

1 Introduction

Mobile apps have carried colossal effect on organizations, social, and way of life lately. The quantity of apps in the store has arrived at 2.2 million in June 2016, outperforming its significant rival Apple App Store [5]. The ascent of Android telephones brought the multiplication of Android apps, bringing about an ever-developing application biological system [6]. As clients depend more on mobile gadgets and apps, the protection and security concerns become unmistakable. Vindictive outsider apps not just take private data, for example, contact list, instant messages, online records, and area from their clients, yet additionally purpose monetary misfortune to clients by making cryptic premium-rate calls and instant messages [8,11]. This gives further impetus to the clients to introduce outsider applications from different apps [2–4], however opens their protection to huge security hazards [5]. All the more explicitly, in the current Android

© The Author(s), under exclusive license to Springer Nature Switzerland AG 2022
S. Joshi et al. (Eds.): SpacSec 2021, CCIS 1599, pp. 303–310, 2022.
https://doi.org/10.1007/978-3-031-15784-4_24

engineering, clients need to choose what sources are given to an app at establishment time. Unapproved interchanges among apps are precluded. Notwithstanding, such consent control system has been demonstrated to be incapable in shielding clients from noxious apps. An examination shows that over 70% of cell phone apps solicitation to gather information unimportant to the principle capacity of the app [1].

Furthermore, such investigation shows that lone a little segment (3%) of clients focus and make right reactions to demands for asset consent at establishment, since they will in general hurry through to will utilize the application. The current Android consent alerts don't enable most clients to make right security choices [3]. Understanding these weaknesses in the current Android engineering, a few endeavors have been made to address the issues. Numerous asset the executives frameworks are proposed such as in [3, 5, 7]. Going down to the framework level, L4Android [4] confines cell phone OS for various use conditions in various virtual machines (VMs). QUIRE [6] gives a lot of augmentations tending to a type of assault, called asset confounded representative assaults, in Android. Consequently, no instrument that accepts clients to have high specialized and security information will be usable for a wide crowd. As brought up in [2, 3], the purposes behind the incapability of the current authorization control framework include: (1) unpracticed clients don't understand asset demands are unessential and could bargain their protection, (2) clients have the desire to utilize the app and might be need to surrender their security so as to utilize the app. Despite the fact that app stores (e.g., Google Play) may eliminate those apps with glitches or bad quality intermittently, many all around created apps with protection infringement are not seen by the stores. As such, app stores discharge the option to end clients to let them conclude if to introduce the apps. In such case, most end clients download and introduce those apps by dismissing the security cautioning. In any event, when a few clients do see the protection issue, as the usefulness and inclination of mobile apps, they actually introduce them into the mobile gadget. Once the apps are introduced, clients' protection data will be spilled when they dispatch those apps.

As mobile apps serve for various functionalities, various sorts of security data might be spilled by clients for dispatching various kinds of mobile apps. For example, an area based assistance (LBS) needs to gather client constant area data from clients. Actually, it is accounted for that clients have developing worry about their security while utilizing mobile apps. An ongoing overview from IDG news uncovers that over 30% of mobile clients want to uninstall those apps in the wake of learning the individual data they gathered.

In this paper, so as to quantify how much protection a mobile client endeavors on the mobile phone and help to suggest apps with less security, we propose a security assessment system by dissecting the app utilization information. The infringement of security depends on the dangers of apps, yet in addition on the client use design. Albeit some apps disregard client security vigorously, client data can't spill if the app has not been utilized. To assess the security spillage, we characterize a peril coefficient to measure the protection and dissect the security infringement appropriation of mobile clients. To lessen the security spillage from mobile gadgets, on one hand, we have to see how much protection a mobile app can uncover. Then again, we have to explore the apps utilization of various clients. Subsequently, we consolidate both the client inclination to mobile apps and the security danger of mobile apps for apps recommendations.

2 Literature Review

In the current Android framework, clients need to choose whether an application is sheltered to utilize or not. Clients are definitely not definitely gifted or they couldn't care less their protection outcomes to settle on kind choices. To direct the hypothetically inadequate group, this undertaking proposes an Android application to discover whether an outsider application is protected to utilize or then again not. In this application, the client needs to enroll and afterward login, the outsider application must be chosen for establishment and afterward it has two modes: Probation Mode and Trusted Mode. Application runs just in the probation mode.

The consents for the outsider application will be given by the client and afterward it will be put away in the information base. At that point by that, the master clients are distinguished utilizing publicly supporting calculations. The consents given by the client are been examined dependent on the master rankings and rating whether to acknowledge the outsider application for establishment or reject it.

With the fast multiplication of cell phones, touchy versatile (applications) are created in the previous scarcely any years. Be that as it may, the elements of portable applications are changed and the plans of them are not surely known by end clients, particularly the exercises and capacities identified with client protection. In this way, seeing how much risk of portable applications as for protection infringement to versatile clients is turns into a basic issue when individuals utilize cell phones. In this paper, we assess the portable application security infringement of versatile clients by processing the threat coefficient. So as to assist individuals with diminishing the protection spillage, we join both the client inclination to portable applications and the protection danger of applications and propose a versatile application use suggestion technique named AppURank to suggest the safe applications with a similar capacity as the "perilous" one for individuals use. The assessment results show that our proposal can lessen the protection spillage by half.

3 Problem Definition

The fast development of applications raises security and protection concerns with respect to untrusted and unsecure applications. Studies have indicated that most applications in business sectors solicitation to gather information unimportant to the fundamental elements of the applications. Conventional consent control plan dependent on one-time choices on establishment has been demonstrated to be not compelling to secure client protection and ineffectively use scant versatile assets (for example battery).

In this work, we propose a framework, a system for smartphone clients to make authorization control continuously and get proposals from master clients who utilize the equivalent applications. This way clients can profit by the master assessments and make right consent conceding choices. We depict our vision on understanding our answer on Android and show that our arrangement is achievable, simple to utilize, and viable.

4   Methodology

In our proposed framework, it will give permits to clients to introduce untrusted applications under two mode: "probation" or a "trusted".

The framework gives the accompanying functionalities:

- In probation mode, an application demands authorization from clients to get to touchy assets (for example GPS follows, contact data, companion list) when required.
- In trusted mode, the application is completely reliable and all consents are totally allowed.
- A proposal framework to control clients with authorization conceding choices, by serving clients with proposals from master clients on the equivalent applications.

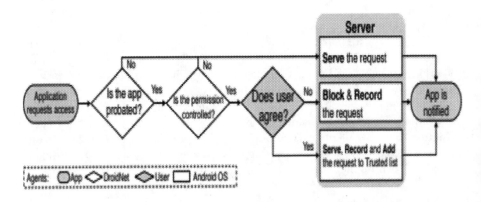

Fig. 1. Proposed framework for permission request

Our overall methodology is to fabricate with four useful cycles, of which two are on portable customers and the staying two are on far off workers. On the customer side, it permits clients to introduce applications in a consent following mode, and gives suggestions to clients on asset authorization demands from portable applications. On the worker side, gathered clients reactions are handled and mined to extricate safe reactions. Specifically,

(1) gathers clients consent demand reactions,
(2) examines the reactions to take out untruthful and one-sided reactions,
(3) recommends different clients with okay reactions to authorization solicitations, and
(4) positions applications dependent on their security and protection hazard level surmised from clients' reactions.

The administration, four principle moves should be tended to:

- How would we instrument the working framework to block asset demands with the least measure of changes to the framework with the end goal that it doesn't influence typical and inheritance activities of the gadget? Simultaneously, how would we make that instrumentation deal with both existing heritage applications and coming applications?
- Given that the reactions from clients are emotional, could be one-sided, and even vindictive, how would we plan the proposal and positioning framework that could recognize and afterward sift through untruthful or one-sided reactions?
- How would we bootstrap and grow the proposal framework? Since this is a participatory help, it is imperative to have a practical and versatile methodology that could give important proposals to all applications.

5 Results

In this section, we included results and survey with the real data. In survey we asked different users to fill in a questionnaire and answer to some objective multiple-choice questions. Figure 1 shows that the majority percentage (66%) people are more worried about their data privacy on mobile applications, while a large percentage (42%) people believe that the smart phone device they use is secure.

We also performed survey on the Ease-of-Use and trustworthiness of the system show in Table 1. We found that the majority (82%) of the participants are satisfied. 70% of the users think that proposed framework is reliable.

Table 1. Recommendation (L = Low, M = Medium and H = High)

Features	L	M	H
Useableness	3%	15%	82%
Reliable and secure	7%	21%	70%

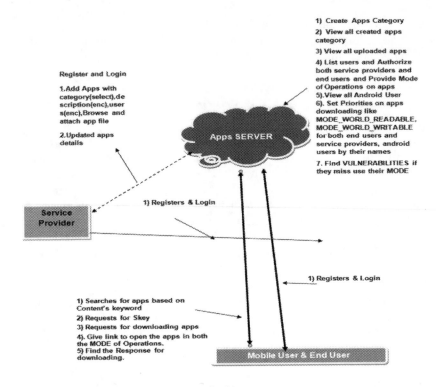

Fig. 2. Architecture

Device Security	Secure	Neutral	Not secure	Total
Privacy Concern				
Concerned	28%	23%	15%	66%
Neutral	11%	7%	3%	21%
Not concerned	3%	7%	3%	13%
Total	42%	37%	21%	100%

Fig. 3. Users' opinion on data and device security

6   Conclusion

We introduced our vision for actualizing a cell phone authorization control and suggested framework which serves the objective of helping clients perform generally safe asset getting to control on untrusted applications to ensure their security and conceivably improve productivity of asset uses (Fig. 2).

The proposed framework permits clients to introduce applications with two modes. In the probation mode, clients are speedy with asset getting to solicitations and settle on choices to concede the authorizations or not. It likewise gives efficient framework on consent allowing choices to decrease the client's danger of settling on bogus choices. We actualized our framework on Android smart phones what's more, exhibit that the framework is achievable and viable (Fig. 3).

References

1. Yan, B., Chen, G.: AppJoy: personalized mobile application discovery. In: Proceedings of the 9th International Conference on Mobile Systems, Applications and Services (MobiSys 2011), Washington, DC, USA, pp. 113–126. ACM, July 2011
2. Yu, K., Zhang, B., Zhu, H., Cao, H., Tian, J.: Towards personalized context-aware recommendation by mining context logs through topic models. In: Tan, P.-N., Chawla, S., Ho, C.K., Bailey, J. (eds.) PAKDD 2012. LNCS (LNAI), vol. 7301, pp. 431–443. Springer, Heidelberg (2012). https://doi.org/10.1007/978-3-642-30217-6_36
3. Zhu, H., Chen, E., Xiong, H., Yu, K., Cao, H., Tian, J.: Mining mobile user preferences for personalized context-aware recommendation. ACM Trans. Intell. Syst. Technol. **5**(4), 58 (2015)
4. Zhu, H., Xiong, H., Ge, Y., Chen, E.: Mobile app recommendations with security and privacy awareness. In: Proceedings of the 20th ACM SIGKDD International Conference on Knowledge Discovery and Data Mining (KDD 2014), New York, NY, USA, pp. 951–960. ACM, August 2014
5. Felt, A.P., Chin, E., Hanna, S., Song, D., Wagner, D.: Android permissions demystified. In: Proceedings of the 18th ACM Conference on Computer and Communications Security (CCS 2011), Chicago, IL, USA, pp. 627–638. ACM, October 2011
6. Au, K.W.Y., Zhou, Y.F., Huang, Z., Gill, P., Lie, D.: Short paper: a look at smartphone permission models. In: Proceedings of the 1st ACM Workshop on Security and Privacy in Smartphones and Mobile Devices (SPSM 2011), pp. 63–67. ACM, October 2011
7. Enck, W., Gilbert, P., Chun, B.-G., et al.: An information-flow tracking system for realtime privacy monitoring on smartphones. In: Proceedings of the 9th USENIX Conference on Operating Systems Design and Implementation (OSDI 2010), Berkeley, CA, USA, pp. 1–6. USENIX Association (2010)
8. Zhou, Y., Zhang, X., Jiang, X., Freeh, V.W.: Taming information-stealing smartphone applications (on android). In: McCune, J.M., Balacheff, B., Perrig, A., Sadeghi, A.-R., Sasse, A., Beres, Y. (eds.) Trust 2011. LNCS, vol. 6740, pp. 93–107. Springer, Heidelberg (2011). https://doi.org/10.1007/978-3-642-21599-5_7
9. Enck, W., Ongtang, M., McDaniel, P.: On lightweight mobile phone application certification. In: Proceedings of the 16th ACM Conference on Computer and Communications Security (CCS 2009), Chicago, IL, USA, pp. 235–245. ACM, November 2009
10. Peng, H., Gates, C., Sarma, B., et al.: Using probabilistic generative models for ranking risks of Android apps. In: Proceedings of the ACM Conference on Computer and Communications Security (CCS 2012), pp. 241–252, October 2012
11. Rashidi, B.: Smartphone user privacy preserving through crowdsourcing (2018)
12. Lin, J., Liu, B., Sadeh, N., Hong, J.I.: Modeling users' mobile app privacy preferences: restoring usability in a sea of permission settings. In: Proceedings of the Symposium on Usable Privacy and Security (SOUPS 2014), Menlo Park, CA, USA, pp. 199–212. USENIX Association, July 2014

13. Liu, R., Cao, J., Yang, L., Zhang, K.: PriWe: recommendation for privacy settings of mobile apps based on crowdsourced users' expectations. In: Proceedings of the IEEE International Conference on Mobile Services (MS 2015), New York City, NY, USA, pp. 150–157, June 2015. https://doi.org/10.1109/MobServ.2015.30
14. Rashidi, B., Fung, C., Nguyen, A., Vu, T., Bertino, E.: Android user privacy preserving through crowdsourcing. IEEE Trans. Inf. Forensics Secur. **13**(3), 773–787 (2018)
15. Safran, M., Che, D.: Real-time recommendation algorithms for crowdsourcing systems. Appl. Comput. Inform. **13**(1), 47–56 (2017)
16. Annachhatre, C., Austin, T.H., Stamp, M.: Hidden Markov models for malware classification. J. Comput. Virol. Hacking Tech. **11**(2), 59–73 (2015)
17. Arp, D., Spreitzenbarth, M., Hubner, M., Gascon, H., Rieck, K.: DREBIN: effective and explainable detection of android malware in your pocket. In: NDSS. The Internet Society (2014)
18. Backes, M., Bugiel, S., Hammer, C., Schranz, O., von Styp-Rekowsky, P.: Boxify: full-fledged app sandboxing for stock android. In: 24th USENIX Security Symposium (USENIX Security 2015), Washington, D.C., pp. 691–706, August 2015

INTELLIBOT - Intelligent Voice Assisted Chatbot with Sentiment Analysis, COVID Dashboard and Offensive Text Detection

Gadiparthy Harika Sai, Meghna Manoj Nair, V. Vani$^{(\boxtimes)}$, and Shivani

School of Computer Science and Engineering, Vellore Institute of Technology, Chennai, India
vani.v@vit.ac.in

Abstract. Chatbot has become an essential crowd puller in the world today and is used in various domains and professions. With increasing technologies and advancements in AI, components of voice assistance have been gaining prolific importance when integrated with chatbots. INTELLIBOT is a smart bot that not only interacts with its users through an interactive and aesthetic platform but also had added features for customized experience. It makes use of speech to text and text to speech processing to listen to the user and speak back to them. This paper would give insights on the various applications of chatbots and existing systems along with the system we have proposed to overcome and curb the challenges posed by them through the INTELLIBOT framework. Further, the paper would elucidate the use of Naïve-Bayes algorithm and pattern matching algorithms for the same.

Keywords: Chatbots · Pattern matching · Naïve Bayes · Sentiment analysis · COVID dashboard · Offensive text detection · Intelligent chatbot

1 Introduction

In the rapidly digitalizing generation, where almost every domain of profession and lifestyle are focusing on automation and interactive components, chatbots have been on the spotlight [1]. In general, a bot is very similar to a software application that mainly aims towards completing and executing tasks without much of a human interference. Chatbots are those bots which are capable of initiating and conversing with humans by speech, text or both by responding to the queries and clarifying doubts [2]. Many a times, chatbots are interchangeably used with conversational agents. However, the key point is that chatbots are much simpler and easier than conversational agents and they can be integrated with Application Programming Interfaces (APIs) to cater to the various needs of the user. Furthermore, it improves branding with less customer effort. Ever since 1990s, a large number of researches have been carried out with regards to conversational systems [3] including those of airline ticketing systems, travel programs, etc. And studies have shown that they have been performing at par with others in the field. ATIS and Communicator systems are designed to understand natural language requests and perform a variety of specific tasks for users, such as retrieving flight information and

© The Author(s), under exclusive license to Springer Nature Switzerland AG 2022
S. Joshi et al. (Eds.): SpacSec 2021, CCIS 1599, pp. 311–323, 2022.
https://doi.org/10.1007/978-3-031-15784-4_25

providing information to tourists. Undisclosed chatbots are four times more productive than novice sales staff, and their ability reaches that of specialized consumer shopping employees. Humans have perceptions and perspectives which often lead to considering chatbots to les viable in terms of emotional intelligence and this can often have adverse impacts especially in those areas of application which involve marketing. In [4], the authors have explored more about the uncanny-valley theory and has elaborated on the awkward senses and emotions a human is exposed to when chatting with a device or application. Personification and contact in people's disclosures on sensitive topics, such as social stressors, have also been examined.

2 Literature Review

With evolving technologies and rapid advancements in numerous fields across the globe, chatbots have become an integral part of majority of applications because of the versatility and convenience it imparts in the domains it is being incorporated into. The very use of a chatbot is to introduce an environment of natural language to the user space with regards to the applications being used, be it entertainment, education, finance, health, etc. One of the very first chatbots that was brought to light was Eliza, which was capable of extracting the context of the user input sentences and generate a response as per the basic rules and guidelines laid out. This technique definitely did grab a lot of attention in the initial stages but on seeking deeper insights of the other features it offers, it was observed that Eliza couldn't retain the history of the messages or conversations it had with its users [1, 2]. Following this came, A.L.I.C.E., a chatbot developed from a novel technology termed as Artificial Intelligence Markup Language (AIML), which took an extensive amount of work and time for curation. A.L.I.C.E. works on the principles of pattern recognition, response template and built-in stimuli for engaging in natural conversations and chats with the users. Once the input is received from the user, the bot makes use of category matching techniques of patterns and further indulges in supervised learning approaches to create and store responses accordingly [3, 4]. With progressing tech strategies and evolving algorithmic paradigms, chatbots have acquired mainstream representation with specifications with respect to the domain of usage and application. One of the other such chatbots is Jabberwacky which is generic in nature and the feature that makes it stand out is its ability to respond back to its users in a humorous and funny way and it keeps improvising its responses each time it learns something new from a recent conversation it had with one of its users. In simpler words, Jabberwacky is a generic conversation bot which doesn't necessarily have an explicit domain of application and usually caters to generic chats and conversations [5]. The above mentioned chatbots are those which were developed in the initial stages of evolving chatbot technology. However, current chatbots are much more sophisticated and consist of intricate and complex strategical approaches for handling various aspects of a well curated chatbot. Few such technologies are so advanced that they often develop a goal driven mannerism. In fact, chatbots these days are inclusively connected with databases, application programming interfaces and application layers for efficient working and additional features [6]. One of the recent innovations in the field of chatbots is the development of a project which involves integrating Internet of Things (IoT) with Natural Language Processing (NLP) techniques for the aquacultural domain. This chatbot also consists of data retrieved from sensors and modular systems along with cloud computational frameworks to provide responses with accurate results in their field of application. This section, hence puts forward the various existing chatbot systems and architectures.

3 Types of Chatbots

Chatbots are of various types and are developed based on the application, use, and necessity. One of the first types of chatbots is the rule based chatbot wherein the communication and interaction with users is based on a predefined collection of rules. This type of chatbot doesn't have much of Artificial Intelligence (AI) involved and hence utilizing such rule-based bots for vast, broad, boundless conversations might not yield accurate responses and results. The next type of chatbot is the menu/button based chatbot, which is quite evidently prevalent in numerous application domains currently [7]. The core data structure used here is that of the decision tree hierarchy which are displayed as buttons for users to chat and interact with the bot. It's often compared to the automated menus which are mainly observed on smart phones and related gadgets. The main use of this menu/button based chatbot is in handling FAQs and support queries and responses. One of the other types of bots is keyword recognition based chatbot which has the potential to respond to the user as per the request and needs of the user, ensuring a user-centric performance. It surely is gaining a lot of popularity off late and has been considered as a mixed combination of menu based and keyword-based type of chatbot [8–10]. Following this, is the contextual chatbot which are surely the most advanced when compared to the above-mentioned types of chatbots, as they make use of Machine Learning (ML) and AI for learning from every new conversation they engage in and also to retain the memory of the previous conversations and chats. This makes the context based chatbots smarter in terms of being able to improvise their responses to the users based on the experiences they gain and from the chats they retain in their memory. Another classification of chatbots is the support chatbot which is majorly used in overcoming a problem or query localized to a certain domain. Apart from this, it also demands the chatbot to be well aware of the contextual background, especially in cases where they might have to explain the entire procedure or business process to the users. Some of the main use cases of the support type chatbots include customer centric service bots, e-commerce bot along with recommendation systems, bots for ordering food, and bots which cater to answering FAQs [11, 12]. Another interesting category of bots is the skills chatbot type which is much simpler when compared to support based chatbots from the awareness aspect. This chatbot is mainly utilized in situation where an action is to executed for a particular command or request that is given to the bot. Then, there are assistant bots which are very commonly used in smart phones for personal assistants like Siri, Bixby, Google Assistant, etc. Transactional bots, information gathering bots, conversation chatbots, etc. are all some of the other types of bots which are currently existing [13]. The key observation to be made here is that there are so many varieties of chatbots such that a particular type of chatbot can be easily adapted to a specific application domain with added features, benefits and characteristics which can be specially curated and attached to the curated chatbot [14]. However, most of the existing chatbot systems have a few disadvantages which restrict their varied and extensive use to a certain extent. Some of these chatbots may not be able to extract the exact essence of what the user is intending to say and might respond back in unexpected ways. Further, some of the chatbots lack a responsive, dynamic and aesthetic user interface presence despite the accuracy in results obtained.

4 Proposed Architecture

Based on the research and analyses of surveys on chatbots, it was observed that majority of the chatbots were specific to a particular domain. In other words, if a chatbot was developed for the health sector, it could only be relatively trained for the health sector and similarly if a chatbot was curated for the educational sector, its utility remains within the boundaries of the educational field. This surely hampers the versatility of the chatbot and urges users to work with many chatbots to get an idea of the chatter bots and to clear their queries in different fields. To overcome this curb and to highlight the versatility and uniqueness of the chatbot, INTELLIBOT is proposed. Like a few other chatbots, INTELLIBOT is an intelligent and smart chatbot which makes extensive use of AI and ML algorithms and concepts for improved behavior with increasing experience and conversations with users. Most importantly, INTELLIBOT has been curated in such a way that it can also cater to the needs and queries of the blind. This is incorporated by using the very important essence of Natural Language Processing (NLP), i.e., speech to text conversion and text to speech conversion. This ensure that, if the user wishes to convey his/her query to the chatbot, they just need to put out the words clearly and INTELLIBOT would grab the essence or context of the said sentence, would apply the necessary pre-processing techniques and would then pick out the respective response and show it to the user. Along with displaying the response, it would also speak out the response which the user can hear and get his/her doubt or query cleared. One of the other aspects and characteristic features of INTELLIBOT is that it isn't restricted to a specific domain of application. It can take up the roles of chatbots in different domains and act accordingly. If the user wishes to have a random generic chat with the bot, INTELLIBOT can take up that role too. But asper the current scenario, there are three pressing issues to be addressed and taken care of which include COVID related queries, offensive text detection and sentiment analysis and INTELLIBOT can embrace and respond to queries related to all these fields as well. This surely is one of the striking features of INTELLIBOT and takes it way ahead than the existing bots in the world.

Figure 1 portrays the architecture of the system used to develop INTELLIBOT. Initially, the user turns on the chatbot application and on being intimidated to speak his/her query or comment, the user speaks. The contextual meaning and logic of the speech is extracted from the spoken words by the bot using the speech to text conversion module. Figure 2 elaborates on the process used for speech to text conversion [15]. Once the input speech is obtained, speech analysis is done by the bot which is preprocessed using the necessary models which are imported from the library. The module from python library called speech_recognition is used for extracting the essence of the text and using the Recognizer.recognize_google (audio) the speech is finally converted to the right textual sense [16]. Once this is done, the next step is for the BOT to parse through the converted text and perform some sort of analysis and preprocessing to understand the exact sense of the speech given by the user. On completing this step, the bot uses the Naïve Bayes algorithm for parsing through the set of predefined pattern-matching based keywords and questions to identify what response needs to be given to the user. There are four possible domains of applications INTELLIBOT offers. The user can chat with the bot from a generic perspective and engage in some humorous and interesting talks. One of the other possible options is to get details related to COVID statistics using the in-built COVID dashboard INTELLIBOT offers. Or, the user can assess the offensiveness of a particular text/comment using the offensive text detection module which is embedded with the bot. And finally, the user can also assess the sentiment of a particular text or comment through the sentiment analysis bot which INTELLIBOT has. The modules apart from the generic/customized text response is carried out on a platform called AI Playground, which is and AI and ML powered framework used for curating such interactive chatbots. After the response for the query shared by the user has been created, the text should now be converted back to speech. Figure 3 elaborates on the procedure involved for the same. The generated text response is preprocessed once

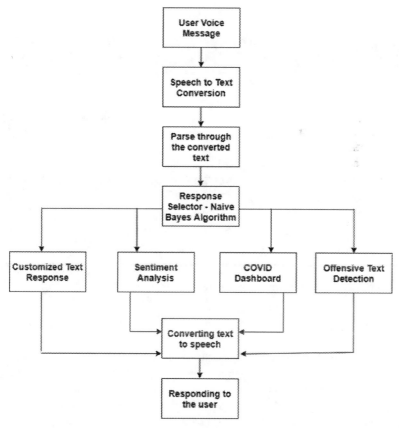

Fig. 1. Proposed system architecture of INTELLIBOT

again and undergoes Unicode conversion followed by segmentation and concatenation of words and syllables. Following which, the prosody and smoothening technique is applied and finally the text is converted back to speech and is given out to the speaker as a response.

The above figure is used for identifying the workflow and modularity of the chatbot framework proposed in this paper.

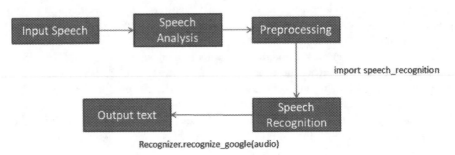

Fig. 2. Speech to text conversion module

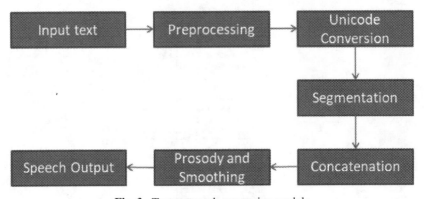

Fig. 3. Text to speech conversion module

Figure 2 and Fig. 3 elaborates on the functioning of the speech to text and text to speech conversion modules for the working of INTELLIBOT.

5   Implementation

Implementation of INTELIBOT has been carried out using the Python programming language for ease of construct, flexibility and dynamic framework related activities. In order to curate the core architecture and conceptual scene of the chatbot, the very first step is to implement the Naïve-Bayes algorithm as per the needs of INTELLIBOT. Firstly, all necessary libraries and packages are imported and installed including those of speech_recognition, pyttsx3, and time. Using the Recognizer() built-in function from speech_recognition library, the user defined function for turning on the input voice resource and extracting the speech given by the user is created. In case of any turbulent noises or extremely unclear speech input, the bot will prompt the user to reiterate the spoken words for better identification. The next main function is the respond() function which is user defined to incorporate the Naïve-Bayes algorithm for giving accurate results to the user. Naive Bayes model is easy to build and particularly useful for very large data sets [17]. Along with simplicity, Naive Bayes is known to outperform even highly sophisticated classification methods [18, 19]. The formula used for curation of the probability of picking the necessary response is as follows:

$$P(c|X) = P(x_1|c) \times P(x_2|c) \times \cdots \times P(x_n|c) \times P(c)$$

wherein, P(c|x) is the posterior probability of getting a particular class c for a given attribute predictor x, P(c) is the initial or prior probability of the class, P(x|c) is the probability of the predictor attribute for a give class and P(x) is the prior probability of the predictor attribute. The dataset used for INTELLIBOT is a large Java Script Object Notation (JSON) file which contains the necessary classes and a set of possible responses as attributes in the form of key value pairs. The algorithm in the respond() function would compare and match the extracted words from the user's speech input and identify the suitable response from the dataset based on the probabilities calculated by the algorithm. Following this, the response is converted back to speech using the user defined speak() function. The function speak() makes use of the pyttsx3 module to convert and transform the response back to audio and the converted speech is then thrown out to the user. The above explanation elucidates the generic working of INTELLIBOT and the integration of the algorithm and dataset used for curating the interactive experience. Moving on to the individual modules of INTELLIBOT which highlight the unique features and characteristics of the bot.

5.1 Sentiment Analysis

One of the major highlights of INTELLIBOT is the sentiment analysis bot which helps the users in identifying the sentiment category or emotional context of a particular text or speech input given. In order to develop this module, the AI Playground framework has been used. AI Playground is a Java Script based platform which allows its users to curate and train models using AI and ML and integrate it with their built-in chatbot called Lexy. As seen in Fig. 4, in order to develop the sentiment analysis bot for INTELLIBOT, the very first step is to train the model for identifying the different classes of sentiments. Initially the different sentiments such as happy, sad and neutral are used as labels for the classes. Each of the classes are then integrated with a sufficient number of words, phrases, and sentences pertaining to the class from the dataset acquired from Kaggle. After the manual updating of the dataset, the model is trained for around 1500 epochs and tested for any glitches and mishaps. Finally, the model is imported to the code base using fetch() and is integrated with INTELLIBOT.

5.2 COVID Dashboard

Over the last year, one of the highly spoken about topic and issue across the globe is the outbreak of the global pandemic – COVID'19. It surely has had a negative toll on

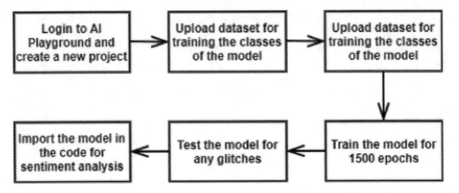

Fig. 4. Steps involved for sentiment analysis model.

majority of the mundane lives and the data inflow in this field has been extremely huge and vast, such that it makes it nearly impossible to interpret the proper statistics with ease and conveniently. INTELLIBOT has been incorporated with a COVID Dashboard which extracts live COVID statistics from a reliable Application Programming Interface (API) and displays the necessary stats for the country. Once the user gives the speech/text input of the country whose details or statistics are needed, the bot would extract the data from the real time updated API and provide information including those of death rates, confirmed cases, positive cases, etc. for the particular country. This module has also been developed using the AI Playground platform. The workflow for this module can be observed in Fig. 5.

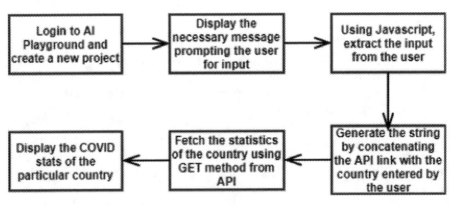

Fig. 5. Steps involved for COVID Dashboard module

5.3 Offensive Text Detection

The next module of INTELLIBOT is the offensive text detection module. With the spike in the use of social media platforms in the society, there has been numerous cases of harassment and unethical events through posts and comments. We wanted to ensure that

INTELLIBOT was close enough to reciprocate to human emotions and hence decided to incorporate the offensive text detection module. Using the AI Playground platform, the model was trained by manually importing the dataset into the two classes of "offensive" and "not offensive". It was trained for 1500 epochs and tested. After developing the accurate model without any glitches, the next step was to integrate the model with the code for implementation. Whenever the user enters a text/speech which involves rude/harsh comments, the bot responds back by telling them that they were mean and if not, the bot would thank the user for being nice to it (Fig. 6).

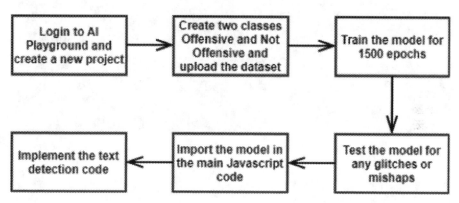

Fig. 6. Steps involved for offensive text detection module

6 Results Obtained

The implementation of the above-mentioned modules and integration yields INTELLI-BOT which is the intelligent voice assisted chat bot. Figure 7 elucidates the snapshot of the implementation using the python code for implementing the Naïve Bayes algorithm and speech to text and text to speech conversion. Figure 8 portrays the snapshot of the training of the model involved in the platform following which the testing can be seen

```
Command Prompt

C:\Users\Meghna\Desktop\Academics\Sem 5\NLP\Chatbot>python demo1.py
How can I help you?
My name is INTELLIBOT
Sun Aug 29 20:19:58 2021
I dont need food for survival :)
What is the location
Here is the location of: India
Bye!

C:\Users\Meghna\Desktop\Academics\Sem 5\NLP\Chatbot>
```

Fig. 7. Snapshot of implementing the Naïve Bayes algorithm for chatbot along with speech to text and text to speech

on the right-hand side column. Figure 9, 10, and 11 gives the snapshot of the implementations of offensive text detection, sentiment analysis, and COVID dashboard using the

Fig. 8. Training the models in AI playground

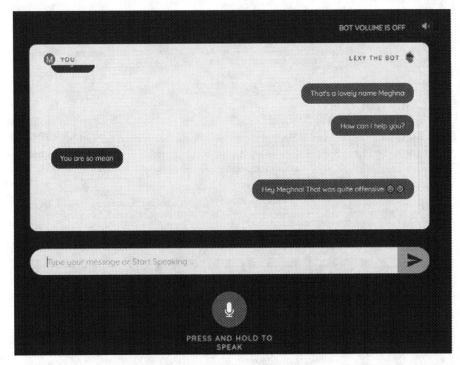

Fig. 9. Offensive text detection analysis

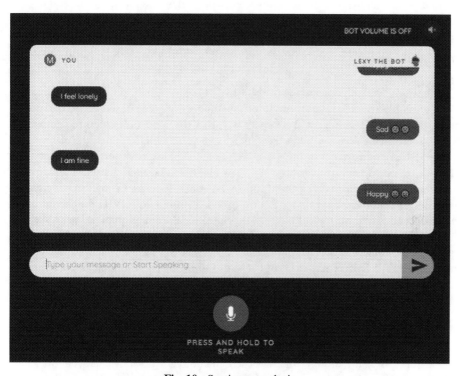

Fig. 10. Sentiment analysis

Fig. 11. COVID dashboard using AI playground

AI/ML powered platform. Further, the built-in chatbot feature integrated with AI Playground is also compatible for detecting speech as well as text and gives the response in both was too.

7 Conclusion

On the whole, the implementation of INTELLIBOT has been beneficial in ensuring that people can clarify their queries and details pertaining to some of the varied and highly important domains within one work space. INTELLIBOT not only caters to people with vision and hearing abilities, but is friendly and smart enough to address the query needs of the visually impaired by using the speech to text and text to speech conversion. Further, the effective and efficient Naïve-Bayes algorithm ensures that the bot responds accurately without much deflectional and deviational responses. In order to integrate the modules of sentiment analysis, offensive text detection and COVID dashboard along with INTELLIBOT, an AI/ML based platform called AI Playground has been used for implementing and training the model. In the current world where chatbots have been gaining predominance over various fields and domains, chatbot systems and architectures like INTELLIBOT have a sure chance of shining bright. From the implementation and detailed analysis on chatbots, it can be observed that there is a pressing need for the development of user friendly and smart chatbots like INTELLIBOT which takes up the role of a virtual friend and covers various aspects and domains of concerns in the current world. This would not only encourage the users to exploit the major advantageous services offered but would also help them be well aware and up to date with the prime concerns. Furthermore, the proposed chatbot provides fast and accurate search responses and responds to the users in a customized perspective by analyzing the behavioral response of the user. The fact that this bot is capable of consolidating data from various APIs and search engines to portray to the user is one of the unique features INTELLINOT possesses.

References

1. Jia, J.: CSIEC (Computer simulator in educational communication): an intelligent web-based teaching system for foreign language learning. In: ED-MEDIA (World Conference on Educational Multimedia, Hypermedia & Telecommunications), Lugano, Switzerland (2004)
2. DeAngeli, A., Johnson, G.I., Coventry, L.: The unfriendly user: exploring social reactions to chatterbots. In: Helander, M., Khalid, H.M., Tham, P.O. (eds.) International Conference on Affective Human Factors Design. Asean Academic Press, London (2001)
3. Bath & North East Somerset Council. Council web site Citizen Information Service Agent (2006). www.bathnes.gov.uk/BathNES/Search/ask/default.htm. Accessed 02 June 2006
4. Wallace, R.S.: Chapter 00. The Anatomy of A.L.I.C.E. http://www.alicebot.org/documenta tion. Accessed 09 Dec 2005
5. Kerlyl, A., Hall, P., Bull, S.: Bringing chatbots into education: Towards natural language negotiation of open learner models. In: Ellis, R., Allen, T., Tuson, A. (eds.) SGAI 2006, pp. 179–192. Springer, London (2006). https://doi.org/10.1007/978-1-84628-666-7_14
6. Ahmad, N.A., Che, M.H., Zainal, A., Abd Rauf, M.F., Adnan, Z.: Review of chatbots design techniques. Int. J. Comput. Appl. **181**(8), 7–10 (2018)

7. Smutny, P., Schreiberova, P.: Chatbots for learning: a review of educational chatbots for the Facebook Messenger. Comput. Educ. **151**, 103862 (2020)
8. Molnár, G., Szüts, Z.: The role of chatbots in formal education. In: 2018 IEEE 16th International Symposium on Intelligent Systems and Informatics (SISY), pp. 000197–000202. IEEE (2018)
9. Ujbanyi, T., Sziladi, G., Katona, J., Kovari, A.: ICT based interactive and smart technologies in education - teaching difficulties. Int. J. Manag. Appl. Sci. **3**, 72–77 (2017)
10. Gogh, E., Kovari, A.: Examining the relationship between lifelonglearning and language learning in a vocational training institution. Appl. Tech. Educ. Sci. **8**(1), 52–69 (2018)
11. Krantz, A., Lindblom, P.: Generating topic-based chatbot responses. Blekinge Institute of Technology (2017)
12. Doshi, S.V., Pawar, S.B., Shelar, A.G., Kulkarni, S.S.: Artificial intelligence chatbot in android system using open source program-O. Int. J. Adv. Res. Comput. Commun. Eng. **6**(4), 816–821 (2017)
13. Goel, A., et al.: Using watson for enhancing human-computerco-creativity. In: 2015 AAAI Fall Symposium Series (2015)
14. Maroengsit, W., Piyakulpinyo, T., Phonyiam, K., Pongnumkul, S., Chaovalit, P., Theeramunkong, T.: A survey on evaluation methods for chatbots. In: Proceedings of the 2019 7th International Conference on Information and Education Technology, pp. 111–119 (2019)
15. Androutsopoulou, A., Karacapilidis, N., Loukis, E., Charalabidis, Y.: Transforming the communication between citizens and government through AI-guided chatbots. Gov. Inf. Q. **36**(2), 358–367 (2019)
16. Kostelník, P., Pisařovic, I., Muroň, M., Dařena, F., Procházka, D.: Chatbots for enterprises: outlook. Acta Universitatis Agriculturae et Silviculturae Mendelianae Brunensis (2019)
17. Hayashi, T., Watanabe, S., Toda, T., Takeda, K., Toshniwal, S., Livescu, K.: Pre-trained text embeddings for enhanced text-to-speech synthesis. In: INTERSPEECH, pp. 4430–4434 (2019)
18. Li, J., Wu, Z., Li, R., Zhi, P., Yang, S., Meng, H.: Knowledge-based linguistic encoding for end-to-end mandarin text-to-speech synthesis. In: INTERSPEECH, pp. 4494–4498 (2019)
19. Serban, I.V., et al.: A deep reinforcement learning chatbot. arXiv preprint arXiv:1709.02349 (2017)
20. Copeland, J., Proudfoot, D.: Turing's test: aphilosophical and historical guide. In: Epstein, R., Roberts, G., Beber, G. (eds.) Parsing the Turing Test: Philosophical and Methodological Issues in the Quest for the Thinking Computer, pp. 119–138. Springer, New York (2008)
21. Setyawan, M.Y.H., Awangga, R.M., Efendi, S.R.: Comparison of multinomial naive bayes algorithm and logistic regression for intent classification in chatbot. In: 2018 International Conference on Applied Engineering (ICAE), pp. 1–5. IEEE (2018)
22. Revathy, S.: Health care counselling via voicebot using multinomial naive bayes algorithm. In: 2020 5th International Conference on Communication and Electronics Systems (ICCES), pp. 1063–1067. IEEE (2020)
23. Eason, G., Noble, B., Sneddon, I.N.: On certain integrals of Lipschitz-Hankel type involving products of Bessel functions. Phil. Trans. Roy. Soc. London **A247**, 529–551 (1955)

Author Index

Abdallah, A. M.   294
Acharya, Saket   51
Althaf, A.   213

Bogatinoska, Dijana Capeska   18
Bohra, Manoj Kumar   201

Chiam, Dar Hung   272
Chiong, Choo W. R.   156
Chowdhury, Dipanwita Roy   105

Desai, Yukta   144
Dhaka, Arvind   18
Dhanare, Ritesh   144
Duddukuru, Krishna Vamshi   283
Dutta, Kamlesh   97

Gadepaka, Latha   117, 130
Gadicha, Vijay   186
Goyal, Hemlata   171
Gupta, Arnav   34
Gupta, Shivani   303

Hablani, Hari   213

Jain, Niyati   34

Kavita   263
Khandelwal, Jyoti   171
Kumar, Krishna   51, 87
Kumar, Ranjeet   303
Kumar, Ravinder   51

Lakshminarayana, Sanjay   283
Lee, Samuel Jia Sheng   156
Lilani, Siddharth   144
Lim, King Hann   239, 272

Maiti, Swapan   105
Malani, Dhrumil   144
Malsaria, Anshika   248
Mathur, Pratistha   263

Mehta, Deval   105
Mishra, Ishan   87
Modi, Jimit   144

Nagpal, Kabir   34
Nair, Meghna Manoj   311
Nandal, Amita   18
Nath, Hiran V.   64

Pal, Triveni Lal   97
Panwar, Neha   75
Patra, Ayush   34
Phang, Jonathan Then Sien   239

Raguru, Jaya Krishna   171
Raich, Anagha   186
Raslan, K. R.   294
Ravipati, Srinivas   303
Rawat, Umashankar   51, 87
Renya Nath, N.   64
Roy, Satyabrata   51, 87

Sai, Gadiparthy Harika   311
Senapati, Kishore Kumar   1
Sharma, Arpit Kumar   18
Sharma, D. P.   75
Sharma, Sachin Kumar   201
Sharma, Vijay Kumar   171
Shivani   311
Singh, Arjun   201
Singhal, Sunita   34
Sinha, Kunal   1
Soliman, A. A.   294
Surampudi, Bapi Raju   117, 130
Syamala, Anjana   34

Thakare, Shubham Bhaskar   283
Tiwari, Kartik   213

Vani, V.   303, 311
Vyas, Pankaj   248

Printed in the United States
by Baker & Taylor Publisher Services